n the Culture of the Cold War

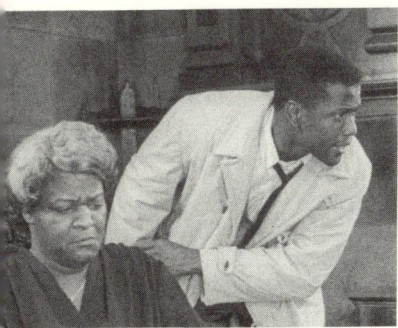

Producing and Contesting

Containment, 1947–1962

Bruce McConachie

University of Iowa Press ψ Iowa City

University of Iowa Press,
Iowa City 52242
Copyright © 2003
by the University of Iowa Press
All rights reserved
Printed in the United States of America
Design by Richard Hendel
http://www.uiowa.edu/uiowapress
No part of this book may be reproduced or
used in any form or by any means without
permission in writing from the publisher. All
reasonable steps have been taken to contact
copyright holders of material used in this book.
The publisher would be pleased to make
suitable arrangements with any whom it
has not been possible to reach.

The publication of this book was
generously supported by the University of
Iowa Foundation.

Printed on acid-free paper

Library of Congress
Cataloging-in-Publication Data
McConachie, Bruce A.
　American theater in the culture of the Cold
War: producing and contesting containment /
by Bruce A. McConachie.
　　　p.　　cm.—(Studies in theatre history and
culture)
　ISBN 0-87745-862-6 (cloth)
　1. Theater—United States—History—
20th century.　2. American drama—20th
century—History and criticism.　I. Title.
II. Series.
PN2266.3.M38 2003
792'.0973'0945—dc21　　　2003052011

03　04　05　06　07　C　5　4　3　2　1

American Theater
in the Culture of the Cold War

American Theater

Studies in THEATRE HISTORY & CULTURE

Edited by Thomas Postlewait

Contents

Preface *vii*

Acknowledgments *xiii*

1 A Theater of Containment Liberalism *1*
2 Empty Boys, Queer Others, and Consumerism *56*
3 Family Circles, Racial Others, and Suburbanization *126*
4 Fragmented Heroes, Female Others, and the Bomb *199*

Epilogue, 1962–1992 *283*

Notes *301*

Index *335*

Preface

Books that present a cultural-historical analysis of representative theatrical events don't usually need a preface. After skimming a short introduction laying out the scope and method of such a study, most readers would prefer to jump into the historical thick of things and work through problems of historiography and theoretical orientation as they occur in the text. I know I would. So I resisted writing a preface for *American Theater in the Culture of the Cold War* until feedback from several readers of my drafts convinced me that I probably needed one. For better and for worse, from their perspective, I was writing a different kind of theater history than most readers were familiar with, so I'd better spend a little more time at the front end of the book preparing them for what lay ahead. This preface, then, is a kind of warning label. Before you swallow my historical medicine, please take a look below at some of my main ingredients to prepare yourself for the consequences.

This book project began conventionally enough. The questions and assumptions about theater, society, and history that shaped my initial investigations into American theater from the late 1940s through the early 1960s were fundamentally the same ones that had guided my work in *Melodramatic Formations* (1992). What were some of the most popular and representative stage productions of this period and which social groups applauded them? How did the experience of enjoying *The Seven Year Itch*, *The King and I*, and *J.B.*, among other shows, intersect with the everyday lives of these playgoers and help to position them within some of the major social, political, and ethical crosscurrents of their time? Finally, were there significant differences between these experiences of theatergoing and similar experiences before and after the period of the early Cold War? If so, how could I explain these historical changes?

These questions and the assumptions behind them continued to guide my research for this book, but I began to lose faith in the conventional definitions of some of the key terms I needed to pursue my work. What, after all, is theatrical "enjoyment" and how does it connect with human "experience"? Beyond semiotics and some warmed-over Freudianism, our current critical and theoretical discourses have very little to say about theatrical pleasure and social experience. And besides, I did not really trust Ferdinand de Saussure or Jacques Lacan to tell me much about enjoyment or experience. Do people really find much enjoyment in reading signs? Perhaps, but it has always seemed like thin gruel to me. And why take the trouble to go to the theater for something you can do anywhere, for free, by yourself? Lacan's theories, by linking human development to language and desire, can help to answer questions about enjoyment and experience, but only if one believes in the Freudian premises of his arguments. Remove those, and the Lacanian house of signs and stages comes tumbling down. Besides, why should the historian attempt to encompass the experience of the theater within such a narrow understanding of enjoyment? More significantly, perhaps, is there any experimental validity to Lacan's conclusions? Or, for that matter, to the psychology of semiosis? Most psychologists work out a tradition of empirical experimentation that Lacan and other Continental philosophers simply reject out of hand. But why should I reject it? Historians have long recognized the importance of empirical investigation as a necessary though partial road to historical truths. Is there an empirically sound psychology and philosophy from which I can derive a better understanding of theatrical enjoyment and social experience?

The foregoing questions and tentative answers did not occur in the syllogistic order in which I have presented them, of course, but they are a fair summary of the logic that led me to cognitive science, specifically the cognitive psychology and linguistics of George Lakoff and Mark Johnson. As I explain more fully in chapter 1, cognitive psychology can give historians access to the ways in which spectators in the 1950s projected themselves onto figures on the stage that gave them pleasure. Further, Lakoff and Johnson have generated a partial taxonomy, which they continue to modify on the basis of further experiments, to identify the ways in which people categorize their perceptual experiences in everyday life. The theater historian can apply these terms with relative ease to discuss the perceptions of spectators in the theater. One of these taxonomic terms is "containment," an "image schema," according to Lakoff and Johnson, that designates what happens when a person categorizes a perceived image as having an inside, an outside, and a boundary between them. *American Theater in the Culture of the Cold War* demonstrates that spectatorial perceptions triggered by "containment" organized much of the experience of theatergoing—indeed, much of the experience of cold war culture—in the 1947–1962 period.

Because this mechanism of categorization occurs largely at an unconscious level, however, I must tell you that there is no direct evidence that this psychological process ever happened in past audiences. (I presume that cognitive psychologists could construct experiments that would demonstrate the occurrence of such mechanisms in present spectators, but as a historian I am out of luck.) Perceiving a mode of acting, a moment of interaction between players, a group of performers within a stage setting, and similar images as types of containers is a gestalt event that occurs instantly. Containment and similar cognitive processes are prediscursive; they work at an unconscious level that precedes and shapes representation. Although direct empirical evidence of the gestalt perceptions of historical audiences is lacking, indirect evidence is plentiful. The consequences of spectatorial cognition leave copious traces in the theatrical events themselves, or what remains of them. By reading the scripts, designs, reviews, memoirs, and other evidence from those productions and receptions through the lens of Lakoff and Johnson's cognitive psychology, we can construct some of the recurring cognitive processes that led audiences to enjoy them. This method involves a version of symptomatic interpretation in which the critic-historian reasons backward from the material results of cognitive processes—in the case of cold war American theater, the success of certain types of productions with audiences—to deduce the kinds of cognitive enjoyments that made them popular.

The version of interpretive history that results from this strategy, however, significantly departs from the usual modes of writing about audiences and theatrical events. These histories, *Melodramatic Formations* among them, generally assume that acts of spectatorial interpretation shape an audience's experience in the theater, in one way or another. *American Theater in the Culture of the Cold War*, in contrast, focuses on cognitive processes that must occur before spectators can form any interpretive judgments at all. Further, these mental mechanisms both enable and constrain the meanings that audiences can make from their experience in the playhouse. Consequently, this book shares some interpretive and rhetorical strategies found in histories built on the premises of Jungian, Freudian, or Lacanian theory, with the important exception that its grounding in cognitive psychology gives it access to a realist validity that these other modes of psychological history cannot claim. That is, this book, like the realist cognitivism of Lakoff and Johnson, takes the empirical evidence as far as possible but also resorts to explanations that no amount of evidence could ever prove or disprove. Resting on the experimental work of cognitive science is no guarantee of historical truth, of course, but it does provide firmer ground for understanding the responses of historical audiences than the often partial, usually contradictory, and always tiny amount of written evidence that suggests how most spectators experienced a play from moment to moment.

This book is weird in another way as well. Soon after I decided to work within the framework of Lakoff and Johnson's cognitive psychology for an analysis of audience response, I realized that the kinds of causes that theater historians normally advanced to explain historical change would no longer do the job in *American Theater in the Culture of the Cold War*. In *Melodramatic Formations*, I had rounded up the usual suspects—economic change, new class formation, major political shifts, new practices intrinsic to the theater itself, and similar causal factors—and deployed them (credibly enough, I believe) to explain why melodramatic theater changed as it did between 1820 and 1870. With cognitive psychology as my base, however, I needed to find structural reasons for shifts in the major cognitive building blocks of a historical culture. If, as I suspected, containment and its many metaphorical extensions organized much American culture during the early Cold War, how did it get there? The American victory in World War II, significant improvements in the economic situation of most citizens, an entirely altered geopolitical order, and an orchestrated campaign against internal subversion had helped to cause some changes in American culture, including the theater, between 1935 and 1950, but how crucial were these factors in altering the type of enjoyment that spectators sought at the theater? These factors might explain some changes in the content of theatrical communication, but I needed a type of causation that could rearrange the tectonic plates of cultural perception and cognition.

From readings in communication theory and history, I began to hypothesize that new media might create reality effects that shape everyday lives in historical cultures at deep, mostly unconscious levels. This led me to examine the cognitive dynamics of photography and audiophony, the dominant media of the 1930s and 1940s. The generation that came to prominence in the Cold War had grown up with these media, especially the audiophonic technologies of the radio and telephone. Perhaps these media had shaped this generation's perceptions of reality, which in turn created new expectations for theatrical entertainment. The more I read about the impact of radio, the surer I was that it was cognitively linked to the movement in cold war theater away from the realism of earlier days and toward the abstraction and allegory that pervaded the theater of the 1950s. The ubiquity of audiophony seems to have elevated to dominance certain cognitive processes that made some kinds of experiences in the playhouse more accessible and pleasurable than before. Here was a possible type of structural causation I might use to explain the cognitive shifts that had occurred between the mid 1930s and the late 1940s. Further, one reason why theater-making and theater-enjoying began to change again in the late 1960s may have had to do with the pervasive cognitive persuasions of television. This type of structural causation did not rule out secondary-level causes of the kind I had deployed before. Indeed, it was becoming clear that the reality effects of radiophony and the new fear of communism, for example, probably reinforced each other in significant ways to alter the culture.

The organization of this book follows from my deliberations and conclusions. After a general introduction in chapter 1 to the theoretical orientations that ground this study, I investigate three major types of containment figures—Empty Boys, Family Circles, and Fragmented Heroes—and the embodiments and narratives that gave them appeal on the Broadway stage. Chapter 2 explores the narcissism of Empty Boys through *The Seven Year Itch* by George Axelrod and *A Hatful of Rain* by Michael Gazzo. The staging of Tennessee Williams's *Cat on a Hot Tin Roof* opposed the closeting of homosexuality in the conventional figure of the Empty Boy. Empathetic mothers energized the Family Circle of *The King and I* by Richard Rogers and Oscar Hammerstein and William Inge's *The Dark at the Top of the Stairs*, both discussed in chapter 3. Lorraine Hansberry contested the privileging of whiteness implicit in these dramas and challenged her audiences to imagine a very different kind of Family Circle. Watching *J.B.* by Archibald MacLeish and *Night Journey*, choreographed by Martha Graham, audiences witnessed the fated struggles of a Fragmented Hero, a figure that crystallized the American response to the threat of nuclear disaster during the Cold War. As chapter 4 relates, *The Crucible* by Arthur Miller opposed the passivity of Fragmented Hero narratives, but at the price of demonizing female sexuality. Each of these chapters also explores the theatrical practices of a major school or figure from the early cold war years—Method acting, the abstract scenography of Jo Mielziner, and the film and play direction of Elia Kazan—within the dominant cognitive categories of the era.

As we will see, theatrical artistry drawing on the economic and cultural capital of Broadway and embedded in the schema of containment produced enormous enjoyment for many spectators during this fifteen-year period. This made it difficult for Williams, Hansberry, Miller, and others to contest the modes of thinking that the Broadway stage, along with the dominant culture, induced. A brief epilogue charts the legacy of the early cold war theater from 1962 to 1992.

Acknowledgments

Most authors embedded in academia, as I have been for all of my professional life, owe a debt of gratitude to the institutions that have supported their scholarship. While I can think of several individuals to whom I must also give thanks, most of their insights and encouragements would not have been available to me had not other institutions, in turn, facilitated their work. Institutional support for this book began with the Department of Theatre and Speech and the Program in American Studies at the College of William and Mary. It also involved, in its early stages, the International Fulbright Fellowship Program and the New York Public Library.

The University of Pittsburgh provided me with a sabbatical leave from teaching for a semester and also financial support for reprinting and securing the rights to the photographs in this book. Because of the flexibility of the Department of Theatre Arts at Pitt, I have been able to teach graduate seminars that allow me to explore my historical interests with my students; their input has been invaluable. Several of my research assistants, in particular Jay Ball, David Himmelreich, and Michelle Sullivan, have given me good advice as well as hours of library time.

Like other scholars, I have benefited immensely from collegial feedback at conferences and in the course of publishing articles in journals. None of this would have been possible without the professional organizations that provide the framework for this ongoing scholarly activity. In particular, I am happy to thank the American Studies Association, the International Federation of Theatre Research, the Association for Theatre in Higher Education, and especially the American Society for Theatre Research. The editors and readers for *Theatre Journal, Assaph,* and *Theatre Survey* also deserve my appreciation.

The yearly summer institutes at the International Centre for Advanced Theatre Studies, affiliated with the University of Helsinki, have provided me with a welcoming forum for the exploration of many new ideas that have found their way into this book. My thanks to Pirkko Koski, director of ICATS, to my colleagues Janelle Reinelt, Freddy Rokem,

Steve Wilmer, and Bill Worthen, and to the many excellent international students who have challenged my thinking over the past eight years.

Finally, I am delighted to be publishing another book with the University of Iowa Press. In particular, my gratitude goes to Holly Carver, Kathy Lewis, and series editor Tom Postlewait, whose knowledge of theater historiography, attention to detail, and concern with accessibility have made this a much better book.

American Theater
in the Culture of the Cold War

A Theater of Containment Liberalism

The Broadway theater of 1947 to 1962 played a small but significant part in the dominant culture of the era. Necessarily bound by the profit motive, theatrical producers on the "Great White Way" sought middle- and upper-class attendance for their shows and generally turned their backs on working class families. Audience surveys done by *Playbill* during the 1950s found that only about 10 percent of the audience identified themselves as working class. Workers stayed away in droves for many reasons. Ticket prices played an important role; a typical show cost about eight times as much as most movies. Second, most workers rightly sensed that they would feel "out of place" in a Broadway theater. As critic and theorist Francis Fergusson noted, Broadway belonged in the "comparatively small 'luxury' class" during the 1950s and early 1960s. "The vision of life which it projects is more like that of the 'after-shave club' than that of the ads, in family magazines, for trusses and detergents," he said. Fergusson's conclusion is confirmed by a glance at the ads in any Broadway program during the period. The playbill for *A Hatful of Rain* for the week of 28 May 1956, for instance, contained advertisements for luxury cars, expensive women's clothes, air and ship travel, nightclub entertainment, and a variety of other high-priced items from liquor to topcoats.[1] While many workers in New York might have enjoyed Gazzo's play about an Italian American family struggling for economic and psychological security, few ever went to see it. Finally, working-class families usually lacked a playgoing tradition. The grandparents might have gone to live theater occasionally; but for most of the twentieth century, movies and later radio and television provided nearly all the professional dramatic entertainment that workers had ever seen or heard.

In 1955 critic Walter Kerr urged the New York theater to leave behind its elitist attitudes and welcome in the millions, because the drama "was not created by a minority for a minority." Kerr conceded the "risk of vulgarity in turning toward what pleases the common customer" but argued that the theater would "continue to shrivel if we do not do it."[2] Like many cultural commentators, Kerr believed that the New York theater was in decline. Certainly when compared to theatrical activity in the 1920s or during the temporary boom years of 1942–1945, the number of shows available on Broadway during the 1950s had decreased. But by most measurements the Broadway theater of the mid 1950s was about where it had been twenty years before. During an average week in February in both 1936 and 1956, theatergoers could choose from about twenty-five different productions. Although more shows opened in the mid 1930s, the successful ones ran longer by 1955. Further, the proportion of productions that recouped their investment remained about the same from 1927 to 1959—roughly 22 percent. If the off-Broadway scene is factored into the comparison, New Yorkers and tourists actually had many more playgoing opportunities available to them than before. From a mere 875 Off-Broadway performances in 1953/54, the number rose to over 9,000 by 1963/64. (In 1963/64 Broadway itself saw only 7,975 performances.) Overall, professional theater in New York increased dramatically from 1947 to 1962, with most of the increase coming in the last half of the period.[3]

Nevertheless, Kerr was correct in assuming that the audience for professional theater in New York was generally elitist in social orientation. Although the audience increased in numbers during the 1950s, its demographic base remained nearly constant. Most spectators lived in the New York metropolitan area, their average age tended to be between thirty-five and forty-five, and they earned above-average incomes. More significant than residence, age, and income, however, were markers of race and class. A 1960 survey found that 68 percent of the audience had been to college or university, a remarkably high number compared to the general population, where, despite the GI Bill and other inducements, less than 40 percent of the population had attended institutions of higher education by 1960. When asked to indicate their occupations, 47 percent checked "professional, semiprofessional, and managerial," and another 22 percent classified themselves as clerks and salespeople. (Because the survey-takers asked heads of households to answer their questions, women—who constituted roughly half of all theatergoers in the 1950s—

2 *A Theater of Containment Liberalism*

were vastly underrepresented. No doubt some of these women worked outside of the home, but most married women in the audience would have been housewives.) Finally, 4 percent of the spectators filling out the questionnaire were students or retired people. Revealingly, the survey did not ask its respondents to indicate their race. For an audience that was probably 98 percent white, this question would have struck most as unnecessary. Nor did the 1960 survey inquire about ethnicity, religion, or political beliefs. If it had, it likely would have discovered a sizable proportion of educated Jews, whose politics were more liberal than those of their gentile cohorts. In terms of class and race, however, over 70 percent of theatergoers in New York in 1960 were white people from the upper-middle class.[4]

Although the term "upper-middle" is appropriate, it would be more accurate to define the majority of theatergoers as belonging to what Barbara Ehrenreich and John Ehrenreich have called "the professional-managerial class." Mostly college educated, these engineers, teachers, managers, accountants, lawyers, writers, and others doing primarily mental rather than physical labor help modern capitalism to function efficiently. This class arose around 1900 as business leaders transformed mostly family enterprises into modern corporations. It found its voice—typically analytical, temporizing, rational, and apolitical—during the Progressive Era and flourished in the large corporations and governmental bureaucracies of the 1920s and 1930s.[5]

The members of the professional-managerial class did not own the means of production, but they distinguished themselves from the working class below them by acquiring a specialized body of knowledge and regulating their careers through professional standards. This allowed them a measure of autonomy from the ruling class, which employed most of them. During the Depression and the war, in fact, progressives in this group of mental workers had often sided with workers in their disputes with capitalists. And many in the professional-managerial group would again ask fundamental questions about the social practices of liberal capitalism in the late 1960s. But the capitalists' victories over working-class interests in the late 1940s, plus the probusiness tenor of public life by 1950, ensured that most professionals, managers, and others in this group would support the ruling class. As historian T. J. Jackson Lears notes, this group was not a class "in any coherent or unified sense." But it was a central part of the dominant "historical bloc" of the 1950s—"a

A Theater of Containment Liberalism 3

coalition of groups which differed in many ways but which were bound together (up to a point) by common interests, common experiences, and a common worldview."[6] During the early Cold War, then, professionals, managers, and other mental workers joined capitalists in what might be called a general business class. This class constituted the majority of spectators at all Broadway shows.

Several theatergoing practices in New York helped to solidify the different groups within this historical bloc. First, there were the productions themselves, which provided a common ground for conversation and camaraderie across group lines. Within the theater, ticket prices and seating arrangements did little to distinguish ruling-class patrons from others. Gone from all Broadway houses were most of the side boxes for elite auditors, and more than half of the orchestra seats were in the high-price range. Thus professional-managerial husbands and wives mixed easily with members of the ruling class in lobbies and seating areas. For most theatergoers, a Broadway show typically involved a "night on the town," with dinner out and possibly drinks afterward. A survey in 1962, for instance, found that fully 71 percent of playgoers living in New York or the vicinity ate at a restaurant before going to the theater.[7] As at the playhouse, this practice meant that members of the professional-managerial group could often mix with their superiors on an equal footing.

This apparent equality, however, was belied when a new show opened. For these occasions, ruling-class New Yorkers, often joined by out-of-town friends and occasional movie stars, came out in force. These spectators were what one survey called the "active theatregoers"[8]—those with much higher incomes than average who attended Broadway shows more than ten times a year. Though not as dominant as they had been in the 1920s and 1930s, the carriage-trade of active theatergoers filled the houses of new shows on Broadway from the late 1940s through the early 1960s, using them as opportunities to parade the latest dress styles, throw lavish theater parties, and perhaps get their pictures in the paper. Because the first few performances were crucial to long-term success in the hit-or-flop system of Broadway production, the ruling class exercised a kind of veto over all shows. In effect they, together with tastemakers and consumer guides in the press, selected what the professional-managerial group and the rest of the theatergoing public might see. Broadway productions during the Cold War had to pass through the eye of a needle held by a conservative ruling class before gaining success and wide distribution. Little wonder, then, that working-class points of view, which surfaced occasionally on the Broadway stage in the 1930s when the ruling class was more politically fragmented, rarely appeared on the Great White Way after 1947.

Indeed, whole areas of working-class life vanished from the theater during the early Cold War. Among different groups of workers in the late 1940s and early 1950s, roller derbies, "jive talk," bowling, rhythm-and-blues music, and group talkbacks to TV found eager participants and audiences, mostly for their parody of the dominant culture and their celebration of working-class grit and collective action. These trends might get a mention, but they never organized the action of a Broadway play or musical. At the same time, *film gris* attracted workers by its cynical response to promises of class mobility, the lures of consumerism, and government-sponsored suburbanization that was dispersing working-class urban communities. Unlike *film noir*, whose paranoiac vision it often shared, *film gris* typically pointed the finger of blame at society, not criminals or women, as the cause of distress. *The Prowler* (1951), for instance, featured a handsome policeman who, despairing of middle-class success, turns to robbery and murder. The difficulties of solidarity and marital love in the midst of a mining strike centered *The Salt of the Earth* (1953). The problems portrayed in *film gris* were not featured in successful Broadway plays. Like the rest of the dominant culture in the 1950s, the Great White Way also ignored the gradual synthesis of African American blues and southern country music that exploded in the rock and roll of Fats Domino, Bill Haley, Chuck Berry, and Elvis Presley. The best Broadway could do to contain the rampant energies of rock and roll threatening to burst national racial categories was *Bye Bye Birdie* (1960), a musical set in suburbia that delivered a paternal pat on the head to rock and featured no African American characters. This strategy of containment and condescension followed the earlier pattern of *The Pajama Game* (1954), which reduced postwar capitalist-labor strife to "Steam Heat" and pretty women in skimpy apparel threatening to strike a pajama factory.[9]

The triumph of capital over labor in the years after World War II underwrote and legitimated the business-class orientation of Broadway theater. Many working-class Americans emerged from the war hoping that postwar life would bring economic security, a better life for their kids, and a world free from fear. Politicians, Hollywood, advertisers, and patriotic business leaders had made these promises during the war, and working-class expectations were high. Instead, after the war many female workers found themselves out of jobs, black workers often got demoted, and even white males in the workforce were sometimes shoved aside by returning veterans. For many, family life seemed more stressful than ever, as the feelings of solidarity generated by the war effort gave way to alienation, marital difficulties, and renewed desire for the good life. With the headlines screaming of Soviet aggression in Europe and remobilization at home, the hope for a peaceful world continued to elude working-class Americans.

Soon after VJ Day, unionized workers in many areas of the economy began demanding more control over their lives on the job — the collective means to shape the conditions and pace of work that many capitalists had promised them during the war. When most business leaders refused to deliver on their promises, workers staged mass mobilizations, slowdowns, wildcat strikes, and general walkouts, often in defiance of their union leaders. Longshoremen in New York City struck in 1945, a general strike shut down much of industrial Pittsburgh in 1946, and women workers led a nationwide walkout against Bell Telephone in 1947. ("We're telling the company we're not part of the switchboard anymore," said one striking operator from Connecticut.)[10] In most of these collective actions, workers sought more independence at the point of production, not simply better wages and fringe benefits.

As George Lipsitz, historian of working-class life and culture, relates, business leaders responded to the postwar strike wave with "concessions, containment, and control."[11] Sometimes assisted by corrupt unions, business bought off worker demands for more control with higher pay and benefits. Indeed, real wages rose dramatically in the postwar years for most workers, but the usual tradeoff was less collective autonomy on the job. Many capitalists actually strove to increase the power of unions and their contracts after 1945 as a way of containing worker discontent and spontaneous action. At the same time, business leaders pushed for passage of the Taft-Hartley Act in 1947, which limited the organizing abilities of unions and banned secondary boycotts, initially a potent weapon in postwar strikes. In the late 1940s, business interests allied with conservative groups to fund an anti-Communist crusade that divided labor's political support, gutted radical labor unions, and moved the national conversation toward values more supportive of big business than it had been since the skewed prosperity of the 1920s.

Lipsitz's conclusion to his narrative of labor's postwar defeat deserves full quotation:

> The postwar triumph of corporate liberalism represents a clear case of a successful struggle for hegemony. Corporate liberals secured control over key resources and institutions by unifying antagonistic elements into an effective coalition. They won widespread support for a worldview that made their view of society synonymous with the general interest. They recruited allies from among competitive-sector conservatives and trade-union liberals by making concessions to the material interests of both groups. Most important, by combining countersubversive rhetoric with policies geared toward economic expansion, they found a basis for uniting the interests and ideologies of groups capable of working together to control the key institutions of the economy.[12]

Controlled by the business class, the Broadway stage also helped to unite "the interests and ideologies" of groups that constituted the historical bloc of the dominant culture in the 1950s.

In part this was because Broadway operated at the center of a centrifugal force field that shaped the entire American theater from 1947 to 1962. Producers of off-Broadway shows rarely competed with Broadway offerings; many, in fact, hoped to move their productions to the Great White Way. There were exceptions, of course, including Julian Beck and Judith Malina's work at the Living Theatre, which began in 1951; Joe Papp's Free Shakespeare in the Park, which started in 1956; and many of the productions at the Circle in the Square. The off-Broadway scene produced some genuinely oppositional theater, mostly toward the end of the 1947–1962 period, including *Sandhog*, a working-class musical by Earl Robinson and Waldo Salt, in 1954; Alice Childress's *Trouble in Mind*, about racial type-casting in theater and society, in 1955; *The Connection*, Jack Gelber's potent mix of jazz and drugs, in 1959; Jean Genet's *The Balcony* and *The Blacks* in 1960 and 1961; Edward Albee's *The American Dream* in 1961; and *Brecht on Brecht* in 1962. But these direct challenges to "corporate liberalism" did not constitute a self-conscious movement, and most had little initial resonance beyond the run of their productions.

Off-Broadway barely dented the financial dominance and cultural preeminence of Broadway in the nation until the mid 1960s. While this book notes these oppositional voices, it is important not to exaggerate their significance.

Other professional companies exercised some regional influence—Theatre '47 in Dallas, the Arena Stage in Washington, D.C., the Actors' Workshop in San Francisco, the short-lived Compass Theatre (1955–1957) in Chicago, and a few more. Even these theaters, however, looked to New York for most of their talent and typically lost talent to Broadway when the siren of success called it back. In addition to playwrights, actors, and designers, Broadway corralled whole cities into its network, effectively stamping out local professional activity in several of the playhouses of Boston and Philadelphia to turn them into tryout venues for its productions. Radiating outward from its center came road shows, hit songs, national stars, honors and awards, published plays, and catalogues instructing schools and community theaters on how to obtain the performance rights for them. Other force fields of entertainment—Hollywood and the major TV networks—wielded more power in the 1950s, but Broadway remained a "player" in the game of shaping America. This was primarily because the concerns of those in the business class who controlled the Broadway stage also set the agenda for "corporate liberalism."

American Theater in the Culture of the Cold War takes the material realities of the Broadway system and the typical theatergoer's search for entertainment within that network of relationships as its starting point. Critics and historians of the American theater during this period, however, have often ignored the material conditions that shaped the kinds of productions and receptions facilitated by the Broadway system and its extensions in the culture. Most scholars have understood the theater and culture of the cold war period in piecemeal fashion. Even though average spectators rarely discriminated between plays that might have lasting value and other forms of enjoyment, researchers have focused most of their attention on canonical works rather than on representative productions. While several scholars have persuasively interpreted the initial performances of the major plays of Arthur Miller and Tennessee Williams, few have attempted to situate these events in the context of similar Broadway productions and within the general cultural dynamics of the early Cold War. Further, spectators sought enjoyment from musicals and dance productions on Broadway, but comments about these forms of entertainment rarely rub shoulders with critical responses to dramatic works. In addition to analyzing several genres of dramatic theater, I discuss musical comedies and a few modern dances and mix popular with canonical theatrical events throughout this book.[13]

■ Lipsitz's term "corporate liberalism" is not inaccurate as a description of the dominant culture of the United States in the early Cold War, but "containment liberalism" may be a more historically specific term. U.S. corporations, after all, had been trading in liberal ideas since 1900. Indeed, as Immanuel Wallerstein notes, liberalism has provided the primary components of the "geoculture" legitimating world capitalism since the French Revolution.[14] With the onset of the Cold War, however, liberalism had to do double duty. Its abstractions of individual liberty, rationality, and freedom had not only to justify the depredations of Big Business within the nation but also to legitimate the struggle of the United States against international communism everywhere in the world—to separate a virtuous "us" from an evil "them" without ambiguity. If the United States were to win the "hearts and minds" of people around the globe, Americans had to practice as well as preach an ideology that had universal validity and appeal.

This led to a particular brand of liberalism that rested on the cognitive logic of containment. This logic can be seen most clearly, perhaps, in the National Security Act of 1947. President Harry Truman had pushed for the act to ensure that the president and secretary of defense would continue to exercise control over the joint chiefs of staff. The 1947 law, however, also created three key agencies that attracted less public attention at the time: the Central Intelligence Agency (CIA) to coordinate spying outside of the United States, the National Security Resources Board to link the needs of the armed services with universities and corporations, and the National Security Council (NSC) to advise the president on all matters relating to the security of the nation. Through these agencies, the law empowered the president to mount propaganda campaigns and conduct covert warfare to protect American interests. In effect, the national security apparatus created by this act separated substantial areas of executive authority from the people it was meant to serve and protect. After 1947 the American people and their representatives in Congress had no legal access to knowledge deemed "top secret" by the security establishment.

The National Security Act marks a significant transition in American history from militant state to cold war nation. According to Michael S. Sherry, historian of American militarization, the 1947 act "embodied the conviction that in an age of instant and total warfare, the vigilant nation must be constantly prepared by harnessing all its resources and linking its civilian and military institutions—indeed, obliterating the boundary between those institutions...." Frederick M. Dolan, a political philosopher, states that the vast expansion of presidential authority implicit in the 1947 act signaled a change in "the constitutional regime" of the United States and gave rise to a "cold war metaphysics" that shaped a range of the nation's tasks from the economy to civil rights. For Catherine Lutz, historian of the ideology of modern psychology, the National Security Act legitimated "denial" at the highest levels of government and led to "ignorance effects" that helped to construct the "epistemology of the bunker."[15]

These disparate insights into the 1947 law gain additional significance and inherent structural similarity when seen through the lens of the cognitive psychology of George Lakoff and Mark Johnson. Lakoff and Johnson's approach to cognitive metaphors can assist the cultural historian in discerning what historian Elizabeth Fox-Genovese has called the "conditions of consciousness and action" that structure the stuff of history. These conditions encompass "systems of social relations, including relations between women and men, between rich and poor, between the powerful and the powerless," and the ideologies that legitimate them. Thus, states Fox-Genovese, "both in the past and in the interpretation of the past, history follows a pattern or structure, according to which some systems of relations and some events possess greater significance than others."[16] Lakoff and Johnson's cognitive psychology holds particular promise for historians because it encourages them to discover these historical patterns in embodied actions centered on primary metaphors, including dramatic performances on the stage.

A metaphorical reading of the National Security Act of 1947 from Lakoff and Johnson's perspective would note that it derives its psychological coherence from the cognitive metaphor of "containment." The figure of "containment" involves necessary relations among an inside, an outside, and a boundary between them. In his book *The Body in the Mind*, Johnson summarizes five entailments embedded in this schema:

(i) The experience of containment typically involves protection from, or resistance to, external forces. When eyeglasses are *in* a case, they are protected against forceful impacts. (ii) Containment also limits and restricts forces within the container. When I am *in* a room or *in* a jacket, I am restrained in my forceful movements. (iii) Because of this restraint of forces, the contained object gets a relative fixity of location. For example, the fish gets located *in* the fishbowl. The cup is held *in* the hand. (iv) This relative fixing of location within the container means that the contained object becomes either accessible or inaccessible to the observer. It is either held so that it can be observed or else the container itself blocks or hides the object from view. (v) Finally, we experience transitivity in containment. If B is *in* A, then whatever is *in* B is also *in* A. If I am *in* my bed and my bed is *in* my room, then I am also *in* my room.

From Lakoff and Johnson's point of view, the human proclivity to structure experience through the concept of containment—like the use of other foundational concepts such as balance, scale, path, and force—is one of several functions of the mind that result from an infant's interaction with her or his physical and social environment. Different historical cultures, however, privilege some of these structures over others to organize their interactions and experiences.[17]

Clearly, the cognitive schema of containment helped Americans to construct much of their culture during the Cold War. Using the five entailments of containment outlined by Johnson to analyze the strictures and implications of the 1947 law reveals its significance as a nodal point of containment culture for postwar America. Taken as a whole, the act maps the nation-state as a unit of containment; inside the United States is secret knowledge requiring protection. Regarding the first entailment above involving protection within containment, the act is designed to safeguard this knowledge from external forces, chiefly the Soviet Union, although theoretically any force in the rest of the world might become an antagonist. In terms of the second, the constrictions caused by containment, the experience of this schema not only limits the ways in which the security establishment handles these secrets, but also puts severe restrictions on the freedoms of all other citizens within the boundaries of fortress America. Next, for the kind of focus involved in the third entailment, the law invites responsible Americans to fixate on people within the United States who have something to do with the secrets being guarded—the president, the security establishment, and potential subversives. For the fourth entailment of the schema, the paradoxes of accessibility, patriotic observers could plainly see some of the guardians and potential thieves of the secrets, but others were hidden in the shadows, protected by the very freedoms that defined the constitutional boundaries of the nation-state. Finally, regarding the fifth entertainment, the "transitivity" of containment meant that citizens in all private organizations within the United States must be suspect—a parent in a local Parent Teacher Association was also a citizen in the nation-state and might be an innocent participant in a cell of subversives. The seeds of what came to be called McCarthyism were not a later growth of the Cold War; paranoiac patriotism had already been planted (and was beginning to sprout) in 1947.

Other containers and their entailments pervaded cold war culture. Business-class Americans during the 1950s tended to regard the self as a container as well, typically an ego of innocence and vulnerability. Thus popular media analysts like Vance Packard (*The Hidden Persuaders*, 1956) convinced many Americans to worry that advertising was piercing the mental boundaries of American selves and injecting them with false values. And psychoanalysts, never before (or since) as popular in the United States, analyzed their patients' dreams to free what had previously been locked within the self. Talking heads and Hollywood films typically understood the white, suburban family as another container, especially insofar as it exerted sexual restraints on its husbands, wives, and teenagers. Imagining the nation as the Chosen People of God encouraged many people to fixate on the presumed qualities of the "American character" during the 1950s. For many Americans, the innocent self, the bunkered family, and the Chosen People provided a series of transitive Chinese boxes within which American morality could be protected and vindicated as a model for the "Free World." Teasing out the entailments of these and other cold war containers could easily consume several volumes of cultural history. In short, containment was at the hub of a vast network of cold war conceptions that structured much of the dominant culture of the era.

What is the performance historian to make of these metaphorical extensions of the spatial image of a container? From a traditional historical and philosophical point of view, metaphors provide a poor road to truth. In Cartesian and empiricist thinking, metaphorical language deviates from the language of verifiable representation. Conventionally, if metaphors are to have any validity beyond poetic evocation or rhetorical flourish, they must express preexisting similarities between phenomena. In short, the traditional notion of metaphor relegates it to a matter of words, not truth. Drawing on thirty years of experiments in cognitive psychology and a desire to construct "empirically responsible philosophy," Lakoff and Johnson completely reject the conventional view of metaphor in their philosophy of "embodied realism." From their point of view, scientific and humanistic truth is impossible without metaphor.[18]

Lakoff and Johnson's embodied realism holds that mental concepts arise, fundamentally, from the experience of the body in the world. As "neural beings," humans must make meaning within certain "basic-level," "spatial relations," and "bodily action" concepts, plus other schemas resulting from the interplay of experience and patternings in the brain. "Primary metaphors" flesh out the skeletal possibilities of many of these foundational concepts. Social stereotypes, prototypical examples, and other modes of categorizing extend basic-level concepts. Regarding spatial relations concepts, the "source-path-goal" schema, for instance, which humans learn at an early age by crawling from a starting point to an end point, undergirds numerous metaphors that organize certain events in our lives as narratives with a beginning, a middle, and an end. "Balance," a bodily action concept, provides many metaphors for mental health, ethical behavior, and public justice. These primary metaphors are "creative," in the sense that they create an analogy linking two phenomena through similarity; they do not rely on the recognition of an inherent, objective similarity between two phenomena. Because these and numerous other primary metaphors link everyday experience to sensorimotor phenomena, most conceptual thinking cannot occur without metaphors.

These metaphors generally work at unconscious levels. People may become conscious of some of their metaphorical thinking, however, through careful analysis of their actions and words; the cognitive unconscious is not the Freudian unconscious of memory and desire. "Conscious thought is the tip of an enormous iceberg," note Lakoff and Johnson. "It is the rule of thumb among cognitive scientists that unconscious thought is 95 percent of all thought—and that may be a serious underestimate." (In this sense, the "cognitive" in "cognitive psychology" moves well beyond the usual definition of the term in philosophy; metaphors do inform conscious, propositional thinking, but they shape most of the iceberg under the water as well.) The foundational concepts and primary metaphors identified by Lakoff and Johnson provide content as well as form to human thinking. Like the spatial relations schema of containment noted above, each of their concepts, together with its associated metaphors, constrains the kinds of meanings that can follow from it. The bodily action concept of "counterforce," for example, entails images that involve a head-on meeting of material forces. This schema organizes much of our perception of football games, historical revolutions, and similar phenomena, but it could not be made to fit much of the content usually organized by other bodily action concepts, such as "full-empty" and "iteration."[19]

According to Lakoff and Johnson, these submerged schemas and their metaphorical extensions are nearly universal to human experience: "Much of a person's conceptual system is either universal or widespread across languages and cultures. Our conceptual systems are not totally relative and not merely a matter of historical contingency, even though a degree of conceptual relativity does exist and even though historical contingency does matter very much." Within embodied realism, cultural relativity and historicity occur in two ways. Lakoff and Johnson note that cultures typically differ in their "worldviews," which they define as a "consistent constellation" of foundational concepts and primary metaphors over one or more cultural domains (such as politics, morality, psychology, etc.). Certain basic schemas and metaphors, in other words, organize significant areas of a culture. Second, new "complex metaphors and other conceptual blends" can arise that facilitate shifts in thinking and historical change.[20] The complex metaphor "time is money," for instance, helped to structure the rise of capitalism in the West — a metaphor largely absent from precapitalist cultures throughout the world.

Hence, for Lakoff and Johnson, all mental operations are built on transhistorical, though not transcendental, sources. That is, human cognition, its potential built into the brain by biological evolution, emerges from every individual's experience with the material world and structures all historical cultures, but it is not a part of some ahistorical, immaterial human nature. The same might be said of such concepts as narrative, gender, and hierarchy — ideas that can be shown to derive from basic-level categories and primary metaphors and that are also universal to all cultures. Human biology and the material world are logically prior to cognition for Lakoff and Johnson. In the source-path-goal example above, for instance, babies must have some experience of human interaction and the pull of gravity to learn to crawl. "At the heart of embodied realism," Lakoff and Johnson state, "is our physical engagement with an environment in an ongoing series of interactions."[21] Thus they reject a strict subject-object dichotomy, which results either in an epistemology of disembodied objectivity or in intersubjective relativism. Embodied realism has affinities with the philosophical realisms of John Dewey, Hilary Putnam, and Ludwig Wittgenstein.

Consequently, historians may join Lakoff and Johnson's embodied realism to cultural theories built on realistic premises, such as systems theory, social practice theory, and hegemony theory and their many combinations and variations. These cognitive and cultural perspectives share a commitment to philosophical realism and its open-ended methodology, which includes hermeneutics and theory-based probes into realities embedded in empirical evidence.[22] To borrow from Lakoff and Johnson's embodied realism, a dominant culture might now be defined as mutually supportive "constellations" of concepts and metaphors legitimating the power of certain social groups and classes. Further, embodied realism suggests that the "meaning" of phenomena in culture and history, though never random or completely relative, is always potentially plural. In this regard, the cognitive semantics that researchers have constructed on the foundation of cognitive psychology affirms the polysemy of all language. Hence, discourse itself, because of its ties to embodied experience, is more like a mansion than a prison house, even though humans in historical cultures spend most of their time in only a few of its rooms.

Merging Lakoff and Johnson's cognitive psychology with hegemony theory theoretically opens up a significant possibility for change in historical cultures. The reserve of concepts and metaphors beyond the constellations of the dominant culture constitutes a potentially enormous reservoir for different cultural constellations; indeed, this potential helps to explain why historical cultures were and continue to be so different around the world. This reservoir needs to be distinguished, however, from what Raymond Williams has called "residual culture," a less-encompassing term that refers to past cultural constellations still current and available for use within a specific cultural-historical tradition. The well of human experience embodied in the brain has room for many residual cultures but also includes concepts and metaphors for all other constellations—past, present, and future. Lakoff and Johnson's cognitive science, consequently, helps to explain cultural innovation. Again to use Williams's terminology, new constellations of cognitive structures, always already available in the mind, may become "emergent" and potentially "oppositional." Given the right agents and circumstances, even "residual" culture can harbor opposition, as occurred in the theater of the early Cold War.[23]

While I have already enumerated the five entailments of containment, it is important to elaborate their wide applicability in shaping interaction in the theater and, more generally, in culture. If figures are perceived as containers, phenomena related to them are understood to be either inside or outside of those figures. This facet of containment affects an enormous range of everyday thinking. If, as Johnson states, "we understand categories metaphorically as containers (where a thing falls within the container or it does not), then we have the claim that everything is either P (in the category-container) or not-P (outside the container)." Thinking with containment as a matrix, in other words, results in either/or propositions that can lead to a "hardening of the categories" in everyday life. Looking at reality through the eyeglasses of containment, the phenomena of the world also seem to possess essences; one or several of the features "inside" a figure can come to represent the essence of that figure. From this perspective, note Lakoff and Johnson, "every entity has an 'essence' or 'nature,' that is, a collection of properties that makes it the kind of thing it is and is the causal source of its natural behavior." They term this the "folk theory of essences" and discuss its pervasive influence in the philosophies of Plato and Aristotle. The "folk theory of essences" and "either/or" thinking are flip sides of the same coin; both derive from conceiving of phenomena as containers with insides and outsides.[24]

If metaphors of containment organized much of the dominant culture of an era, one would expect to find numerous examples of either/or and essentialist thinking across many fields within its constellation. Several scholars have noted that this was indeed the case during the early Cold War. Cultural historian Jackson Lears points to one consequence of essentialism in the dominant culture of the 1950s, the pervasive "reification of abstract concepts into things which [in the theories of social scientists, especially] acted autonomously on people."[25] Talcott Parsons's abstract notion of a "social system" with the ability to push people about like chess players on a board is a salient instance cited by Lears. He also notes as examples the concept of "modernization" in the discourse of economists and modal personality types common in anthropological and sociological studies. In each of these discourses, reifying the essence of a social science category leads to imagined effects in the material world.

In *Allegories of America: Narratives, Metaphysics, Politics*, Frederick M. Dolan links the widespread influence of modern versions of Platonism to the "metaphysics" of the Cold War. Dolan suggests that the pervasive "fear of simulation," a concern that "outward appearances do not correspond to inner essences," generated multiple strategies "to distinguish the apparent from the genuine, simulations from representations," throughout cold war culture. "Taken to an extreme," Dolan continues, "it is a fear that no judgment, no distinction is any longer possible; a fear, as Jean Baudrillard has expressed it, that there is no God." Behind Baudrillard's thinking is the Platonic metaphor "categories of thought are containers": either categories represent their true inner essences or they simulate the surface of an empty shell. Dolan recognizes that without essences controlling the appearance of categories, it is impossible to distinguish representations from simulations; hence Platonic judgment is at risk. (Lakoff and Johnson would argue, of course, that the distinction between representation and simulation is erroneous to begin with, since both proceed from the folk theory of essences.) For Dolan, however, the dialectic between discourses of representation and simulation characterized cold war culture: "In Cold War America, ideologists of representation [i.e., modern Platonists] simultaneously stimulate the fear that representation is at risk from simulation and reassure us that the recovery of representation, the equation of sign and meaning, of public and private, is still possible. . . . In fact, the symbiosis of simulation and representation is central to postwar American political culture and, more specifically to the Cold War—as distinguished from Soviet-American conflict, which it promises to outlive."[26] In popular culture, this dialectic often took the form of a conflict between surface and essence, which typically distinguished the "phony" from the "real."

Finally, rhetorician David Campbell links this desire to represent essences to a recurrent American anxiety about national political identity. Believing that history provides them with no fixed identity, Ameri-

A Theater of Containment Liberalism 17

cans, says Campbell, have stirred up several "cold wars" over time in which they reified an evil Other in an anxious attempt to define themselves: "In these terms, 'cold war' signifies not a discrete historical period, the meaning of which can be contained, but an orientation toward difference in which those acting on behalf of an assumed but never fixed identity are tempted by the lure of otherness to interpret all dangers as fundamental threats that require the mobilization of a population." Drawing on the scholarship of Benedict Anderson, Campbell notes that the identity of "America" has always been fragile; "America is the 'imagined community' par excellence," he states.[27] Consequently, concerns about "un-American" activities have proliferated in times of crisis, as occurred among the Puritans in the late seventeenth century, between Federalists and Republicans in the 1790s, between the Radical Republicans and their enemies during Reconstruction, and in the 1950s — to name a few of the major American "cold wars." During these "ages of anxiety," as several commentators termed the 1950s, many Americans struggled over either/or definitions of law and order, the family, religion, sexuality, and gender roles. Fear of Others who might simulate "Americanness" drove self-styled patriots to essentialize "America" and to idealize (in both the conventional and philosophical meanings of the word) its representations. If "America" is understood as a container of national identity, categories of "us" and "them" follow naturally from this metaphor.

My debts to Lears, Dolan, and Campbell are apparent in the following pages. Like them and others, I argue that containment and its inherent Platonism shaped significant domains of the dominant American culture during the Cold War — in particular the Broadway theater. Images emanating from this concept and its constellation crossed theatrical genres to inform domestic melodramas, musical theater, Broadway comedy, biblical dramas, and modern dance. Metaphors of containment saturated all of the dramas and dances from the dominant culture discussed in this study — *The Seven Year Itch*, *A Hatful of Rain*, *The King and I*, *The Dark at the Top of the Stairs*, *J.B.*, and *Night Journey*. "Containment" not only did cultural work through the form and pressure of dramatic narratives centered on contained figures; it also shaped the vocal and physical choices of Method actors like Marlon Brando, the images created by Jo Mielziner and similar designers, and the total *mise en scène* of directors like Elia Kazan. As I demonstrate, the rhetorics and aesthetics of containment liberalism on the stage wove together acting style, playwriting, design, and audience expectations to generate unified theatrical events of significant influence. Spectator enjoyments induced by these events prepared Americans to participate in the dominant culture as consumers, family members, and witnesses. At the same time, some stage performances encouraged audiences to contest the dominant culture of the era—performances drawing on the residual culture of traditional orality and on metaphors current during the Popular Front years of the late 1930s and early 1940s.

■ From the point of view of Lakoff and Johnson's embodied realism, theatrical rhetoric cannot be separated from aesthetic style. Before undertaking an analysis of cold war theater, it is necessary to rejoin rhetoric and aesthetics through cognitive psychology, a merger that entails a new understanding of audience response in the theater. In conventional theory, the rhetoric/aesthetic distinction assumes a radical dichotomy between experiencing subjects and objectively knowable objects. Although Lakoff and Johnson do not comment directly on this analytical separation, their discussion of the errors of "disembodied scientific realism" is relevant to it. This way of doing science, they state, "create[s] an unbridgeable ontological chasm between 'objects' which are 'out there' and subjectivity, which is 'in here.'" They continue: "Once the separation is made, there are only two possible, equally erroneous, conceptions of objectivity: Objectivity is either given by the 'things themselves' (the objects) or by the intersubjective structures of consciousness shared by all people (the subjects)." As Lakoff and Johnson point out, what "disembodied realism," like most aesthetic and rhetorical theory, "misses is that, as embodied, imaginative creatures, *we never were separated or divorced from reality in the first place*" (emphasis in original).[28] Restated in theatrical terms, the "response" of the audience was never separated or divorced from the "reality" on stage. Consequently, humans can gain no objective understanding about the formal properties of theatrical objects on the stage or about a separable, discrete response to them from members of the audience. The relationship connecting spectators to the stage and events on the stage to the spectators must be understood as a single phenomenon.

This differs from the dualistic view of semiotics and similar approaches in which the audience interprets theatrical signifiers to understand the signifieds that they represent. Rather than looking at a performance as a kind of text through which to view an absent fictional world, spectators at a play experience dramatic fiction directly through the cognitive game of theater. Drawing on the phenomenon of "seeing as" described by Wittgenstein and on the aesthetic ideas of Kendall Walton, theorist David Saltz adapts Walton's key proposition that viewers use art as "props in games of make-believe" to understand how audience members use the theater. Like children playing with action figures, spectators engage in a cognitive game when they choose to "see" actors "as" characters; they likewise "implement a metaphorical restructuring of reality" to experience the fictitious world of the play. As Saltz acknowledges, "the way metaphor functions in the theory I am proposing is . . . closely related to the function of metaphor in Lakoff and Johnson's theory." For Saltz, semiotics misleads critics about an audience's experience in the theater: "Spectators do not always, or even usually, treat theatrical performance as a text from which to extract details about a fictional world. The focus of their attention is on the performance itself, and on the significance and force of the performers' actions within the world the performers have created on stage."[29]

Cognitive science provides insight into the possible relationships between the "force of the performers' actions" and the spectators. Drawing on experiments from several researchers, Lakoff and Johnson discuss the primary means by which humans imaginatively identify themselves with others in fictitious, "seeing as" situations. The ability to imitate another person that is learned in childhood involves imagining oneself as inhabiting the body of the other—metaphorically projecting the self onto someone else. Combining Wittgenstein, Saltz, and Lakoff and Johnson, it is clear that metaphorical projection is the basis of theatrical enjoyment. Cognitively, this occurs in two primary ways: advisory projection and empathetic projection. In advisory projection, state Lakoff and Johnson, "I am projecting my values onto you so that I experience your life with my values. In the other type, empathetic projection, I am experiencing your life, but with your values projected onto my subjective experience."[30] In theatrical terms, both kinds of projection involve spectators' imaginatively occupying the bodies of actors (and potentially others) in the performance. The difference involves "values," one's own or an Other's.

While the mechanics of projection are simple enough, the results can be quite complex. Most performances of drama involve the audience in numerous moments of advisory and empathetic projection, a distinction that is further complicated when the spectator's values are nearly identical with the values of the figure identified with on the stage. And who or what is this figure? In realist plays, in which the presence of the actor mostly "becomes" a fictitious character for the audience, spectators primarily imagine themselves projecting their subjectivity onto the body of the "character." In some modes of theater that encourage the audience to separate the actor from the character, however — productions of Bertolt Brecht and Luigi Pirandello are obvious examples — spectators may mix their projections between actors and "characters." But "characters," of course, have no bodies without actors; the possibilities for complexity in advisory and empathetic projection multiply.

The approach to theatrical rhetoric embedded in Lakoff and Johnson's philosophy comes closest to the phenomenological materialism advocated in *Theatre and Everyday Life: An Ethics of Performance* by Alan Read and *The Fate of the Object: From Modern Object to Postmodern Sign in Performance, Art, and Poetry* by Jon Erickson. Read locates the process of theater in the interplay of spectating and performing bodies. "Theatre is an expressive practice that involves an audience through the medium of images at the centre of which is the human body," he states.[31] Although *The Fate of the Object* leaves unquestioned the conventional subject/object dichotomy of conventional semiotics, rhetoric, and aesthetics, Erickson's understanding of an actor's "presence" is useful for teasing out an implicit theatrical rhetoric within Lakoff and Johnson's embodied realism. Actors, says Erickson, can never fully become or fully erase a spectator's perception of them as both corporal beings and signs of some Other person; they are, consequently, both bodies and characters, simultaneously. In fact, alleges Erickson, "the tension between the *body as object* and the *body as sign* gives birth to an awareness of *presence* as the tension between basic corporal being and the becoming of signification" (emphasis in original).[32] Following Lakoff and Johnson, one might emend Erickson's statement to note the gestalt nature of audience projection. That is, spectators project themselves onto the "presence" of actors, a presence constituted both by the body of the actor and by the actor's fictional significance in the performance. This significance might range from the meaning of the persona a Brechtian actor presents to the audience as "herself" to the meaning of a fully embodied male "character" portrayed by a Method actor. Hence, spectators project their subjectivity onto the presence of an actor on stage. In advisory projection, the spectator reads his or her own values into that presence. When the projection is empathetic, spectators take what they perceive are the values of that presence and read them into their imaginative experience of it.

Projection onto the presence of an actor is the first step in the dynamics of dramatic rhetoric on stage. Spectator identification of a narrative binding these actor-characters together is the second. Like projection, narrative imagining is a foundational part of human cognition. As literary-cognitive theorist Mark Turner notes, "storytelling is a constant mental activity . . . essential to human thought." The urge to narrate proceeds from the source-path-goal image schemata and frames numerous events in everyday life, from pouring a cup of coffee to imagining a journey. Rather than being "optional" or merely "literary," narrativity "appears to be inseparable from our evolutionary past and our necessary personal experience," states Turner.[33] This human proclivity to imagine stories prompts theatergoers to look for narrative links among the events on stage and connect them into cohesive series and wholes. As in all narratives, what critic Peter Brooks terms "the structuring force of the ending" pulls spectators through the story line of a play.[34] Like spectatorial projections onto the presence of actors, the preferred forms and genres of narrative imagining often vary widely among periods and cultures. Hence certain kinds of actor-characters and specific stories about them gain popularity in a given historical period. A wily hero and his voyage home had significant valence for ancient Greeks listening to the story of Odysseus. Cold war Americans needed stories about Empty Boys growing up to be men, Family Circles bunkered to defend themselves against dangerous Others, and Fragmented Heroes struggling to pull themselves together.

If imaginative projection and narrative expectation couple spectators to the presence of actors embedded in stories and if the rhetoric of the theater can no longer be separated from its aesthetics, how can an expanded sense of rhetoric and aesthetics be forged for interpreting and explaining the linkage between audiences and performers during the cold war theater? Rhetoric in this larger sense must now encompass not only how but what audiences projected themselves onto and what stories were told through these actor-characters when they went to the theater. Plays were aesthetically pleasing and rhetorically persuasive, then, insofar as they encouraged spectators to project themselves onto "figures that mattered," to adopt a phrase from philosopher Judith Butler—figures involved, as well, in "stories that mattered."[35] This sense of rhetoric approaches Kenneth Burke's understanding that persuasion is always preceded by identification; for rhetoric to work in the theater, spectators must be able to identify the story they are watching and be able to identify with it—in Lakoff and Johnson's terms, to project themselves onto it.[36] Burke's sense of rhetoric gets us closer to embodied realism, but the notion of projection as identification still involves subjects operating on objects. For the kind of interaction that Lakoff and Johnson envision, the figures projected onto must, in effect, push back; the specific content of the actor's presence—both his/her corporality and significance in the narrative—must empower and constrain the kinds of identification and projection possible for spectators in the theater. Because of this interplay of projection and actor content embedded in narrative, the rhetoric of dramatic theater is always a local affair, difficult to generalize about except as groups of theatrical events in which certain kinds of audiences meet specific kinds of figures and experience particular stories on the stage. As a result of this interaction, certain kinds of performances fashion certain groups of spectators and vice versa.

How is the historian to proceed, then, in determining how these various interactions, these rhetorical genres of theater, occurred within a historical period? As Lakoff and Johnson recognize, humans use basic-level categories, schemas, and primary metaphors thousands of times each day to make sense of their world. With so many category types and metaphors at play, how can the historian know which ones shaped the specific enjoyment of a particular rhetorical genre in the theater and also achieved more relative importance than others during a specific historical period? Luckily for the theater historian, performances tend to be "condensational events" in which certain primary metaphors, condensed from cultural-historical interaction, emerge as dominant and significant.[37] The first step, then, is an analysis of representative instances of these performance genres with close attention to the kinds of inducements for identification and projection specific to them and an interest in the kinds of figures and narratives that spectators enjoyed projecting themselves onto. Next, the historian must move from the micro- to the macro-level of analysis, checking to make sure that the kinds of projections and metaphorical mappings induced by these performance genres occurred with some frequency in the everyday lives of the spectators. If the broader culture induced analogous enjoyments, spectators, even those relatively new to the game of theatergoing, would have an easier time involving themselves in the rhetorical inducements of the performance event. The historiographical process that results is the familiar hermeneutic circle, with the historian tacking between specific and general evidence, making interpretive adjustments, and finally arriving at an adequate explanation of the cognitive processes involved, the material consequences of these mechanisms, and their larger historical significance.

Since theatergoing is a subspecies of imaginative game playing, an analogy to the enjoyment of American football may be helpful. Football was popular among pockets of the American business class before World War II, but it did not achieve the status of a major national sport until the mid 1950s. Most spectators watching Johnny Unitas and the Baltimore Colts win the 1958 and 1959 National Football League championships, whether at the stadium or on television, identified with one of the teams and empathetically projected themselves onto specific figures during the action. In so doing, they engaged in thousands of cognitive processes; but among these the spatial relations concepts of containment and part-whole and the physical action concepts of compulsion, iteration, and counterforce frequently recurred. Football involves the use of guile and physical force to gain territory or contain an opposing team; there is little ambiguity about the cognitive mechanisms involved in comprehending the agonistic mode of this "condensational event." What most spectators (and nearly all ardent fans) might call their enjoyment of the game was cognitively processed through these categories, though other primary metaphors may have been involved as well. Indeed, it is difficult to imagine football spectators understanding the game at all, much less enjoying it, without their minds working unconsciously in these ways. The cognitively attuned sports historian attempting to explain the popularity of football with the American business class in the 1950s might look to similar public events at the time (including stage performances) that entailed a massive investment in these cognitive modes.

Arguably, spectatorship at a specific genre of theatrical performance involves more cognitive complexity and ambiguity than a football game (though football enthusiasts would probably disagree). Nonetheless, for a production on stage to "work" with its spectators, the audience members must invest in most of its cognitive inducements; they must "play the game" or sit in silent boredom. In this important sense, enjoying plays and enjoying football games are similar. On one level, of course, spectators can think whatever they please in the playhouse. Frequent random acts of cognition are unlikely, however, simply because the environment of the auditorium and the events on stage invite certain kinds of identifications and projections and not others. As Lakoff and Johnson understand, the world pushes back against human perceptions; consequently, the minds of audience members, shaped by evolution, the experience of living on earth, and historical culture, will tend to take well-traveled routes of cognition to gain comprehension. Faced with certain kinds of stimuli, the cognitive unconscious tends to click onto "containment" rather than another primary metaphor to make sense of what is perceived.

Since this happens at the unconscious level, there can be no hard evidence of its occurrence. But the historian can know that the results of such projections and cognitions in popular, successful theater led to the creation and enjoyment of similar projections and cognitions in subsequent theatrical events. Thus the indirect evidence for such cognitive experiences is substantial. Analyzing the scripts, reviews, and designs of rhetorically successful theatrical genres can lead the historian to an understanding of the major cognitive mechanisms in any period that generated theatrical entertainment. This historical method cannot produce certainty, but it can lead to valid judgments that rely on what I have termed "cognitive probablity."[38] The argument of this book is not that early cold war spectators always processed their theatrical involvement through metaphors of containment. An analysis of representative popular performances and their historical context, however, shows that containment and other primary metaphors of the period shaped significant interactions between the stage and most spectators during the 1947–1962 period.

Cognitive processes are presemiotic. While containment and other metaphors shaped the meanings that spectators in the 1950s took away from their experiences in the theater, the later articulation of these meanings (in reviews, memoirs, letters, etc.) must be separated from the theatrical experience itself. Play reviews, for example, are shaped by journalism and other discursive protocols; they never analyze the moment-to-moment response of the critic to the performance, much less her or his engagement at the level of the cognitive unconscious. Nonetheless, reviews, like other primary sources from the theatrical past, can be moderately helpful in the historical task of imaginatively constructing a typical performance and the response it generated. Critical reviews can also be read symptomatically to understand what a few spectators, perhaps more sensitive than most to the rhetorical inducements of a particular genre, may have experienced at the cognitive level while watching the performance. That is, a review may reveal attitudes and values that suggest how the critic projected him/herself onto a performer-character and the metaphorical mappings the reviewer used to comprehend the narrative of the play. In this sense, critical interpretation and evaluation—what a critic thinks a play was "about" and how well it was written and produced—is less interesting to me than the traces left in the review that reveal the critic's cognitive engagements with the initial theatrical experience. If an analysis of several reviews reveals similar suggestive evidence, this insight must be factored into any broader historical explanation. Symptomatic interpretation, in fact, must inform the cognitive historian's understanding of all of the primary documents relating to a popular genre.

Cognitive performance history asks different questions about spectator response in the theater than the questions most semioticians and historians have usually posed.[39] Assuming a presemiotic, preinterpretation level of audience engagement, the cognitive historian needs first to understand the primary cognitive mechanisms that bonded spectators to actors and their actions in the playhouse. If Lakoff and Johnson and other cognitive scientists are right, these mechanisms must be animated before spectators can make any meanings at all out of their experiences. Because the kinds of projections and metaphorical mappings triggered in the game of theater both animate and constrain the kinds of meanings most spectators make, these mechanisms provide a firm guide at the next stage of historical interpretation, the attempt to understand how spectators may have connected the protomeanings of the performance they just witnessed to their everyday lives. Here I am guided by the insights of Stanley Cavell's *The Claim of Reason* (1979), which demonstrates, largely through a rereading of Wittgenstein, that most people share the same experiential world, in which "good enough" knowledges allow them to construct satisfying and intelligent lives. For the historian interested in audience engagement at the theater, Cavell's book suggests that most spectators' meaning-making in the theater flows through conventional, historically constructed channels of truth-telling and is generally untroubled by the complications and contradictions that later critics and historians may discover in their response. This is not to discount the possible historical significance of such disjunctures in spectators' making of meaning; it simply acknowledges the transformation that occurs when critic-historians take the relatively straightforward evidence of spectatorial cognition and interpretation and subject it to contextual analysis and explanation.[40]

■ The specificity of aesthetic and rhetorical dynamics in the theater necessarily throws theatrical production and response into the arena of history. Cognitive metaphors such as containment, together with related groups of metaphors, may structure the "conditions of consciousness and action" within a historical period, but the hegemony of such a nexus of metaphors must be initiated by other factors.[41] As several theorists and historians have argued, changes in the major communication practices of a culture alter how people conceive of reality. According to Walter J. Ong, for instance, media "define what really is." The effects of new media on older forms of communication in a culture, including live theater, however, cannot be charted in straightforward, cause-effect patterns. Writing about the impact of print on the plays of William Congreve and late Restoration theater, Julie Stone Peters notes: "There is no direct and necessary set of equivalences between orality and the live theater, and literacy and the printed drama. It is thus impossible to make two neatly divided lists that would detail a perfect dichotomy. Some of the more interesting elements of Congreve's relation to orality, literacy, print, the live theater, and the published dramatic text defy all categorization and qualify substantially the more generalized conclusions at which I have arrived."[42] Similarly, the disparate effects of print, photography, radio, and television—the major communication media of the early Cold War—on the theater of the period defy easy generalization.

An observation by critic-director Harold Clurman provides an initial approach to this problem. Writing in 1967, Clurman lamented the general change from the realist dramas of the 1930s to the "poetic or 'stylized'" plays of the postwar era. The former leader of the Group Theatre believed that the pressing problems of the real world—the need "to remedy unemployment, feed the hungry, alter the economy, combat Fascism"—had led to realist treatments of characters and situations in social dramas and even many comedies before the war. Today, he cautioned, "the world still exists [and] acts upon us, no matter how resolutely we flee it," but "the drama of our recent past has suffered intellectual and emotional attrition through its exclusion of the specific, the spectrum and spectacle, the *body* of reality" (emphasis in original).[43] The shift that annoyed Clurman has puzzled subsequent critics and historians. Several have noted the change away from the generally photographic conventions of stage and dramatic realism in the prewar period toward increasing subjectivity, abstraction, and allegory after 1945, but no one has adequately explained why this shift occurred.

Looking at the reality effects of new media on theatrical constructions of the real, one clue to explaining this shift may be the ubiquity of radio by the 1940s. Under pressure from print, photography, and films, the dominant media of the 1920s and 1930s, the plays of those decades generally crafted their version of reality within the constraints of the visual culture. The successful plays of the 1950s were no less "real" for their spectators, of course, but perhaps they were responding to a notion of reality shaped in part by radiophony. If the cold war theater seemed to ignore the "*body* of reality," in Clurman's words, it may have been because artists and spectators assumed that aural images from the disembodied medium of radio might be just as real (or even more real) than the "spectacle" of the material world.

Recent theoretical work by Tobin Nellhaus on changing modes of communication and the historical generation of metatheatricality provides some helpful guidance for the critic-historian eager to trace the disparate effects of radiophony. Nellhaus points out that metatheatricality has occurred primarily during eras when new forms of communication are challenging older ones. Following Nellhaus, metatheatricality and metacommunicative artistry in all media proliferated in the twentieth century because radiophonic and other aural modes of communication continued to unsettle the representational authority of print and photography, the dominant media by 1900.[44] Nellhaus notes that this ongoing tension creates particular difficulties for the "agents" of performance, by which he means playwrights who craft scripts for the theater and actor-characters, the dramatic agents in the fictional world on stage. Aware that older conventions of representation no longer carry full legitimacy, playwrights add narrative frames to foreground their agency as storytellers while their characters, Hamlet-like, worry about their own possibilities for action within the world of the play. Perhaps the prime examples of this dynamic on the modern stage are the plays of Bertolt Brecht. Brecht intended his plays-within-plays and split characters to involve his spectators directly in the question of historical agency. By refusing to allow his actors to disappear into an iconic representation of his scripted roles, Brecht tried to keep alive his own agency and that of his ensemble in the midst of performance. According to Nellhaus, the critic-historian could expect to find more instances of metatheatricality and heightened concern regarding the legitimacy of theatrical and dramatic agency, especially evident in playwriting and acting, whenever new modes of communication are challenging older ones.

Apart from this general level of historical change that occurs when any new medium reaches dominance, the critic-historian might also look for more specific kinds of influence traceable to the reality effects of the new mode of communication itself. The realities stemming from new media rarely cause anything directly, of course, but they do establish structural "conditions of consciousness and action" that can shift the modes of cognition of the dominant culture, allowing new schemas to emerge into prominence and suppressing the frequency and valence of others. When writing challenged orality in ancient Greece, according to historian Jennifer Wise, it "established new standards of ideality, repeatability, and sameness for words, abstract qualities that spoken language, tied as it is to particular instances of utterance and engagement with unique constellations of perceptual data, never attains."[45] From Wise's point of view, the theater itself could not have occurred without the invention of writing. Similarly, the advent of print and the proliferation of books and newspapers gave rise to a culture that prized individual subjectivity, a value evident in the elevated status of authorship and the private act of reading. In turn, photographic culture (including the "moving" pictures of the silent film era) was dislocating notions of reality around 1900. These gradual shifts in perceptions of "the real" suggest that the technologies of audiophony, and radio in particular, may have moved the tectonic plates of human cultural cognition in similarly fundamental ways after 1920.

The advent of commercial radio broadcasting in 1920 caused both the general effects predicted by Nellhaus and specific changes in the dominant culture's orientation to reality that the work of media historians has led us to expect. Radio challenged the reality effects of photography and silent film that had complemented or partly replaced those of print during the previous forty years. According to Walter Benjamin and others, the advent of photography in 1839 marked a significant turning point in modern history. Susan Sontag links the popularization of photography to multiple processes of rationalization and secularization, the primary engines of modernity. The gradual shift from a belief in unseen forces that could only be indicated but never made manifest through print—political, religious, and economic forces—to a belief in visual realities actually seen through photographs leveled political hierarchies, eroded religious faith, and advanced capitalist consumerism. Because photographs and moving pictures are necessarily linked to the world of objects, they tend to enhance the solidity and factuality of material realities. By recording a single event in time, photography (though not film) also arrests the temporal flow of experience that may appear relatively seamless in a printed novel. Consequently, according to Benjamin, photography underwrote the possibility of modern historiography. As Roland Barthes has remarked, it is not accidental that "the same century invented history and photography."[46] The nineteenth century also conceived of realist theater, the primary response of the stage to the growing influence of photography. When theater artists tried to make their stage images more true to life through innovations in playwriting, scenery, acting, and lighting, their model of verisimilitude by 1900 was usually the photograph.[47]

Other technologies of communication, however, challenged the growing hegemony of the photograph soon after it was invented. By 1940 modern modes of sound production, evident in the telephone and the phonograph but most influential in the enormous popularity of radio, were undercutting the implicit materialism and historicity of photography. Talking pictures played an ambivalent role in this challenge. Although the films of the 1930s and 1940s generally kept audiophony subservient to visuality, filmic sound borrowed extensively from the growing sophistication of radio.[48] Where it had taken photography sixty to eighty years to undercut the ontology of print, audiophonic technologies were reorienting notions of the real established by photography in less than twenty years and would share dominant media status with photography during the middle years of the twentieth century. The ontology of radio and related sound media differed sharply from the ontology of the photograph. As Walter J. Ong suggests, this difference derives from the distinction between human hearing and seeing. "Sound situates man in the middle of actuality and in simultaneity, whereas vision situates man in front of things and in sequentiality," he states. Unlike the experience of vision, "hearing makes me intimately aware of a great many goings-on which it lets me know are simultaneous but which I cannot possibly view simultaneously and thus I have difficulty dissecting or analyzing, and consequently of managing."[49] Where the photograph (a technologizing of vision) privileges materiality, analysis, and historical writing, the radio (a technological extension of the voice and the ear) enhances more emotional and amorphous behaviors, such as religious ecstasy and the exercise of power. Not surprisingly, as more Americans made radio listening a part of their everyday lives, this disjuncture between notions of the real began to shift the dominant cognitive culture of the United States.

The reality effects emanating from the earlier technologies of audiophony shaped the ripple effects of radio in the culture. Media historian Friedrich Kittler has demonstrated that the historical conjunction of the phonograph and the telephone with Sigmund Freud's "invention" of the unconscious around the turn of the twentieth century was no accident. For the philosopher G. W. F. Hegel, as for many scientists and philosophers in the nineteenth century, all sounds—from instrumental music to the human voice—were "a saturated expression of the manifestation of inwardness." Freud's "talking cure" depended on his patients' involuntarily revealing their own subconscious "inwardness" through the puns, slips, parapraxes, and jokes during their talking on the couch. The doctor would then repeat these "slips of the tongue" back to his patients to trigger new associations until, by continuing this process, the patient could express the previously unspeakable truth of her or his condition. In his "Recommendations to Physicians Practicing Psycho-Analysis," Freud mandated that the doctor "must turn his own unconscious like a receptive organ towards the transmitting unconscious of the patient. He must adjust himself to the patient as a telephone receiver is adjusted to the transmitting microphone." Further, Freud recognized that the ability of Thomas Edison's phonograph actually to record and play back the sounds emanating from patients' mouths could provide the physician with a kind of objective report of their unconscious that the doctor's own notes, necessarily filtered through the conscious act of writing, could only approximate. In effect, Freud understood sound recording as a potentially superior mode of psychoanalysis because of its ability to provide absolutely accurate feedback to patients. As Kittler concludes, "In the talking cure known as psychoanalysis, [the real] has the status of phonography."[50]

From the start of commercial radio broadcasting in 1920, listeners understood that radio gave them access to a kind of "inward," psychological reality that other media could not replicate. By 1931 over half of American homes owned a receiver. Radio purchases and regular programming, led by popular music and comedy shows, increased rapidly during the decade, despite the Depression. For adult Americans who had grown up with print and photography, radio was mostly a pleasant amusement that did little to alter how they made sense of their lives. For their children, however, radio was beginning to reshape their cognitive world. As occurred with the advent of other new media in world history, the first twenty-five years of commercial radio in the United States generally imitated the forms and content of its media predecessors. Radio programming recycled the conventions of newspaper reporting, realist theatrical representation, musical concert programming, and filmic montage.

Nonetheless, radiophony altered even as it replicated past cultural practices. The news, music, and drama might have had the ring of familiarity on the new medium, but radio put these old formats in a new space, both more abstract and more intimate than any before it. As communications historian Richard Butsch notes, "[By 1940] no longer did the announcer enter the listener's home. Rather, the announcer drew the listener out of the family into a personal conversation in 'radioland.'" "Radioland" might begin in the listener's front parlor or living room, where the Philco or Westinghouse sat in its cabinet, but it transported the auditor into a Platonic shadowland, "an imaginary space, at the heart of a dreamy, utopian activity," according to radiophonic artist Rene Farabet.[51] This imaginary space might spark family conversations, but it could also facilitate personal, inward journeys into the dreamland of the unconscious.

Events in this "noplace" generally corresponded to listener ideas about the material world; but they could have only a typified and abstract, never a mimetic or photographic, relationship to that reality. Unlike most films and much theater before 1940, the complex materiality of physical action and real space simply disappeared on the radio, in favor of signature sounds that presented an emblematic conception of the real.

The junk falling out of Fibber McGee's closet every time someone opened it on *The Johnson Wax Hour* was generalized and abstract enough, for example, so that listeners across America could imagine different paraphernalia making the noise. And as Ray Barfield notes in *Listening to Radio, 1920–1950*, many listeners named a particular closet or drawer in their own house a "McGee's closet"; this jam-packed container became "Every-closet," and its crashing sounds signaling the breakdown of neighborly communication on the program gave American listeners a handy metaphor for many of their own squabbles. Radio, termed by critic Joe Milutis "a Platonic cave," encouraged such casual allegorizing.[52]

In addition to spatial abstraction, radio dematerializes the human body and privileges the mental over the physical, another of its Platonic effects. Radio broadcasting splits the voice from the body, leading to a situation in which the material source of representation, typically a body in a studio in front of a microphone, is absent for the audience. During the 1920s, when radio was still in its infancy, some listeners viewed this process as powerful and unnatural; the ability to "pull voices out of the air" challenged age-old notions of reality and theology. When Rudyard Kipling first listened to a radio, he compared the experience to a séance. Barfield reports examples of several radio-age children who often looked behind the family set to catch the "little people" as they were speaking. The disembodied voices of newscasters and public personalities emanating from radio speakers gave them a kind of authority that was unprecedented in other media. One listener reported that when he and his family "heard news of the great world from H. V. Kaltenborn, Gabriel Heatter, or our family favorite, Lowell Thomas . . . [they] made it clear that whatever [they] said was The Truth."[53] For many listeners, President Franklin D. Roosevelt's radio voice, during his "fireside chats" and on more formal occasions, lent significant gravity and majesty to the New Deal and the war effort. In the United States and across Europe, the radio was the dominant news medium during World War II, more immediate and intimate than newspaper photos and newsreel footage.

Indeed, the intimacy of radio could make events from far away seem more dangerous than they were. During the war, radio announcers brought the fighting in North Africa and Guadalcanal directly into family living rooms. As one historian has remarked, Edward R. Murrow's broadcasts from London during the blitz "made Americans think of the Battle of Britain as a prelude to the bombing of New York or Washington."[54] Crime and terror shows deliberately heightened the kind of moderate paranoia made possible by radio and indirectly produced by newscasters. Orson Welles extended the limits of radio-induced paranoia in his broadcast of "The War of the Worlds" on Halloween night in 1938. Understanding that the real source of radio voices is always hidden from listeners—that alien Others could believably "take over" a broadcast—Welles tricked many Americans into imagining that invaders from Mars had landed in New Jersey. By the 1940s many regularly scheduled radio programs, including *Lights Out, The Shadow, Inner Sanctum Mysteries,* and *The Whistler,* used the imagination-based rhetoric of radiophony to induce paranoiac thrills and chills for their listeners.

Similarly, radio heightened the fear of un-American simulators and the need to identify a Platonically essential America in the late 1940s. On the radio, the whining baritone of Senator Joseph R. McCarthy sounded authoritative and ominous. Reunited with his bloated body and smarmy smile on television by Murrow, McCarthy shrunk into pathos and petulance. Because radio hides bodies, it creates the desire for full presence, for a stable identity, both national and personal. Radio raised questions about the collective nature of the American polity that earlier media did not induce. As media critic John Durham Peters notes, the lack of physical interaction in radio communication led to such worries as "How binding is a relationship that lacks any contract of mutuality?" and "What kind of moral or political obligation can ethereal contact compel?"[55] The need to affirm an essential "us" that might counter a threatening "them"—whether Americans vs. Communists or humans vs. Martians—drew on the categories-are-containers metaphor. Consequently, the desire for true Americanness voiced by numerous political speakers and by crime and mystery radio programs proliferated images of containment.

Several kinds of radio dramas, including soap operas, comedies, dramatic serials, and terror shows, used the voice-over technique in which the voice of a single actor would play both the narrator of a story and the central character in all of its dramatized episodes. Occasionally, this single voice would also play one or more duplicitous roles in the drama, as in the alter-ego of the Shadow and the three characters (one also doubling as narrator) in *I Led Three Lives for the FBI.* All of these dramatic programs, however, carefully segregated the essential, Platonic personality of the protagonist from the other roles that he—most multiple-role figures were male — might be playing. Usually the narrators/protagonists in these voice-over programs separated an essential, sincere self from other selves by sharing with auditors the intimate thoughts and feelings of their true, Platonic selves. While conventional programming kept these several selves in carefully delimited boxes and implicitly assured listeners that the narrative voice was telling the truth, the mere existence of several selves and the impossibility of knowing any truth apart from the narrative voice opened up possibilities for psychological ambiguity and even a kind of vocal schizophrenia. Again, the reality effects of radiophony and the assumptions of psychoanalysis overlap. After all, how could a voice with such an evil laugh as the Shadow's be trusted? Narrators like the Shadow could claim a kind of dematerialized reality and superior knowledge, akin to that of a manic psychoanalyst, that the visual, material world, absent on radio, could not contradict. Later radio artists such as Samuel Beckett and Harold Pinter would move beyond these conventions to explore the dark Platonism of radiophonic schizophrenia.[56]

The Platonic ontology of radio worked its way into other media during and after the war. Sci-fi and *film noir* movies borrowed the voice-over from radio and used it to enhance their claustrophobic point of view. Like radio drama in the 1940s, much *film noir* tightened its focus on the psychology of its protagonist, whose narrative speech usually hinted at constraint and confinement. The slow strangulation of William Holden's voice at the hands of a faded movie queen in *Sunset Boulevard* (1950) is perhaps the best example. For much of its first decade, between 1947 and 1957, commercial television was little more than radio with a picture. This was partly because the major networks transferred many of their most popular evening shows from radio to TV in the early 1950s with few changes in their writing, singing, acting, announcing, and joke-telling conventions. Further, the blurred, black-and-white picture limited the kinds of environments that TV shows could utilize and kept most camera work to medium shots and close-ups. The intimacy of the voice-over continued from radio, with the voice of Jack Webb, for instance, narrating *Dragnet* on television just as he had done on radio. Other performers effectively visualized the voice-over; in the *Burns and Allen Show*, for example, George Burns (following narrative techniques he had used on radio and in vaudeville) found opportunities to break out of the ongoing dramatic action and address the audience directly on camera with jokes and commentary.

Of course television viewing did reunite performers with their bodies and kept the imagination of spectators tethered to the picture tube. This was not always a welcome change, however. The need to visualize formerly imagined environments led many auditors to wonder if TV could ever be as entertaining as radio. Barfield interviewed several radio listeners who complained that the picture of Jack Benny's vault on television was a letdown from the one in their minds created by the clanging chains, squeaking doors, safety alarms, and echo effects on the radio. The Platonic inducements of radio listening were sometimes more fun than the rematerialized reality of TV. But listening to the radio, especially to musical programming, continued through the 1950s. Further, its ontological effects, which had massively shaped the generation of Americans that came into prominence and power during the early Cold War, put ongoing pressure on other media and on the cognitive structure of the dominant culture.

Radio probably increased the frequency and significance of containment thinking in the culture not only through the inherent Platonism of its reality effects but through the metarealities of much radio communication. Storytelling on the radio typically framed one level of reality inside of another, using the voice-over technique to move auditors from the present tense of the narrator into a story about his past, which then became the present tense of the drama within the narration. This framing of realities within realities occurred in most detective and thriller shows on the radio and spilled over into *film noir*. From the point of view of Lakoff and Johnson's cognitive science, a person's ability to perceive one kind of reality within another is a function of the transitivity of containment. The world, in this mode of perception, becomes a series of Chinese boxes; open one box and a smaller one appears within, ad infinitum. Or the logic can operate the other way, from small containers to larger ones, as in the letter scene of Thornton Wilder's *Our Town*. Recall that the address on the letter placed New Hampshire in the United States, the United States in North America, North America in the world, the world in the universe, and the universe in "the mind of God." Wilder evidently hoped that the transitivity of his containers would induce his audience members to climb out of their provincialism toward a mode of Platonic abstraction that might humanize his spectators.

When such realities within realities are given concrete representation on the stage, the result is metatheatricality. By locating one drama within a larger drama and enjoining the audience to watch actors playing characters who play other characters, theater artists rely on the transitivity of the containment metaphor to give cognitive logic to their creations. One level of reality in such theatrics is only a part of a larger container, and that apparent reality may turn out to be simply a part of a more encompassing one. Pirandello's *Six Characters in Search of an Author* is the modernist example *par excellence* of such transitive exfoliation. On a simpler level, adaptations of well-known novels for the stage also set up the expectation of transitivity for the audience; spectators look to the adaptation on stage to work within their idea of the text, which remains (much like Wilder's "mind of God") the larger container representing the "true" novel. Following Nellhaus's theory of metatheatricality, the historian might expect that varieties of theatrical transitivity would proliferate on the cold war stage, both because the emergence of any new media should spark such variety and, more specifically, because radio itself engages in transitive modes of storytelling. Metatheatricality was especially popular in musical comedy, in such hits as *Finian's Rainbow* (1947), *South Pacific* (1949), *The King and I* (1951), *Me and Juliet* (1953), *My Fair Lady* (1956), and *Gypsy* (1959). It flourished as well in successful "straight" plays like *Joan of Lorraine* (1946–1947), *Camino Real* (1953), and *J.B.* (1959).

South Pacific, *The King and I*, and *Joan of Lorraine* were also adaptations of longer works of fiction or history whose stories were well known to the reading public. Similar adaptations crowded the cold war stage during the 1950s: *The Member of the Wedding* (from Carson McCullers, 1950), *Point of No Return* (from John P. Marquand, 1951), *The Teahouse of the August Moon* (from Vern Sneider, 1953), *The Immoralist* (from André Gide, 1954), *The Diary of Anne Frank* (from a censored version of her diary, 1955), *Look Homeward, Angel* (from Thomas Wolfe, 1957), *Jane Eyre* (from Charlotte Brontë, 1958), and *Advise and Consent* (from Allen Drury, 1960). And these were only some of the more prominent examples. Many productions between 1947 and 1962 had metatheatrical elements, and most seasons featured dramatic adaptations of several novels.

In addition to giving prominence to the cognitive schema of containment, radio broadcasting also shifted cultural cognition toward the schema of "compulsion." As Nellhaus has suggested, periods of media transition and conflict often proliferate feelings of powerlessness in the dominant culture; agency is at risk because historical subjects are unsure of their grounding in reality. This is not to imply that radio alone produced cultural anomie, of course; business-class Americans had many reasons for feeling anxious about their ability to take concerted action between 1930 and 1960. But the structural tensions between the realities implicit in photography and radio—in brief, between the materiality of history and the ideality of interior subjectivity—legitimated fears about agency within the dominant culture. Perceiving reality through the schema of "compulsion" was a logical extension of this concern. Like "containment," "compulsion" and its metaphorical extensions derive from physical experiences in the material world, in this case the experience of being swept along by a strong external force like water or wind. Mark Johnson explains that this cognitive structure has two components, a vector of physical force and the object that force is acting against. "Sometimes the force is irresistible . . . [while] at other times the force can be counteracted or modified," he writes. Sometimes the compulsion comes from an external force, and sometimes it seems to emanate from within.[57]

In the theater, as we will see in more detail, "compulsion" shaped the characterization of driven, anxious figures and narratives that pitted apparently weak characters against seemingly overwhelming odds or structured dramatic outcomes according to some external, deterministic force. Such characters and plots were not new to the American theater, of course, but they proliferated on the cold war stage in such widely diverse productions as Euripides' *Medea* with Judith Anderson (1947), *Mr. Roberts* (1948), *Come Back, Little Sheba* (1950), *The Caine Mutiny Court Martial* (1954), *The Bad Seed* (1954), Martha Graham's *Clytemnestra* (1958), *The Visit* and *The Disenchanted* (both 1958), *How to Succeed in Business without Really Trying* (1961), and *Moby Dick* (1962). In addition, compulsion structured major actions in all of the productions from the dominant culture discussed in the following pages. *A Hatful of Rain*, *The King and I*, and *Night Journey* leaned especially heavily on "compulsion" for their cognitive coherence. No doubt several immediate factors helped to cause these emanations of "compulsion" in cold war culture, but the long-term tensions among the reality effects from different media also generated their salience.

The cognitive logic of typification, a subset of the schema of containment—also boosted into prominence by the reality effects of radio—shaped significant areas of cold war culture as well. The believability of radio broadcasting hinges on typification, the distillation of a complex sound into a simpler essence to enhance communication. The sounds of crunching footsteps in a radio play, for example, served to typify the complex aurality of a man walking through the snow. With only sound to indicate characterization, radio writers, directors, and actors also had to rely more on "type characters" than their counterparts in film and the theater did. Characters that conform strongly to "type"—the term derives from the word "stereotype" in print culture, but is appropriate for all modes of phonography as well—are intended and usually interpreted as representative essences of a diverse social group. Type characters, of course, have been common to many periods of theatrical history, but the typification of major characters in serious plays tended to retreat with the popularity of dramatic realism in the 1920s and 1930s. The cold war era reversed that trend with representative types in major roles in such generally realist productions as *Command Decision* (1947), *The Traitor* (1949), *Billy Budd* (1951), *The Shrike* and *The Seven Year Itch* (both 1952), *A View from the Bridge* (1955), *The Cave Dwellers* (1957), *The Tenth Man* (1959), and *Gideon* (1961).

In addition to type characters, the containment schema and its entailment of typification also undergird the ability of an audience to perceive one narrative as an allegory of another. Again, the cognitive logic of this operation is straightforward: spectators map a narrative with which they are familiar onto one that engages them; they read the present target narrative as a representative type of an older source narrative that presumably carries universal meaning. Readers do this, for example, when they map the biblical story of original sin onto *Paradise Lost* to understand John Milton's poem as an allegory. The formal name for this act of perception and interpretation is *allegoresis*. Several critics have usefully distinguished between allegory (a genre of writing) and *allegoresis* (a mode of reading). Gordon Teskey, for instance, notes that "to allegorize a poem—to say it says something other than what it does say—does not make that poem an allegory."[58] The obverse of Teskey's statement, however, is incorrect; allegorical poems do evoke allegorical readings. *Allegoresis*, then, is a common mode of reading deployed to interpret a wide variety of texts and performances, both allegorical and otherwise. Readers who allegorize always discover type characters and representative situations in their fictions. In effect, *allegoresis* moves typification from the level of characterization and event to the more encompassing level of narrative.

Allegorizing spectators presume that some meanings—those they can link to the familiar ur-narrative behind their immediate experience of a text or play—are significant while others are peripheral; *allegoresis* suppresses plural and competing meanings. Further, meanings derived from allegorizing are nearly always conservative and traditional. Critic Sayre Greenfield points out that "allegorical reading is seldom capable of radicalism precisely because it provides a metaphoric mechanism of escape from any uncomfortable associations."[59] With *allegoresis*, readers who know the source text—the ur-narrative essence validating the truth of the typical example—never leave familiar ground. Because allegorizing encourages readers to presume that a source text contains essential and universal truth, this mode of interpretation works with the other Platonic inducements of containment. Assuming that a past master narrative holds the "true meaning" of a present one, the "Platonizing" spectator will usually refuse to consider meanings that depart from conventional belief. Nonallegorical interpretation, in contrast, can surprise readers with unconsidered combinations of ideas. Cold war playwrights eager to challenge the cultural status quo needed to involve their audiences in narratives that did not trigger the typifications of containment cognition.

They had much to contend with, however. Many plays evoking *allegoresis* enjoyed widespread popularity on the cold war stage. T. S. Eliot's Christian comedy *The Cocktail Party* enjoyed a respectable run on Broadway in 1949, as did Christopher Fry's allegorical ruminations on the recurrence of biblical figures in history in *A Sleep of Prisoners*. G. B. Shaw's foray into allegory in the middle of *Man and Superman*, "Don Juan in Hell," ran professionally in 1951 as a dramatic reading, without benefit of scenery or stage action. Several popular musical comedies, including *Brigadoon* (1947), *Call Me Madam* (1950), *Damn Yankees* (1955), *L'il Abner* (1956), and *Camelot* (1960), invited audiences to link enjoyment of their characters and situations to previous "universal" narratives with which they were already familiar. Many plays drew directly on the most popular American text of all time, the Bible: *Magdalena* (1948), *Design for a Stained Glass Window* (1949), *The Flowering Peach* (1954), and *J.B.* (1959), among others. Several, such as *A Streetcar Named Desire* (1947), *Picnic* (1953), and *Toys in the Attic* (1960), evoked psychological narratives that many spectators presumed to be universal through the popularization of Freud. Other serious dramas asked audiences to connect their plots with well-known and purportedly universal narratives of recent political events—*Darkness at Noon* and *Barefoot in Athens* (both 1951), for instance. To judge from the popularity of these productions, cold war spectators frequently encountered figures and narratives on the stage that they could typify. They also expected to enjoy metatheatrical situations, plus characters and plots that rested on compulsion.

Theatrical involvements centered on typification, metatheatricality (both products of containment cognition), and compulsion helped to produce the general shift from realism to abstraction noted by Clurman.[60] As we will see in subsequent chapters, the schemas of "counterforce," "part-whole," and "restraint removal" also played a role in this transition. It is probable that the experience of listening to the radio and looking at photographs over a lifetime had validated and heightened the modes of cognition that set up these spectatorial expectations and stage productions.

The schemas of containment and compulsion, plus their many metaphorical extensions in the culture, had not always shaped the theatergoing experiences of American audiences. The sentimental plays of the eighteenth century generally worked through type characters to evoke Enlightenment hopes for universal virtues but rarely led their spectators to fear that external powers might be controlling their fate. In the wake of the American and French Revolutions, a desire for Platonic essences, type characters, and plots that involved rescue from a compulsive power animated audiences to attend some forms of melodramatic theater from the 1790s through the 1820s. Romantic forms of melodrama popular after 1830 and types of theater such as minstrelsy that privileged satire induced other modes of cognitive engagement. Romanticism in general moved readers and spectators away from *allegoresis* in its insistence on grounding its symbols in concrete materiality rather than in Platonic abstractions.[61] The Romantic concern with organicism and higher forms of consciousness led Romantics to privilege bodily action concepts such as "process" and "merging" rather than containment and compulsion.

The rise of realism later in the nineteenth century moved audiences further away from modes of containment but often continued to engage them in metaphors of compulsion. Environment and heredity, which served as typical cornerstones of causation in realistic and naturalistic plots, had transferred compulsion from human villainy to natural deter-

A Theater of Containment Liberalism 41

minism. After 1900 the influence of photography, with its implicit cognitive inducements of "surface" and "mass-count," pulled the plays of Rachel Crothers, Laurence Stallings, Susan Glaspell, and others toward empirical specifics and historical context. By the 1930s American realists as diverse as Philip Barry, Robert E. Sherwood, George Kelly, Clifford Odets, Lillian Hellman, and S. N. Behrman were deploying Ibsenesque techniques to focus on money, political power, social class, and foolish idealism. Their dramas often entertained audiences with compulsive characters and historical typifications but generally did not seek to engage them with the multilevels of metatheatricality or to induce the Platonism of *allegoresis*. (There were significant exceptions, of course, including *Hotel Universe* [1930] by Barry and *The Petrified Forrest* [1935] by Sherwood.) Meanwhile, the musical stage before 1940 was purveying such cognitive joys as "attraction," "balance," and "iteration" with its plots, jokes, and dancing.

While the main cognitive ingredients of the cold war theater were present before 1947, they had not been mixed into many theatrical dishes that appealed to the tastes of the American business class. Ironically, working-class theater during the early years of the Depression, in such productions as *Newsboy* by the Workers Laboratory Theatre, for example, drew heavily on the cognitive mechanics of the containment and compulsion schemas (as well as "surface" and "iteration") but made little impact on commercial theater. Thornton Wilder, perhaps the most Platonic of American playwrights, engaged audiences with allegory and metatheater (though he shied away from the melodramatics of compulsion) but gained few disciples among other playwrights. The injunction to typify through characterization and allegory evident in many of the plays of Eugene O'Neill, plus his continuing investment in dramatic determinism, may have offered the best precedent for cold war playwrights. Not surprisingly, O'Neill's combination of the inducements of containment and compulsion in such plays as *The Great God Brown*, *The Hairy Ape*, and *The Emperor Jones* enjoyed renewed fame during the O'Neill revival of the 1950s.[62] In 1940, however, before the war moved American culture toward the militarization that would change it for the rest of the century, the major genres of the American theater consistently offered few of the cognitive enjoyments that would come to dominate the American stage in the 1950s.

■ A brief comparison between the productions of Clifford Odets's *Awake and Sing* and Arthur Miller's *Death of a Salesman* underlines the general shift that occurred after the war in the cognitive inducements of American theater and suggests the structural importance of radio (and audiophony generally) in undergirding and legitimating this shift. No two productions, however representative of their eras, ever encompass all of the dynamics of a major historical change, but a comparison of *Sing* and *Salesman* can at least point to some of the significant differences separating one cultural period from another and prompt questions about causation. In this regard, I suggest that the tensions between photography and audiophony and the new reality effects of radio helped to establish the believability and popularity of *Salesman*. Although my discussion of these two plays cannot develop in detail how new modes of communication shaped the American cold war theater—this larger concern shapes the next three chapters—this comparison can at least summarize some of the major cognitive differences separating the theater of the 1930s from that of the 1950s.

Both *Awake and Sing* and *Salesman* are primarily social dramas, focused on a lower-middle-class family's struggle for economic success in New York City. Produced only fourteen years apart, in 1935 and 1949, the plays have much in common in terms of their domestic settings and familial disputes, plus a general concern about the ethics of the American dream. Nonetheless, *Salesman* is significantly different from *Sing*; and the differences primarily cluster around the cultural shifts produced, in large measure, by the popularity of radio and its clash with the reality effects of photography. Unlike *Awake and Sing*, *Death of a Salesman* features major characters who look to their psyches, not to society, for self-realization and encounter difficulties exercising their agency in the world of the play. While *Salesman* self-consciously examines the possibility of narrative truth-telling through daydream sequences, *Sing* tells its story in a straightforward manner, with no recourse to metatheatrical strategies. Finally, *Sing* invited its audience to understand its characters, situations, and meanings through the frame of history. *Salesman*, in contrast, induced typification through its playwriting and staging, challenging its spectators to find universal, ahistorical truths.

While both plays problematize the agency of their sympathetic characters, the figures in *Sing* overcome their difficulties and the protagonist of *Salesman* sinks into compulsion. Bessie Berger's smothering concern for her family's economic well-being is the chief obstacle blocking her adult children, Hennie and Ralph, from achieving self-realization. Although both Hennie and Ralph occasionally focus on their psychological shortcomings as a reason for their problems, both form alliances with others inside the household to achieve their goals. Both also achieve a measure of freedom by the end of the play. In *Salesman*, however, Willy Loman cuts himself off from any help he might get from his neighbor, his sons, and his wife. Unsure even of his performance as a salesman — should he act the rugged individualist or play at casual charm? — Willy feels deeply guilty about his past performances as a breadwinner, father, and husband. The pressure to perform — in business, sports, and sex — has warped the values of the Loman family and left the protagonist unsure of his identity. Anxiety especially about "what happened in Boston," when son Biff discovered his father's marital infidelity, hobbles Willy's ability to take concerted action in the present and drives him compulsively into memory scenes where he can seek vindication in a partly imagined past. Following Miller's script, the 1949 production realized these daydreams on stage, giving material reality to Willy's guilty conscience and the compulsions it activated.[63] In the end, Willy abandons his agency to Uncle Ben, his imagined but physically present brother, and Ben advises his suicide so that Willy's son Biff might inherit the insurance money. The sound of a car pulling away and crashing caps the compulsions driving Willy, literally, to his death. History, embedded in family relations, constrains the agency of Hennie and Ralph in *Sing*. The primary obstacles to Willy's goals, however, occur "inside of his head," Miller's original title for his drama.

Where *Salesman* assumes that characters should have an essential psychological and moral identity to guide their actions, *Sing* allows its sympathetic characters more agency to shape themselves over the course of the play. Odets presents Ralph and Hennie as malleable, in the process of "becoming" rather than stuck in "being," to adopt a Romantic dichotomy. The villains and victims of the play, too, from the dominating mother to the idealizing grandfather, have been shaped by history; none of them has a fixed inner essence transcending historical change. The 1949 production of *Salesman*, however, relied on the foundational concept of containment to understand and depict moral identity. While Biff finds his moral essence during the course of the play, Willy's identity,

Uncle Ben/Thomas Chalmers gives advice to Willy Loman/Lee J. Cobb and his sons, Biff/Arthur Kennedy and Happy/Cameron Mitchell, in a daydream scene from Act I of Death of a Salesman. *Eileen Darby photo, courtesy New York Public Library.*

like that of many protagonists in *film noir* and radio drama, falls apart. As critic Ward Morehouse put it, Arthur Kennedy's Biff "finally decides that he knows who he is" by the end of the play. Divided by guilt over Biff's failures and shame over losing his job, the container of Willy's identity fragments over the course of the action. Critics variously spoke of Lee J. Cobb's Willy as "breaking," "broken," "disintegrating," and "com[ing] apart" — phrases implicitly acknowledging the primacy of the container metaphor for his identity. Indeed, the contrast between Cobb's large physical size and the shattered image of his Willy emphasized what most took to be the character's tragic fall. Because Cobb/Loman cannot "pull himself together" and is blinded by his continuing hope of success for Biff, Willy's agency breaks down and the force of Ben's advice propels him to suicide.[64]

Compounding the problem of agency within the characters' world of *Salesman* is its self-critical stance toward the playwright's agency on the metatheatrical level of the play. The play's memory sequences implicitly question the ability of any agent to tell a story truthfully. Each of the daydreams emanating from Willy's imagination begins as a wish-fulfillment and ends as a guilt-ridden nightmare. By comparing characters and situations from Willy's enacted memories to their counterparts in the realist scenes of the play, the audience learns that it cannot trust Willy's scripting of his past. Perhaps the biggest contrast between memory and reality is the character of Bernard: Willy remembers him as a tattle-telling crybaby, but he appears in a later realist scene as a distinguished lawyer about to argue a case before the Supreme Court. *Salesman*'s metadramatic daydreams also highlight the corrosive effects of performing for others. In the first memory scene, for example, Willy is clearly performing the role of the successful salesman for his family, and his sons — emulating their father — are showing off their sports abilities to impress him. Later on, Willy remembers — likely misremembers — when his rich older brother, Uncle Ben, taught Biff a lesson through performance. In short, as in many radio plays, the audience frequently cannot know if the protagonist's memory of his past is accurate. Performativity corrupts agency in *Salesman* at the levels of both practical and narrated action. Miller's nervous reflexivity about agency and performativity is absent from *Awake and Sing*.

While a great deal of critical attention has been paid to the psychological and performative aspects of *Salesman*, less interest has been shown in the initial response to Miller's play, a response shaped significantly by *allegoresis*. The Group Theatre production of *Awake and Sing* in 1935 had immersed its audience in the empirical and historical realities of the Berger family—its environment, language, and the social and economic problems of Depression-era America—and evoked little *allegoresis*. The setting for Odets's play, the interior of the Berger household, drew on audience knowledge of its photographic likeness to numerous rooms in Jewish middle-class apartments in New York. While spectators were encouraged to make generalizations about the characters as representative of their historical time and place, the play did not establish the figures as universal types deriving from a master narrative. The cognitive logic of typification was operative in both productions, but in *Sing* it worked at the level of character and history, not narrative and universality. Odets and the Group Theater offered the Bergers and their problems to the audience as metonyms for historical processes with which they (and the audience) might merge and help to shape. In sum, the romantic realism of Odets's play probably dissuaded most audience members from allegorizing their experience in the theater.[65]

Compared to the onstage world of *Awake and Sing*, the universe of *Salesman* was dematerialized and abstracted. Jo Mielziner's setting, a barebones outline of the Loman house with few properties and furniture (which critic Brooks Atkinson tellingly described as "skeletonized"), informed the audience that this was less a play about the effects of the social and economic environment on Willy Loman than it was about the abstractions that flooded his imagination.[66] Much of the density of empirical reality was also stripped away from the costumes and sound effects; the initial flute music, for instance, set a mood of somber remorse but took the play out of the reality of 1949 Brooklyn. In relation to *Awake and Sing*, Miller's dialogue is similarly generalized; the Lomans use many expressions from popular American culture, not usually from any ethnic subculture (although some critics have noted the prominence of Jewish American locutions in Miller's phrasing). In this abstract space and time, a "salesman"—the audience never learns what Willy sells—drives his family and himself to pieces trying to live up to a deeply contradictory idea of success, evidently put into his head by mainstream American culture.

Within this world of abstractions, Willy Loman became an "Everyman" figure. Critic Robert Garland stated the metaphor directly: "If

A Theater of Containment Liberalism 47

Everyman will forgive me, in Arthur Miller's Salesman there's much of Everyman." While no other Broadway critic put the equation so baldly, several others (William Hawkins, Robert Coleman, and Brooks Atkinson), plus Garland himself, also described Willy as a "tragic" character. In the critical discourse of 1949, a tragic figure was also a universal one. Later cold war critics, too, allegorized the abstracted drummer as a symbolic American male whose fate was broadly representative of the failure of the dream of economic success.[67] Miller's play enjoins its spectators to typify Willy Loman; somewhat contradictorily, the drama suggests that he is both psychologically unique and typical of all American salesmen. An Everyman figure who pursues worldly success but fails to live within traditional moral values is at the center of many narratives, most notably in the drama of *Everyman* itself and its immensely popular Puritan rendition, John Bunyon's *Pilgrim's Progress*. In *Salesman*, good and bad angels—Linda and Charlie on one side, the Woman from Boston and Uncle Ben on the other—tug at Willy's conscience to move him toward regeneration and life or the lure of success and death. Indeed, Uncle Ben's function and meaning in the play are startlingly similar to the role of Death in the medieval morality play. Miller, Kazan, and the other artists connected with the production made it easy for spectators to map the general narrative pattern of humanity's progress toward Judgment in the midst of trials and temptations onto *Salesman*.

Because much of Willy's search for psychological integration and positive agency must occur "inside of his head," Mielziner's design and Kazan's direction found ways of scattering Willy's mind all over the stage in the 1949 production. What critic-historian Brenda Murphy terms the "subjective realism" of the production style gave concrete shape to Willy's subjectivity through sound, lighting, movement, and acting.[68] This mode of expressionism was more indebted to radiophony than to most experiments with expressionism popular on the U.S. stage in the 1920s and 1930s. Strategies to externalize a character's internal psychology that had proliferated on the radio found their way into *Salesman*. Just as Uncle Ben's voice seems to emanate from inside the protagonist, the Woman from Boston's off-stage laughter, which haunts Willy at several moments during the play, is essentially a radio effect. A wire recorder with the chirping sounds of his boss's children chillingly reminds Willy of his own failure with his sons. Audiences familiar with the radio convention of the voice-over had no trouble following Willy's transitions from present time and place into his daydreams located in the past. As in many radio plays, the protagonist's voice, temporarily serving as both character and proto-narrator, led listeners through the transition. This mode of segue into Willy's psyche differed sharply from earlier American experiments with expressionism. In the 1920s, before the widespread influence of radiophony and psychoanalysis on the culture, *Machinal* and *The Adding Machine* signaled expressionistic effects primarily through visual means. Social and economic circumstances that could be depicted in photographs, not in the oral exchange of a psychoanalytic session or a radio program, shaped most of the earlier dramatic nightmares of expressionism. (In this regard, O'Neill's more psychoanalytic use of expressionism in *The Emperor Jones*, for example, was ahead of its time.)

Of course radiophony alone cannot explain the popularity of *Salesman* in 1949. But it is significant that this widely hailed production of the era embodied the three major attributes of radio-influenced theater — a protagonist of diminished and troubled agency, a level of metatheatricality in the daydream sequences that explored the difficulties of narrative truth-telling, and a movement away from romantic-realist conventions toward Platonic abstractions that involved the audience in the practices of typification. As previously noted, these inducements are linked to the cognitive mechanisms of containment and compulsion. Although the script and staging made it relatively easy for audience members to make sense of *Salesman* by mapping the moral fable of Everyman or one of its numerous variants still circulating in American culture onto it, spectators probably left allegorizing to explore other meanings in the play as well. For *allegoresis* to work, audiences do not need to find an equivalent in the ur-narrative for all of the characters and events of the present one. Nor will they always be conscious that they are deriving meanings for present characters and stories from previous ones. There is much is *Salesman* that does not "fit" the narrative of Everyman, of course, but the major figure and general pattern were apparently close enough for allegorizing to occur.

The pressures of radiophony are apparent in the aesthetics and rhetoric of all of the productions examined in this book. Outside voices crowding into the protagonist's mind populate the plays centered on an Empty Boy. In *The Seven Year Itch*, in fact, an authoritative voice from a radio-phonograph cabinet enters into conversations with the protagonist. Countering the psychologized voice of the radio with the folk tradition of orality, Tennessee Williams finds a way through the narcissism of Empty Boy plays in *Cat on a Hot Tin Roof*. Plays about the Family Circle often empowered a mother figure but diminished male agency and appealed to audiences through the dynamics of metatheater. *The King and I* and even William Inge's *Dark at the Top of the Stairs* betray an interest in metatheater that suggests the influence of radiophony. *A Raisin in the Sun*, in contrast, returns to an earlier, preradio dramatic form to emphasize the significance of material circumstances on a black family. In part because representing an atomic explosion exceeds the conventional capabilities of radiophony, productions about Fragmented Heroes generally lean more heavily on visual codes. MacLeish's *J.B.*, however, finds that the power and mystery of the Voice of God can best be presented, in effect, over the radio. Miller's *The Crucible* is less invested in radiophony than *Salesman*. Even the protagonist's desire to protect his "good name" finally depends on a visual gesture, not a spoken enunciation that might place it closer to radiophony.

■ As the preceding section makes clear, competing media and the reality effects of radio helped to structure the formal and aesthetic attributes of the dominant theater of the early Cold War. Perceptions of the real tied to containment and compulsion also generated significant content and rhetoric in the 1947–1962 theater. Following a general introduction to the relevant historical context for each chapter, I investigate three major types of containment figures on the Broadway stage, the dramatic narratives that animated their situations, and the cognitive mechanisms that they probably induced from spectators eager to engage with the reality of these fictions.

The intertwining of military build-up and popular psychology in postwar America provided a context in which the figure of the Empty Boy exerted significant influence on Broadway audiences. Chapter 2 examines how and why spectators identified with the Empty Boys of *The Seven Year Itch* by George Axelrod and *A Hatful of Rain* by Michael Gazzo. Axelrod and Gazzo eased male spectators, especially, into allegorizing their plays as endorsements of boyish, heterosexual innocence. Axelrod's and Gazzo's Boys are Empty, passive, and driven, in part, because the photographic delights of consumer culture clash with their radio-induced desire for authenticity. Will the mature male of *Itch* take a permanent vacation from adult responsibilities? Will the young husband in

Hatful overcome his Oedipal problems, stop taking heroin, and grow up? Or will both remain in the ambiguous role of the Boy, a social role crucial, yet dangerous, for American freedom? Method acting as taught at the Actors Studio made the pain and compulsiveness of Empty Boys significant on the stage and legible for American spectators. Despite these plays' apparent rejection of consumerism for authenticity, the primary mode of spectatorial projection induced by these productions positioned audiences as ethical egoists eager to take part in the consumerist delights of the postwar American economy.

The Family Circle—sometimes protecting Mom, Dad, and the kids in a bomb shelter, at other times embracing the "Family of Man" in an empathetic gesture of humanitarian goodwill—was another significant figure of containment in the early Cold War. Militarization, new female gender roles, the baby boom, and the suburban ideal shaped the figure of the family from 1947 through 1962. The production of *The King and I* by Rodgers and Hammerstein expanded the Family Circle to include nonwhite peoples, while *The Dark at the Top of the Stairs* by William Inge contracted the Circle to heighten tensions within a nuclear family. Will the embattled mother of both the musical and the melodrama muster enough counterforce to preserve her family from the forces of dissolution? Or will aggressors outside of her contained family puncture the Circle and collapse her hopes for world peace (in *King and I*) or for a normal home (in *Dark*)? Both productions encouraged spectators to understand their dramatic fictions as allegories that validated universal values for troubled times. In several Family Circle productions, the set designs of Jo Mielziner underlined the naturalness of the suburban ideal as the appropriate setting for family trauma and reconciliation. Primarily through empathetic projection, spectators identified with mothers and their children on stage to arrive at an embrace of liberal utilitarian ethics. In effect, both plays positioned their audiences as nurturant caregivers. Although spectators' experiences of Family Circle plays may have helped them to become better parents, these theatrical events also encouraged them to legitimate a postwar American empire that many of them believed was inherently benevolent and white.

In the shadow of the Bomb, the will of God and the commands of reason provided the best asylum most Americans could imagine for themselves and their loved ones during the 1950s. Contradictory beliefs that positioned mature American males as Fragmented Heroes, men who were both powerful masters of their fate and impotent in the face of nuclearism, set the stage for the Broadway success of *J.B.* by Archibald MacLeish and *Night Journey*, choreographed by Martha Graham. These productions used allegory, a modernized version of the Book of Job and Jocasta's story from the myth of Oedipus, to universalize the stories of jeremiad or apocalypse that structured these events. In both productions, the compulsory force of superhuman power played a central role, driving the protagonists toward a fate they could barely comprehend or resist. Will the Fragmented Heroes of these dramas fall apart in the wake of catastrophe or will they manage to pull themselves together to face their mortality? *J.B.* and *Night Journey* invited their audiences to project themselves onto witnesses who could observe the Fragmented Heroes at the center of these plays, an interaction that resulted in legitimating liberal, rationalist ethics. Elia Kazan translated these nuclear dynamics into some of the most celebrated stage images of the early Cold War. The rhetoric of Fragmented Hero plays allowed for limited forms of protest against the excesses of containment liberalism, but at the cost of branding women as irrational Others.

As in most other periods of Broadway history, a residual theatrical culture flourished during the 1947–1962 period that generally avoided the inducements of containment and compulsion in the new era to entertain its spectators with cognitive enjoyments from the past. Stars from previous decades—Katharine Cornell, Helen Hayes, Charles Laughton, Tallulah Bankhead, Alfred Lunt, Lynn Fontanne, and others—mounted vehicles crafted as much to enhance their public personas as to satisfy cold war tastes. While some of these productions played to contemporary concerns (Lunt and Fontanne in *The Visit*, for example), many more of them (such as Bankhead's revival of *Private Lives* in 1948) sustained a traditional residual culture. The early Cold War may have been the golden age of the book musical, but girls, gags, and songs never really went out of fashion. Two of the best of these old-fashioned musicals, *This Was Burlesque* and *A Funny Thing Happened on the Way to the Forum*, opened in 1962. Glamorous revues, high-toned Shakespeare, and conventional bedroom farces also dotted the theatrical landscape. Then as now, Broadway audiences tended to be middle-aged and older. Many were happy to renew their acquaintance with older stars and took delight in the familiar theatrical rhythms of nostalgia.

With full-throated oppositional theater relegated to a few productions on the margins of Broadway, professional playwrights trying to make a living at their craft but eager to contest aspects of the dominant culture often had to couch their concerns in residual forms. Typically, oppositional playwrights in the twentieth century had explored new styles as well as innovative content and rhetoric to confront the status quo, but the hegemony of Broadway nearly closed down that option in the United States during the 1950s. Consequently, some of the most radical plays on Broadway in the 1947–1962 era returned to the apparently safe mix of realism and romanticism from earlier decades, sometimes tweaking its photographic surface to heighten dramatic effects but remaining true to its materialist premises and allowing substantial room for historical agency. These plays included Miller's *All My Sons* (1947), *A Streetcar Named Desire* (1947), John Van Druten's *I Am a Camera*, (1951), *The Crucible* (1953), *Cat on a Hot Tin Roof* (1955), Hellman's adaptation of Jean Anouilh's *The Lark* (1955), *A Raisin in the Sun* (1959), Williams's *Sweet Bird of Youth* (1959) and *The Night of the Iguana* (1961), and Albee's *Who's Afraid of Virginia Woolf* (1962). Ironically perhaps, most of these dramas had more in common with *Awake and Sing* than with *Death of a Salesman*. As we will see in greater detail, however, several of these plays did not receive productions that highlighted their oppositional possibilities. Director Elia Kazan reversed the gendered sympathies of Williams's *Streetcar* and undercut the materialism of *Cat*. Further, the initial production of *The Crucible* smothered it in the costumes and scenery of a creaky historical epic, robbing the play of some of its anti-McCarthyite punch. While the staging of *Raisin* largely lived up to the oppositional orientation of Hansberry's socialism, American racism and cold war liberalism prevented most audiences from understanding what she had written. Nonetheless, the romantic realism of the past did provide a familiar base upon which these politically sensitive writers could build their critiques of containment liberalism.

Substantial sections in each of the following three chapters examine play productions that partly contested hegemonic constructions of the Empty Boy, the Family Circle, and the Fragmented Hero. In *Cat*, *Raisin*, and *Crucible*, Williams, Hansberry, and Miller succeeded, to some degree, in turning the tables on cold war culture by focusing attention on the figure of the abject Other that stood behind the Empty Boys and other images of containment at the center of mainstream plays. This abject Other informed through antithesis the figure of spectatorial concern in hegemonic types of drama. From the point of view of Lakoff and Johnson's cognitive psychology, an abject Other is not a necessary part of all discourse and culture. Rather, it is a secondary effect of containment thinking, resulting from the contrast between "inside" and "outside" that structures all figures of containment. Because the cognitive logic of containment required an outside Other to delimit an inside Same, abject Others proliferated during the Cold War. The image of the homosexual shadowed the character of the Empty Boy, the black Family Circle stood behind its white counterpart, and the threat of the fecund female shaped the Fragmented Hero. These abject Others were not peripheral to containment liberalism, but constitutive of its constellation of concepts and metaphors.[69]

Ironically, the two playwrights most successful in using residual culture to contest containment theater, Tennessee Williams and Lorraine Hansberry, are usually celebrated for breaking new ground. Their romantic realism in *Cat on a Hot Tin Roof* and *A Raisin in the Sun* deterred spectators from allegorizing. Perhaps the more significant question, however, is how Williams and Hansberry may have depicted sexuality and race as relative rather than Platonic categories to undermine the inside/outside dichotomy that distinguished the Empty Boy from the homosexual and the white Family Circle from the black one. What rhetoric did Williams deploy to defuse the "Are you now or have you ever been a homosexual?" question asked about Brick in *Cat*? And how did Hansberry relativize the category of race to open up questions about class and U.S. imperialism in *Raisin*? Although critics during the 50s embraced the plays of Arthur Miller as statements of social conscience, *Crucible* was less successful in opposing the reach of containment liberalism. Miller used two of the major rhetorical tools of Fragmented Hero plays—spectator projection onto witnesses and the denigration of sexualized women—to argue against the political paranoia of McCarthyism. Despite its modestly progressive political effects, *The Crucible* upheld several of the fundamental values of the dominant culture through its endorsement of a rationalist jeremiad, the same kind of narrative behind the success of *J.B.*

Although the American theater changed in some ways after 1962, the containment liberalism spawned by the early Cold War continued to shape the dominant culture of the United States, and hence commercial theater, for the next thirty years. In the early 1960s off-Broadway productions of disturbing plays by Albee, Genet, Amiri Baraka, and others and new modes of modern dance, plus the stirrings of a nonprofit regional theater movement, began to contest the hegemony of Broadway. Despite these challenges, the dominant contents and modes of acting, storytelling, and spectating that had emerged in the fifteen years after 1947 continued to shape the New York stage and, through it, theater across the United States. A brief epilogue examines this legacy by looking at some of the representative successes of the American theater from 1962 through 1992. This epilogue passes a cognitive Geiger counter over several popular plays to track the continuing cultural fallout from the Cold War.

Empty Boys, Queer Others, and Consumerism

Two kinds of sci-fi horror films filled American movie screens in the early and mid 1950s. In *Them!* (1954), *The Thing* (1951), *The Day the Earth Stood Still* (1951), and *The Blob* (1958), extraterrestrial invaders threatened wholesome Americans and their self-reliant values. Several of these films, including *Them!* and *Godzilla* (1954), featured science and the military working together to expel or kill the aliens. The second kind of film, exemplified in *Invaders from Mars* (1953) and *The Invasion of the Body Snatchers* (1956), focused on subversion from within. In these, the extraterrestrials found a means of simulating real Americans with replicants, compulsive automatons who would do their bidding. The aliens in *Body Snatchers*, for instance, grow duplicate bodies of citizens in pods to take control of a small town in California, the first step in planetary conquest. These pod-people look just like those they replace; only their loved ones can tell that something is "wrong."[1]

These sci-fi thrillers allegorize the two kinds of threats to national authenticity perceived by many Americans during the early Cold War—external invasion and internal subversion. To counter the first, Americans spent billions of dollars to establish a "military-industrial" complex for "national security." The second threat was more elusive, its defense harder to devise. The Central Intelligence Agency (CIA) and the Federal Bureau of Investigation (FBI) could arrest spies; local McCarthyites could root out union leaders, teachers, and journalists who might be Communist sympathizers; but finally there was very little difference on the outside between pod-people and genuine Americans. How could patriots tell the simulators apart from the authentic people? The "science" of psychology offered some answers, with its claim to be able to gaze beneath the surface of simulation into the depths of a person's true, essential self. Psychology could both detect "deviants" and help "normal" people to conform to the ways of a "freedom-loving" nation. Not surprisingly, perhaps, the provisions of the National Security Act of 1947—passed to guard the container of the nation from both within and without—joined psychological manipulation to national security by allowing the government to propagandize its own citizens. Containment liberalism facilitated a linkage between the militarization and the "psychologization" of the nation.

Among the many cold war constructions of these two cultural processes was the "American boy," a mixture of innocence and independence, vulnerability and strength. Nineteenth-century Americans generally understood boyhood as a time of transition for males from childhood to manhood, which might last from the teens through the mid twenties. By the twentieth century, however, the dominant culture had begun to celebrate the extension of boyishness into manhood through such figures as Teddy Roosevelt, Babe Ruth, and the male heroes of Frank Capra films. In the 1950s the figure of the boy was even more popular but also more indeterminate than before. Responding to the general demand for the type, Hollywood produced a variety of boys during the early Cold War: tough, sexy boys like Marlon Brando, sensitive rebels like James Dean, the boys-next-door like Rock Hudson, sophisticated playboys like Frank Sinatra, and shy but talented boys like Danny Kaye. These Hollywood boys were not as yet the primary breadwinner for a family, although they might become one by the end of their films. Like that of their stage counterparts, the identity container of these boys was fundamentally empty; it had not yet been filled with an adult personality. Indeed, while the dominant culture of the 1950s praised adult males who preserved their boyishness, it generally separated fulfilled men from Empty Boys when males married and began to provide for their families.

In the popular imagination, the American boy represented the potential strength of the nation. During the war, Americans used the term to designate all young men who went off to fight for their country. Interviewing veterans for his oral history of World War II, Studs Terkel discovered that the former combatants referred to themselves and others like them during the war as boys, regardless of whether they had been teens or mature males during the fighting. The popular mythology surrounding the "good war" tended to conflate American boys with America itself. The suddenness of the Japanese attack on Pearl Harbor shocked

Americans into an image of themselves and their enemies that would stay with them for a generation: innocent, vulnerable Americans faced treacherous enemies in a world where the distances provided by two oceans no longer mattered. American innocence and vulnerability may have been a convenient half-truth, but few citizens wanted to question the foundational self-image motivating a righteous war. After 1945 this image of vulnerable innocence, coupled with the brash toughness of the patriotic soldiers who had saved America, would transform all the boys of the 1950s into potential military heroes. Most believed that the American boy, an embodiment of what was best in the nation, was the first line of defense in the Cold War.

In the postwar quest among public intellectuals to identify an American "national character," the figure of the Empty Boy often stood behind their characterizations. The notion of national character was itself a Platonic abstraction intended to define the essence of Americanness in the expectation that this essence would be sharply different from its Soviet counterpart. In addition to confronting an external danger, the construct of national character posed an internal question of authenticity: Are we being true to ourselves? Typically, the national character texts of the 1950s and early 1960s ignored the variety of American life to single out professionals and managers in the business class as representative Americans. In his overview and analysis of this literature, Rupert Wilkinson points to "the fear of *being owned* (including fears of dependence and of being controlled and shaped by others)" (emphasis in original) as a significant reason for the popularity of these national character texts.[2] Concerns about conforming to the will of others—in school, at the office, in suburbia—drew on the schema of "compulsion" for their cognitive sense. Would the adolescent, the junior exec, and the female shopper simply follow the crowd or exert some independence and self-control? Films like *Blackboard Jungle* (1955), novels such as *The Man in the Gray Flannel Suit* (1955), and numerous articles in the *Ladies' Home Journal* flagged "conformity" as a major problem of the decade and urged Americans to maintain their individuality and freedom in the face of social pressure. National character texts offered some reassurance against this fear. The image of America as an independent, vulnerable, innocent, and strong American boy assuaged this concern. Authentic boys would not become alien pod-people.

Like most authors of national character texts during the Cold War,

David Riesman, David Potter, and R. W. B. Lewis gave America a mixed review. Riesman's critique of "inner-directed" and "other-directed" individuals in *The Lonely Crowd* (1950)—people motivated by inner principles or by the influence of peers—led him to celebrate a boyish third type, the "autonomous person." This person, evidently gendered as a male, gained autonomy by remaining unattached, adventurous, and sensitive to the needs of others. In Riesman's estimation, however, "other-directed" pressures to conform made autonomy difficult to maintain. In two important essays, "The Quest for the National Character" (1962) and "American Individualism in the Twentieth Century" (1963), historian David Potter was more optimistic than Riesman had been in assessing the possibilities for individual authenticity. Drawing on his 1954 history of the effects of increasing prosperity on the national character, Potter distinguished between nineteenth-century self-reliance and twentieth-century individuality. Contemporary abundance, Potter believed, encouraged present Americans to value the boyish qualities of creativity, nonconformity, vulnerability, and even dissent. *The American Adam* (1955) by R. W. B. Lewis revealed that innocent vulnerability defined the most significant characters of the American literary past. One of the main problems for the authors of Natty Bumppo, Huck Finn, and their progeny, according to Lewis, was how their characters could learn about the world yet preserve their Adamic innocence. "Ours is an age of containment," wrote Lewis in his last chapter. "We huddle together and shore up defenses; both our literature and our public conduct suggest that exposure to experience is certain to be fatal."[3] For these writers and many more, the American boy (however problematic in Lewis's estimation) became the guarantor of national authenticity.

Protecting "our boys" from future world wars underwrote massive budgets for national security. The militarization of America escalated in the late 1940s in response to perceived threats from Soviet Russia. Although the National Security Act and a new draft law were enacted in 1947, President Truman had to "scare hell out of the American people," as he admitted, to get Congress to pass his Truman Doctrine for the defense of Europe from the Russians.[4] The Communist coup in Czechoslovakia and the Berlin blockade in 1948 impelled American policymakers to voice more dire Manichean predictions about the Communist menace to the "Free World," which led to passage of the Marshall Plan, the North Atlantic Treaty Organization, and other institutions that would structure the foreign policy of containment for the next fifteen years. These same external pressures, continuing in 1949 with the Soviets' explosion of a nuclear bomb and the Chinese Communist victory over the Nationalists, led to a series of actions that consolidated and vastly expanded what President Dwight D. Eisenhower would later term "the military-industrial complex." If any one of these international situations led to war, American citizens assumed that "our boys" would soon be on the front lines. The "police action" in Korea, of course, confirmed the importance of American boys for national defense. By the early 1950s the nation was deeply invested in its Empty Boys.

Historian of U.S. militarization Michael S. Sherry calls attention to the "militarization of social relations" that resulted from the ongoing expansion and consolidation of "the military-industrial complex" amidst national security fears: "It involved not only conscription of social resources but the recasting of social relations in light of national security, and a complex deployment of the language, models, and modes of warfare. While it often advanced a centrist, liberal, assimilationist agenda — no mean feat in the social climate of the [late] 1940s — its significance went much further."[5] Sherry points to the increased concern about the rights of African Americans, the urge to assimilate previously excluded immigrant groups, such as Eastern Europeans and Jews, and the lower status of women — all of these pressures were partly the result of the "militarization" of social life. The elevation, even adulation, of the American boy was another example.

For other groups and figures, however, heightened concerns about national security and defense meant new visibility and the label of "deviant." The GI Bill that opened educational and home-owning opportunities to thousands of returning boys excluded many gay men who had served in the armed forces. Even though homosexuals were not accepted as volunteers, many young men awakened to a gay sexual identity in the service and, when discovered, were dishonorably discharged. The war raised American consciousness about sexual orientation; while gays and lesbians learned that their numbers were much larger than they had supposed, many others in submarines, war industries, and lonely outposts who identified themselves as heterosexual discovered that their sexuality was more fluid than they had suspected. The Platonic necessities of the Cold War, however, mandated that such knowledge be repressed. Males were either hetero- or homosexual; any blurring of these containers of identity could lead to chaos. And the ongoing celebration of boyhood, in which sexual identity might still be untested, widened the distance between straight and gay identities into a chasm.

When the Kinsey Report of 1948 identified homosexual behavior as an "inherent physiological capacity" in all males, the dominant culture hastened to label the report as subversive. Claiming gays lacked will power and might easily be blackmailed, the government vilified "sex perverts" and purged them from the military, the State Department, and other agencies. According to a 1950 report from the Senate Appropriations Committee, a single homosexual could "pollute a government office" by enticing others to enjoy his perverted practices.[6] Militarization thus helped to identify and politicize "the homosexual," giving new impetus to antigay hostility by defining the presumed problem in national-security as well as moral terms. The antigay campaign also sparked organized opposition with the founding of the Mattachine Society in 1950, the first gay and lesbian rights group started in the United States.

Postwar psychiatry worked hand in glove with militarization to demonize homosexuality. Before 1940 most psychologists classified homosexual behavior as a form of sexual depravity, but they did not usually type the homosexual as a different kind of person. Partly as a result of the need to classify homosexuals as unfit for military service, most psychologists by 1945 came to understand the homosexual as an abnormal personality type. Edmund Bergler, the leading postwar psychoanalyst in the field of homosexual "pathology," claimed that gay men were unconsciously "trying to extinguish the race." As for his critics, Bergler threatened that their statements "will be politically and propagandistically used against the United States abroad, stigmatizing the nation as a whole in a whisper campaign."[7] Bergler could be confident of his critics' silence; classifying the homosexual as a deviant personality and then demonizing this type were now matters of national security.

Reinforcing Bergler's authority was the immense prestige of psychology in the postwar years. Knowing that modern warfare involved the hearts and minds of the troops and civilians on both sides of the conflict, the military had employed thousands of psychologists and clinicians during the war. Psychologists used case studies, surveys, and interviews to evaluate and boost the patriotic morale of soldiers and citizens. Clinicians screened out recruits predisposed to mental problems, provided psychological self-help manuals and lectures near the front, and treated thousands of soldiers suffering from mental breakdowns induced by combat. Treating the returning boys for the traumas of peacetime adjustment kept hundreds of psychiatrists and counselors busy after 1945. Psychologists and clinicians believed they had provided a vital national service during the war years; a grateful nation saw no reason to disagree.[8]

Psychology and psychotherapy boomed during the Cold War. Truman's signing of the National Mental Health Act in 1946 gave new power and more money to the Mental Hygiene Division of the Public Health Service and opened federal funding to several mental health associations. The Department of Defense poured research dollars into psychological warfare, intelligence operations, military training, clinical techniques, and even psychological studies of revolution. The apparent Chinese Communist "brainwashing" of American prisoners-of-war during the Korean conflict led to more millions for psychological countermeasures. By one estimate, 5 percent of the American Psychological Association worked full-time for the Department of Defense in 1957, with a similar number employed by the Veterans Administration. Many more were funded by government grants in universities and research centers like the RAND Corporation.[9] As in the militarization of many businesses, the incorporation of large areas of psychology into the apparatus of national security created a common culture that erased distinctions between civilian and military control and generated mutual interests and agendas. By the early 1960s the Department of Defense was spending about fifteen million dollars annually on psychological research.

Psychoanalysis was never more respectable in the United States than during the 1950s. In addition to American-trained psychiatrists, emigrants from Europe, especially Germany, filled the ranks, adding their own stature to the profession. The school of "ego psychology," a conservative version of Freudianism, dominated American psychiatric practice in the 1950s. Adapted from the ideas of Abraham Cardner and Harry Stack Sullivan, ego psychology held that personal rebellion against accepted social roles rarely led to individual happiness; social conformity was the key to psychological success. Because Sullivan was the training analyst for new psychiatrists in New York City, his positive valuation of conformity had great influence on the national practice of psychoanalysis in the 1950s. Ego psychology had progressive connotations in the 1930s when Cardner and Sullivan first enunciated its principles. At that time, conformity involved the norms of secular liberalism put forward during the New Deal or the even more radical role-playing facilitated by the norms of the Popular Front. By the 1950s, however, the hegemony of containment liberalism had drained most progressive possibilities out of social norms and roles; the conformity preached by ego psychology primarily led to an acceptance of the status quo. The ties linking psychological research to national security and psychoanalysis to containment liberalism helped psychological thinking to permeate the business class.[10]

The ideology of "the psychological" during the Cold War has important implications for the construction of the postwar Empty Boy. Sociologists Philip Rieff and Christopher Lasch and historians Jackson Lears and Richard Fox have demonstrated a causal link between the rise of the professional-managerial group in the twentieth century and what they term a "therapeutic culture."[11] In brief, therapeutic culture established the importance of an inner, in-depth self as a key to social and cultural success. Like Lakoff and Johnson, these sociologists and historians assume that identity cannot be reduced to an inner essence; the performance of self depends upon a variety of cognitive, social, and historical factors. In the 1920s introspective selves gained access to cultural capital often denied to classes that did not privilege "the psychological" in their construction of the self. In this regard, psychoanalyst Joel Kovel notes that "within our [American] culture, introspection signifies participation in a particular class and social relation.... I am not saying that working-class people do not develop insight, but for them to do so in analysis means pursuing an activity foreign to their experience of the world."[12]

Twentieth-century business-class Americans claiming sensitivity to levels of "reality" within themselves marked their class and racial distinctiveness with psychological discourse. This began early in the century when the professionals and managers of corporate America realized with mounting anxiety that they could no longer be "self-made men." According to cultural historian Joel Pfister, a new "ideology of self" emerged in the 1910s and 1920s to assure the business class that, although external validations of their masculinity and success might be lacking, there were other treasures to be mined internally, in the depths of their psyches, that could salve their self-esteem. "Troubles or anxieties, their representation in 'psychological' language and narratives, and their treatment in therapy were now constitutive of a new ideology of self—the middle- and upper-class performance of a 'psychological' identity," states Pfister.[13] This emergent psychologization of identity achieved widespread legitimacy in the dominant postwar culture. Nearly all of the boys popularized by cold war Hollywood were introspective, with some driven by a sensitivity that tied them in psychological knots. Further, with the boy as a symbol for American authenticity, military preparedness, and potential greatness, psychologizing the figure became a cultural imperative. The construction of the boy as a sensitive loner, his identity still unformed, vulnerable to internal as well as external threats (even when embodied in a putatively working-class character) suited the class distinctions of the postwar dominant culture. The Empty Boy became one of the most important "psychological identities" available to cold war Americans.

The cultural expectations loaded onto the American boy, however, guaranteed that performances of the role would be fraught with difficulties. Embedded in the boy were tensions and contradictions that crisscrossed the fault line of gender in the Cold War. The vulnerability of the boy feminized the role, rendering him more emotional and even more neurotic than the hegemonic male of the era. Likewise, the openness and innocence of the boy allowed for a casualness in body language and a tenderness with others that ill suited the controlled toughness of the "normal" breadwinner. Because of his presumed immaturity and emptiness, the boy could become a passive victim of forces beyond his control, a feminizing situation intolerable for the mature male. At the same time, the boy as future combat soldier had to display evidence of his potential for courage and leadership. His "feminine" side—vulnerable, tender, and passive—had to be kept in check by a more powerful performance of "masculine" physical control, emotional stoicism, and practical activity. Otherwise, the performed boy would be classified as homosexual, destroying his power to stand as an authentic symbol of the nation. Put another way, the boy had to embody psychological complexity but lay his problems aside when "the going got tough" and it was time for "the tough to get going."

The ambiguous gendering of the boy could be a source of great attraction for audiences, a fact strikingly evident in the public image and success of Montgomery Clift. A closeted bisexual, Clift helped Hollywood image-makers to mask his sexual ambivalence through roles and publicity that emphasized the "masculine" side of his boyish persona. At the same time, Hollywood took full advantage of Clift's "feminine" traits—his small body, psychological vulnerability, and emotional intensity—in leading roles in *The Search* (1948), *A Place in the Sun* (1951), and *From Here to Eternity* (1953). Widespread publicity about Clift's training as a "Method actor" helped his fans to believe that Clift was an authentic American boy who had simply transferred his true self to the roles he played on the screen. Yet, as Steven Cohan points out in *Masked Men: Masculinity and the Movies in the Fifties*, Clift's fan discourse alluded to his bisexuality in numerous ways, playing up the enigma of Clift and his characters as tense, confused young men without ever acknowledging the source of the actor's appeal. Several critics have noted the boy-man homoeroticism of *Red River* (1948), involving Clift as young cowboy paired with John Wayne as older cattleman. Although the hegemonic masculinity of Wayne, plus the fighting spirit of Clift's character and his romantic involvement with a woman, allows the film to repress its homoerotic subtext, Cohan persuasively argues that the "love" between Clift and Wayne accounted for much of the film's popularity. He concludes that "the bisexual performativity structuring Clift's persona is what determined his value—in the fan discourse and, hence, in the star system as a whole—as the representation of a boyishness different in kind from the seemingly unproblematic, literally straightforward masculinity of an older star like John Wayne."[14] Ambivalently gendered boys like Clift were simultaneously desirable and dangerous: necessary figures for patriotic and psychological purposes, but Empty Boys that could just as easily explode hopes for a strong and individualistic America.

Many of the Empty Boys on the cold war stage reflected the gradual aging and psychologizing of the figure that had occurred since the 1920s. Booth Tarkington's *Clarence* (1919), Ralphie in *Awake and Sing*, and George in *Our Town* exemplified the boys of the prewar period. Typically heart-whole, though at odds with the older generation, these boys struggled to find a place for themselves in the adult world; their problems were primarily external to themselves, and they were eager to grow up. This figure continued in some postwar plays, such as *No Time for Sergeants* (1955) and *Take Me Along* (1959, a musical version of *Ah, Wilderness!*), but most Empty Boys in the American theater of the 1950s tended to be more internally conflicted, in part because the adult world ahead of them seemed to promise less freedom and more compulsion. Cold war boyhood was both a temporary cocoon of safety and an aimless limbo;

better to remain "empty," many plays suggested, than get "filled up" with the hypocrisies and conformities of middle-class life. Several plays about this ambivalence centered on the problems of the returning veteran, including *Home of the Brave* (1945) by Arthur Laurents, *Truckline Cafe* (1946) by Maxwell Anderson, *All My Sons* (1947) by Arthur Miller, and *Sundown Beach* (1948) by Bessie Breuer. Other lads in uniform, in such disparate shows as *Mister Roberts* (1948), *South Pacific* (1949), and *Billy Budd* (1951), suffered similar psychological conflicts in the service. After 1950 most Empty Boys in Broadway plays came from situations removed from military life—Hal's problems in *Picnic* (1953) came from poverty and Tom's in *Tea and Sympathy* (1953) from an over-ambitious father, for instance—but the veteran as needy neurotic remained a staple of popular fiction through the decade. He recurred in 1955 in *A Hatful of Rain* by Michael Gazzo and in 1956 in *Time Limit* by Henry Denker and Ralph Berkey, for example, both dramatic responses to the "brainwashing" of veterans returning from the Korean War. Spectators at these plays, like audiences watching Biff and Happy in *Salesman*, were prompted to ask whether these aging boys would ever grow up.

Another type of Empty Boy, relatively new to the American stage, gained popularity in the 1950s—the sympathetic adult male who reverts to boyhood as an escape from the pressures of the grown-up world. A mature man making a fool of himself over a pretty young woman had long been a figure of fun in American comedy, but the cold war stage psychologized and sentimentalized this character, finding deeper meaning in the sexual fling of a married man than had most earlier plays. The prototype of this figure was Richard Sherman in *The Seven Year Itch* (1952) by George Axelrod, even though Rodgers and Hammerstein had put a confused (and adulterous) young married man on stage five years before in *Allegro* (1947). Axelrod followed *Itch* with another adult male as born-again-boy in *Will Success Spoil Rock Hunter?* in 1955, the year that also saw the enormous success of *Damn Yankees*. Although the middle-aged man, transformed in a Faustian bargain with the Devil into a young pitcher for the Washington Senators in *Yankees*, successfully resists the sexual temptations of "Whatever-Lola-Wants-Lola-Gets" Lola, the figure at the center of the musical was the same bored, confused, sexually anxious married mouse as in *Itch*. Other boyish, unmarried older males populated later cold war musicals, including *The Music Man* (1957) and *Fiorello!* (1959). *Faithfully Yours* (1951) and *Oh, Men! Oh, Women!* (1953) rang new changes on the figure of the male sexual dupe by placing a psychiatrist in the role. Other plays later in the decade, such as *Two for the Seesaw* (1958) and *Silent Night, Lonely Night* (1959), treated the adult male boy in need of sexual reassurance with more psychological complexity and sentimentality. The central dramatic question animating most of these shows was not when the Empty Boy would accept adult responsibilities but how the Empty Man-Boy would ever return to them.

■ Michael Gazzo's *A Hatful of Rain* opened at the Lyceum Theatre on 9 November 1955 and played for over two hundred performances. Ben Gazzara cut short a successful run as Brick in *Cat on a Hot Tin Roof* to play the leading role, Johnny Pope. Shelley Winters, already renowned for her Academy Award nominations in two films, rearranged her Hollywood schedule to play Celia Pope, Johnny's wife. In supporting roles were the veteran Broadway performer Frank Silvera as Johnny's father and relative newcomer Anthony Franciosa as his brother. Gazzo had developed his script with Gazzara and Winters, who improvised some early scenes as part of their work with Lee Strasberg at the Actors Studio in New York. With different casts (including a young Steve McQueen on the road), *Hatful* enjoyed a London run, a road show in 1956–1957, and eventual production as a film.[15]

Premiering on 20 November 1952, *The Seven Year Itch* by George Axelrod was the blockbuster comedy of the early 1950s, running in New York through March 1955. Tom Ewell, who had played a variety of supporting comic roles in television, film, and musical revue, established his stardom with Richard Sherman, the sex-struck dreamer with an "itch." Film ingénue Vanessa Brown played "The Girl," while Neva Patterson, celebrated on Broadway for her charming insouciance, played Ewell's wife and Robert Emhardt appeared as a pop-eyed psychiatrist. Elliott Nugent, who had co-produced the show, played Ewell's role on the road, as did Eddie Albert and, for a time, Ewell himself. In addition to road companies in the United States, *Itch* enjoyed foreign productions in London, Paris, Stockholm, Milan, and Lima, Peru. The comedy might have run on stage throughout the decade had it not been for the release of the film in the summer of 1955, which starred Tom Ewell and Marilyn Monroe.[16]

In one sense, Johnny Pope of *Hatful* and Richard Sherman of *Itch* have opposite problems: Johnny is trying to leave his boyhood behind to become a mature breadwinner for his pregnant wife and their future daughter, while Richard—already a successful adult male with a wife and son—struggles to recover the boyishness of his premarital youth. In another sense, though, both are Empty Boys at heart, their Platonic essence evident in their situation and psychology. In *Itch*, no sooner are the wife and son of a paperback publishing executive out of the family's New York apartment for a summer up north than the husband begins fantasizing about three women he has wanted to sleep with over the seven years of his marriage. Through "dream lighting" (306) and a setting with several hidden entrances, simulations of these women appear before him, tempting the "summer bachelor" with their beauty and availability. Though played by flesh-and-blood actresses, these women are dematerialized fantasies, emanations (like Uncle Ben and the Woman in *Salesman*) from the protagonist's mind. Soon enough, an actual "Girl" appears in his living room—a beautiful model subletting the apartment upstairs who has lost her keys. By the end of Act II, Richard has wooed and bedded her. The Kinsey Report on male sexuality, mentioned in *Itch* and a sensation in 1947 when it appeared, had noted the decline in sexual potency among males after their teens. At thirty-eight, Richard Sherman, who believes, "I don't look a bit different than I did when I was twenty-eight" (310), still has the hormones of a healthy boy!

Richard's relation to two other male characters in the comedy also relegates him to the emblematic role of an Empty Boy. As he gets more involved with the Girl (just as much a type character as the protagonist), Richard seeks counseling from Dr. Brubaker, a psychiatrist working with him on the upcoming publication of his book, *Of Man and the Unconscious*. The better he gets to know Richard, the more Dr. Brubaker treats him like a child; he is already calling Richard "my boy" by the middle of Act II. The other major male character is the "Voice of Richard's Conscience," played by a separate actor, who talks to him out of the speakers of his radio-phonograph cabinet. A kind of Freudian "reality principle," the Voice undercuts Richard's fantasies by reminding him of his past cowardice with women, the unlikelihood of his chances with the Girl, and, finally, his fear of his wife's retribution. Throughout, the Voice treats Richard with condescension, calling him "Dickie boy" when he first speaks (328). Despite his success as a breadwinner and his thirty-eight years, Richard Sherman remains a boy.

While the Voice from the radio-phonograph cabinet demonstrates

The Girl/Vanessa Brown stands over a guilt-ridden Richard Sherman/Tom Ewell in a fantasy scene from Act I of The Seven Year Itch. *Talbot-Giles photo, courtesy New York Public Library.*

the direct influence of the radio on *Itch*, the comic premise of the entire play is essentially radiophonic. In good radio-play fashion, Richard tells his problems directly to the audience while voices bombard him from without and intrude upon his conscience. Two levels of metatheatricality are at work here: the level of the dramatic present, and, within it, the level of Richard's fantasies. Some of these voices on the fantasy level proceed from real people (Dr. Brubaker, the Girl, his offstage wife), while others come from imagined figures (the three dream women, the Voice from the Cabinet, and others), external projections of Richard's interior psychology. Within Richard's conscience, however, images from his mind have as much effect on his mood and actions as do the real people. The similar status of real and imagined characters effectively dematerializes all of them. As in *Salesman*, where Linda Loman and Uncle Ben claim equal reality in Willy's mind, the fundamental comedy of *Itch* takes place "inside of his head."

Although Richard is the nominal seducer in the plot, "The Girl," whose lack of an individuating name increases her emblematic power, pulls most of the strings. She fetches champagne to celebrate her birthday with Richard, shows him a nude photograph of herself in *U.S. Camera*, reveals that she likes married men as sexual partners because they don't fall in love with her, and plants the first kiss. All of this is performed with a breathless innocence that types the Girl as an eager and excitable ingénue, not a conspiring vamp. At the end of Act II, when Richard thinks he has failed a second time to seduce her, she takes the initiative by opening up an entrance in the ceiling of Richard's living room (his apartment had once been a duplex but now the stairs to the second floor dead-end at the ceiling). The Girl tiptoes down the stairs to sleep with him. Richard, initially oblivious to the action behind him, finally sees her standing next to him, a small claw hammer in her hand. He can only manage a drop-jawed "Hi . . ." (356) before the curtain falls. Richard's passivity when faced with the sexual determination of a beautiful woman turns him into a boy. His vulnerability and relative innocence in this situation, the climax of the comedy, probably disarmed most moral conservatives in the audience who might otherwise have condemned the character's breach of marital fidelity. With Richard reduced to a boy, his passivity in arousal is comically forgivable.

The Girl's descent from above to take control of the sexual situation is also significant. While this may have suggested the delightful materialization of an angel to some men in the audience, others probably linked the hammer in the Girl's hand to the "bombs" unknowingly launched by her earlier in the action. Soon after the comedy begins, "an enormous iron pot with a plant in it" (312) plummets onto the chaise longue of Richard's balcony terrace, landing on the spot where he had been sitting just moments before. Watering the plants on the terrace above, the Girl had accidentally pushed the pot over the balcony railing, nearly killing Richard. Just to be sure the audience gets the point that the Girl is the same kind of dangerous "bombshell" as the iron pot, Axelrod runs the joke again at the end of the act. A potted geranium crashes at Richard's feet, and the Girl apologizes that she "was just taking them in so there wouldn't be another accident" (335). The double incident, of course, provides a metaphor for the entire comedy. A "bombshell" accidentally falls into the life of poor Richard, exploding a sexuality previously contained by his marriage, and our boy must pick up the pieces before his wife discovers the accident.

Many spectators in the 1950s probably recognized the metaphor. As Elaine Tyler May points out in "Explosive Issues: Sex, Women, and the Bomb," the designation of beautiful young women as "bombshells" had been a popular locution since the 1930s, heightened during the war when American flyboys painted cartoons of sexy women on their bombers and sometimes on the bombs themselves.[17] When a hydrogen bomb was dropped on the Bikini Islands in 1954, American flyers attached a photograph of Hollywood sex symbol Rita Hayworth to the weapon. Soon afterward, designers of women's swimwear decided to name their skimpy suit a "bikini" to celebrate the explosive potential of the female body inside. *Itch* featured a similar bombshell. Hollywood had already capitalized on Vanessa Brown's fresh, girl-next-door face and her Rita-Hayworth torso before she appeared in her first adult role on Broadway. In the film, with Monroe as the Girl, American culture had the bombshell of the decade to desire. Putting the Girl "on top" was not a fundamental problem for the masculinity of Richard Sherman within the culture of the 1950s because the character had already proven his heterosexuality by providing for his family and fathering a son.

Nonetheless, Empty Boy Richard had to exert some counterforce against the Girl or the figure would be too feminized to induce audience identification. The image schema of "counterforce," in fact, was nearly as important as containment and compulsion in shaping the dramatic world of *Itch*. Empty Boys could not initiate a conflict, but if they did not fight back they would be worthless for American defense. Axelrod carefully balances his characterization and plot to demonstrate that Richard is not the complete plaything of his fantasies, his hormones, and the Girl. He argues with the Voice from the cabinet, actively recruits the psychiatrist to help him with his bad conscience, and confronts a man he believes is trying to seduce his wife. Invigorated by Dr. Brubaker's advice, Richard transfers the remains of his anxiety into a verbal attack on Tom MacKenzie, a large man apparently invented by Axelrod to demonstrate to the audience that Richard is not a wimp. Like all good adult boys in Hollywood movies, Richard lays aside his anxieties to fight for what he believes, even though it is soon apparent that MacKenzie has no designs on his wife. This comic reversal, however, is irrelevant to the validation of Richard's fighting spirit. The mouse roars in the end to protect his marriage; his counterforce reconfirms his manhood.

Johnny Pope in *Hatful*, in contrast, has yet to prove his manhood, even though he is a combat veteran from the Korean War. The melodrama uses several realist devices to relate his situation. The setting of *Hatful*, for instance, demonstrates that Johnny has tried to play the role of responsible breadwinner for his wife, Celia, by refurbishing the woodwork and masking the old plumbing in their Lower East Side apartment. Next the play's exposition reveals that after a hospital stay when he returned from Korea, Johnny went to college on the GI Bill, took a job as a machinist, and got married. But in the present time of the drama, he has lost the last of several jobs, has stopped attending college, and refuses to make love with or even talk seriously to his wife, even though she is about to have their baby. Near the end of the first scene, the audience learns the reason for his recent behavior—Johnny has become a heroin addict. The rest of the drama explores his attempts to break his compulsive habit, mend his marriage, and reconcile with his father and brother. As in *Itch*, the image schema of "counterforce," principally embodied in Johnny's and his family's attempts to fight against the problems that threaten to overwhelm him, shapes significant moments in the dramatic action. *Hatful* climaxes in a tempestuous scene when Johnny, hallucinating and badly in need of a fix, breaks out of his bedroom and must be restrained by his family. In the last minutes of the drama, his wife calls the police to take Johnny to the hospital.

In his review of *Hatful*, Brooks Atkinson called Ben Gazzara's Johnny "a manly performance, moody but free of whining." *Boston Globe* critic Elliott Norton noted that Gazzara's Johnny "carries a burden of anguish manfully except in those moments when the drugs wear off. . . ."[18] To designate a performance as "manly" or a moment on stage when a "manful" performance slips into something else suggests that the play evoked some anxiety about gender roles. Any actor performing a credible Johnny Pope might have induced this kind of dubious praise from a critic because the character was posed at a crisis point of cold war masculinity. Since adult masculinity was synonymous with the role of breadwinner, notes social historian Barbara Ehrenreich, "the man who failed to achieve this role was either not fully adult or not fully masculine. In the schema of male pathology developed by mid-century psychologists, immaturity shaded into infantilism, which was, in turn, a manifestation of unnatural fixation on the mother, and the entire complex of symptomatology reached its clinical climax in the diagnosis of homosexuality."[19] Johnny Pope is a case study of this type, an adult boy tending toward infantilism and homosexuality who cannot reach manhood until his childhood and wartime traumas are resolved. His drug addiction, while the focus of the drama, is not the source of his problems, which are mired in his search for the mother he never had and the Oedipal rage he still feels toward his father. Gazzo has created what Pfister would call a "psychological identity" for his type character.

To plumb the depths of Johnny's complex "individuality," Gazzo deploys three male pushers who both supply and harass Johnny and typify different aspects of his neurosis. Two of them, Apples, an infantile, giggling homosexual who plays with weapons, and Chuch, an apelike, slow-moving zombie who crushes his victims, are partly alter-ego emblems of his disintegrating personality. The third, Mother, a reptilian figure in an exquisite suit and dark glasses, is a metaphor for the real mother Johnny lost as a young child. Their names are ironic signifiers of their true nature: "Apples" connotes a fall from grace, a perverted innocence; "Chuch," close in sound to "church," is the bestial opposite of a churchman; and "Mother," whose only milk is the white powder of heroin, encourages a dependency that could lead to death. Together, they are a family of pod-people, the desiccated, zombielike figures from *Invasion of the Body Snatchers*, who become eerie symbols for Johnny's past family and imply a possible fate for his future familial relationships. More directly, they also suggest that Johnny has regressed to a substitute mother who is turning him into a perverted monster. Johnny may look normal on the outside for much of the time, but his authenticity as a free individual and his boyhood potential as an American man are in crisis. These allegorical figures threaten to empty him out and replace the "real" him with a simulation.

The Broadway reviewers did not comment on the suggestive connections between Johnny and his pushers, but they did register the horrified pleasure they took when these three were on stage. For John Chapman, the actor playing Mother was "magnificently chilling." Robert Coleman found the pushers "fascinating"; their antics were "like watching a bunch of nasty snakes crawling about the premises." Richard Watts devoted nearly a third of his review to describing this group of "perversely interesting monsters." He wrote: "There is, for example, the leader of the gang, a fellow who hides behind dark glasses, is given to reading while he waits for his prey, and goes by the name of Mother. Then there is his toady, a young man known as Apples, who has a child mind, feminine instincts, and reaches for his knife when crossed by his pals. Or, to take the third of the gang, there is Chuch, who sometimes sympathizes with his victims while he is throttling them." Watts's conclusion summed up for most of the critics the importance of the pushers *vis à vis* the rest of *Hatful*: "The family episodes are the core of Mr. Gazzo's play, but it is the peripheral sections dealing with the monsters that hold the attention."[20]

The subtext of *Invasion of the Body Snatchers* centered on subversion from within by Communists. Gazzo's family of pushers may also have reminded spectators of the same radical Other in the American cold war imagination. In the early 1950s novelists, politicians, churchmen, and others imagined a variety of "Commies" that continued to circulate in the culture long after the ravages of McCarthyism had passed into memory. Communists were likened to robots such as Chuch, infantile homosexuals like Apples, Mafioso hoodlums similar to Mother, even — in the words of Cardinal Francis Spellman — to "the world's most fiendish, ghoulish men of slaughter," a designation that easily applies to all three of Gazzo's pushers. Senator McCarthy had conflated homosexuals and intellectuals with Communists in such phrases as "dilettante diplomats" and "the prancing mimics of the Moscow party line." In the immensely popular novels by Mickey Spillane in the early 1950s, "commies" were the opposite of wholesome, healthy, and tough Americans. They were decadent, degraded, and soft—"dumb as horse manure," for instance, and easily deserving to die in *One Lonely Night* (1951). Spillane's rhetoric of kill-'em-all *machismo* traveled widely, infecting even the sober political analysis of *The Vital Center* by Arthur Schlesinger, Jr. Schlesinger praised the "new virility" that American postwar leaders had brought to public life, contrasting it to the "political sterility" of the old-guard leftists and the "emasculated" ruling class. For Schlesinger, communism was "something secret, sweaty, and furtive, like nothing so much . . . as homosexuals in a boys school."[21]

Like Schlesinger, most anti-Communists agreed that the Red Menace brought with it sexual perversion and chaos. To heighten the latent sexual threat already posed by his monsters, Gazzo introduces Putski, a strung-out, rich young woman wearing nothing more than shoes and a fur coat, into the final appearance of his pushers. The audience probably classified Putski as a "nymphomaniac" because of her sexually suggestive body language. A picture from the souvenir program for the Broadway production shows her sitting in profile on a kitchen chair: her upstage foot is propped on another chair revealing a bare leg, bent at the knee, thus opening a view of her crotch to the three men sitting and standing above her. The pushers, however, remain numb to her proffered charms. (See the photo montage from the souvenir program.) Putski's presence on stage pointed up Johnny's precarious sexual relationship with his wife. His addiction-induced impotence is driving his wife into the arms of his brother, a temptation both are resisting but neither seems able to ignore. Because of Johnny's boyhood traumas and dependencies, sexual chaos is subverting the domestic happiness of an American family. If this Empty Boy turns passive and soft, this key to future national strength could fatally weaken American society from within. How to mount an effective counterforce against the pushers—and by metaphorical extension against communism and sexual perversion—is the chief dramatic problem of the play.

Johnny's wartime experiences sharpened the relevant historical context for the Broadway audience from the general problems of domestic anticommunism to the specific difficulties faced by returning boys who had been "brainwashed" in Korea. At the end of the conflict in 1953, the American public was startled to learn that twenty-three American prisoners-of-war refused repatriation, "converted" to communism, and stayed in North Korea. And it was feared that the many other POWs who did return to the United States might have been psychologically

A collage of photos from the souvenir program of A Hatful of Rain. *Clockwise, from upper left corner: Celia Pope/Shelley Winters embracing Johnny Pope/Ben Gazzara; Polo Pope/Anthony Franciosa talking with Johnny; Mother/Henry Silva restraining Polo while Celia looks off; Celia ironing and talking with Johnny; Polo grabbing John Pope, Sr./Frank Silvera; Apples/Paul Richards and Chuch/Harry Guardino with Johnny and Mother; Johnny and Apples. In the center: Polo dancing and Mother and Putski/ Christine White in the kitchen. Courtesy New York Public Library.*

damaged beyond repair. Some soldiers were even tried in military courts for their prison camp behavior. This led to a wide-ranging public debate on the psychology of "brainwashing," a term introduced into American journalism by a CIA operative under cover as a reporter. Did the Communists have more advanced psychological techniques than ours? Might better-trained American soldiers have used their free will to resist them? The debate heated up in August 1955 when President Eisenhower signed into law a new code of conduct for the military, requiring that the soldier "never surrender of [his] own free will, . . . never forget [that he is] responsible for [his] actions" and that he is bound to give only his name, rank, service number, and birth date when captured.[22] Most journalists applauded the new code, but significant questions remained. Among them: would our boys have the psychological strength to obey the new regulations? Or would conformity and compulsion ease them into traitorous behavior?

Opening only three months after the establishment of the new code of military conduct, *Hatful* probably animated several spectators to consider the domestic consequences of the Communist brainwashing of POWs in Korea. Some critics rightly complained that Johnny's capture and imprisonment — the events that triggered his drug addiction — were not adequately explained in Gazzo's drama. Nonetheless, the play does make it clear that the Communists pulled him out of a cave in which he had been hiding for fourteen days, tortured him physically, and played with his mind to get him to confess the secret location of his sergeant. For giving them nothing but his name, rank, and serial number, Johnny returned to the United States a decorated though traumatized hero. The sad irony of Gazzo's play, of course, is that Johnny's resistance to brainwashing in Korea set him up for an equally savage brainwashing by drug pushers in the United States. *Hatful*'s input into the brainwashing debate of 1955 and 1956 was the pessimistic insight that commanding American boys to use their free will was not enough; we would lose the Cold War on the domestic front unless measures are taken to prevent subversive scum from infecting all of our boys with their poison. (Concerns about brainwashing continued into the 1960s, evident in the popularity of *The Manchurian Candidate* [1962], arguably one of Hollywood's most virulent contributions to cold war paranoia.)

The underlying cognitive assumptions about brainwashing and Johnny Pope's heroin addiction in *Hatful* are identical. Both the play and the public debate legitimated and enhanced "the psychological" as the only relevant mode of explanation; neither even considers causes that do not rest on the personal problems of Johnny and other POWs. In this regard, both rely on what Victor Braitberg has called a "hypodermic model of influence." In this containment conception of how to shape human behavior, bad people can alter good people's actions very quickly by injecting them with evil ideas and attitudes. This, it seemed, was what the Communists had accomplished in Korea. Fears of brainwashing and addiction link the schemas of containment and compulsion; once the container of the mind or body has been pierced, the individual loses his or her freedom. Many journalists and psychologists were concerned that American television programs and advertisers might also be injecting viewers with false values that undercut their free will. The "truth serums" ubiquitous in the spy stories of the 1950s represented another expression of this anxiety. As cultural historian Catherine Lutz notes, "This model's automatic quality was Janus-faced — it promised innocence of responsibility for those caught in its snare, but it also threatened a sudden and terrifying lack of self-control and authenticity."[23] This is Gazzo's point of view about Johnny's situation in *Hatful*: the boy cannot be blamed for his addiction, but he needs help to shake it before he becomes a shell of his former self. And the play positions its spectators to adopt Gazzo's liberal, therapeutic ethos as their own.

Johnny's innocence and relative lack of agency are key to his allegorical significance in the melodrama. As did Axelrod in *Itch*, Gazzo makes it clear that his protagonist is doing his best to fight against his oppressors, but his willpower is insufficient to overcome them. *Hatful* induces its audience to read Johnny's situation first as the problem of Everyboy beset by temptation and second, at the end of the play, as the crucifixion of Christ. Gazzo's conflation of the Everyman narrative with the Passion of the Son of God was hardly a new idea; both the anonymous medieval play and *Pilgrim's Progress* figured their hero as a kind of Christ, a tradition that continued in such dramatic allegories as *The London Merchant* (1731) and *The Drunkard* (1844). The escape from moral responsibility offered by the pushers, of course, is the main source of temptation in *Hatful*. For Gazzo, these perverts represent what Johnny's father, early in the drama, calls "the age of the vacuum" (321). This powerful containment metaphor, echoed throughout the play, suggests that "the age" has somehow vacuumed the life out of individuals and turned them into pod-people. Consequently, the Father and Celia assert, the American people have lost faith in themselves and their families and "the psychiatrists [have] struck oil" (321). By Act III, Mother and his gang have moved into Johnny and Celia's apartment to wait for eight hundred dollars owed them from past drug deals. "Brainwashed" on their own drugs, "they appear [in Gazzo's stage directions] to be either in slow motion or hopped. There is a sense of a vacuum . . . and then, coming from nowhere a sense of chaos and speed" (374). Polo, Johnny's brother, prevents the pushers from draining his brother of the last vestiges of his individuality in this episode, but the danger that Johnny may become another victim of "the vacuum age" remains until the end of the play.

Not content to generalize about the emptiness of American life in his drama, Gazzo pushes his allegory further into the realm of the universal by figuring Johnny as an emblem of Christ. Christian imagery pervades this play about an Italian American family named "Pope," deeply immersed in their Catholic faith. Gazzo has the Father, like the apostle Peter after the crucifixion, deny three times that he any longer knows his son. The pregnant Celia becomes a modern Virgin Mary when she hears Johnny's prayers and tenderly forgives him for his past sins. Polo, who has sacrificed his savings and much of his personal life in an attempt to help Johnny, is finally able to tell their father, "I'm my brother's keeper more than you know" (380). This Christian allegory climaxes at the end of the play when Johnny is raving for a fix. "Pop. Watch over me—watch over me," says Johnny. "For crissakes, Polo, he's dying," shouts the Father. "Hold on, for the love of God," urges Polo (383). At the climax of the melodrama, the realistic trappings of Gazzo's play fall away to reveal the universal abstractions underneath: in *Hatful*, "the vacuum age" is crucifying the American Boy, potential savior of the nation and of humanity.

Hatful is less directly indebted to the radiophonic than *Itch*, but as in the comedy the general situation of the melodrama draws from the ontology and strengths of radio drama. Again, voices outside of the protagonist crowd into his conscience, tempting him in *Hatful* to change his real family for the false family of the pushers. Mother, Chuch, Apples, and Putski are not imaginary characters, but they do externalize real psychological traits of the protagonist. Like *Itch*, but to melodramatic rather than comic effect, *Hatful* plays on the schizophrenia that can occur when contradictory aspects of one's personality become embodied and externalized. The result, again as in *Itch* (and *Salesman*), is a morality play in which the good aspects of Johnny's personality are at war with the bad. Vacuumed out, their bodies "snatched" by drugs, Johnny and the pushers are disembodied, literally out of touch with their physical needs. At moments when these characters are "hopped," the material environment of the apartment does not constrain them. Celia Pope may struggle to bring Johnny back to the material world of concrete reality, but for much of the play the mental world of Johnny's addiction is just as "real."

The Seven Year Itch also used the protagonist's emblematic value to generalize about the human condition. Specifically, Axelrod encouraged the audience to read Richard's situation with the Girl as the comic rediscovery of Edenic bliss for a modern Adam and Eve. In this sentimental rendering of the biblical story, Richard/Adam lives in the garden of his fantasies, his imagination untroubled by reality outside of Eden. As in James Thurber's story "The Secret Life of Walter Mitty" (and in the Mitty scenes in the stage adaptation, *A Thurber Carnival*, produced in 1960), Richard is actually a repressed mouse — one reviewer called him a "housebroken hubby"—whose dreams of heroism come to life on stage.[24] In *Itch*, these fantasies center on scenes of sexual prowess and conquest: a Lascivious Voyeur watching women undress; a suave, Sophisticated Lover who kisses the Girl passionately; a Clever Husband who romances his wife; and a Man of Cool Machismo who treats all women as one-night stands. In effect, Ewell/Sherman's body could be anything his mind might dream up. As the ur-male of all men, this Adamic figure contained mental multitudes.

When the Eve-Girl, her natural goodness sentimentally untainted by her sexual knowledge, introduces Richard/Adam to the possibility of flesh-and-blood sexuality, the reality of Guilt produces a comic Fall. Alexlrod used Dr. Brubaker's Freudian pronouncements to ease Richard's lapse from fantasy into infidelity. Their first conversation ranges from rape ("the case of Gustav Meyerheim") to the desire to commit wife murder ("repressed uxoricide") (319–21). In their second encounter, Richard confesses his attempted seduction and admits he would like to kill the Girl "with [his] bare hands" if she talks about their fling (340). Finally, the doctor helps Richard to analyze his guilty conscience ("sexomasochistic excitement") and seeks to allay his anxiety that his wife will "kill us both" (369–70) if she discovers his deed. In all of these incidents, Axelrod comically links Richard's compulsive fantasies of primal sex and violence to Brubaker's pseudo-Freudian analyses and prescriptions. While the playwright satirizes the psychiatrist's pomposity, he never undercuts his Freudian pretensions to universal truth and psychiatry, generally, as an appropriate counterforce to the anxieties of modern life. Axelrod encouraged spectators to couple modern psychiatry and Judeo-Christian mythology to allegorize *Itch*.

Like Axelrod, Gazzo positioned his spectators to recognize the need for expert intervention. Significantly, it is Celia who calls the police to take Johnny to the hospital at the end of the play. She is Gazzo's main line of defense against the simulations of "the vacuum age." As a good cold war wife and future mother, Celia offers "belief" in families, children, and the nation as the best antidote to addiction and inauthenticity. Her influence prevents Polo from seducing her, helps Johnny and his father to forgive each other for their past antagonisms, and saves her marriage. But in the end, the righteous influence of a wife and mother-to-be is not enough to save Johnny. Nor is the love of his family; Celia understands that Polo, attempting to help his brother, has actually been enabling his habit. Polo and the Father want to keep the police out of it, but Celia knows their love for Johnny may prevent them from forcing him to quit. In the necessary fight against "the vacuum age," the family must turn to the state. "Give me the police," says Celia into the telephone. "I'd like to report a drug addict. My husband. Yes, he's here now" (384). The weapons of the state provide the ultimate counterforce against the threat of simulation.

The ending of *Hatful* replays the dynamics of McCarthyism and underlines the confluence of the militarization and "psychologization" of American culture during the Cold War. As in *On the Waterfront* (1954) and numerous McCarthyite narratives of the 1950s, the point of view in *Hatful* celebrates the decision of an "informer" (Celia) to turn against those closest to her or him in order to bring to justice a boy or man who endangers America. *Hatful*, in fact, closely parallels the ending of *My Son John* (1952), a film in which a mother decides to turn in her son to the FBI when she realizes that he is a Communist. Here, too, Catholicism plays a significant role in strengthening patriotic vigilance, a patriotism that finally trumps traditional family loyalties. In both *Hatful* and *My Son John*, the liminal "psychological identity" of the Empty Boy allows the narrative to suggest that he has been victimized by forces beyond his control, which have first vacuumed him out then injected him with un-

American beliefs and habits. With a boy's psyche so malleable, any hint of inauthenticity could be a threat to national security. America had to protect itself from pod-people.

Although lacking the underlying hysteria of Gazzo's play, *Itch* relied on much the same rhetoric and several of the same assumptions. The comedy dropped a sex-bomb on a "normal" marriage, allowing an Eve-Girl to infect the mind and heart of the male spouse. Will the Boy become "addicted" to more girls; is the "itch" just a skin rash or has it penetrated the container of his soul? Because Broadway audiences believed that marriage was a bulwark against communism, Axelrod needed to assure them that Richard and Helen's marriage could be saved. As in *Hatful*, the conventional resolution of the problem lay in restoring the protagonist's authenticity, his ability to act in accordance with an inner Platonic essence that is fundamentally good. Luckily for Richard, the Girl is not Gazzo's vampirelike Mother. Though probably able to vacuum him out and inject him with more desire, the Girl decides she would rather get married to someone her own age, so she skips out of Richard's life as quickly as she dropped into it. In the end, Richard's comic counterforce against Tom MacKenzie reconfirms his manhood. With psychiatric help, Richard has conquered the danger of becoming another victim of the vacuum age and can rejoin "normal" life in America.

Itch and *Hatful* primarily encouraged what Lakoff and Johnson understand as advisory projection from cold war audiences. Both productions offered spectators numerous opportunities to project their own desires and concerns onto the figure of the boy. "What would I do if I stepped in to Johnny's or Richard's situation and chose to act according to my own values?" is the dramatic hook of *Hatful* and *Itch*. Both plays discouraged empathetic involvement. For empathetic projection to work, spectators must be able to discern the values of an actor-character and be willing to adopt those values as their own. As Empty Boys, both characters lack clear ethical orientations; they have needs, even addictions, but their values and behavior are a mass of contradictions. Johnny lurches between indifference and affection toward his family. His crucifixion climax carries little salvific grace; it is almost entirely self-centered. Richard's hormones, fantasies, and conscience twist him into a hundred comic knots, his values equally contorted. In conventional rhetorical terms, pathos, not ethos, is the key attraction of both boys, evoked melodramatically for one character and comically for the other. Both playwrights invite spectators to feel pity and sympathy for their boy protagonists, but neither character has enough of a stable ethical identity to sustain empathetic response.

■ In terms of the range of ethical orientations available in the hegemonic culture of the time, *Itch* and *Hatful* primarily positioned their spectators as ethical egotists, even narcissists. From Lakoff and Johnson's point of view, the ubiquity of containment liberalism in the United States during this period could be attributed to its combination of "strict father" and "nurturant parent" morality.[25] In their discussion of ethics and its ramifications, Lakoff and Johnson note that most abstract moral concepts are defined by metaphors that relate them to family governance. In his research into this problem, George Lakoff has discovered persuasive cognitive evidence linking conceptions of the ethical family to more general notions of political, social, and even theological justice. Strict father morality, as the name implies, projects the notion of a strong male presence able to protect his family from external dangers onto other ethical realms in which order, hierarchy, and abstract authority are prized. The nurturant parent model, in contrast, tries to mediate internal family problems and values the happiness of the children and the mutual responsibility of family members for each other. Both models of parenting, notes Lakoff, can be pathological if carried to an extreme: the strict father may become rigidly authoritarian and the nurturant parent (usually a mother but occasionally a father in the modern West) excessively permissive. If these two models are considered as a continuum, *Itch* and *Hatful* ranged near the extreme end of nurturant parent morality.

The morality of nurturant parents played significant roles in the society and imaginations of cold war Americans. Traditionally, liberalism had provided reforms to ensure some progress in the social and economic welfare of citizens and to defuse the threat of violent revolution. Although no longer as numerous and progressive as New Deal reforms, modest initiatives in social security, veterans' benefits, and other social programs continued to trickle through the 1947–1962 period. As historian Immanuel Wallerstein notes, instead of democracy, in which the lower classes would share in power according to their numbers, liberals promised meritocracy, the rule of experts. The nurturant parent was the conventional role model for experts in the schools, in medicine, social welfare agencies, and local government, and even in some corporations during the 1950s. In part because there seemed to be so many managers and professionals looking out for their welfare, many Americans believed that there was a natural harmony of interests among all classes and ethnicities. Even race relations, some whites assumed, could be fixed by enlightened social science, reform programs, and an attitude of patient nurturance toward "Negro" citizens, most of whom (they believed) were struggling to assimilate to white norms.

Mark Johnson notes that the moral theories of utilitarianism and ethical egoism have flourished within the general orientation of nurturant parent morality. The rewards and punishments of utilitarianism are primarily social-familial—fellow feelings of benevolence and togetherness or isolation and alienation. Ethical egoism, the moral theory at the center of *Itch* and *Hatful*, results from what Lakoff calls a "pathological" form of the nurturant parent family. Individuals come to believe that it is ethical to maximize their own well-being; self-nurturance and self-interest become more important than a sense of one's virtue and the well-being of others. Liberal notions of individual freedom and the "Invisible Hand" mechanism of a "rational" market can justify ethical egoism. Within this orientation, individuals may gain self-esteem from their own success, but the downside of such narcissism is a feeling of one's essential worthlessness.[26]

Projecting themselves onto Richard Sherman and Johnny Pope, the audience identified with two narcissists who were much more concerned with their own problems than with the well-being of others. Contemporary psychiatrists understood narcissism as a common malady of the postwar era. During the 1950s many therapists agreed with psychoanalyst Melanie Klein that narcissism sprang from an anxiety that the self might fall apart. Narcissistic individuals, according to Klein and others, never develop a healthy self-esteem and inner resilience because of unresolved traumas in early development.[27] This leads narcissists to fantasize that they are at the center of attention and in total control of others and/or that they are powerless to control themselves and others unless they merge with an authority figure. Consequently, narcissists tend to swing between feelings of optimistic overconfidence and anxious depression, between grandiosity and emptiness. Because they constantly regress to an infantile stage in their lives, narcissists supposedly have trouble distinguishing their desires from the separate needs and personalities of others. This often leaves narcissists pathetically vulnerable, hypersensitive to the moods of others, and either full of anger or depressed because of the rage they disavow.

While Klein and other psychoanalysts located the postwar rise of narcissistic disorders in problems that occurred in infancy, social historian Christopher Lasch pointed to an American "culture of narcissism" that facilitated their proliferation. Part of the reason for the spread of this culture, argues Lasch, was the success of psychiatry and other therapeutic professions in convincing Americans that traditional forms of psychological assistance—families, friends, the church, even local bartenders—could no longer serve their needs. A whole range of therapeutic services proliferated during the 50s, as the rich paid for expensive psychotherapy, businesses and schools hired counselors, and cities turned the poor over to social workers. For Lasch, this dependency on specialists generated perverse effects:

> As therapeutic points of view and practice gain general acceptance, more and more people find themselves disqualified, in effect, from the performance of adult responsibilities and become dependent on some form of medical authority. The psychological expression of this dependence is narcissism. . . . Since modern society prolongs the experience of dependence into adult life, it encourages milder forms of narcissism in people who might otherwise come to terms with the inescapable limits of their personal freedom and power—limits inherent in the human condition—by developing competence as workers and parents.[28]

Lasch's social history makes it clear that mild forms of narcissism pervaded the culture.

Lasch did not mention the side effects of radiophony on the culture, but this mode of communication also contributed to the rise of narcissism in the business class. A person listening to the radio, rapt in radioland, can shut out the world and may assume that sounds emanating from the speaker are meant for his or her private enjoyment. The rapid spread of television in the 1950s furthered this privatization of cultural communication, initiated by radio and the telephone. As media historian Richard Butsch notes, "television was not so much the culprit as an accomplice" in the privatization of American life after the war.[29] Other factors that led to a long-term decline in the value and practice of public and community activities included suburbanization, the emphasis on home and family, and the positioning of Americans as consumers rather than citizens. Privatization led to the separation of the self from others not of one's choosing and facilitated the kind of alienation and self-involvement that could result in narcissism. Radiophony alone cannot be blamed for this, of course, but it was part of the problem.

Not surprisingly, cold war spectators applauded many narcissists on Broadway stages, from Brando's Stanley in *A Streetcar Named Desire* to Robert Preston's Harold Hill in *The Music Man*. Johnny Pope is a vacuumed-out, empty self whose moods swing wildly from grandiose dreams of success to the depths of self-pity and despair. Gazzo uses his other characters to keep audience attention circling back to Johnny, either by restricting them to the immediate family (father, brother, wife) and keeping their focus on their son/brother/husband or by depicting others as symbols of Johnny's emptiness (the drug pushers). Richard Sherman in *Itch* has so little sense of a coherent identity that he populates his mind with Walter-Mitty fantasy figures who play out a full range of infantile anxieties. Axelrod puts the audience members inside Richard's head at the start of the show and rarely lets them out; if spectators do not quickly identify with Richard, they may as well leave the theater. Significantly, Gazzo and Axelrod bring in outside authorities — psychiatry and the state — as counterforces to conclude their plays. These *dei ex machinae* confirm the power and legitimacy of the culture of narcissism. Both plays suggest that ordinary people are too mixed up and traditional modes of care-giving too unreliable to solve personal problems; people must turn to therapeutic and medical specialists.

■ When audiences identified with Johnny Pope, they projected themselves onto Ben Gazzara, already renowned in the mid-1950s as a new Method star. Gazzara had won the Drama Critics Award as the "Most Promising Actor of the Year" in 1954 and received more critical praise for his Brick in *Cat on a Hot Tin Roof*, which he left to star in *Hatful*. The critics termed his performance as Johnny Pope "admirable" (Chapman), "quite brilliant" (Watts), and "titanic" (McClain). In an interview in *Cue* magazine in 1955 — one of several given by Gazzara in the mid 1950s — the actor credited Lee Strasberg for his success. Strasberg, he said, was "a bonafide genius" and "working with him was equivalent to studying with Stanislavsky in an earlier period." The article introduced Gazzara as "typical" of the new Method stars: "They noisily eschew glamour, dress carelessly, are intensely intense. They endlessly discuss motivation, integrity, the search for values, tab our times the age of anxiety." As if to confirm the cliché of the Method actor, Gazzara admitted his therapeutic need to find relaxation through painting: "These are tense times and we are all taut."[30]

Walter Kerr's review suggests how the actor used Method technique to develop his embodiment of Johnny Pope: "Ben Gazzara's hopelessly 'hooked' veteran is a brilliant tour de force. The alarming tensions of the evening are his to elaborate and to control. Whether he is cocking his head to one side and twisting his mouth into a sick, self-pitying smile, or diving headfirst into a bed in anguish, the control is there. The spine-tingling eruptions are violently credible; the ordinary man behind them is credible too."[31] Gazzara's control as a performer allowed for sharp contrasts between the authentic Johnny Pope, full of determination, self-pity, and occasional affection, and the inauthentic Monster Addict compulsively threatening to take over his soul. Like other Method performers of the period, Gazzara knew how to heighten those theatrical moments when physical and psychological pain is reduced to an image of universal, emblematic emotion.

Audiences came to the theater expecting Gazzara's presence to embody a Method performance. For many spectators, the authenticity that was synonymous with Method acting easily merged with narcissism. By the mid-1950s, several famous Method actors had already played many narcissistic young men—Marlon Brando in *A Streetcar Named Desire*, Montgomery Clift in *A Place in the Sun*, and James Dean in *Rebel without a Cause*, among others. Because these stars were widely classified as Hollywood Method actors, the public believed that they had played a side of their natural selves in these roles. The personas of these performers stood as models of American boyhood; applauding them had elevated youthful narcissism to popular eminence. Audiences and critics were already pressing Gazzara's image out of the same mold. By 1957, after his success in *Cat* and *Hatful*, numerous television appearances, and a major film role, Gazzara had joined the pantheon of male Method stars. A newspaper puff on Gazzara casually noted that "the same names come up" whenever the Actors Studio is mentioned: "James Dean, Marlon Brando, and, nowadays, Ben Gazzara."[32] At the opening of *Hatful* in 1955, Gazzara's performance as a narcissistic Johnny Pope confirmed a stereotype audiences already knew.

Further, the public was beginning to identify the Method actor himself, apart from any role he might play, as a type of narcissistic personality. In 1960 critic Theodore Hoffman limned this dismissive outline of the type:

> Method actors seem more intense than others. . . . There is a tautness to their voices which makes them inaudible or monotonous. . . . They like to scratch themselves, rub their arms, brush their hair, count their buttons. They keep on doing these things even when other actors are the center of attention. . . . They like to play scenes wherever they choose, frequently in odd pockets of the stage. They apparently don't like to deliver lines towards the audience. . . .
> When a piece of business like lighting a cigarette or pouring a drink comes up, the play seems to stop while the actor carefully examines the cigarette to find out what brand it is or looks for germs on the glass. One gets the impression that a great deal is happening to the characters but one isn't always sure just what. And in the end, one gets a kind of cheated feeling, as if the actors were going through all that rigmarole for their own pleasure and really weren't the least bit interested in communicating anything to the audience.[33]

Hoffman's catalogue of Method sins, a summary of the complaints of many other theater- and filmgoers about "the Method," centers on the male performer's compulsiveness and narcissistic self-involvement. Similarly, Norman Mailer (no stranger to narcissism himself) chided Method actors for elevating their own authenticity over the presentation of a playwright's character. In wry amusement, he quipped "how disagreeable" and "even brutal" it was for the Method actor "when his role is not adequate to him, when he cannot act with some subtle variations of his personal style."[34] When spectators came to watch Gazzara in *Hatful*, many expected a narcissistic performance even before they knew anything about Johnny Pope. Some of them may have been disappointed—Gazzara did not scratch and mumble his way through the role—but for others the narcissism of the character probably helped them to confirm their image of the Method boy.

The ideas and techniques of Lee Strasberg are key to understanding the public image and actual practice of Method acting. Despite the fact that Strasberg's Method—his concept of Konstantin Stanislavski's system—had influenced the early triumphs of the Group Theatre, Kazan and other founders of the Actors Studio did not invite Strasberg to join them when they began teaching in 1947. They believed he had been too domineering during their Group Theatre days; Strasberg's tyranny and intransigence, in fact, had led to his forced resignation from the Group Theatre in 1937. Nonetheless, Kazan and co-founder Cheryl Crawford asked Strasberg to teach a few workshops at the Actors Studio in 1948; and soon Strasberg began taking on more responsibilities, as Kazan's filmmaking career kept him away from New York for longer periods. By 1951 Lee Strasberg had become the guiding spirit of the Actors Studio; he controlled the admission of prospective students, and his beliefs shaped the curriculum of the workshop. During the decade, Strasberg made his name synonymous with Method acting and the Actors Studio the recognized headquarters of the Method in America.[35]

Working within Strasberg's Method, actors could assure themselves that they were connected with the platonically "real." To breathe life into his characters, "an actor must deal with deep, firm things inside himself," stated Strasberg. Studio-trained director Jack Garfein noted that Strasberg made all the actors feel that they had "great inner treasures." Strasberg's most notable exercises took for granted the existence of an essential self, less conscious but more genuine than the mask worn on the outside for public display. Affective memory, for example, assumed that past memories locked within held the essential truth about a person's identity. And the "private moment" exercise encouraged performers to withdraw from the ongoing work of a rehearsal to engage in an activity normally performed in private as a means of ensuring that their emotions were flowing from an authentic center. In short, for Strasberg, the "inner emotional experience" of every actor was the contained core of his or her being as an artist. Actors who learned how to open this treasure chest and utilize those "deep, firm things inside" could perform their characters with sincerity and spontaneity.[36] Actors who did not draw on their authentic selves to create their roles might expose their lack of genuineness in front of an audience. Strasberg's fundamental advice was to rely on your Platonic identity or risk inauthenticity on stage.

Stanislavski, too, had recognized the importance of an actor's work on the self. Nonetheless, he believed it was possible and necessary for actors to experience both themselves and their characters simultaneously on the stage. Strasberg, however, emphasized the projection of the self into the character; the role should disappear into the self in performance.

Much of Stanislavski's technique, especially in his later writings, drew the actor's attention back to the play script, limiting the extent to which the performer could rely on his or her self as the entire basis for characterization. Stanislavski called on actors to focus on the "problem" of their characters' situation by analyzing the "given circumstances" of the play and then attempt to solve this problem through the creation of "actions." For Stanislavski, the author's characters were best understood as real people with a past, living out their lives in the midst of an environment that also derived from the historical circumstances in the world of the play. In addition to using himself or herself, the modern actor had to give voice and body to this other "person," alive in the mind of the author if not yet on the stage.[37]

For Strasberg, characters were more abstract, less preexistent in the script and hence lacking a firm connection to a historical past within the fiction of the play. Kazan had urged Actors Studio actors to play the "actions" of their scripted characters, but Strasberg concentrated on the actor's search within the self for genuine emotion. While Strasberg never denied the importance of Stanislavski's given circumstances and actions, his discourse effectively configured the relationship between actor and character differently than had his mentor. In Strasberg's conception, actor, character, and play were like three Chinese boxes resting inside of each other: the inner self of the actor nested inside the character she or he was playing, which, in turn, was contained by the largest box of the three, the fictional world of the play. Many apparent contradictions in Strasberg's language disappear when the transitivity of his containers is recognized. Thus Strasberg could tell Keir Dullea "to learn to live on stage simply and believably, within the logic of your character" in one breath and then urge him "to provide a basis for yourself, of how you would be inside that character" in the next. The inner self is always the smallest of these nesting blocks, and actors must learn to project its essence into the blocks encapsulating it. When these containers within containers are properly aligned, the walls between them tend to disappear for audiences. Therefore, Arthur Penn could say that Method acting can give spectators "a sense of a character's inner life, all radiating from the actor's genuinely personal core."[38] Whereas Stanislavski understood dramatic characters as living out a personal and social history, Strasberg placed characters within a spatial metaphor that deemphasized their relation to historical processes and grounded them in projections from the actor's self.

Strasberg's emphasis on the performer's Platonic authenticity as the proper basis of characterization loosened the actor's presumed allegiance to the playwright's intentions, however they might be interpreted. Meade Roberts, a playwright who joined the Studio's Playwrights Unit (an experiment that soon folded) in 1955, recalled that Strasberg's discussion of an actor's character work made him nervous because it suggested "that the actor is a creator more than an interpreter." Rather, believed Roberts, "A method [should not be] an end, it is a means to dramatic truth." Cultural critic Robert Brustein agreed. "[The Actors Studio] has inflated the importance of the actor's calling at the expense of the author's," he concluded.[39] All practitioners of the Method believed that actors needed to play the "subtext" of their speeches, the real meanings beneath the words of the dramatic text. But how far could an actor go in ignoring, ironizing, or even contradicting the apparent, denotative meaning of the playwright's dialogue? Stella Adler told her students to derive subtexts that worked within the "given circumstances" of the play. Strasberg, however, encouraged much more latitude, advising his students to use affective memory to trigger the subtexts of their lines.

Strasberg's desire to privilege the actor's subtext over the author's text gets at the possibilities for narcissistic expression inherent in Method acting. If, as historian Sharon Carnicke concludes, "the Method treats the play as a springboard for the actor's personal work,"[40] actors become creators as much as interpreters, using the author's characters to represent a side of their own essential identities on stage. Thus many Method actors in the 1950s could believe that performing was primarily a means of self-realization and self-representation, only secondarily the simulation of some other reality articulated in the script. Audiences might conflate the author's character and the actor's characterization, but the Method performers did not; they had to use their own bodies and minds as the basis of the creative work. Urged by Strasberg to keep their work "honest," "spontaneous," and "genuine," Method actors constructed an interior, Platonic self that they believed could animate their authenticity. Because this essence was forever elusive, however, Method actors pressed to authenticate their authenticity.

The phrase "authenticating authenticity" comes from film historian

Richard Dyer, who uses it to discuss fan discourse about Hollywood stars from the 1930s through the 1950s:

> There is a whole litany in the fan literature surrounding stars in which certain adjectives endlessly recur—sincere, immediate, spontaneous, real, direct, genuine, and so on. All of these words can be seen as relating to a general notion of "authenticity." It is these qualities that we demand of a star if we accept her or him in the spirit in which she or he is offered. Outside of a camp appreciation, it is the star's really seeming to be what s/he is supposed to be that secures his/her star status, "star quality" or charisma. Authenticity is both a quality necessary to the star phenomenon to make it work, and also the quality that guarantees the authenticity of the other particular values a star embodies (such as girl-next-door-ness, etc.). It is this effect of authenticating authenticity that gives the star charisma. . . .[41]

Although the Method's ideology placed the ethics of authenticity in the context of European high art, most American actors were already prepared to accept it through their experience of Hollywood movies.

Well before the founding of the Actors Studio, Hollywood publicists had been crafting "star images" for the studs and fillies of the studio stables—a mélange of biographical details, photographic stills, and media coverage that congealed (often in odd ways) with the roles they actually played. It was an article of Hollywood faith that star actors only performed roles that were somehow "right" for them, even if a departure in casting from their usual type required an altered image. Real stars, it seemed, always represented themselves, not some mere character dreamed up by a writer. Clark Gable, for example, cannot speak with a southern accent in *Gone with the Wind*; he must sound like Gable to his fans. The elevation of the actor at the expense of the author in Hollywood had already provided the core of the ideology of authenticity and potential narcissism that Method actors would follow. While Hollywood would continue to link external image to internal personality in the creation of a star's authenticity, however, Strasberg located the center of an actor's appeal solely on the inside; Method authenticity became a Platonic essence fundamentally unchanged by external appearances. Nonetheless, when American stage actors embraced the Method in the early 1950s, they confirmed the Hollywood credo, embedded in the culture of narcissism, that a star's authenticity provided the foundation of his or her art.

Marlon Brando's performance as Stanley Kowalski in *Streetcar* in 1947 solidified the connection between narcissism and Method acting on the Broadway stage. The response to Brando in that role is worth examining in some detail, for the light it sheds both on the likely audience response to Gazzara's Johnny Pope and on the cultural ripple effects of the performances of all of the Method boys during the 1950s.

Brando's presence in *Streetcar* evoked a significant narcissistic response from many theater critics. This was partly because Brando followed Elia Kazan's directions to play Stanley as a desperate hedonist. Before rehearsals began, Kazan commented in his *Streetcar* notebook: "Stanley is supremely indifferent to everything except his own pleasure and comfort. He is marvelously selfish, a miracle of sensuous self-centeredness. He builds a hedonist life, and fights to the death to defend it." Kazan surrounded Brando's Stanley with a variety of props he could use to demonstrate his compulsive self-involvement, especially his need for oral gratification—cigarettes to manipulate in his mouth, beer to sip and nurse, fruit to eat, cigars to suck on. "[Stanley] is going to get very fat later. He's desperately trying to drug his senses . . . overwhelming them with a constant round of sensation so that he will feel nothing else," recorded Kazan.[42] (Ironically, Brando's bloated physique in middle age would later mirror Kazan's prediction about the fate of the actor's most famous character.) The emblematic moment of Brando/Kowalski as hedonist, of course, is his ripped-T-shirt embrace of Stella after wailing her name outside their apartment. Desperate hedonism—the attempt to reassure an empty self of its own coherence and worth—is a clear sign of narcissism.

In a recent article that analyzes Brando's physical strategy in characterizing Stanley for both the film and stage versions of *Streetcar*, John Gronbeck-Tedesco notes that his poses and gestures copied the confident, coiled, often bare-chested images of American soldiers during the war. These images were widely available in print journalism and film, and still prevalent in 1947 when *Streetcar* premiered. Brando understood Stanley as a veteran, suggests Gronbeck-Tedesco, a master sergeant who had enjoyed obedience from his men and survived the invasion of Salerno: "Stanley's body is fraught with signs of the insecurity and terror of battle—insecurity and terror he cannot face but which continue to provoke his aggressive responses to others. His soldierly body formations are literally holding him together, although only barely."[43] For Gronbeck-Tedesco, one of the larger arcs of *Streetcar*'s action is Stanley's reestablishment of male authority in the postwar American family through the violence of rape. The moment when Stanley carries Blanche to his bed at the climax of the play is an emblem of the Empty Boy as violence-prone veteran. As either violent soldier or desperate hedonist, Brando/Kowalski is an empty shell, held together by kinesthetic body language learned in the military or in the consumption of goods. This presence needs constant sensation to stave off depression.

While several of the reviewers of *Streetcar* noted aspects of Brando's characterization of Stanley that might be termed narcissistic, only one of them was troubled by the point of view that the production seemed to take toward Stanley's hedonism and violence. In his critique for *Tomorrow*, Harold Clurman praised Brando's performance but noted that his "combination of an intense, introspective, and almost lyric personality under the mask of a bully endows the character with something almost touchingly painful." This was unfortunate, he believed, because Kowalski "is the unwitting antichrist of our time, the little man who will break the back of every effort to create a more comprehensive world in which thought and conscience, a broader humanity, are expected to evolve from the old Adam. His mentality provides the soil for fascism. . . ." Nonetheless, for nearly two-thirds of the play, stated Clurman, "the audience identifies itself with Stanley Kowalski. His low jeering is seconded by the audience's laughter, which seems to mock the feeble and hysterical decorativeness of [Blanche's] behavior. The play becomes the triumph of Stanley Kowalski, with the collusion of the audience, which is no longer on the side of the angels."[44] When Clurman later directed Anthony Quinn as Stanley for the road show of *Streetcar*, Quinn and Clurman characterized Stanley as much more brutish than had Brando and Kazan.

While no other reviewer focused specifically on the disruptive effects of Brando's performance, several used language that suggested that their own sense of the sympathetic balance between the positive and negative attributes of Blanche and Stanley had indeed been altered by Brando's portrayal. Most of the Broadway newspaper reviewers happily crossed the line from what Clurman regarded as the "side of the angels" to stand, with some minor reservations, with Stanley Kowalski. Their reviews typically characterized Brando's Stanley as rough, even brutish, but realistic, warm-hearted, and spontaneous. For Ward Morehouse, for instance, Stanley, "an ex-G.I. of Polish parentage," though "a brute of a boy," was also "simple and hardworking." Robert Garland called him "toughly tender." For Louis Kronenberger, Stanley/Marlon was a "no-nonsense roughneck." "A stalwart Polish-American" and a "realist," said John Chapman. William Hawkins tended to conflate the actor and the role. The speech and anger of Brando's Stanley, he said, were "ingeniously spontaneous, while his deep-rooted simplicity is sustained every second." For these reviewers, Brando/Kowalski's presence embodied an ethnic version of the emblematic American boy, no longer innocent but good-at-heart. Only two reviewers dissented from this consensus, Brooks Atkinson and Robert Coleman. Atkinson called Stanley "quick tempered, scornful, and violent." For Coleman, he was "aggressive and ruthless."[45]

Most of the reviewers described Jessica Tandy's Blanche Dubois as a neurotic, sexually predatory female, a figure out of *film noir*. All agreed that Blanche was psychologically disturbed: "Neurotic and desperate," stated Morehouse; and "unfitted . . . for reality," admitted Atkinson. Several condemned her sexual promiscuity. "She is the hat rack of her Mississippi town, a generous, loving accommodator of any yearning stranger," said Chapman. Most reviewers were less forgiving: "nymphomania posing as straight-lacedness" (Kronenberger), "a boozy prostitute who gradually loses her mind" (Barnes), and "a paranoic-nymphomaniac" (Coleman). While a few reviewers expressed the belief that Blanche was more sinned against than sinning, most avoided mentioning Stanley's role in driving his sister-in-law to madness. When reviewers noted the rape at all, they usually couched it in euphemism and evasion: Kronenberger wrote that Stanley "takes her to bed," and Coleman stated that he "had an affair with her." For most, Blanche evoked some sympathy (although Hawkins found her pathos "repellent rather than sympathetic"), but her neuroses and decadence doomed her to destruction.[46]

Of course this was not the response that Williams and Kazan had hoped for and expected. Stanley's rape of Blanche, said Williams, was "the ravishment of the tender, the sensitive, the delicate, by the savage and brutal forces in modern society." Though deeply drawn to the pathos of his Blanche, Williams also realized that he had created in Stanley a character who was not wholly a villain and looked for a complex response

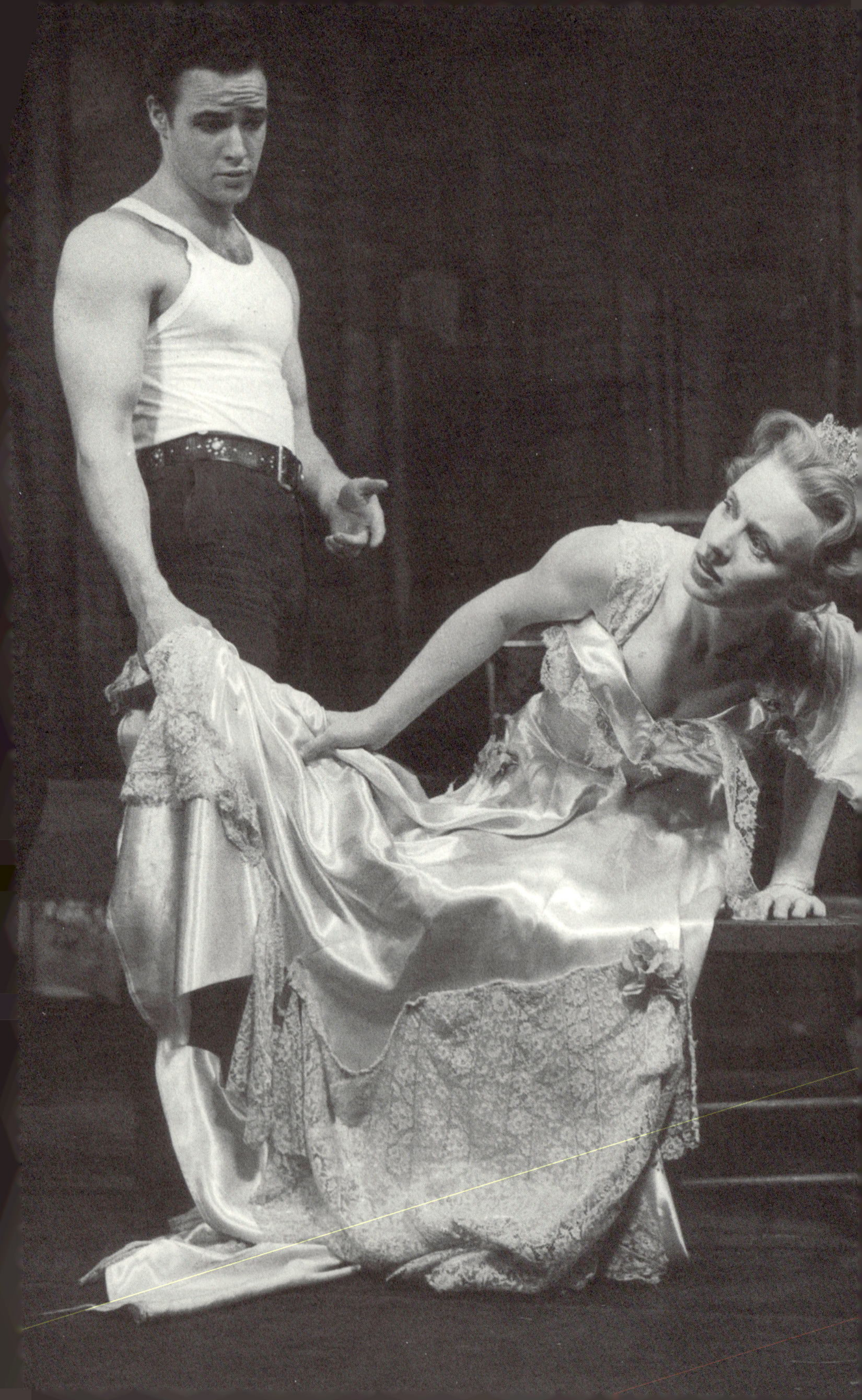

to him from his spectators. Kazan expected the audience to side with Stanley in the initial scenes of the play but hoped that their sympathies would gradually shift to Blanche. By the time of his autobiography (1988), Kazan defended the ambivalent effect that he thought the play had produced on viewers in 1947. Brando in his autobiography was more self-critical. "I think Jessica [Tandy] and I were both miscast," he admitted, "and between us we threw the play out of balance . . . she was too shrill to elicit the sympathy . . . the woman deserved. This threw the play out of balance because the audience was not able to recognize the potential of her character, and as a result my character got a more sympathetic reaction than Tennessee intended."[47]

For most spectators, the balance of sympathies tilted sharply toward Stanley. Several reviewers refused even to be drawn into the ethical conflict between the two characters because they were mostly repulsed by Blanche and accepted Stanley's hedonism and violence as inevitable facts of nature. Hawkins summed up this general point of view about Stanley when he termed him "an honest animal who needs no motivation for anything he does other than he wants to do it at that particular time."[48] This discourse effectively subtracts agency, and consequently blame, from the character. In this understanding of the play, Stanley is a simple brute who cannot help himself and Blanche should not have gotten in his way. Chapman, Garland, Kronenberger, Morehouse, and Hawkins—five of the nine newspaper reviewers of the play on opening night—express variations of this interpretation. While they do not applaud Stanley's narcissistic revenge against Blanche, they are eager to ignore or excuse his behavior since, in their analysis, it was driven by forces beyond his control. During the war, the American public excused similar sexual exploits by American servicemen overseas; "the boys" could not help themselves. Either because these critics were mild narcissists themselves or because their response to Stanley simply followed the conventional reaction of many Americans to soldier-boy indiscretions during the war (or for both reasons), these five reviewers encouraged a narcissistic response to the presence of Brando's Stanley Kowalski.

Stanley/Marlon Brando grabs at Blanche/Jessica Tandy's tattered satin evening gown in scene 10 of A Streetcar Named Desire. *Eileen Darby photo, courtesy New York Public Library.*

No doubt many Americans responded narcissistically to Brando/Kowalski in the film version of *Streetcar*, also directed by Kazan, which was released in 1951. Kazan found numerous opportunities for Brando to invite a gaze from male and female viewers that sexualized his body, thus encouraging narcissistic identification. More than most other people, narcissists desire to elevate and eroticize the bodies of others as a means of affirming their own sexuality. The film induced this gaze most memorably in the scene after the "Poker Night" fight when Blanche begs her sister not to "hang back with the brutes." The camera follows Stanley, who has been secretly listening to Blanche's harangue, as he saunters into the room, flashes a boyish smile, and invites Stella (and the spectators) to admire his sexy, boyish physique. In response, Stella embraces him fiercely and Stanley grins, presumably at Blanche, but straight into the camera.

Publicity stills of Brando on the set of *Streetcar* released by Warner Brothers also eroticized his masculinity. Film historian Steven Cohan notes that two shots in particular — both featuring Brando in T-shirt and slacks — divided his body "into zones of erotic interest," emphasizing the relaxed strength of his muscular arms, the rounded sensuality of his shoulders and pectorals, and the forward thrust of his hips and pelvis. Such photographs underlined what Elia Kazan called "the bisexual effect of Brando's image." In a *New Yorker* profile of Brando, Harold Brodky commented on the androgyny of the actor's film persona: "Brando [in *Streetcar*] took over the vanity and posing and sheer willfulness of a good-looking woman and developed . . . an anti-version of a diva's romantic sexuality. He gave it a male twist, using the rigorously male energy of his director, Elia Kazan." Brando's Stanley, in other words, participated in the "transvestite effect" that Steven Cohan has concluded underscored the presence of many male performances in Hollywood films during the 1950s.[49] This sexualized, androgynous presence invited a narcissistic gaze from film viewers. It is likely that Kazan and Brando deployed many of these same strategies to invite this gaze from audience members in the stage version of *Streetcar* as well.

Colin Counsell's semiotic reading of Method performing generally confirms its narcissistic effects and helps to locate it firmly within the culture of the Cold War. Counsell notes four general attributes of Method signification from actors on stage and film, three of which have already been discussed: a physical ease that audiences understood as a sign of naturalness and authenticity; eruptive and often unpredictable emotions (e.g., anguish, trauma, joy) usually read by spectators as psychological intensity and/or disturbance; and signs from the actor such as behavioral tics, "spontaneous" vocal inflections, and nuances of gesture that indicated a complex inner life. These "three consistent features of the Method performance," states Counsell, "form the core of its iconography, for although Strasbergian actors often employ their own unique performance personae, their mannerisms nevertheless fall into predictable categories, proffering the same orders of meaning."[50] These mannerisms were so readily observable in the performances of Brando, Gazzara, and numerous other Method Boys that they could be parodied by the end of the 1950s.

Comic mockery by Hoffman and others, however, did nothing to alter the general impression that the Method actor was somehow more adept at portraying the essence of the human condition than others were. This was because the model of the self embedded in Method performance conformed to the contained, psychologized self of cold war culture. As Counsell notes, Method signification sent the same message to audiences about the self as *Hatful* and *Itch*: an authentic, inner essence trapped inside a repressive outer shell. The struggle of the essential self to break free—from social codes, a tortured past, drug addiction, a restrictive conscience, or any of numerous other oppressions—constituted the primary conflict of Method performance, what Counsell calls "the iconography of neurosis." Counsell explains: "When we see characters wrestling with language, fighting to communicate their emotions and failing, we read this as an indication that language is inadequate to convey them, that their thoughts and feelings run deeper than words can express. In inferring the existence of 'blocked' feelings, then, the failed attempt at expression signals to spectators that the character possesses dimensions which cannot be seen."[51] The result, says Counsell, is that spectators perceive fractured characters, divided against themselves, in the grip of neurotic struggle.

Counsell may be largely correct regarding the meanings that spectators attributed to the spectacle of Method performance, but he slights the valuation of those meanings on the part of cold war spectators. More likely, when watching a struggling Empty Boy on stage (i.e., actor conflated with character), audiences projected their own assumptions about him onto the actor-character to compensate for the apparent ethical and psychological confusion of the image; in effect, this is what most of the critics had done in their reviews of Brando as Stanley in *Streetcar*. Following Counsell, Brando/Kowalski may have seemed somewhat neurotic; but, more importantly, most critics and audiences viewed his psychological intensity and eruptions positively. Brando/Kowalski's apparent emptiness, his absence of a clear psychology, invited audiences to fill in the blank through advisory projection with ethical attributes that they ascribed to themselves and to the general figure of the American boy. The narcissistic gaze did not reject stage narcissists as neurotic; it sympathized with them as fellow sufferers and even stars.

The narcissism inherent in spectator response to Method Boys like Brando and Gazzara had many consequences in the 1950s and 1960s. As Christopher Lasch details in *The Culture of Narcissism*, narcissistic identification at the theater and elsewhere influenced Americans to worship heroes, depend on bureaucrats, abdicate parental authority, dread old age, and trivialize personal relationships. It also helped to induce consumerism, the belief that commercial products can fulfill psychological needs, which rose dramatically during the 50s. According to cultural historian Philip Cushman, the postwar economy was largely successful in constructing Americans as "empty selves" to facilitate the consumption of products necessary to sustain growth and prosperity:

> Without the empty self, America's consumer-based economy (and its charismatically oriented political process) would be inconceivable. New fields such as advertising and psychology have responded to and further developed the new configuration of the empty self. . . . Americans in the post–World War II era came to pursue self-improvement in a form and to a degree unknown before. As the individual's growth, enjoyment, and fulfillment putatively became the single most valued aspect of life, several industries grew up to minister to the newly created needs: the cosmetics industry, the diet business, the electronic entertainment industry, preventive medical care, and the self-improvement industry (including mainstream psychotherapy, pop psychology, and pop religion).[52]

Along with charismatic politics and psychotherapy, these industries used advertising to create a need for their products. As never before in American life, commercials helped to hollow out an empty self by facilitating status anxiety, personal insecurity, and other fears that nag at even the mildest of narcissists. Madison Avenue crafted ads that promised to fill the aching void with commodities that could overcome alienation, promote illusions of protest and freedom, and create a grandiose self that would be the center of envious attention. In addition to advertising, other social forces in postwar America—suburbanization, radio listening and television watching, white-collar conformity, professionalization—colluded to position individuals as narcissists and consumers. As Riesman and other postwar commentators realized, the dynamics of cold war society were flattening the work ethic.

The rhetorics of *Hatful* and *Itch* encouraged their spectators to worry about consumerism but gave them nothing to counter its blandishments. Instead, both plays recognized that the self of their male protagonists is an empty, anxious, and compulsive one, waiting to be filled. In *Hatful*, Celia complains that her dull job as a secretary provides no challenges, only money to buy things. Polo, when drunk, mocks his own material comforts: "We don't need anybody. I got . . . Florsheim shoes . . . Paris belt. . . . I got everything I need . . . except a Bond suit. I dreamt I fell asleep in my Bond suit" (335–36). Gazzo is aware that consumption can become just another addiction, like heroin, to fill an empty self, but no state intervenes in *Hatful* to stem the ravages of consumerism. Likewise, *Itch* pokes fun at Richard's compulsive consumption of cigarettes and alcohol as soon as the Girl animates his narcissistic neurons. Since she is as much of a narcissist as he is, however, they can consume each other and walk away from the affair, their egos temporarily sated, in the same way that readers discarded the paperback books peddled by Richard's firm once they were read.

By treating each other as consumables, the Boy and the Girl of *Itch* foreshadow the prime example of the synthesis of consumerism and sexuality in the 1950s, the *Playboy* phenomenon. The first edition of Hugh Hefner's *Playboy* magazine hit the newsstands in 1953, roughly a year after the premiere of *Itch*. Promising from the first to free men from the confines of marriage, *Playboy* also offered "freedom" through consumption. Through stereo sets, imported liquor, the right clothes, and other products, the playboy could declare his independence from the family values of the fifties and enjoy (at least in fantasy) the "playmate of the month," the ultimate in pleasurable consumption. Though hardly a playboy at heart, Richard Sherman backs into the "playboy lifestyle" and comes out a new boy/man. And the Girl seems to have been manufactured to fit into one of Hefner's foldouts: not only was she photographed in the nude, but the production costumed and made up Vanessa Brown to appear already air-brushed for a bounce in bed.

Hefner and Axelrod capitalized on a new consumer ethic for men that was just beginning to succeed in postwar America. The basic problem for cold war prosperity, as a motivational researcher told businessmen, was finding a way "of permitting the average American [male] to feel moral . . . even when he is spending; . . . to demonstrate that the hedonistic approach to his life is a moral, not an immoral one." The answer lay in converting the average American male to what one contemporary sociologist called "fun morality"—convincing him that a life of pleasurable consumption was his just due.[53] "Fun morality," of course, is simply another name for the narcissism that Lakoff and Johnson term "ethical egoism." The campaign to promote "fun morality" succeeded beyond anyone's wildest hopes in the 1950s. Between 1947 and 1961, as the Gross National Product increased by over 60 percent, consumer spending on non-necessities (purchasing a television, fixing up the house, buying a second car, etc.) doubled. If "fun morality" made hedonism normal, the Stanley Kowalskis of America were justified in protecting and enjoying their piece of the pie. And the Richard Shermans had a right to an occasional fling. "Fun morality" encouraged Empty Boys to recline in La-Z-Boys.

Nationalistic discourse during the 1950s linked consuming more and better goods to patriotic duty. Far from being immoral, the "freedom" to consume distinguished America from Soviet Russia. At the American Exhibition in Moscow in 1959, Vice-President Richard Nixon trumpeted the virtues of American consumption in his conversation with the Soviet premier, Nikita Khrushchev. In what came to be called the "kitchen debate" because it was televised in the kitchen of a model home at the exhibition, Nixon pointed to the American family's ability to choose among a variety of kitchen appliances on display as a primary reason for the superiority of free enterprise over communism. The Soviets might be ahead of the United States in missiles, Nixon admitted, but American commodities topped Russian ones in providing individuality, security, and abundance for American homes. As liberal capitalism eased Americans into a culture of consumption in the 1950s, the Cold War hastened the process. And the Empty Boys of Broadway did their part to animate narcissistic anxieties and quicken American consumerism.

■ In *Cat on a Hot Tin Roof*, which premiered on Broadway in 1955, Tennessee Williams erected an ironic shrine to the comforts of narcissistic consumerism. According to his stage directions, the single setting for the play, a spacious bedroom in a plantation mansion, features "a monumental monstrosity peculiar to our times, a *huge* console combination of radio-phonograph (hi-fi with three speakers), TV set *and* liquor cabinet, bearing and containing many glasses and bottles, all in one piece. . . . This piece of furniture (?!), this monument, is a very complete and compact little shrine to virtually all the comforts and illusions behind which we hide from such things as the characters in the play are faced with. . . ." (emphasis in original).[54] *Cat* exposes the "monstrosity" of Williams's characters' "comforts and illusions" but does not rid the stage of them. Like the console itself, the playwright's grotesque characters and situations obdurately refuse to go away; their monstrosity endures (and even multiplies) to the end.

Williams deploys the rhetoric of the grotesque in *Cat on a Hot Tin Roof*. As Mark Fearnow points out in his study of the theater of the 1930s, the genre of the grotesque "fixes experience but does not convert it to meaning. A grotesque representation provides a degree of distance from a contradictory moment but does not resolve the contradiction."[55] Audiences can enjoy grotesque plays in the theater because they take pleasure in the "naming" of a contradictory person or situation; their fascination with the grotesque object thus carries an electric charge of recognition, horror, and delight. Unlike more normative dramatic genres, grotesque plays provide the audience with no stable subject position from which to enjoy and judge dramatic action. Audiences alternately identify with and reject the major characters who are the carriers of the grotesque. From Lakoff and Johnson's point of view, the grotesque works when spectators engage in advisory projection with a surrogate onstage, reading their own values onto the character in the hope that this Other will somehow live up to their expectations. In the next moment, however, these expectations are invariably shattered and the spectators' hopes are thrown back in their faces. Fearnow traces the whiplash effect of the grotesque in a variety of films and plays from the 1930s, including horror films and the movies of the Marx Brothers, *Tobacco Road*, and the tragicomedies of Robert E. Sherwood. Tennessee Williams continued this residual dramatic tradition into the 1940s and 1950s.

By 1955 Williams had explored a variety of grotesque characters and situations in several of his major plays. *The Glass Menagerie* (1945), for example, named the grotesquerie of Tom's guilt, keeping the memory scenes of the play at an ironic distance from the present through Tom's monologues, "magic-lantern slides," and the ambiguous characterizations of Amanda, Laura, and the Gentleman Caller. Although *Streetcar* was closer to melodrama, the open-ended quality of the concluding scene suggests that Williams wanted his audience to refrain from moral judgments and focus on the grotesque incoherence of Stanley's triumph, Blanche's madness, and Stella's baby. In *The Rose Tattoo* (1951), the obsessions of its protagonist, Serafina, constantly threaten to push the action from sexual comedy into farcical grotesquerie. Critics have generally understood *Camino Real* (1953)—another play featuring a disoriented soldier-boy hero—as an allegory about the endurance of romantics confronted by the corrosions of time. But time, according to Williams himself, has always been a motive for the grotesque. "The influence of life's destroyer, time, must be somehow worked into the context of [a play]," said Williams in 1978. "Perhaps it is a certain foolery, a certain distortion toward the grotesque which will solve the problem."[56] As in *Camino*, the weight of time distorts the actions of all the major characters in *Cat*.

Williams also understood the Broadway potential of the "southern grotesque" and used it to advantage in *Cat*. By the logic of Broadway, Williams had suffered three flops in a row by 1953, with *Camino* damned or dismissed by nearly all of the critics who mattered. As Albert J. Devlin relates, Williams decided to give the Broadway audience what it wanted on the surface of *Cat* but to plant some explosives under its facade that would destabilize and perhaps (for some spectators) even destroy normative cultural assumptions. Consequently, *Cat* has many of the trappings of a southern romance: the plantation house, dutiful "darkies," minor characters trimmed to fit regional stereotypes, decadent wealth, an aging patriarch, encomiums to "the land," and, of course, frustrated sexuality. On initial inspection, *Cat* probably seemed to the Broadway audience of 1955 a combination of mint julep and "corn likker," brimming with equal portions of a sunny and a benighted South, of *Gone with the Wind* and *Tobacco Road*. Stylistically, too, Williams hewed closer to realism than he had since *Streetcar*. Flannery O'Connor notes that "anything that comes out of the South is going to be called grotesque by the Northern Reader, unless it is grotesque, in which case it is going to be called realistic."[57] Knowing his prospective audience for *Cat*, Williams opted for realist grotesquerie.

Like O'Connor, Williams understood the regional prejudices of his northern spectators and used them to trap his audience into questioning many of the primary assumptions of containment liberalism. In effect, Williams deploys realist grotesquerie in *Cat* to challenge the cultural imperialism of the North. When Williams introduced himself to his agent Audrey Wood in 1939, he called himself a wily "descendent of Indian-fighting Tennessee pioneers." Like Oscar Wilde in the midst of imperial London, Williams cajoles his spectators into embracing their prejudices and then explodes them. His primary counterforce against consumerism is southern orality, embodied in two of his most grotesque characters, Maggie and Big Daddy. As postcolonial scholar Helen Gilbert affirms, "performative orality" has the potential to defamiliarize conventional language and to focus audience attention "on 'voice' itself as a site of contestation."[58] In *Cat*, grotesque personal narratives challenge fact-based language as the only mode of truth telling. The result is polyvocality—what M. M. Bakhtin termed heteroglossia—that disperses meaning, especially the kinds of univocal meanings enabled by *allegoresis*. *Cat*'s emphasis on the grotesque relativity of truth undercut the Platonic certainties of the 50s.

The grotesque runs riot through *Cat*. Characters constantly compare each other to animals—Big Mama charges like a "rhino," Big Daddy eats like a "horse," Mae and Gooper's children are either pigs, monkeys, or "no-neck monsters," and Maggie, of course, is a cat. Like jackals and vultures watching a dying elephant, these animals feint and threaten each other in an attempt to bite off the biggest piece of Big Daddy's estate following his imminent death. As Big Daddy notes, a powerful odor of "mendacity" pervades the play, and no major character escapes its stench. Big Daddy's firstborn and his wife, Gooper and Mae, may be the most mendacious, but Brick lies to Big Daddy about his colon cancer, Maggie lies about being pregnant with Brick's child, and Big Daddy lies to his family to support Maggie's lie. Even the final scene in the bedroom, when Maggie declares her love for Brick and determines to make the lie of her pregnancy come true, may also be mendacious. In short, the play adamantly refuses to allow spectators to make dramatic meaning out of its major theme; if all of the characters are mendacious and mendacity encompasses life itself, the term defines everything and nothing. The audience, implicitly mendacious as well, is allowed no stable ethical position from which to judge the mendacity of others.[59]

Williams's embrace of the grotesque is best seen in the preproduction scripts of *Cat* and in his reading version of the play, which contains two third acts—one preferred by Williams and the second, the "Broadway Version," taken directly from the stage manager's prompt book for Act III of the 1955 production.[60] In a "Note of Explanation" added to the published play in 1955, Williams praised the collaborative efforts of director Elia Kazan, whose suggestions for script revisions had helped to shape the final texts of *Streetcar* and *Camino Real* as well as *Cat*. Williams also reported, however, that he and Kazan had differed substantially on revisions of *Cat*. In his "Explanation," he listed three major reservations that Kazan had noted in a letter to him commenting on the first draft of *Cat*: (1) Big Daddy's disappearance from the play after Act II; (2) Brick's intransigence, even after his conversation with Big Daddy in Act II; and (3) Maggie's lack of sympathetic appeal to the audience. Williams stated that he had agreed with Kazan about Maggie and revised the script accordingly but had resisted Kazan's first two suggestions: "I didn't want Big Daddy to reappear in Act Three and I felt that the moral paralysis of Brick was a root thing in his tragedy, and to show a dramatic progression would obscure the meaning of that tragedy in him . . ." (125). In the end, Williams compromised on the first two points as well; Big Daddy makes a brief appearance in Act III, and Brick moves toward a reconciliation with his father and his wife in the Broadway version of the play. Apparently Williams felt that he needed Kazan—even though Kazan had presided over *Camino*'s "flop"—and was willing to accede to his suggestions in order to get him to direct the production.

Whether Williams violated his artistic integrity by compromising with Kazan, whether Kazan was partly to blame for insisting on changes before he would agree to direct the play, or whether, as Brenda Murphy alleges, this mode of collaboration simply continued their past working relationship, it is clear that Williams's preferred version(s) of the script embraced a vision of theatrical grotesquerie that Kazan did not wholly share.[61] Kazan's suggested changes, if entirely carried out, would have moved the play into a melodramatic father-son conflict based on the revelation of a "guilty secret." As David Savran emphasizes, Williams, like Anton Chekhov, resisted the dramatic conventions of liberal tragedy, in which a secret from the past dooms a bourgeois subject (e.g., Hedda

Gabler, Willy Loman) to destruction. In the melodramatic version of this structure, the subject is threatened by the secret's revelation but finally triumphs over its devastating effects. *A Hatful of Rain*, for example, deployed the melodramatic possibilities of these conventions. Lillian Hellman, William Inge, Arthur Miller, and many other cold war playwrights relied on the structural devices of liberal tragedy.[62]

From Kazan's perspective, *Cat* evidently shared enough affinities with the conventions of liberal tragedy and its melodramatic offspring to lead him to suggest revisions that pushed the play sharply in that direction. In his "Note of Explanation," Williams implied that Kazan urged the three changes to make the play more commercially acceptable, a charge that Kazan denied later in his autobiography.[63] While Kazan may indeed have believed that his suggestions would improve the play artistically, they also had the effect of molding the play into the kind of melodrama that had been successful on Broadway. As in a dozen other dramas focused on a troubled Empty Boy, the revised *Cat* seen by Broadway audiences suggested that Brick was on his way to resolving his guilty secret about his past problems, settling his relationship with his father, reforming his addictions, and "proving" his heterosexuality with his wife. These changes led to what critic Eric Bentley, in his review of the production, termed the "uncoordinated double vision" of *Cat*.[64] Although Williams, under Kazan's prodding, sanded down some of the grotesque edges of his characters and painted over the homosexual hues of Brick's past relationship with Skipper, the Broadway script did not alter the fundamentally grotesque situation of the Pollitts' squabbling while Big Daddy dies. Kazan's direction, however, generally sought to impose stable meanings where Williams's script reveled in irony and contradictions. The result, as Bentley noted, was a production that pulled the audience in two different directions—on the one hand toward an open fascination with these modern grotesques and their cynical values and on the other toward a closed, melodramatic appreciation that patriarchy must survive regardless of the cost.

The "uncoordinated double vision" of the production was apparent in the response of the opening night critics. Several reviewers reacted primarily to Williams's grotesquerie. "The play functions like a snake charmer," said William Hawkins. "It holds one's hypnotized and breathless attention, while it writhes and yowls and bares the souls of its participants with a shameless tongue." "You are torn between fascination and revulsion, but you are held," stated John McClain. Richard Watts noted *Cat's* "sadistic probing into lost souls, its neurotic brooding, its insight into decadence, its torrent of language, both lyric and lewd." Like Hawkins and McClain, Watts was fascinated with the characters and situations but rarely moved to melodramatic pity. Watts confessed, however, that he had "great difficulty" believing in the final reconciliation between Maggie and Brick: "It seems almost a happy conclusion, yet the final impression is one of doom." Watts could name the contradiction but did not attempt to resolve its inherent grotesquerie.[65]

Other critics, led by Kazan and probably their own history of playgoing to expect dramatic closure, were put off or frustrated by the apparent moral relativity of the play. Robert Coleman complained of the play's "cynical finish"; and John Chapman, who called *Cat* another of Williams's "perceptive and sympathetic dramas of frustration," wrote: "When it was over I felt frustrated myself—felt that some heart or point or purpose was missing." Expecting to experience pity and compassion for an Empty Boy caught up in a melodramatic situation, Coleman and Chapman did not know what to do with the grotesque elements of the play that did not point toward clear dramatic meaning. Brooks Atkinson's review, however, ignored the play's grotesquerie to focus on its revelation of "honesty." Classifying *Cat* as liberal tragedy in the tradition of Henrik Ibsen and O'Neill, Atkinson wrote: "To say that it is the drama of people who refuse to face the truth of life is to suggest a whole school of problem dramatists."[66] The Broadway critics, then, were divided in their understanding of the generic nature of *Cat*. While most gave the production favorable notices, some experienced the show as theater of the grotesque, while others responded to it as liberal tragedy or melodrama.

Stylistically, Williams had conceived of *Cat* as a realist play, with a setting that looked like a bedroom and stage movement that approximated real life. Kazan, however, worked with his designers and actors to give the production mythic proportions. Kazan convinced Jo Mielziner to design a bed-sitting room in a plantation mansion that featured a diamond-shaped raked stage with only a few pieces of furniture on it and Greek columns painted on a scrim background. The relative openness of the ground plan allowed Kazan to arrange his performers in a series of formal poses. In his review, Bentley suggested that Kazan's staging was an

Jo Mielziner's set design for Cat on a Hot Tin Roof. *Peter A. Juley and Son photo, courtesy New York Public Library.*

attempt to "conquer that far outpost of the imagination which we call Grandeur":

> Just as there is less furniture and less scenery, so there is a less natural handling of actors, a more conscious concern with stagecraft, with pattern, with form. Attention is constantly called to the tableau, to what, in movies, is called the individual "frame." You feel that Burl Ives [cast as Big Daddy] has been *placed* center stage, not merely that he *is* there; in the absence of furniture, a man's body is furnishing the room. When the man lifts his crippled son off the floor, the position is held a long moment, as for a time-exposure. My wife nudges me at his point, and whispers, "Why, it's a Michelangelo." (emphasis in original)[67]

The grandeur of Kazan's (neo)classicism worked against the play's grotesqueries.

These tableaux vivants also smothered much of Williams's mocking irony. At the turning point of the play, for instance, when Maggie lies about her pregnancy to the assembled Pollitts, Williams crafted dialogue that parodied the biblical Annunciation of Christ. "I have an announcement to make," states Maggie. "A child is coming, sired by Brick and out of Maggie the Cat! I have Brick's child in my body, an' that's my birthday present to Big Daddy on his Birthday" (153). Rather than underlining the joke, Kazan had Burl Ives stand behind Maggie and press his hands into her belly as though he were passing the life force from his dying body into hers. In Kazan's handling of the scene, this was a mythic moment, with Ives in a flowing white robe, looking God-like in his majesty, and Barbara Bel Geddes as Maggie, the passive recipient of His power. Such "grandeur," however, ignored the absurdity of figuring Big Daddy as the Holy Ghost and Maggie as the Virgin Mary.

The moment, like the other formal tableaux of the production, also betrayed Kazan's itch to involve his spectators in conventional allegorizing. Williams's delight in grotesquerie was an outgrowth of his romantic orientation, hence generally incompatible with *allegoresis*. As Brenda Murphy relates, Kazan began to shift the general focus of the production from the Brick-Maggie storyline to the father-son relationship soon after he read Williams's preproduction script in 1954. On his copy, Kazan crossed out a quotation from W. B. Yeats that explained the initial title that Williams had given his play, "A Place of Stone," and penned a note linking the play to the poetry of Dylan Thomas. Williams took up this suggestion and changed the epigraph in the printed play to Thomas's well-known passage: "And, you, my father, there on the sad height, / Curse, bless, me now with your fierce tears, I pray. / Do not go gentle into that good night. / Rage, rage against the dying of the light."[68] The raging, cursing, and finally the blessing of his son by Big Daddy would be the focus of Kazan's production. Of course romantic treatments of this theme are possible, but the passing of patriarchal authority from one generation to the next clearly evoked allegorical meanings for Kazan.

Several of the tableaux that Kazan arranged depicted the Platonic power of patriarchy. These pictures had wide cultural resonance, appearing in newspaper advertisements for the production and pictorial spreads in *Life* magazine as well as on stage. The picture of Maggie in a slip on her knees clutching at Brick's legs as he balances on a crutch and pats her head was widely reproduced. Visually, it suggests a dutiful, if frustrated, wife and a long-suffering but dominant husband, perhaps irritated by his wife's sexual demands. By emphasizing Maggie's sexual frustration and Brick's physical disability, the picture effectively avoids the problem of Brick's lack of attraction to his wife; their sex life, it appears, will be fine as soon as Brick gets off his crutches. The two images of Big Daddy knocking the crutch out from under Brick's arm and sending him sprawling and of Big Daddy cradling Brick's head on his chest as he raises him from the floor suggested the power and perversity of the patriarch and the dependency of his son. Here was an Old Testament deity of unknowable wrath and enormous love; sons might curse or embrace such a father, but they must finally obey him. These images of physical strength deter any questions about Big Daddy's homosexual past. The images of Maggie on her knees in front of the standing figure of Big Daddy and of Big Daddy infusing Maggie with life clearly subordinate Maggie's interests to Big Daddy's desire to preserve the family name through a male grandson. These are archetypal images of women serving as counters in an economy of exchange controlled by men. Maggie's final purpose in the play is reduced to her biological ability to carry a Pollitt heir.

To turn *Cat* into a play about patriarchal power, Kazan needed actors who could embody the emblematic type as well as enact the psychological complexities of their characters. So eager was Kazan to fill the role of Big Daddy with an actor who looked the part as he had conceived it that

Big Daddy/Burl Ives grabs Brick/Ben Gazzara in Act II of Cat on a Hot Tin Roof. *Fred Fehl photo, courtesy Fred Fehl.*

the director took a chance with Burl Ives. When Williams objected that a folk singer in his first major acting role on stage might not be able to handle the challenges of the part, Kazan brushed aside the problem and insisted that Ives would be fine. His casting hunch paid off. Ives's power and presence impressed nearly all of the critics; William Hawkins, for example, called him a "rock mountain" in the role.[69] In the film version of *Cat*, which closely mirrored Kazan's and Ives's stage interpretation of Big Daddy, Ives sacrifices subtlety for massiveness of emotion and effect. With Ives in the role, Big Daddy becomes a mythic patriarch who can, without irony, lay just claim to "twenty-eight thousand acres of th' richest land this side of the valley Nile!" (65).

Kazan's decision to cast Barbara Bel Geddes as Maggie was also a gamble, but a strategic one on his part to contain the grotesquerie of the role. In his preproduction script, Williams had made Maggie a more desperate and calculating character, more "poor white trash," than Kazan had wanted. His casting of Bel Geddes, like his suggestion to Williams that Maggie be more sympathetic, was part of Kazan's general strategy to shift Maggie from a greedy and conniving woman to a wholesome mother-wife eager to help her husband regain his heterosexual desire. Before *Cat*, Bel Geddes had played naive ingénues, such as the girl too-sweet-to-be-seduced in *The Moon Is Blue* in 1951. (Soon after *Cat*, she would play motherly helpmates, like Jimmy Stewart's left-behind girlfriend in *Vertigo*.) While subsequent Maggies, following Elizabeth Taylor in the film version, have often been known for their steamy sensuality, none of the Broadway reviews used language that came close to that description for Bel Geddes. Instead, she was "appealing and authoritative" (McClain), "vital, lovely, and frank" (Atkinson); her monologue in Act I was a "scene of devastating honesty" for one reviewer (Kerr) and "a luminous and appealing job" for another (Chapman).[70] In the hands of Bel Geddes and Kazan, Maggie had become the kissin' cousin of Celia Pope, the motherly wife who both confronts and nurses husband Johnny back to familial and social responsibility; her cat had more purr than scratch.

The model for this Maggie in Kazan's mind was probably Laura Reynolds in *Tea and Sympathy*, which Kazan had recently finished directing before reading and commenting on the preproduction draft of *Cat*. In Robert Anderson's melodrama, a sexually frustrated young wife leaves her husband to seduce and comfort an Empty Boy confused about his sexual identity. Williams's initial ending of *Cat* unambiguously positioned Maggie "on top" in her relationship with Brick, an ironic reversal of her attempt to incite Brick's advances in Act I. Under Kazan's urgings, Williams played with different endings for the drama, finally settling on dialogue for the "Broadway Version" that essentially positioned Maggie as another Laura seeking to help another confused boy toward heterosexual manhood: "You weak, beautiful people who give up with such grace. What you need is someone to take hold of you—gently, with love, and hand your life back to you. . . . I can! I'm determined to do it—and nothing's more determined than a cat on a tin roof—is there? Is there, Baby?" (158). Bentley commented that the ending of the play carried "the outward form of that *Tea and Sympathy* scene without its content."[71]

Tea and Sympathy had raised the accusation of homosexuality but dodged its full cold war implications. Because the boy in question is not homosexual after all, the play could treat the false accusation as if it were simply another McCarthyite witch hunt motivated by fear. Williams, fully aware of the homophobia of containment culture, crafted a play that explicitly endorsed the toleration of sexual deviance and implicitly suggested that sexual orientation cannot be contained by the hetero-homo binary. In *Homosexuality in Cold War America*, Robert J. Corber effectively argues that Williams, like Gore Vidal and James Baldwin, "stressed the construction of gay male subjectivity across multiple axes of difference, thereby promoting a model of political solidarity that was rooted in a collective experience of oppression rather than membership in a particular community." Instead of promoting a gay male consciousness in isolation from other oppressed groups, says Corber, Williams drew on the experience of radical groups in the 1930s to write plays and short stories that might appeal to others who crossed conventional lines of race, class, and gender. Consequently, Williams was "not interested in establishing that homosexuality constituted a fixed minority identity but looked forward to the end of 'the homosexual' as a category of individual."[72]

In retrospect, Williams's strategy of theatrical grotesquerie might have provided an acceptable rhetoric for some Broadway spectators to question their culture's construction of sexuality. An audience reacting, by turns, in horrified disgust and comic delight to Big Daddy's sexual voraciousness and Maggie's attempts to work off her frustrations might have viewed Brick's innocence about his sexual identity as simply one more problem of animality in the family barnyard. Critics complained that Williams had failed to clarify Brick's past relationship with Skipper, but in truth the Broadway script is just as straightforward about Skipper's attraction to Brick and Brick's horror in discovering it as it is about Maggie's failed attempt to seduce Skipper and Big Daddy's liaison with Jack Straw and Peter Ochello. The preproduction script, however, does provide more details about these matters than the dialogue that spectators heard in the theater in 1955. In it, Big Daddy speaks fondly of the sexual relationship between Jack Straw and Peter Ochello, the two lovers who owned the plantation before him and with whom he shared his own body to become their heir apparent. The early script also clarified the triangular relationship that evolved among Skipper, Brick, and Maggie after their marriage. Cut from the production was Maggie's long speech about how shut out she felt from the affection shared by the two boys, who continued to play football together after college. In the preproduction version, Brick is more withdrawn and volatile, suggesting that his despair over Skipper's suicide had as much to do with his loss of a potential lover as with his guilt over his own refusal to prevent Skipper's death. Significantly, however, the early script is no more forthright about pinning Brick to a single sexual orientation than the later one.

Nonetheless, by pushing the script toward liberal melodrama, Kazan invited the critics to probe the play for the originary moment in the "guilty secret"—possibly Brick and Skipper's lovemaking—from which the plot of the play, in the conventional structure of liberal tragedy, should unfold. Brick does reveal one "guilty secret" in the course of telling his story to Big Daddy: he hung up after Skipper confessed his sexual attraction to him, and this rejection soon led to Skipper's death. Several critics, however, believed that Brick's confession held other secrets yet to be told. Among the first-night reviewers, McClain, Chapman, and Kerr were puzzled—Kerr was even annoyed—that the production had not spelled out the entire truth about Skipper and Brick. Kerr found in *Cat* a "tantalizing reluctance—beneath all the fire and all the apparent candor—to let the play blurt out its promised secret." In a follow-up Sunday editorial in the *Herald Tribune* entitled "A Secret Is Half-Told in Fountains of Words," Kerr continued to pick at the play: "The boy who has lost a friend and abandoned a wife cannot say what private wounds and secret drives have crippled him." Finally for Kerr, the production evaded its responsibility to the audience: "Listening, we work at the play in an earnest effort to unlock its ultimate dramatic meaning, but the key has been mislaid or deliberately hidden."[73] Building on the psychological truism for his time that essential truth might best be found in "private wounds and secret drives," Kerr simply asked the production to meet the expectations it had aroused. His complaint was the logical response to Kazan's decision to direct the play as though it were a liberal melodrama. Behind the evasions of Kerr's own rhetoric was a simple question: is Brick now or has he ever been a homosexual? If so, this "hidden key" would unlock the play's apparent mysteries and evasions. Animated to expect an essentialist answer to the question of Brick's sexual orientation, Kerr pursued McCarthyite tactics in his dogged probing of the play for dramatic truth and meaning.

The "is he or isn't he" response to Brick's problems countered Williams's hope that *Cat* might promote a more fluid understanding of human sexuality. It also sunk Kazan's desire to lead the audience to answer the question in the negative when they witnessed Ben Gazzara in the role. During his short career as a Broadway actor, by 1955, Gazzara had gained the most renown as a bully in a play set in a military school. Certainly Kazan had other reasons for casting Gazzara, but the actor's rugged good looks and deep voice must have figured in his choice of the relative newcomer; Gazzara was the complete opposite of effeminate. Further, Kazan knew that Method actors like Gazzara could project a confused sexual identity as a part of their general narcissism—a confusion Gazzara would deploy later the same year in *Hatful*—without losing, and potentially even enhancing, audience sympathy for the actor-character. While only one of the opening-night critics decided that Gazzara's Brick was a "queer" (Chapman), several others, like Kerr, questioned his sexual identity in either/or terms.[74]

The chief exemplar in the play of male desire undefined by the homo-hetero binary, of course, is Brick's father, Big Daddy. As he tells Brick in the published version of the play, he "knocked around" (85) in his youth and, despite his disgust for Big Mama, dutifully laid her "regular as a piston" (80) during their long marriage. Even on his deathbed, he continues to have a "lech" (19) for Maggie and dreams of a young mistress that he could "hump" from "hell to breakfast" (72). Although Williams softened this language for Broadway, the production still made it clear that Big Daddy's homosexual attachments as a young man did not define or contain him; his lusts were gargantuan enough to override all conventional categories of sexual positionings and couplings. David Savran notes that Williams probably intended Big Daddy's bowel cancer to represent the devastating results of his early sodomy.[75] This may be so, but it is not clear that many in the audience would have made this connection between homosexuality and disease. Further, the play generally presents Big Daddy's death not as the preventable result of some past sin but as the inevitable fall of a giant; mortality is simply a part of *Cat*'s grotesque world. Big Daddy's bowel cancer adds a note of absurdity to his imminent death, but it does not undercut the play's commitment to tolerance. If Big Daddy cannot be classified as a homosexual, the play suggests, neither can Brick.

Rather than incite the audience members to pigeon-hole Brick's sexual orientation, *Cat* wants them to examine the effects of his homophobia. Brick's need to cling to a rigid binary between homosexuality and heterosexuality—his wish to elevate his relationship with Skipper to a "pure an' true thing" (90) above sexual desire—has deformed him. Brick's disgust with Skipper and himself has led him to compulsive alcoholism and self-mutilation; his broken leg and broken soul are the result. The Empty Boy of *Cat*, Brick has all the innocence, grit, vulnerability, and physical strength of his postwar type; but these qualities, rather than evoking the spectators' guarded hope for Brick's eventual enrollment into heterosexual manhood and patriarchal prosperity, arouse the audience's suspicion that Brick may never be fit to assume the place his father and wife initially expect him to fill. If the Empty Boy remains a compulsive, wounded narcissist, the play asks, who will take his place in the patriarchal order? As grotesque realism, *Cat* does not need to answer this question forthrightly; Williams's refusal to resolve the problem, in effect, throws it back into the audience's face.

Sexual innocence in most plays about American boys was typically an endearing quality. For the comedy in *Itch* to work, for example, the American Adam must be less experienced and less eager than the Girl. Williams, in contrast, shows the corrosive results of perpetuating an innocence that verged on willful ignorance about male sexual orientation. The culture of liberal containment turned its back on the Kinsey Report and information provided by the Mattachine Society to demonize homosexuality as a threat to cold war national unity. *Cat* demonstrates that Brick's ignorance and rigidity not only affect him; they also paralyze major institutions of American society—marriage, the family, and the mechanisms of patrilineal inheritance. As occurs in many of Williams's dramas, the characters are stuck in stasis while time, the destroyer, marches on, forcing the characters into ever more absurd contortions. Arthur Miller famously critiqued *Cat* for Brick's indecisiveness on social issues. Like all grotesque plays, *Cat* is finally, formally indecisive; but along the way it also demonstrates the perverse results of "ignorance effects" about sexual orientation.[76]

Despite Kazan's desire to knead the play into liberal melodrama, the yeast of Williams's grotesquerie caused it to rise into odd shapes in performance. Early in his thinking about *Cat*, Kazan decided to stage the play more presentationally than Williams had written it. In Mielziner's slightly raked setting, a corner of the bedroom floor jutted beyond the proscenium arch and into the auditorium. Kazan wanted Burl Ives as Big Daddy to be able to walk downstage, ignore the other characters, and address the audience directly during several of his long speeches in Act II. Kazan probably expected that this staging would increase spectators' sympathetic response to Big Daddy and to his point of view; he may also have wanted the folk singer to be able to tell stories in a mode that was comfortable for him. Kazan gave Barbara Bel Geddes several opportunities for presentational storytelling during her long speeches in Act I as well. One result of such staging was to pull the audience members out of their immediate involvement in the plot and characters of the play and encourage them to enjoy the immediacy of a good story well told. Ironically for Kazan, his presentational staging probably made the "liberal tragedy" of Brick's dilemma less interesting to the spectators by decentering and dispersing the energies of the drama even as it heightened their enjoyment of Bel Geddes's and Ives's tales of southern grotesquerie.

Nearly a third of Williams's dialogue in Acts I and II is taken up with storytelling. Like Chekhov, Williams's favorite playwright, his major characters in *Cat* need to narrate events about their past to come to terms with a present that is frustratingly, absurdly static; their tales, in other words, are realistically motivated. Maggie's stories include her narration about Mae and Gooper and the no-necks at dinner, the tobacco juice tale about an embarrassing incident for a cotton carnival queen, Sonny Boy Maxwell "burning holes" in Maggie's clothes with his eyes (38), several stories focused on the poverty of her youth, and her versions of what happened with Skipper. Big Daddy relates tales about his own past with Straw and Ochello, his trip with Big Mama to Europe and Africa, and his battles with mendacity. Their storytelling, especially Big Daddy's, finally leads Brick to tell his version of what really happened in his last telephone conversation with Skipper.

Preceding Brick's confession that his refusal to help Skipper led to his suicide, then, are many other stories that shape audience expectations about the kinds of truth that storytelling can reveal. In effect, Williams used the oral tradition to undercut the hegemony of literate speaking; he destabilized the kind of enunciation that legitimates the credibility of a revealed secret in the performance of a play. According to the linguistics of Emile Benveniste, there are two possible modes of utterance on stage, as in all social situations: *histoire* and *discours*.[77] The mode of *histoire* implicitly claims transparency and objectivity, the kind of utterance that underwrites the reliability of statements about the past in well-made plays. In contrast, *discours* is subjective and specific to place and time; listeners can never be sure if its truth claims transcend the immediacy of the speaking situation. Although modern plays usually deploy a mix of both modes, playwrights are generally careful to mark some speech as *histoire* during moments of exposition, reversal, and revelation. In *Cat*, however, Williams anticipated Harold Pinter and other late modernists by refusing to provide reliable information about the past of his characters. Consequently, even Brick's tortured revelation about Skipper's sexual orientation and his own refusal to provide help cannot be understood by spectators as stable knowledge, uninflected by the subjectivity of Brick's memory. Most realist plays encourage spectators to believe that they can attain an objective, dispassionate understanding of the action. Williams's reliance on *discours* and his undercutting of *histoire* during *Cat*, however, reposition the audience as subjective interlopers with incomplete information, a positioning that heightens the grotesquerie of the play. The dominance of personal narrative and the impossibility of objective knowledge in *Cat* finally call into question the reliability of hegemonic forms of cold war information.

Maggie's story about the cotton queen and the tobacco juice typifies Williams's use of *discours* in Act I of *Cat*:

> Why, year before last when Susan McPheeters was singled out fo' that honor, y'know what happened to her? Y'know what happened to poor little Susie McPheeters?
> Brick (Absently). No. What happened to little Susie McPheeters?
> Margaret. Somebody spit tobacco juice in her face.

> Brick (Dreamily). Somebody spit tobacco juice in her face?
> Margaret. That's right, some old drunk leaned out of a window in the Hotel Gayoso and yelled, "Hey, Queen, hey, hey there Queenie!" Poor little Susie looked up and flashed him a radiant smile and he shot out a squirt of tobacco juice right in poor Susie's face.
> Brick. Well, what d'you know about that?
> Margaret (Gaily). What do I know about it? I was there, I saw it.
> Brick (Absently). Must have been kind of funny.
> Margaret. Susie didn't think so. Had hysterics. Screamed like a banshee. They had to stop th' parade an' remove her from her throne.... (21–22)

To tell her tale effectively, Williams gives Maggie many of the stylistic devices of "personal narrative": complex rhythms, tonal patternings, alliteration, and repetition.[78] These devices mark her storytelling as *discours* rather than *histoire*. While most spectators will probably believe that something like this event really did happen to Susie McPheeters, they will also understand that Maggie has stretched and altered the story to make it more entertaining. Moreover, they will realize that the point of the tale has to do with the ongoing relationship between Brick and Maggie, not with the weight of a real past incident on present circumstances.

Likewise, Williams gives Big Daddy several stories in the mode of *discours* that also point toward present and future relationships rather than the formative influence of an objective past bearing down on a tenuous present. In the middle of his story about a trip abroad with Big Mama, Big Daddy recalls a specific incident in Morocco:

> But listen to this. She [an Arab woman] had a naked child with her, a little naked girl with her, barely able to toddle, and after a while she set this child on the ground and give her a push and whispered something to her. This child come toward me, barely able t' walk, come toddling up to me and—Jesus, it makes you sick t' remember a thing like this! It stuck out its hand and tried to unbutton my trousers! That child was not yet five! Can you believe me? Or do you think that I am making this up? I wint back to the hotel and said to Big Mama, Git packed! We're clearing out of this country . . .
> Brick. Big Daddy, you're on a talkin' jag tonight.

> Big Daddy (Ignoring this remark). Yes, sir, that's how it is, the human animal is a beast that dies but the fact that he's dying don't give him pity for others, no, sir. . . . (66)

Given Burl Ives/Big Daddy's massive presence on stage, plus his often orotund and didactic language, his stories probably carried more authority than Maggie's. Audiences confronted with "Do you think I'm makin' this up?" likely credited the general truthfulness of Big Daddy's statements about this past event. Nonetheless, they also realized that the present rhetorical situation—a father trying to rescue his son from paralyzing guilt about an unusual sexual encounter—probably influenced Big Daddy's memory. His utterances, whether in storytelling or earnest conversation, were centered more often in the mode of *discours* than of *histoire*.

Further, as with Maggie's tales about her poor childhood, the audience listening to Big Daddy came to understand the transformative potential of personal narrative. By telling tales about his past poverty and relations with Straw and Ochello, Burl Ives/Big Daddy transcended a desperate past that might have continued to haunt him but is now safely storied away. In performance, Bel Geddes and Ives used *discours* to transform the past problems of their characters into present opportunities for instructive stories. Both actor-characters set an implicit example for Ben Gazzara/Brick Pollitt; he must be able to tell "the tale of Brick and Skipper's phone call," to transform it into personal narrative, before he can put the event behind him and live in the present. His falteringly confession at the end of Act II thus prepares him for further transformations at the end of the play. It is important to underline here that Williams is not advocating the transformation of facts about the past into fictions for the present. All the storytellers of *Cat* tell a truth about past events, even if it is not the entire truth based on all the facts. In effect, the play demonstrates the moral triumph of *discours* over *histoire*, the humanistic necessity of transforming objective truths into personal ones through storytelling. The primary agents of dramatic counterforce in both *Itch* and *Hatful*, psychiatry and the state, are thoroughly imbedded in *histoire*. Williams, in contrast, suggests that dwelling on objective truths about the past can damn individuals to guilt and recrimination. Personal narratives, however, can liberate.

Indeed, the world of *histoire* in *Cat* is the world of mendacity. When literal, objective statements are made, devoid of personal narrative—

when the truth is only a matter of "just the facts, ma'am," as it was in the popular radio and television hit *Dragnet*—Williams demonstrates that no one can be trusted. Utterances from characters that would usually stand as *histoire* in most Broadway plays are not reliable in *Cat*. The audience soon learns that both the reverend and the doctor, typical *raissoneurs* in a well-made play, do not speak the truth in *Cat*. Nor do lawyers and their wives, also normally credible; Gooper and Mae, the chief advocates of literal truth-telling, consistently select objective facts which suit their purposes. Of course Maggie's lie about her pregnancy and Big Daddy's affirmation of it are the biggest whoppers of all! What makes their mendacity acceptable to the audience is its timing and Williams's rhetoric. By affirming the value of *discours* and undercutting the importance of *histoire* throughout the action, plus demonizing Gooper and Mae, Williams prepares the audience to wink at Maggie's lie and even to celebrate her acquisition of Big Daddy's estate. The triumph of Maggie and Brick felt "right" to the audience because of the truth of their *discours*; they may have lied within the world of *histoire*, but so did everybody else.

By validating the live performance of personal narrative over the telling of objective facts, *Cat* also challenged the authority of radiophony on the cold war stage. If the ontology of radio implicitly celebrated the dematerialization of knowledge, the privatization of public relationships, and the externalization of individual psychology, *Cat* manifestly opposed all of these tendencies. On stage, the knowledge available through *discours* came out of the very material bodies of Bel Geddes/Maggie and Ives/Big Daddy. Although *discours* may seem, like the radio, to privatize relationships through its reliance on subjectivity, the opposite is true in periods when *histoire* cannot be trusted. In *Cat*, the sharing of oral stories puts private experience into at least a semipublic sphere and potentially frees Empty Boys from the radiolike isolation of self-involvement. *Cat*, unlike *Itch* and *Hatful*, does not pay a compliment to the anxieties of a narcissistic protagonist by externalizing them through allegorical figures or a voice from a radio-phonograph system. The more rigorous morality of *Cat* rejects the ethical egoism of Empty Boy plays. In effect, the implications of radiophony stay encased with the television, high-fi, and liquor in the monstrous entertainment console that dominates Brick and Maggie's bedroom. The only technological advance in communication implicated directly in the play is the telephone, and it usually carries messages of mendacity from doctors and relatives. That Skipper and Brick spoke on a telephone, rather than face-to-face, for their final, fatal conversation is but one of Williams's many ways of telling his audience that live *discours* is always more reliable than technologized *histoire*.

Cat's implicit rejection of the ontological effects of radiophony is a part of its "performative orality." In "De-Scribing Orality: Performance and the Recuperation of Voice," postcolonialist scholar Helen Gilbert notes that "the appropriation and abrogation of the colonizers' linguistic codes are essential to post-colonial writing." Gilbert discusses the effectiveness of Aboriginal plays and actor-storytellers, with their distinctive tonalities, rhythms, and accents, in subverting the official English of the dominant culture in Australia. Their alterity, she writes, "prevents the seamless application of writing to the oral [and] enacts an important mode of resistance for oral cultures against the hegemony of literate ones."[79] Hence, "performative orality" becomes "the endless deferral of the authority of writing." As in the current dominant culture of Australia, containment liberalism in the United States in the 1950s depended on the authority of writing and counted on orality to be easily translatable into the black-and-white objectivity of the written word. *Cat*, however, featured two garrulous southerners, Maggie and Big Daddy, whose peculiar accents and rhythms gave voice to stories that were much more alive in the onstage telling than they could ever be in silent reading. By winning the ears and hearts of northern audiences with their grotesque personal narratives, Maggie and Big Daddy challenged the authority of *Dragnet*-voiced *histoire*, the voice of liberal culture in the North.

As Gilbert affirms, the *discours* of personal narrative disperses the validity of official, fact-based language less by overturning *histoire* than by its mere existence as another mode of truth-telling. The polyvocality of *Cat*, central to the play's embrace of the grotesque, undercuts the possibility of *allegoresis*. Kazan may have been reaching for univocal, allegorical "grandeur," but the reviews suggest that Williams's storytellers frustrated the desire for narrative closure. To be sure, some in the audience tried to force the round peg of the play into the square hole of *Dragnet* positivism and patriarchy, the same hole occupied by *Itch* and *Hatful*. But others seem to have enjoyed its grotesquerie and consequently may have been led to a more mature understanding of the fluidity of cultural and sexual identities. Williams could not directly confront the domination of liberal containment culture, any more than he could openly question the homo-hetero binary and expect his plays to flourish on Broadway.

Through the residual path of the grotesque and its voice of personal narrative, however, he could examine the ignorance effects of the worship of the American boy, the consumerism fueled by boyish narcissism, the self-disgust and mendacity at the heart of cold war homophobia, and the positivistic basis of patriarchal power. Moreover, Williams could open these wounds without appearing to "take a stand" on any of the issues he had raised. The grotesque has its uses in politically repressive times.

After opening on 24 March 1955, *Cat on a Hot Tin Roof* played for 694 performances. No doubt its reputation for sexual titillation helped to keep it alive. George Jean Nathan advised New Yorkers who craved "a dirty show" in June 1956 not to go out of town in search of one but to "stay right here on Broadway in New York and go to *Cat on a Hot Tin Roof*."[80] Nathan was hardly alone in emphasizing *Cat* as a sexual turn-on; advertising for the show featured an attractive man in pajamas and an alluring woman in a slip. The critics also anointed *Cat* with several prestigious awards. For the 1955 season, Williams's play won the New York Drama Critics' Circle Award, the Donaldson Award, and the Pulitzer Prize. The promise of high culture and sleazy (hetero)sex in an exotic milieu has often proven a potent combination in luring audiences to Broadway shows. How many of them left *Cat* with their cold war expectations and assumptions destabilized or even undercut cannot, of course, be known. Williams's southern grotesquerie and, ironically, Kazan's presentational style had provided the ingredients for a different kind of experience than most of the spectators probably anticipated.

■ Edward Albee's one-act play *The American Dream*, performed off-Broadway in 1961, aimed a more frontal attack against the conjunction of Empty Boys and consumerist society than Williams was able to mount on Broadway. In Albee's comedy, modeled on *The Bald Soprano* but adding social satire to Eugene Ionesco's absurdist humor, the playwright contrasted the pioneering independence of the past to the impotent conformity of the American present. As Albee explained in his "Preface," *The American Dream* was "an attack on the substitution of artificial for real values in our society, a condemnation of complacency, cruelty, emasculation and fatuity; it is a stand against the fiction that everything in this slipping land of ours is peachy-keen."[81] The conflict of the play centers on Mommy and Daddy's quest for consumerist "satisfaction" and the morality of Gramma, a symbol of the "real values" of self-reliance and independent thought noted by Albee in his preface. As in *Cat*, rambling orality (Gramma's) provides the primary counterforce to the efficient but vacuous dialogue of the mendacious. The audience soon learns from Gramma that Mommy and Daddy killed an adopted son because he did not conform to their fantasies and now wish to adopt another one to fill their empty lives. Disgusted by their amorality and destructive power, Gramma finally packs up her life and exits at the end of the play, presumably to her death.

The American Dream of the title is another symbolic character in the play—a beautiful Empty Boy without empathy for others. "I no longer have the capacity to feel anything," says the Young Man. "I have no emotions. I have been drained, torn asunder . . . disemboweled. I have, now, only my person . . . my body, my face. I use what I have . . . I let people love me . . . I accept the syntax around me, for while I know I cannot relate . . . I know I must be related to" (115). The Young Man's physical beauty and bland narcissism incite the consumerist desires of Mommy and Daddy, who mistake him for their replacement son from the Bye-Bye Adoption Service and take him into their family for the social prestige and sexual pleasure that he offers. "To satisfaction," crows Mommy, drink in hand at the end of the play. "Who says you can't get satisfaction these days!" (126).

The American Dream pushed the grotesquerie of Williams's *Cat* beyond realism and into absurdist satire. The hollowed-out, compulsive, narcissistic, and sexually ambiguous Young Man is a two-dimensional version of Brick Pollitt, beamed out of the Mississippi Delta and reconstituted as a horrific pod-person cartoon in Ionesco-land. Like Williams's mendacious animals, Albee's empty shoppers rest their vicious values on ethical egotism. Unlike Broadway-bound Williams, however, Albee provided his audience with a satiric point of view on his amoral world. Where the rhetoric of the grotesque prevented Williams from taking a stand, Albee's Gramma reminded off-Broadway spectators of residual though fading values that directly contested cold war consumerism. In *Who's Afraid of Virginia Woolf* a year later (1962), Albee continued his attack, challenging Broadway audiences to scrutinize their mendacities in the light of traditional humanistic values. Significantly, however, *Virginia Woolf* succeeded with critics and spectators more as emotional exorcism than as apocalyptic satire.[82]

Family Circles, Racial Others, and Suburbanization

In the imaginations of cold war Americans who defined themselves as "white," the contained image of the Family Circle contracted and expanded to meet their fears and hopes for the present and future. At one extreme, the business class pictured the nuclear family as a fortress protecting family members from the evils of urban blight, teenage crime, and racial Others. At the other end of the continuum, the Family Circle in their minds expanded to include all of humankind in a warm embrace of Others who were "just like us under the skin." The realities of the nuclear age pushed imagination to both Platonic extremes; for many, either the world would agree to ban the Bomb or the bunkered family would have to survive atomic warfare on its own. Most white, business-class American families tried to ignore these realities, however, and relied on friendships, neighbors, and religious and civic institutions to locate themselves somewhere in the middle of this imagined continuum between survival in a fortress and the Family of Man. Nonetheless, few doubted that the nuclear family must center their lives. The cold war politics of race and the contained image of the family reinforced these choices; it was difficult for white Americans to imagine adult life outside of a normative family circle or beyond a continuum connecting its survival to all humanity.

The purity of both polarities exerted a continuing fascination during the early Cold War. In 1961 *Time* ran a story entitled "Gun Thy Neighbor" in its religion section. The article reported the growing number of owners of fallout shelters who were arming their bunkers with machine guns to repel their neighbors after the Blast. Responding to the general problem of shelter selfishness, anthropologist Margaret Mead underlined the idealization of suburban family life that had backed Americans into this ethical cul-de-sac. She also pointed to several "dread[s]" that had led to this contraction of the spirit: "dread of the strain of living always related to distant and still alien peoples," "dread of the surging mass of young people . . . turning to drugs and crime," and "dread of our crumbling, dangerous cities." Consequently, said Mead, many Americans turned inward to protect their families: "Drawn back in space and time, hiding from the future and the rest of the world, they turned to the green suburbs, protected by zoning laws against members of other classes or races or religions, and concentrated on the single, tight little family. They idealized the life of each family living alone in self-sufficient togetherness, protecting its members against the contamination of different ways or others' needs. . . . The armed, individual shelter is the logical end of this retreat from trust in and responsibility for others."[1] In the atomic age, the image of the bunkered family turned togetherness into dystopia.

Widening the Family Circle to embrace the Otherness of Mead's "alien peoples," while ethically ennobling, seemed nearly impossible to many Americans. Edward Steichen understood this difficulty when he assembled the photographs for "The Family of Man" exhibit at the Museum of Modern Art in New York in 1955. He insisted that all 503 of the exhibit's images, many culled from the archives of *Life* magazine, represent the universal human condition so that viewers could form an immediate, empathetic response to the pictures without stumbling over historical, national, and racial Otherness. Steichen had borrowed the phrase "family of man" from Carl Sandburg's epic poem *The People, Yes*, his paean of Whitmanesque praise for human diversity and potential. MOMA's installation of international humanity was organized around such themes as courtship, marriage, child-rearing, education, strife, loneliness, and war, with a preponderance of images depicting family life from around the world. Near the end of the exhibit and occupying a separate space, Steichen placed a large color photograph of an exploding hydrogen bomb—the only color image in the show. No one at this immensely popular exhibit could miss the point: the Family of Man could perish unless humanity worked together to prevent nuclear war. As American Studies scholar Eric Sandeen remarks, Steichen hoped that people's emotional response to the installation would encourage them to "form a compensatory community to combat the impersonalized, highly technological conflict of the Cold War. This assumption was both the exhibit's strength and its weakness." Steichen's Platonism was heavily influenced by American notions of technological progress and what was assumed to be the universality of the nuclear family. Roland Barthes, among others, criticized the show for suppressing "ethnic particularity" and "the determining weight of history."[2] But a Platonically inclined public embraced Steichen's sentiments and made it the most popular exhibit of the decade at MOMA.

When it came to the Family Circle, the hegemonic imagination of citizens in containment liberalism ran to extremes partly because of the militarization of American society. Governmental policies to reward veterans through low-interest loans and to improve military defense by building new highways helped to spur the rapid growth of suburbs after the war. During the 1950s, 85 percent of new home construction occurred in the suburbs; the number of suburban dwellers nearly doubled in a decade. While there were many reasons for urban couples to start families in the suburbs that had little to do with militarization—the desire to escape crowded apartments in central cities, the fear of urbanized minorities, the quest for better educational opportunities for their children, the dream of home ownership—the rush to the suburbs was facilitated by a variety of governmental policies linked to the Cold War. By 1960 the suburban population in the United States equaled that of the central cities.

Militarization also played a role in constructing the white suburban family, especially the role of the cold war mother. U.S. policy during the war had been ambivalent toward women; the government encouraged women to work outside of the home but also reminded them of their subsidiary role in the war effort, even branding single women as potentially dangerous to the nation. Many women lost their jobs to returning veterans after the war and bowed to pressure from big business and the government to stay at home and raise a family. By 1955 presidential candidate Adlai Stevenson could declare, to wide applause, that the female college graduate's primary job was to keep her husband "truly purposeful" and help "defeat totalitarian, authoritarian ideas" in the home. When Betty Friedan claimed in *The Feminine Mystique* (1963) that there was a conspiracy to trap women in the "comfortable concentration camp" of the home, she was partly right.[3]

The social and cultural forces limiting women to the domestic roles of wife and mother during the postwar years came from many sources, however. The Depression of the 1930s, when many business-class fathers failed as breadwinners, left many Depression-era children yearning for a return to more "normal" gender roles within the family. Many young wives, knowing they were only temporary Rosie the Riveters, gladly left their wartime jobs to make a home for their children and returning husbands after VJ Day. And the tensions of the Cold War, especially the outbreak of the Korean conflict, encouraged women to search for security in their homes. (Because marriage and children excused men from the draft throughout the 1950s, raising a family had additional appeal for young-marrieds.) Cultural pressures from popular psychology, print media, and Hollywood also influenced women to limit their sights to domesticity.

The result of these constraints was what historian Elaine Tyler May has called a domestic version of containment: "Within [the home], potentially dangerous social forces of the new age might be tamed, where they could contribute to the secure and fulfilling life to which postwar men and women aspired. Domestic containment was bolstered by a powerful political culture that rewarded its adherents and marginalized its detractors. More than merely a metaphor for the Cold War on the home front, containment aptly describes the way in which public policy, personal behavior, and even political values focused on the home."[4] Domestic containment also limited the social lives of white adults outside of nuclear families, especially homosexuals, bachelors, and divorced women. As well as constraining women's aspirations, the liberal idealization of the home and family contained the lives of all Americans.

Universalist definitions merging the norms of the postwar American family and its gender roles with all families throughout history were widely paraded in academic and popular discourse. Family historian Arlene Skolnick remarks that "sociological theories portrayed the middle-class family of the 1950s as the most evolved version of a timeless, universal nuclear family, its division into gender and generational roles 'functional' to the psychological needs of family members and to those of the larger society."[5] In the sociology of Talcott Parsons, for example, the categories of sex and gender were conflated in narrowly Freudian fashion to naturalize and prescribe complementary but inequitable roles for mothers and fathers. Likewise, liberal psychoanalysts assured women that a "maternal instinct" had programmed their bodies and minds for motherhood. Women who attempt to rival men in the business world, stated American Freudians Ferdinand Lundberg and Marynia Farnham in 1947, would develop masculine characteristics "wholly opposed to the experience of feminine satisfaction."[6]

With sexuality ideally contained in marriage, sexual satisfaction for married couples gained new importance. In 1954 an editorial in *McCall's* magazine urged marital "togetherness," an "ideal" that was already regulating many business-class marriages. "Togetherness" meant that the tasks of the home, including parenting, household chores, and even inducing sexual pleasure, should be shared. Couples were advised that they needed to "work" at their marriage; sexual compatibility—usually an unknown for couples before marriage—could be achieved through mutual effort. Young-marrieds were also told that most couples achieved marital happiness through their children; liberal experts saw children as a means of both keeping Father at home and taming Mother's potent sexuality. The result, from the late 1940s through the 1950s, was that Americans wed at an earlier age, produced babies sooner, and raised more of them to maturity than any earlier generation in the United States in the twentieth century. With the divorce rate stabilized—in part because many feared the social wilderness awaiting divorced adults—a higher percentage of the adult U.S. population was married in 1960 than at any time before (or since). Some Americans may look back to the 1950s as the last "normal" decade in the century, but with regard to marriage, families, and children it was the most abnormal era in American history.

Motherhood anchored the contained family of the 50s. Father remained the nominal head of the house; but despite the ideology of "togetherness" he generally stayed on the periphery of the Family Circle, posted there to protect it from intruders but frequently exiting for work. The ideal business-class mom, in contrast, remained in the center to manage the home, organize the family's social life, and raise the children. Experts glorified Mother's role and Hollywood invested it with honor and prestige, renewing the Victorian "cult of motherhood" that had flourished in the late nineteenth century. Cold war mothers, however, faced challenges unknown to their grandmothers. Threats to family stability and mental health now seemed more ubiquitous and omnipotent than ever. Margaret Mead, for example, warned that children now faced "a world suddenly shrunk to one unit, in which radio and television and comics and the threat of the atomic bomb are everyday realities."[7] The general belief that mothers could and should shape the personalities of their children led to widespread anxiety among women, especially since mothers were now asked to monitor a child's inner psychology, not simply control her or his outward behavior. Parents turned to experts for advice, but even the immensely popular *Baby and Child Care* (1946) by Dr. Benjamin Spock, who admonished parents to trust their instincts but also (implicitly) to "read my book," could not allay concern.

Liberal experts advised American families to move into ideal ranch-style suburban homes. Historian Clifford Clark, Jr., underlines the Platonic desires that animated the elevation of a ranch-house utopia: "The 1950s housing crusade was . . . a central part of a larger perfectionist impulse that swept through postwar American society. Like the crusade to halt the spread of communism and the belief that antibiotics would eliminate germs forever, the justification for the postwar housing boom was part of a one-dimensional frame of mind that stressed the possibility of creating the perfect society."[8] Architects designed suburban ranch houses to enhance familial "togetherness." Master bedroom suites emphasized the importance of conjugal satisfaction; and "family rooms"—a postwar innovation—provided a common space for parents and children, typically pictured seated around a new television. Convenience, comfort, and flow were the hallmarks of the suburban ranchhouse. Where the flow of the prewar house might move outward toward a front porch, the more private suburban backyard, typically mediated by a breezeway, back porch, or patio, now oriented the house to the world beyond. Indeed, picture windows and sliding glass doors helped to create a sense of continuity between the home and the natural world, now cut, trimmed, and controlled in an impossible attempt to eliminate anything wild or irregular from the suburban landscape. Nonetheless, suburbanites substantially accepted the perfectionist ideals of their domestic lives. When surveyed, most reported that ranch-house, suburban living had improved familial "togetherness" and even enhanced their civic commitments.

Beyond problems with crabgrass, however, living out the utopian family dream in suburbia harbored nagging problems and contradictions. The antiseptic model of suburban space eliminated much of the pleasing variety and casual neighborliness of city streets. In the home, picture windows and "window walls" allowed Others to look in as well as family members to look out, creating a fishbowl effect more conducive to bunkered conformity than to family fun. Isolated "togetherness" left independent teens with little to do nearby, leading to exaggerated concerns about juvenile delinquency during the 1950s. Within the Family Circle, fathers were urged to help with household tasks but ridiculed as unmasculine if they put on an apron to wash the dishes, as occurred in a notable scene from *Rebel without a Cause* (1955). Moreover, no amount of suburban security, not even a fallout shelter in the backyard, could protect nuclear families from the Bomb.

The contradictions of the era fell most heavily upon women. As Arlene Skolnick notes: "Motherhood was glorified, yet women were denigrated. Sex discrimination flourished, yet women were regarded as the privileged sex of America. Attitudes that today would be regarded as embarrassingly sexist were taken for granted as part of everyday life. Women were entering the workplace in increasing numbers, yet work for women was denounced as unnatural." Given the ideals essentializing the liberal concepts of marriage and the home, most couples had difficulty imagining alternatives to their lives. Typically, they struggled to work through familial difficulties and contradictions rather than abandoning their contained notion of the family. Summarizing the results of a study of six hundred white, middle-class couples surveyed about their cold war marriages, Elaine Tyler May reports that "compromise, accommodation, and lowered expectations" characterized most of them. In part because domestic containment had reshaped their lives, May concludes, the women of the survey were more willing than the men to make sacrifices in order to maintain a stable family life.[9]

Throughout the early Cold War, most suburbs effectively excluded racial minorities through racist zoning restrictions and real estate practices. Abraham Levitt and Sons, builders of several suburban "Levittowns" along the east coast, for instance, refused to sell to blacks until forced to do so by court order in the mid 1960s; like most developers, they feared that admitting African Americans would lead to the same "white flight" that had initially populated their new neighborhoods. Cautious builders were hardly alone in segregating the suburbs; by restricting mortgage loans to whites buying homes in racially defined "good neighborhoods," federal government policies during the 1950s also worked to prevent racial mixing. Unable to move from inner cities, many black Americans, like groups of Puerto Ricans, Appalachian whites, Native Americans, and Mexican migrants, were caught up in the gradual decline of once thriving urban centers. When wealthy and middle-income white families departed for the suburbs, they left behind a shrinking tax base, a deteriorating transit system, and antiquated schools. The liberal "urban renewal" projects of the late 1950s and 1960s typically packed poor minorities into high-rise ghettos to make room for expressways, civic projects, and expanded business districts. By the late 1950s African Americans were challenging the de jure segregation of the rural South, but the de facto segregation, urban blight, and erosion of economic opportunity in the cities of the North would prove much harder to overcome.

As novelist Ralph Ellison understood, black Americans were generally "invisible" to the white majority, especially to those living in segregated suburbs. When they thought about African Americans at all, business-class whites typically viewed them as a "problem" to be solved through assimilation; "Negroes" would have to learn to behave "normally," like "Caucasians," before they would be widely accepted. Historian Matthew Jacobson notes that the capaciousness of the "Caucasian" category grew during the twentieth century to encompass many social groups that had previously been understood as a separate race. By the 1930s, the "Celtic race," the "Jewish race," and other racialized immigrant groups— formerly in competition with the "Anglo-Saxon race"—had become the "Caucasian race" in public discourse. The need for national unity in the fight against fascism also worked to enlarge the category "Caucasian" and to reduce "race" to skin color. On the eve of the Cold War, remarks Jacobson, American liberalism "was already deeply structured in black and white."[10]

Indeed, because international competition with communism rendered American racism a continuing source of embarrassment to American liberals, the Cold War made assimilation more urgent than before. By the late 1940s the Soviets were eagerly circulating stories of racial discrimination, lynchings, and "race riots" in the United States to newspapers in Asia and Africa. Alert to the possibilities for change, African American leaders pressed their advantage. In 1947 A. Philip Randolph threatened a March on Washington and W. E. B. Du Bois led the National Association for the Advancement of Colored People (NAACP) to file a petition in the United Nations denouncing American racial injustice. Truman justified his executive order desegregating the armed forces in 1948 on the grounds of national prestige and security. As Eleanor Roosevelt noted at the time, civil rights "isn't any longer a domestic question—it's an international question." Within an hour after the *Brown v. Board of Education* decision ordering the desegregation of southern schools in 1954, the

Voice of America broadcast the news to Eastern Europe. The liberal elite needed to demonstrate for international eyes that America was moving toward racial justice. Even as the Cold War helped to motivate civil rights reform, however, it also ruled out of bounds a broader critique of economic injustice and racism. As historian Mary Dudziak notes: "Racism might be an international embarrassment. Class-based inequality, however, was a feature of capitalism, an economic system Americans were proud of. . . . Once America's image seemed secure [by the mid 1960s], Cold War concerns dropped out as one of the factors encouraging civil rights reform."[11]

An American Dilemma: The Negro Problem and Modern Democracy (1944), by Gunnar Myrdal and other sociologists, shaped the postwar liberal consensus to use "social engineering" to defuse racism at home and hence prevent it from undermining the image of the United States abroad. Myrdal based his hope for interracial democracy on the ideas of Robert Park, an influential sociologist at the University of Chicago who argued that assimilation was a necessary part of the modernizing process. From Park's point of view, ethnic and racial newcomers to American cities needed to leave behind their premodern, dysfunctional behaviors and beliefs and conform to cosmopolitan, American modernity. Park's grand narrative of modernization made no distinction between African Americans and other immigrant groups; his abstractions ignored massive differences of historical oppressions and present inequities. Myrdal's book extended Park's thesis of modernization through assimilation.

The American Dilemma also psychologized racial dynamics, concluding that the key to overcoming racism was to play upon white psychological guilt. A product of the same therapeutic assumptions that classified thousands of Americans as victims of psychological forces beyond their control, Myrdal's book spawned a host of related research projects built on the belief that racism had indelibly pathologized black personalities and families. Ironically, these studies occasionally produced progressive results in the short term, even if their long-term consequences were deleterious. A study entitled "The Effects of Segregation and the Consequences of Desegregation: A Social Scientific Statement," purporting to demonstrate the low self-esteem experienced by black children in segregated schools, anchored Thurgood Marshall's attack on segregation in the *Brown* v. *Board of Education* case of 1954. For the most part, however, cold war social science encouraged blacks to view themselves as helpless victims and whites to view blacks, especially black males, as disturbed and dangerous. In the conclusion to her chapter on "The Damaging Psychology of Race," historian Ellen Herman attributes the psychologized focus on black male self-esteem that drove most social science research during the early Cold War to the therapeutic ethos of the era, assumptions about universal sexual and gender differences, "a social context hospitable to turning psychology into public policy," and, ironically, "the progress of the civil rights movement."[12] Most liberal social scientists sincerely believed they were contributing to the easing of racial tensions and the progress of integration. Their psychologized assumptions, Platonic categories, and assimilationist agendas, however, probably had the opposite long-term effect.

The social science discourse about racial Others overseas suffered from similar shortcomings. From World War II into the mid 1960s, the federal government funded many research projects to discover how the United States might use psychological insights to modernize the governments and economies of "third-world" countries. Several social scientists focused on the possibility of changing the personalities of emerging generations of foreign elites to induce them to accept a capitalist path for their country's modernization. Leonard Doob, for instance, conducted numerous psychological experiments based on the assumption that "civilization," which to him meant Western society and culture, was the product of psychological development, not the result of such material realities as economic systems and political institutions. Doob found that "uncivilized" personalities were rigid and lacked empathy, compared to the rationality and fellow-feeling of civilized peoples. Nonetheless, he believed that elites in many traditional societies were eager to become more civilized and listed several ways that the United States could encourage them to assimilate to American values. Like Park and Myrdal, Doob based his research on the liberal premises of modernization theory. The abstractions of modernization theory, with its notion of "nation building," also set the stage for American intervention in Vietnam.[13] The narrative of modernization appealed to cold war liberals in the 1950s because it seemed scientific and progressive—plus it countered the Marxist-Leninist idea of world revolution on the same ground of universal history.

Whereas the image of dangerous blacks bursting out of inner cities and moving next door to their daughters led many nervous white families to bunker down in suburbia, the prospect of white policymakers leading racialized Others in distant lands toward civilization inspired thoughts of the Family of Man. Although the racism of both attitudes was rooted in similar causes, the fact of distance, the apparent opportunity for greater control, and the resulting self-image for the liberal white male made imperial patriarchy abroad far superior to gradual racial integration at home. Historian Emily S. Rosenberg demonstrates that most cold war white Americans understood nonwhite foreigners as "emotional, irrational, irresponsible, unbusinesslike, unstable, and childlike."[14] Nonetheless, American leaders such as John Foster Dulles, secretary of state under Eisenhower, were eager to educate them in the ways of capitalist modernization to save the world from communism. Despite the success of the Communist Revolution in China, the majority of Americans continued to regard Asians as particularly susceptible to Western tutelage. American missionaries had practiced in Asia for decades, and many continued to live and work in Asian countries other than China after 1949. By embracing Others in Christian community and gradually assimilating foreign nonwhites to Western ways, missionaries remained a potent symbol of the expansive family in the 1950s. Racialized Others encountered fortress suburbia in the United States but might enjoy paternalistic encouragement and even a house in the same neighborhood as U.S. citizens in foreign countries.

These anomalies of cold war whiteness, of course, were directly linked to the imperial ambitions of the United States after the war. Members of the American business class, however, made reluctant imperialists; few even supposed that the extension of American hegemony abroad through military treaties, trade and financial agreements, and assistance to former imperial powers Britain and France (notably in Vietnam) constituted "imperialism" at all. The similarities between U.S. foreign policy and the actions of the United Nations in the early Cold War, plus the need to prevent yet another totalitarian nation from world conquest, made the worldwide thrust of U.S. power appear to be a simple extension of the objectives of World War II. Once again, innocent Americans had to assume new power and responsibility to rebuild and protect free nations from dangerous aggressors. As historian Geoffrey Perrett remarks, the earnest internationalism of the postwar era (that nonetheless trumpeted American values and institutions as the path to freedom and prosperity) amounted to "little more than the old-fashioned boosterism on a global scale."[15] Though generally innocent of imperialist intentions, U.S. liberals created a world environment that produced many of the benefits of preceding empires for their imperial powers. By the mid 1950s the "free world" was enriching the imperial center, client nations bowed to the will of the United States, and the mostly nonwhite elites of "developing" nations lost power to U.S. policymakers.

The American media generally portrayed imperialism in Family of Man tropes. Feature films and news reports about the Korean conflict, for example, depicted American soldiers taking care of orphaned Korean children. During the 1950s Protestant church groups and the American media nearly canonized Dr. Albert Schweitzer, the African missionary. James Michener won the Pulitzer Prize for Literature in 1947 with *Tales of the South Pacific*, which showed exotic islanders and the children of French planters welcoming the Americans who intruded into their lives to fight the Japanese. Joshua Logan, Richard Rodgers, and Oscar Hammerstein II would later turn these tales into one of the longest-running musical hits of the postwar era. Michener's 1953 bestseller, *Sayonara*, became a popular film in 1957 starring Marlon Brando. He played an American officer who rescues a Japanese woman from bigots in the Air Force to return with her to the United States, where she will be a model of ethnic assimilation.

While some media events focused on the bunkered nuclear family, many more depicted a white Family Circle that expanded to encompass distant relatives, neighbors, and friends around the nuclear core. Two popular Walt Disney movies, *Westward Ho the Wagons!* (1956) and *Swiss Family Robinson* (1960), dramatized the threat to the bunkered family from nonwhite Others. In these films, Native Americans attacked a wagon train and Asian pirates assaulted a family's island fortress. Television situation comedies, the most popular family genre of the postwar era, however, primarily demonstrated the flexibility of the Family Circle. On *I Love Lucy*, for instance, the Mertzes effectively became an older brother and sister to Lucy and Desi Ricardo. Even the Hollywood stars on *Lucy* who "just dropped in for a visit" became instant family. Likewise, the suburban home of the Nelsons on *Ozzie and Harriet* easily encompassed neighbors and friends; Harriet served cookies to them all. By the end of many sit-com episodes, the camera focused on the now reconciled husband and wife, assuring viewers of the ongoing viability, indeed the Platonic universality, of the nuclear family. "Alice, you're the greatest" told spectators of *The Honeymooners* (one of the few sit coms not set in suburbia) that if the Kramdens could settle their differences, the marriage of any American couple was meant to survive.

In the 1950s, of course, these extended sit-com families were entirely white, even if the household included a black maid or gardener. Through the containment logic of Otherness, African Americans helped to define the universality of whiteness in the society and culture of the nation. Occasional reports in the media about the "Negro problem," as Myrdal had termed it, primarily served to reinforce black marginality and normalize white privilege. Cold war Broadway gave blacks somewhat more visibility than did mainstream television, but some productions—such as revivals of *The Green Pastures* and *Tobacco Road*, both presented with an all-black cast in the early 1950s—simply continued the segregation of U.S. society on the stage. Other plays, including *Deep Are the Roots* (1945), *Forward the Heart* (1948), and *Member of the Wedding* (1949), did little to challenge the liberal assumptions of white entitlement, paternalism, and assimilation. The situation began to shift toward a recognition of the need for racial equity with Louis Peterson's *Take a Giant Step* in 1953, followed by the success of James Earl Jones in Papp's Shakespeare in the Park and Lena Horne in *Jamaica* (1957). Off-Broadway, *Trouble in Mind* by Alice Childress (1955) and Loften Mitchell's *A Land beyond the River* (1957) argued forcefully for racial justice. It was not until 1959, however, with *A Raisin in the Sun* by Lorraine Hansberry that Broadway audiences saw a play that challenged the underpinnings of American racism. *Purlie Victorious*, which boosted Ossie Davis to stardom, continued the attack in 1961.

The liberal view of race left hegemonic American culture in the 1947–1962 period with three narrative options for constructing dramas centered on the contained figure of the Family Circle. First, situation comedies, many soap operas, and sentimental family plays such as *I Remember Mama* (1944) offered one popular solution: keep conflicts within a modestly expanded white Family Circle that includes friends and neighbors but excludes all racialized Others from significant roles. Early cold war plays in this category included *The Heiress* (1947), *Life with Mother* (1948), *Mrs. McThing* (1952), *The Shrike* (1952), *The Bad Seed* (1954), and *The Cave Dwellers* (1957). The long-running off-Broadway hit *The Fantasticks* (1960) was built on the premise that fathers could control family conflicts by having exotic Others stage pretend battles. *The Member of the*

Wedding, which starred Ethel Waters, and *The Grass Harp* (1952), a fantasy by Truman Capote which featured an outspoken black servant, bent the rule about excluding racialized Others from important roles somewhat by featuring strong black women in traditionally subservient parts. Of course keeping all conflict in the (white) family did not necessarily guarantee a sentimental evening at the theater. Revivals of two O'Neill family plays, *Long Day's Journey into Night* and *A Moon for the Misbegotten*, both staged by José Quintero, seared playgoers in 1956 and 1957.

Second, dramatic constructions could push against the Family Circle from the outside, watch it contract to its nuclear core and perhaps even disintegrate. This strategy might have involved African Americans doing the pushing, but a safer construction of this option for cold war Americans excluded blacks and featured an exotic outsider threatening family integrity. Numerous films and plays of the 50s took this route, including *The Long, Hot Summer* with Paul Newman as the outsider (1958) and Disney's animated feature *Lady and the Tramp* (1955), in which two Siamese cats undermine the household of Jim Dear and Darling. William Inge, the most popular melodramatist of cold war families, placed threatening outsiders in the midst of troubled Family Circles in *Come Back, Little Sheba* (1950), *Picnic* (1953), *Bus Stop* (1955), and *The Dark at the Top of the Stairs* (1957) and then documented the social and psychological fireworks that followed. Intrusive outsiders also powered the dramatic conflicts of such disparate "family" plays and musicals as *Autumn Garden* (1951), *The Rainmaker* (1954), *The Music Man* (1957), *The Miracle Worker* (1959), and *Camelot* (1960). Some had a biological family at their core, while the Family Circle of others was more metaphorical but no less psychologically contained. The smothering physical and psychological confinement forced on the Frank family and their boarders by the external evil of Nazism in *The Diary of Anne Frank* (1955) may have been the closest that many American spectators came to imagining the possible reality of life in a bomb shelter. Typically, these plays featured a strange outside force pressuring or entering the circle of a mostly normal family. As he had done in *The Glass Menagerie* (1945), Tennessee Williams reversed the usual formula in *The Rose Tattoo* (1951) by placing a "normal" intruder in the midst of an abnormal family.

Accommodating dramatic structure to the liberal view of race also generated a third option for Family Circle plays in the 1947–1962 period. Characters inside a white or nonwhite family could attempt to push out its boundaries to make it more inclusive. In *West Side Story* (1957), for instance, Tony and Maria try to expand the tight "families" of two ethnic gangs, which can only join together in a more inclusive circle of humanity after the deaths of the two lovers. Rodgers and Hammerstein began bringing together Eastern exotics and Western humanitarians with *South Pacific* (1947) and continued in *The King and I* (1951) and *The Flower Drum Song* (1958), which featured a Chinese immigrant to America and assimilated Chinese Americans. Pushing out the Family Circle to incorporate a type of exotic Other was also a prominent feature of *The Teahouse of the August Moon* (1953), *The Flowering Peach* (1954), *My Fair Lady* (1956), *Auntie Mame* (1956), and *The Sound of Music* (1959). As these examples illustrate, the Family of Man strategy of this option worked best for comedy and musical plays. Given the liberal construction of the family and the politics of race, family dramas in the postwar period that strayed outside of these three structural options rarely gained popularity.

The family dramas of William Inge and Rodgers and Hammerstein helped to legitimate the "family values" of containment liberalism. While Inge used the device of outsiders threatening the Family Circle, Rodgers and Hammerstein frequently deployed significant characters attempting to expand the Family Circle from within. Although none of Inge's exotic intruders are African American — such a direct acknowledgment of white fears would probably have sunk his plays at the box office — his dramas do explore the central problem that exotic Others posed for liberal Americans: how to respond when the Other comes knocking at the family door. In *Dark at the Top of the Stairs*, the exotic Other is a young Empty Boy who combines homo- and heteroerotic allure, more a sexual than a racial threat, which nonetheless temporarily backs a typical family into a psychological bunker. The racially mixed protofamily in *The King and I*, in contrast, attempts to climb out of its shelter to whiten humankind. At a safe remove from the inner-cities of the United States and innocent of imperial intentions, the Americanized protagonist of this musical drama yearns to universalize the attributes of Western whiteness by including de-racialized Others in her expanding Family Circle.

■ When *The King and I* opened in 1951, it capped a string of Broadway hits for Rodgers and Hammerstein, which had begun with *Oklahoma* in 1943 and included *Carousel* (1945) and *South Pacific* (1949). Their fifth collaboration starred long-time London and New York stage personality Gertrude Lawrence as Anna Leonowens, a widowed English schoolteacher, plus relative newcomer Yul Brynner as the King of a mid nineteenth-century, half-mythical Siam. The show ran for 1,246 performances and swept the Oscars and box office records as a film in 1956. By 1958, after further hits from Rodgers and Hammerstein, the *New York Times Magazine* dubbed the team "more like a durable institution than a pair of human beings."[16] *The King and I* was a bulwark of their musical empire.

Since *Oklahoma*, Rodgers and Hammerstein had explored numerous ways of suggesting a conflict between outward appearance and inner emotion in their major characters. The book musical, with its tighter integration of character, music, and plot, made such explorations possible; indeed, the cold war interest in exploring psychological depth helped to produce and legitimate this new musical form, just as it popularized Method acting. Both pitted an essential inner self against outward show. Lawrence's hoop-skirted gowns contained her body and added masculine forcefulness to her character's brisk actions. When they first meet her, the King's wives suppose that "you wear big skirt like that because you shaped like that." They also call her "sir" because she is "scientific."[17] These male attributes, made more legible to the audience because of the response of the Siamese characters on stage, were belied, of course, by many of Anna's later actions. The audience soon learned that underneath her efficient and massive exterior beat the heart of a typical mother longing to love Siamese children.

In contrast to Lawrence's gendered conflict between outer masculinity and inner motherliness, Brynner's characterization embodied generational tensions, suggesting a conflict between potent masculinity on the outside and prepubescent child within. Despite the implicit sexual threat of his bald head and bare chest, "no child in the court," noted one reviewer, echoing several others, "is as precocious or petulant as his royal highness, the King."[18] Rodgers and Hammerstein focused audience attention on the King's true self by paralleling his desires and situations with those of his son, the heir to the throne. The Crown Prince reprises the King's "A Puzzlement," for example, even repeating his father's bow to Buddha for the final verse. By the early 1950s audiences had come to expect that inner truth would eventually triumph over outward show in a musical. Thus, at the climax of *The King and I*, when Anna tries to stop the King from beating Tuptim's lover, outward masks fall away and a mother's conscience confronts the petty tyranny of a little boy.

Further, both Lawrence and Brynner played out the tensions between inner reality and outward pretense in their characterizations. Commenting on Gertrude Lawrence's Anna in *The King and I*, John Mason Brown noted the "quiet inner strength" that restrained the energy of her outward buoyancy and charm. In such numbers as "I Whistle a Happy Tune," Lawrence suppressed her inner fears through outward *bravada*, a form of suppression expressed physically and vocally that recurs for the character throughout the musical. As the King, Yul Brynner devised a similar characterization centered on the dynamics of containment. Said one critic, "His king is a veritable tour de force of animal energy, with a protective armor of pride hiding a basic humility. . . ." Newspaper critic Elliott Norton contrasted Brynner's outward pretense of authority with his inner trepidation: "He is sometimes making noise to keep up his own courage. He is not without inner fear. Though he cannot admit it, he hungers not only after knowledge, but also after wisdom."[19] In "A Puzzlement," sung in soliloquy, Brynner embodied and explored the conflict between his necessary show of power and his lack of emotional security. To heighten the conflict between his appearance of ferocity and the reality of his "puzzlement," Brynner designed a Kabuki-like mask for his makeup as the King. It heightened both the typicality and the psychological dynamics of his character.

The ideological consequence of this generational split in the King's inner and outer character for the audience justified and reinforced a condescending attitude toward Southeast Asia. Siam was reduced to the status of a child in need of Western schooling. Critic Arthur Pollock, like several others, was unapologetically patronizing in his view of the King's need for education: "[He] yearns to let his mind go out and meet the rest of the world or that part of it more civilized than his little section of it, to get in step with progress, to know, to help his people to evolve." Even Harold Clurman was won over by what he termed "the fatherliness of feeling" for the Siamese that pervaded Hammerstein's book. The belief that Asians in positions of authority were essentially wide-eyed children fundamentally eager to join a civilized Family of Man would have tragic consequences in Vietnam.[20]

Beckoning the King to join this "universal" family throughout the musical is a Mother. Although Anna has her own English son, she becomes the mothering schoolmarm to all of the King's fourteen children. Anna occupies the center of the symbolic Family Circle in *The King and I*; as in typical cold war families, the nurturance and success of "her" children depend on Mom. Whereas the primary metaphor of containment made the Family Circle legible and significant in the musical, the schema of "part-whole" gave Anna preeminence within it. Simply put, Anna is the usual "part" of the family that represents the "whole" of it. A dancing, singing synecdoche, Anna often embodies in her actions the present and future good of the King, the children, and herself as a family unit. Occasionally, Anna's private life or her concerns as the biological mother of Louis erase her larger symbolic role, but never for long; the musical quickly returns her to the status of Primal Mother in the Family of Man. Other figures might temporarily take her symbolic place—the King, Lady Thiang, and the young King-to-Be in the final scene—but none can compete with her moral authority in the Family Circle.

Anna's abilities as a teacher complement and enhance her symbolic role in the family. Many reviewers spoke glowingly about the cuteness and spontaneity of the King's offspring, the "kids who begin creeping into your heart the minute you get to Siam," according to the *New York Journal American*. But Rodgers and Hammerstein's book and musical numbers rigorously controlled their behavior (and consequently enhanced their charm) by featuring them in scenes where they must take orders from adults, primarily their father and Anna. Efficient as well as warm, Anna rehearses them as a group in their school song and involves them in repetitive hand shaking, marching, and singing for "Getting To Know You." To many reviewers, and likely to many in the business-class audience as well, this was pedagogy for progress. Citing the similarities between the historical Anna Leonowens and the character in the musical, Robert Coleman remarked: "One of the most important of [Anna's] achievements was the schooling of the Crown Prince, who was, on his ascension to the throne, to stand for progress."[21] In *The King and I*, children, especially Asian children, are *tabulae rasae* on which may be written the dictates of the West. A motherly teacher can make the world one.

If in Rodgers and Hammerstein's *South Pacific* a Western mother successfully adopted two Asian children, Anna in *The King and I* implicitly adopts fourteen. In fact, the long-distance, symbolic "adoption" of Asian children by business-class couples was a popular program in the early

Cold War, pushed by the Christian Children's Fund through print advertisements that encouraged Americans to view all Asians as helpless children. By 1955 the CCF, with a budget of nearly two million dollars, was funneling American money to support children in fifteen Asian countries. As cultural studies scholar Christina Klein demonstrates, the CCF program, like *The King and I*, offered "a ready-made subject position and visual model of global responsibility" for Americans through its advertising. Co-author Hammerstein went further than symbolism in adopting an Asian child. In 1949 James Michener approached Oscar Hammerstein about supporting Pearl Buck's Welcome House, a program the novelist had established to facilitate the adoption of mixed-race children of Asian and Western couples. Hammerstein gave generously, and his daughter Alice adopted a baby girl, making him one of the first grandfathers of a Welcome House child. Programs like the CCF and Welcome House, plus the immensely favorable press given to both, encouraged a Family of Man response to the Cold War in Asia; Americans could support anticommunism and humanitarian relief to children simply by widening their Family Circles. In advocating assistance to the new "nation" of South Vietnam in 1956, Senator John F. Kennedy said, "If we are not the parents of little Vietnam, then surely we are the godparents. . . . This is our offspring—we cannot abandon it, we cannot ignore its needs."[22] By 1956 "familializing" international relations in Southeast Asia already entailed future obligations.

When *The King and I* was produced in 1951, the trope of mother-as-hero was relatively rare in popular culture, but it rapidly gained in influence in the mid 1950s. Viewed as threats to male power during the war, female desire and fecundity centered many filmic images of evil women in *film noir* and the sci-fi movies of the 1940s and early 1950s. The predatory vamp of *Sunset Boulevard* (1950) and the female ants of *Them!* (1954), whose procreative power threatens all humanity, shaped the depiction of mothers in many domestic melodramas and comedies. Jim's mother in *Rebel without a Cause*, for instance, is cold, materialistic, and manipulative. (Little wonder that the film rejects both of the hero's parents to project an ideal family formed by its three sympathetic teens.) Signaled by a shift in the image of Marilyn Monroe from *noir* predator to "innocent" playmate, the general transition from manipulative to loving Mom might be dated at mid decade. Hefner's monthly playmates, of course, which began with Monroe, helped ease the transition. With female sexuality no longer a major threat to family life, mother-love could be either ignored or celebrated. The manipulative mother of Alfred Hitchcock's *Strangers on the Train* (1951), for example, was giving way not only to Harriet Nelson and June Cleaver, but also to Julie Andrews in *The Sound of Music* (1959).

Actually, most musical mothers after the mid 50s combined outrageous manipulation with sacrificial love, sublimating their sexual energies to push their "children," biological or not, to success. These included, most famously, Chita Rivera in *Bye Bye Birdie* (1960), Carol Channing in *Hello, Dolly!* (1964), Angela Lansbury in *Mame* (1966), and, preeminently, Ethel Merman in *Gypsy* (1959). As D. A. Miller remarks, "The Broadway musical is the unique genre of mass culture to be elaborated in the name of the mother; a name, however, that it dare not quite speak...." In these musicals too, Mom achieves synecdochal power in the Family Circle; for much of the time, her force is the only option for family togetherness. For Miller, the classic musical's fixation on a powerful mother explains its contradictory appeal to homosexuals: "Call her Dolly, Mame, or the Spider Woman; even call her Lola, Peter Pan, or Annie; by any other name she is still a Rose [the stage mother in *Gypsy*], a Momma who returns each of us to the dependent condition of a Momma's boy fearful she will leave him and take with her all his pleasure and even his continued vitality."[23] Miller also acknowledges that the best way to retain the liveliness of Mom is to become her yourself.

Following Miller, it is clear that many musicals in the 1950s and early 1960s offered spectators two major positions of empathetic involvement: mother and child. Imaginatively putting yourself in the place of a Merman, an Andrews, or a Lawrence and singing a show stopper was certainly one inducement to keep audiences coming back for more. Identification with a performer working in the "self-expressive mode," as Bert States calls it, has always been a reason to empathize; through such involvement the spectator instantly acquires the virtuosity of a star.[24] In numbers like "I Whistle a Happy Tune" and "Getting to Know You," however, the rhetorical appeal from the stage is made initially to the child inside each spectator. From this position, audience members can enjoy being mothered. During the course of the songs, it is likely that many spectators alternated between the two positions. Shifting between the pleasures of mothering and being mothered effectively creates a third position—empathizing with a mother-centered family. In both numbers, finally, mother and child have become brave together and "gotten to know" each other.

Many show tunes address audiences in the first-person plural, helping to constitute the family feeling that mothers and children extend from the stage and audience members return from their seats. Even when the mode of address is primarily second-person singular, as in "There's No Business Like Show Business," the "we" often enters for the finale: "Yesterday they told you you would not go far / That night you open and there you are / Next day on your dressing room they've hung a star / Let's go on with the show." When Merman sang this in *Annie Get Your Gun* (1946), she was initially mama assuring all of her children in the theater that they could be stars. With "Let's go on with the show," the rhetoric shifted to "we"; we could be troopers together, mama and the rest of us, a family. What Miller terms the "mothered performance" of the musical positions the willing audience member as both securely coddled infant and super-talented adult; "we," Mom and child together, can transcend all obstacles and succeed against the odds. Empathize in a musical and join an instant family! As Miller notes, this position for spectators was typically as "vacuous" as it was energizing.[25]

Several of William Inge's plays also induced empathetic projection through a variation of the "mothered performance." Inge was the most popular playwright of serious dramas about the American family during the early Cold War. His first success, *Come Back, Little Sheba*, opened in 1950 and played for a respectable 190 performances. With direction by Joshua Logan and a design by Jo Mielziner, *Picnic* ran for a year and a half after its 1953 premiere and gained immense popularity as a film starring William Holden in 1955. *Bus Stop* enjoyed a similar transformation from pleasing play (478 performances) in 1955 to hit movie, starring Marilyn Monroe. Elia Kazan directed *The Dark at the Top of the Stairs*, which opened in December 1957. Like its popular predecessors, it played for roughly a year and a half and then made the transition from Broadway to Hollywood. Significantly, Inge's mother figures grow in complexity and sympathy during the decade; his shifts in depicting Mom followed contemporary trends. Despite a string of successes during the 50s, Inge never had another Broadway hit after *Dark*, though some of his film scripts, including *Splendor in the Grass* (1961), continued to win him recognition.[26]

Cora Flood/Theresa Wright on the stairs, yelling at Rubin Flood/Pat Hingle in Act I of Dark at the Top of the Stairs. *Friedman-Ables photo, courtesy New York Public Library.*

Like most family dramas in all cold war media, *Dark at the Top of the Stairs* features a Family Circle centered on Mom. The Floods live in a small town near Oklahoma City in the midst of the 1920s oil boom. Cora and Rubin Flood have two children, ten-year-old Sonny and sixteen-year-old Reenie. The Family Circle also includes Lottie Lacey, Cora's older sister, who comes to visit after Rubin leaves in anger at the end of Act I. Kazan cast Teresa Wright in the role of Cora Flood, a Hollywood actor well known for spunky teenagers and sparkling young wives in fourteen films before 1957. Broadway reviewers praised her Cora Flood for its emotional warmth and vulnerability. Henry Hewes in the *Saturday Review* called Wright "a nucleus of normality around which Mr. Kazan sends his charged particles,"[27] confirming her centrality within Inge's nuclear (and psychologically radioactive) circle.

Before slapping his wife and leaving his family at the end of Act I, Rubin Flood accuses Cora of "pampering" their kids (228), and the audience knows that he is right. In part because Rubin works as a traveling salesman and is frequently away from home, Cora has lavished excessive attention on the children. Neighborhood boys taunt Sonny as a "sissy," and Reenie hides from social interaction through compulsive attention to her schoolwork and piano lessons. Inge leads the audience to see that Cora, seeking to satisfy her own desires through concentrating on her children, has slighted the sexual and psychological needs of her husband. With Rubin's angry exit, their marriage is on the brink of collapse. Indeed, the integrity of the Flood Family Circle is at stake, and Cora — the only "part" with the authority to represent the "whole" of it — must take action on several fronts at once. "Can Cora save her family?" is the major dramatic question motivating the action.

As in *The King and I*, the dramatic structure and theatrical style of *Dark at the Top of the Stairs* partly induced the audience members to identify with and empathetically project themselves onto a mother. Instead of becoming mother-stars, however, Inge's spectators were invited to transform themselves into mother-psychiatrists, specifically the kind of psychologically attuned mother elevated to cultural stardom in *Baby and Child Care* and the numerous spinoffs of Dr. Spock's book. Consequently, spectators' relation to Cora shifts back and forth between empathetic and advisory projection. At those moments when she is following correct parenting procedures, the audience is encouraged to "become" Cora, taking her values and point of view as their own. In the next moment, though, Inge asks the audience to stand back from Cora and judge her according to psychologically appropriate standards—values that he assumes the audience shares with him but that Cora may not momentarily meet. The final rhetorical effect of these shifts is much the same as in mother-centered musicals: an audience of "we"s becomes the Flood family, empathizes with its plight, and judges the actions of all actor-characters in terms of its happiness.

Dark at the Top of the Stairs is embedded in Benjamin Spock's theories of child-rearing. Influenced by the identity theories of psychologist Erik Erikson and notions of progressive education deriving from John Dewey, Spock believed that happy, outgoing children would make good team-players as adults. Parents, especially mothers, said Spock, had a responsibility to raise a child "to be sociable and popular."[28] By this measurement, postwar American audiences could see that Cora Flood was failing as a mother. According to Spock's psychology, both Sonny and Reenie suffered from arrested identity formation. Socially shy and jealous of her brother, Reenie was hanging onto her position in the family as "Daddy's little girl." Inge, who was undergoing psychoanalysis when he wrote the play, drew Sonny as a ten-year-old in the midst of an intense Oedipal crisis struggling to break free from his mother's influence and to identify with phallic masculinity. Following Freud, Spock believed that án Oedipal crisis was a "normal" part of male development and cautioned mothers to be ready to cut the apron strings when the boy pulled against them. Spectators could see that instead of encouraging the gradual resolution of Sonny's Oedipal problems, however, Cora was exacerbating them. Needing her son's affection in her hurt and loneliness following her husband's desertion, Cora demands, "Do you love me, son?" and hugs him to her. Next, in Inge's stage directions, "mother and son lie together [on the floor] in each other's arms" (249–50).

The moment hints at incest, but Inge is more interested in Sonny's arrested development due to what cold war culture called "momism," a term coined by Philip Wylie in *Generation of Vipers* (1942), which remained a best-seller during the 1950s. Wylie argued that mothers who smothered their male children with too much affection raised "sissies" who were likely to become homosexuals. Spock also implied as much in *Baby and Child Care* but emphasized that love and positive reinforcement could overcome these problems to shape a successful heterosexual personality. Mothers who read both experts, however, could never be sure

Cora Flood/Theresa Wright hugs her son, Sonny/Charles Saari in Dark at the Top of the Stairs. *Friedman-Ables photo, courtesy New York Public Library.*

of how much affection was too much. Though relying mostly on the insights of Freud as filtered by Spock, *Dark* sides with Wylie on this important point. Inge wanted spectators to understand that Cora Flood's parenting of Sonny might lead him into homosexuality—Inge's own sexual orientation, about which he felt deeply ashamed. If the mother is a synecdoche for the family, her own mental health stands for the psychological intergrity of all family members. When "mother and son lie together in each other's arms," a symbol of the whole infects a needy part of the family with her psychological weakness.

Indeed, the drama suggests that Cora's mistakes could drive her son to the same fate as Sammy Goldenbloom, an attractive boy whose loneliness leads to his suicide. Sammy is the outsider Inge introduces to push the Flood family problems into crisis. The magnetic presence of Sammy, written as a teenage Valentino rendered even more exotic by his Jewish Otherness, awakens desires and recognitions that threaten the evasions and repressions holding family members back from their full potential. Kazan, however, chose not to cast a darkly sensual teenager in the role. Although the script links Sammy Goldenbloom to Rudolph Valentino through stage directions, dialogue, costuming, and sound effects—a player piano near Sammy grinds out "The Sheik of Araby" soon after his entrance, for example—the reviewers complimented Timmy Everett for his innocent, charming, and vulnerable Sammy. Kazan's sensitivity to ethnic prejudice—from his own experience and from directing the film *Gentleman's Agreement* on anti-Semitism (1947)—probably led him to this casting decision. As a sweet boy-next-door, Sammy posed little threat; his unloved plight evoked more sympathy than desire. While understandable, Kazan's choice of Everett pulled the production toward Sammy's situation and away from the dilemma of the family. Sammy's visit in Act II to take Reenie to a dance was meant by Inge to provide the turning point of his plot, revealing to Cora the extent of her children's fear and immaturity as well as awakening her own desire for her husband's return. Without an exotic Sammy, the revival of Cora's sexuality—which motivates many of her actions for the remainder of the play—remains abstract and somewhat unconvincing. Wright/Flood's decisions to save her family became mostly the necessary strategies of a good mother, not, as well, those of a desiring wife. Like *The King and I* and much of the culture of the 1950s, the production of *Dark at the Top of the Stairs* slighted the sexual desires of older women.

Nonetheless, Kazan's directing, by focusing most of its central images away from Cora and onto the Oedipal problems of Sonny, did emphasize the *allegoresis* induced by the production. Inge and Kazan expected the public to read the play through the Freudian narrative of a Boy's struggle to become a Man. The playwright and the director used Sammy's relation to Sonny—the similar sound of their names is not accidental—to spark psychoanalytic recognition within the characters and, they evidently hoped, in the individual spectators. Sammy enters the Flood household as a blind date to take Reenie to a local dance. While there, he plays affectionately with Sonny, and the young boy responds to him with more physical assertiveness than he has shown before. Attracted by the dress sword worn as a part of Sammy's military uniform (he attends a nearby military academy), Sonny pretends to be impaled on it, in a comic but revealingly "Freudian" moment that could not have been lost upon the audience. Sonny may not realize that he is working through his Oedipal crisis, but his mother sees the general outline of the problem. Not in psychoanalytic terms, of course—Inge does not presume that a 1920s provincial woman would have read Freud. Nonetheless, Cora acts according to the doctor's precepts. "You mustn't come crawling into my bed anymore . . . You can't expect me to mean as much to you as when you were a baby" (289–90), she tells Sonny in their next scene together. The lesson is clear: good parents must place the template of Freudian psychoanalysis over their children's problems if they hope to interpret their difficulties and help them toward responsible adulthood.

In a 1954 article in *Theatre Arts*, the playwright forthrightly admitted his therapeutic designs on American spectators. As well as enjoyment for his audience, Inge said he wanted his plays to provide an experience "which shocks them with the unexpected in human nature, with the deep inner life that exists privately behind the life that is publicly presented."[29] Inge intended *Dark at the Top of the Stairs* as shock therapy. To effect this, Kazan and Inge presented the audience with emblematic moments when truths derived from Freudian allegory show through the thin veneer of commonplace naturalism that covers Inge's plays. These moments reduce the wealth of signs on the mimetic stage to a single image that the playwright and director evidently hoped would awaken spectators into an understanding of "the deep inner life" of the psyche. Cora holding Sonny in her arms at the end of Act I is not simply one more moment in the everyday lives of an Oklahoma family in the 1920s. The past clues about their relationship come together in this image; rather suddenly, the stage picture confronts the audience with a Freudian essence: Mother Arrests Son's Natural Development. In the moment of essentializing their relationship, the image also universalizes it: All Mothers Can Endanger Their Sons. The result, as *Cue* magazine said of the play, was that "[Inge's] so-called ordinary people have universal meaning."[30]

Dark at the Top of the Stairs concludes with a similar "Freudian" tableau. Throughout the production, the "dark" at the top of the stairs has been both a real physical space, a hallway in which the audience can see standing or walking characters from the knees down, and a metaphor for adult sexuality. In the last moments of the play, the audience saw Cora stop on a landing of the stairs, at the top of which wait the "naked feet" of her aroused husband. She gazed at Sonny standing below her, who gave her a look of "confused understanding." Then the tableau melted into physical action and dialogue. Sonny headed out the front door; and Cora said, "I'm coming Rubin. I'm coming," on her way up the stairs (304). Another emblematic moment: Cora, perched between her son and her husband, Chooses Marital Togetherness over Momism. In *Freud on Broadway*, W. David Sievers complimented Inge's early plays for their ability to draw upon Freudian insights "without succumbing to the obvious or the trite."[31] Most of Inge's contemporary spectators during the mid 1950s would likely have agreed that his construction of "Freudian" characters and situations was subtle and believable. It is only in retrospect that the allegorical strings are apparent.

The King and I also invites allegorizing. Its ur-text is Harriet Beecher Stowe's *Uncle Tom's Cabin*, which the musical moves from background to foreground with the production of "The Small House of Uncle Thomas" at its climax. "Small House," imaginatively choreographed by Jerome Robbins to suggest a Siamese interpretation of a staging of Stowe's novel, encouraged spectators to pull together all the major themes of *The King and I* and explain them through this single narrative. On one level, the production of "Small House" demonstrated Anna's success in "civilizing" Siam. Within the narrative of the musical, the reason for the play performance is to convince British emissaries to the King's court that Siam should not be incorporated into the British empire. (The faulty logic of this reasoning — that Great Britain would not offer the "civilizing" influence of empire to an Asian country already civilized — reveals the musical's deep investment in American innocence

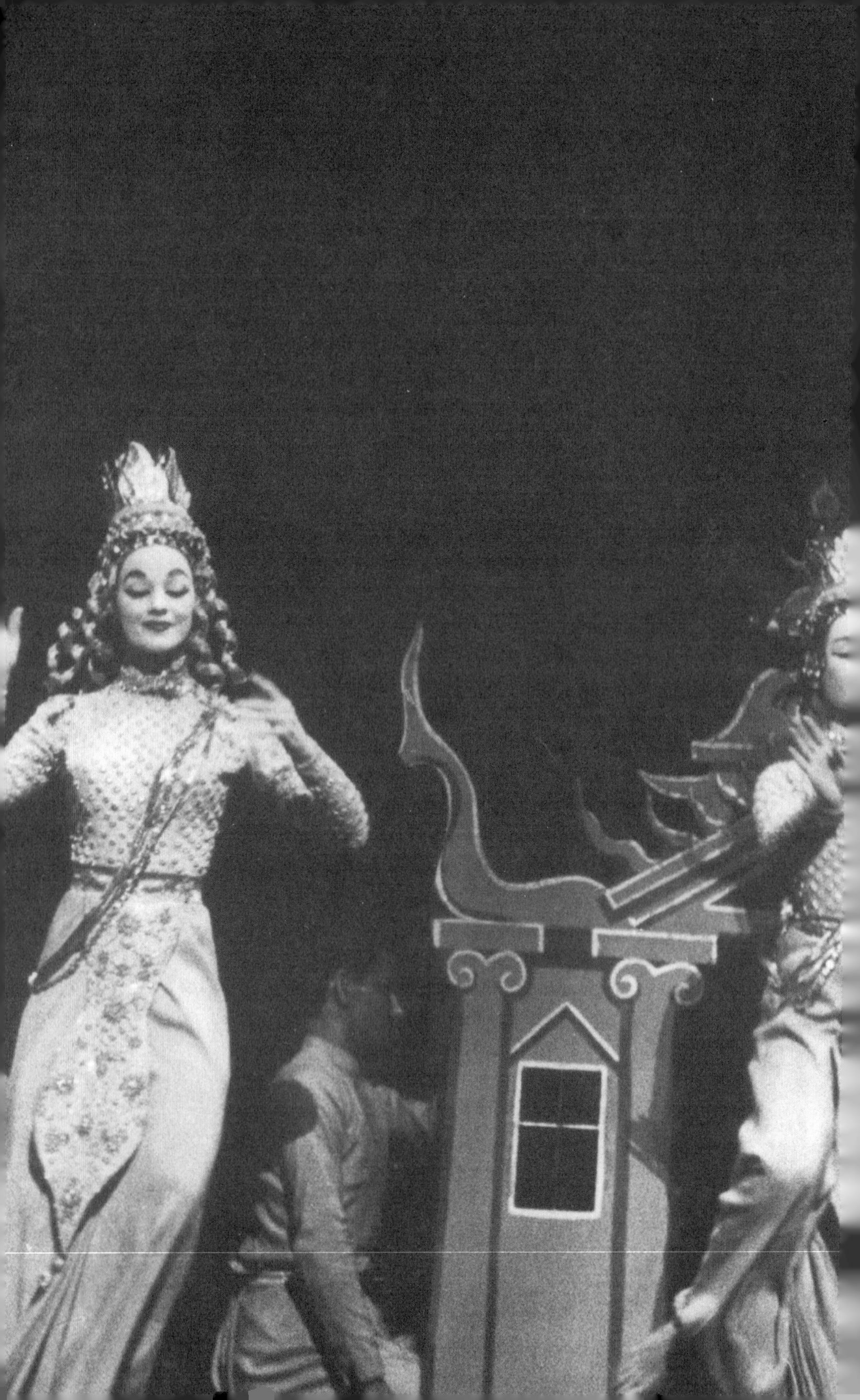

about imperialism.) Significantly, the "proof" of Siamese civilization is its ability to mimic a historically popular American, rather than an English, stage production. Second, spectators could link "Small House" to the romantic subplot of the musical involving Lun Tha and Tuptim, a recent addition to the King's harem. Like the slaves George and Eliza in "Small House," the Siamese lovers are separated by a despot—"Simon of Legree" in "Small House" and the King in the musical. Finally, the parallel plots of the play-within-the-play and the musical directly connect to Anna's desire for her own "small house." Since arriving in Siam, she has been trying to make the King live up to his promise that she would have her own house outside of the palace walls. In addition to Hammerstein's dialogue reminding the audience of this problem, the musical relied on Rodgers's weaving of the melody of "Home, Sweet Home" into his score. The production of "Small House," then, presented a metatheatrical summation of the play, encapsulating in microcosm the themes of civilization, freedom, and home depicted in the macrocosm of the musical. The inducement to read microcosm into macrocosm, of course, is a direct invitation to *allegoresis*.

Siam's need for Western civilization is demonstrated throughout the musical. Early in the action of *The King and I*, Anna gives the King's children a lesson in geopolitics. Seeing an old map of Asia on the wall in which Siam occupies an area roughly the size of China, she rolls out her own visual aid to cover it. Anna's new map is a Mercator projection of the world with Siam reduced to dimensions drawn in London and surrounded by land masses colored to denote the encroachments of European imperial power. The children object to the shrunken size of their kingdom, but the King commands them to recognize that Anna's version of their nation is the correct one. Within the world of the musical, the British map is just as real as snow, which the children also deny; both naturalize the superior civilization of the West.

In his book *American Foreign Policy*, Henry Kissinger drew a sharp distinction between Western and third-world views of reality: "The West is deeply committed to the notion that the real world is external to the observer, that knowledge consists of recording and classifying data—the

---

Dancers in "Small House of Uncle Thomas" scene from The King and I. *Vandamm photo, courtesy New York Public Library.*

more accurately, the better. Cultures which have escaped the early impact of Newtonian thinking have retained the essentially pre-Newtonian view that the real world is almost entirely internal to the observer."[32] Without the aid of Western advisors, believed Kissinger, the people of Southeast Asia could not understand their lives and their place in the world. Anna Leonowens, avatar of numerous American advisors to Asia, taught objective reality to the people of Siam.

Simply civilizing Siam, however, is not enough for *The King and I*; it must also be secured for the non-Communist "free world." "Small House" ensures that American family values rather than the artificial and militaristic ones of mid-Victorian England will be the measure of civilization in the musical. Until the production of Stowe's novel at the King's court, the British occupied an ambiguous position in the action. Anna and her son represent the civilizing force of English culture, but Britain is also an offstage villain threatening to gobble up little Siam and spread more pink ink (the map color of the British empire) across the globe. How to use civilization to contain an expanding imperial power is one of the major questions of the show. The relevance to American international interests in 1951, with Joseph Stalin's new empire in Eastern Europe, the recent "fall" of China, and the ongoing Korean conflict, must have been apparent to all in the audience; once again, pink ink, now deepened into red, threatened to overflow attempted containment and engulf more nations. Like the change that occurred in Anglo-American relations during the 1940s, *The King and I* effectively passes the prestige and responsibility of world empire from British into American hands in return for a "special relationship" which acknowledges the wisdom of British civilization and its legacy in the United States. In addition to containing the march of empire, "Small House" demonstrates that proto-American Anna, with can-do ingenuity, is able to trick the decadent British into believing that show matters more than substance.

Rather than endorsing British imperial might, *The King and I* saves Siam for the seemingly softer empire of American modernization, primarily by naturalizing the values of American capitalism. In the ideology of the Cold War, Communism was not only wicked and powerful; it was also unnatural. Historian James Wilson Gibson remarks that "Communism as the ultimate foreign Other had a theoretical position already prepared for it" by American capitalism: "Capitalists, both the old variant called 'laissez faire' and the new capitalist order coming into existence during the war, understood themselves as being modeled on *nature*. If capitalism was nature, then communism by definition had to be *anti-nature*. By logical extension, if capitalism represented the natural economic structure of all nations, then by definition a Communist movement could only be *foreign*; it had to come from the *outside* because nature itself occupied the *inside*" (emphasis in original).[33] Gibson's logic rests on the notion of categories as containers, an either/or logic that grounded much cold war thinking. Business-class spectators, of course, easily identified capitalism as the "natural" condition of the world.

Like nearly all musicals, *The King and I* takes no obvious "stand" on American capitalism. Nonetheless, as in most musicals, Rodgers and Hammerstein arrange things so that nature aligns with capitalism and triumphs over arrangements of power constructed as arbitrary and artificial. Historian Thomas Haskell has convincingly demonstrated that the promise-making and promise-keeping of verbal and written contracts was fundamental to the development of capitalism in the West.[34] While the musical underlines the King's desire for commerce with the West, it also makes it clear that his commitment to slavery and tyranny undermines it. Much of Anna's struggle with the King hinges on his unwillingness to keep his promises to her — his desire to retain his traditional power as an arbitrary despot. "Small House" dramatizes their conflict when King Simon of Legree destroys the happy home of Uncle Thomas, Little Eva, and Little Topsy in the Kingdom of Kentucky to persecute the slave Eliza for running away. In addition to its other lessons, Hammerstein's version of *Uncle Tom's Cabin* argued the superiority of contractual agreements over tyrannical power. His choice of Stowe's novel and Abraham Lincoln's Civil War is particularly significant in this context, since both signaled the end of traditional economics and the rapid expansion of contractual relations in industrializing America. In the last scene of the musical, when the King's son is preparing to take power, the audience is led to believe that promises, contracts, and eventually the rule of law will ensure the moral and material progress of Siam. Legally binding contractual arrangements are natural in the world of *The King and I*; despotic power and the rule of force, whether Siamese or British, are not.

Further, natural feelings hold the key to the utopian Family of Man in the musical. Sympathetic Asian characters, although culturally "Other" on the outside, fall in love just like Americans when their predestined heartthrob touches them on the inside. When Anna sings "Hello, Young Lovers" for the King's wives, the audience is in no doubt about the universality of romantic love. Touched herself by the young love of Tuptim and Lun Tha, Anna risks her position in the palace to aid them. Her production of "Small House" is intended as a direct challenge to the King's presumably unnatural right to take numerous wives. It also motivates Tuptim, performing as the narrator of the show, to interrupt the production to exclaim: "I too am glad for death of King [Simon of Legree]. Of any King who pursues a slave who is unhappy and wish to join her lover" (56). Later that evening, Tuptim and Lun Tha attempt to flee the King's palace, much as Eliza fled from Legree. *The King and I* understands romantic love as the natural expression of an inner self beneath an outer facade of cultural and racial difference. In matters of the heart, culture and race are only skin deep.

The casting of the musical also encouraged American audiences to believe that Asian culture could easily be shed when "universal" values were at stake. As producers of *The King and I*, Rodgers and Hammerstein apparently exercised no consistent policy articulating relationships among the ethnic features of a performer, the ancestry of his or her character, and the general importance of the performer and/or character to the production. Yul Brynner's King may have become, as Frank Rich noted recently, "as much a part of our collective unconscious as the Statue of Liberty," but Rodgers and Hammerstein considered several others for the role—all, including Rex Harrison, ethnically "Caucasian"—before auditioning the bald Russian.[35] A white American played the Crown Prince while an Asian American performed the counterpart role of his sister, Princess Ying. According to an article in *Collier's*, Rodgers and Hammerstein cast "children of Oriental, Negro, and Puerto Rican extraction" for the King's Siamese offspring.[36] A few critics tut-tutted these random matchups of performer and character, but it is evident from several reviews and articles that most Americans, long accustomed to a variety of actors playing "Oriental" roles, were not troubled by the casting. Of course they would have responded quite differently had Asian American or black performers been cast in "white" roles. In this regard, Rodgers and Hammerstein continued the traditional double standard regarding casting and race.

One result of this double standard for the representation of Siamese characters, however, was to disembody the culture of Siam ostended in the production. Audiences could not watch a performer and know from his or her ethnic features alone which culture the performer was representing. Spectators needed the aid of costumes, makeup, and the dramatic narrative to figure it out. In effect, spectators were induced to understand "Siamese" as a performance in itself, a matter of external role-playing involving a darker or lighter shade of grease paint and other theatrical trappings. With Western characters, however, the audience could presume that the "inside" matched the "outside"; the actor underneath the role always looked the part. Since essentialism in casting was the norm for Western characters, Rodgers and Hammerstein's characters from other cultures appeared to lack an essence, an "inside." Following the cognitive logic of containment in characterization, when any performer can play Siamese, the "inside" of any Siamese character can be anything at all. Hence, the lack of discernible casting conventions contributed to the audience's belief that Siamese people already were or could easily become just like "us," like white Americans.

By naturalizing and universalizing economic and romantic relationships, *The King and I* helped to legitimate and extend the myth that the creators and characters of musical theater are just plain folks. In her book *The Hollywood Musical*, Jane Feuer points to the paradox of movie musicals masquerading as folk art. The Hollywood musical, she says, tries to cancel out the alienating effect of its mass art relations "by creating humanistic 'folk' relations in the films."[37] Movie musicals, for example, generally pretend that their acting and dancing are spontaneous, not rehearsed, that amateur entertainment is better than the professional kind, and that backstage communities can be a microcosm for world community. In this regard, the production of "Small House" within *The King and I* followed the conventions of the Hollywood musical. Like the shows thrown together in an old barn by Judy Garland and Mickey Rooney in their films together, "Small House" trumpets its connections to folk traditions by its joyously "amateur" joining of Siamese storytelling and dance conventions and American popular fiction. (Robbins's choreography, Jo Mielziner's settings and lights, and Irene Sharaff's costumes, of course, made it one of the best amateur productions ever mounted on any stage.) By rehearsing and producing a show together, the musical suggests, Anna and Tuptim forge a community that transcends race, culture, and privilege; their metatheatrical backstage family provides a better model for international relations than does the artificial pomp and circumstance of the King's ambassadorial dinner. As in most shows-within-the-show in Hollywood musicals, "Small House" suggests that a utopian Family of Man is just around the corner if only folks will recognize their common natural humanity.

Like *The King and I* and other backstage musicals, the plays of William Inge also featured "performed" moments within the larger enactment of the play. Although these are instances of social performance in which actor-characters never directly address the auditorium audience, they occur at significant moments in all of his major plays from the 1950s. Frequently, character-spectators secretly gaze at the physical beauty of others temporarily placed on view. In *Come Back, Little Sheba*, for instance, Lola (the mother-figure of the plot) spies on their boarder, a lovely college girl, and her muscular boyfriend, who strikes artistic poses in his underwear for his art-major date. Lola even watches them "spooning" and encourages her husband to join in her voyeuristic pleasures. While *Sheba* moved toward moments of metatheatricality in 1950, *Bus Stop* at mid decade clearly distinguished between two levels of role-playing on the stage. More than *Sheba*, it also encouraged the audience — both the other characters on stage and the spectators in the Broadway theater — to enjoy them. Set in a small midwestern cafe where the major characters wait out a snowstorm before continuing their trip, *Bus Stop* featured a "talent show" to pass the time. One character plays his guitar, two others struggle through the balcony scene from *Romeo and Juliet*, and Cherie, a nightclub singer, performs "That Ole Black Magic." The performances in both of these plays revealed psychological information about their character-spectators and character-actors; but, just as importantly, they invited the Broadway audience to examine role-playing interaction as a significant force in the shaping of personality.

Dark at the Top of the Stairs is painfully ambivalent about the power of play-acting. Sonny's fascination with Hollywood stars and parlor performances is crucial in this regard. Initially, the drama uses Sonny's desire to collect photographs of 1920s Hollywood stars and perform monologues at family gatherings as evidence of his need to escape into pre-Oedipal fantasies. When Sammy arrives, Sonny pulls him into this private Hollywood world with pictures and swashbuckling death scenes involving Sammy's sword. Soon after Sonny presents his rendition of "To be or not to be . . . ," Sammy promises to take him to Hollywood to meet his mother, a film actress. By the middle of Act III, after Sammy's suicide has been reported, performing parlor monologues and dreaming of Hollywood stardom have been firmly linked to death. Nevertheless, near the end of the play, when Sonny has nearly resolved his Oedipal problems, Inge approvingly sends him out to perform his *Hamlet* monologue for the neighbors. And Rubin, now returned to the Family Circle, compliments his son for "gettin' to be a regular Jackie Coogan" (301), a Hollywood child star in the 1920s. The play remains conflicted about the ethics of role playing, the injection of theatricality into everyday life.

Part of the ambivalence toward self staging in *Dark at the Top of the Stairs* has to do with the racialized position of actor-characters who intentionally perform for others. As critic Richard Dyer notes, rationality and spirituality, the essential attributes of whiteness in American culture, are fundamentally disembodied and invisible; whiteness may be a skin color, but its cultural claim to truth resides in the mind and the spirit. "Coloredness," in contrast, has been manifest since slave auctions and blackface minstrelsy in sexualized bodies performing for Others. Dyer concludes that "the ultimate position of power in a society that controls people through their visibility is that of invisibility, the watcher."[38] Hence the invisible voyeurism of spectating has been inherently "white" in American culture, while performing runs the risk (and opens the transformative possibility) of positioning the actor as a racialized Other. As both outsider and performer, Sammy Goldenbloom in *Dark* occupies two positions normally accorded to blacks. Suddenly in Inge's script (if not fully in Kazan's production), a darkly handsome Jewish boy is performing in the front parlor with all the panache of Al Jolson or Eddie Cantor. Like those blacked-up Jewish entertainers from the 1920s, Sammy embodies the energy and sexuality of the racial Other.

Inge's fascination with but ambiguity about the performing self, however, had more to do with sexual orientation than with race. A closeted homosexual during the 1950s, Inge was hypersensitive to his own social performances and the role-playing of others. While publicly donning the mask of available bachelor, privately Inge suffered from bouts of alcoholism, depression, and thoughts of suicide. Although the "talking cure" of psychoanalysis helped to steady his social performances, Inge remained shy and withdrawn, even with directors and most actors, throughout the decade. In *Dark at the Top of the Stairs*, his most autobiographical play, Inge seems to have used both Sonny and Sammy to represent different aspects of his personality. Like Sonny, Inge's portrait of his own childhood, he remained a "mama's boy," feeling most at home in the company of motherly women. Sammy, however, is the consummate social performer of the play; like Inge in adulthood, Sammy kept thoughts of his Otherness at bay through good manners, bursts of energy, and the illusion of effortless charm. Inge carefully monitored his social performances to keep from betraying the guilty secret of his sexual orientation. For Inge, role-playing was both necessary and dangerous. *Dark* is primarily a Freudian allegory resting on essentialist premises of identity. But a secondary, covert theme of the play suggests that social performance may be just as important as psychobiology in the construction of the self.

Musical comedy in the 1950s resolved the cold war conflict between the performing self and the essential self through the ideology of stardom. Because stars always "played themselves" and performing was a part of their essential natures, it was no problem for Gertrude Lawrence and Yul Brynner to become Anna and the King in their scenes together and then shift from representational into self-expressive mode when they sang and danced. And within the drama of the musical, strategic role playing is one of the keys to Anna's success. In "I Whistle a Happy Tune," as in numerous other instances in the musical, the mask can become the self if properly acted. *King and I*, however, framed Anna's acting differently from the King's in ways that preserved her whiteness and underlined the racial Otherness of the Siamese monarch. While the audience could see that Anna was self-consciously enacting several roles to win the King's favor and bend him to her will, the King never saw Anna as a performer. She, in contrast, was allowed to gaze on the King's awkward playing of Western roles as a patient mother might watch her child trying on adult shoes in a struggle to grow up. Broadway spectators saw that Anna could always fool the King with her performances, but he never could fool her with his.

A master stage director and acting teacher, Anna also instructs the King's wives in the performance of whiteness in "Small House" and nearly whitens the King himself in "Shall We Dance." When the new boy-king bows in Western style to Anna at the end of the play, her lesson in racial assimilation is complete: racialized Others have learned to perform like whites to gain civilization. Significantly, however, the boy-king remains an "Oriental" because Anna and the audience can see that he is still performing. His whiteness is not yet internalized and invisible. Indeed, his skin color means that the new king can only be a similitude of whiteness, a bad Method actor of another racial position, because his inside psychology can never take over the performance of his outside behavior. Nonetheless, the new king's attempt to embody whiteness is enough to gain him entrance into the Family of Man, if not, eventually, into the bedrooms of a bunkered American family. Anna retains superiority and agency in the world of her expanded family; she is the only part of her Family Circle that can always represent the whole of it. Indeed, performances of family dramas like *The King and I* and *Dark at the Top of the Stairs* proffered a relatively simple answer to the problem of historical agency in cold war America: focus your energies on the bunkered family at home or the Family of Man abroad and you can change the world! That this mode of agency was contained by the Family Circle bothered few business-class Americans during the 1950s.

This celebration of female agency within the family partly accounts for the placement of compulsive characters in these plays. *The King and I* deploys the schema of compulsion to depict type characters in the thrall of tradition, such as the King's prime minister and some of his wives. Unlike Anna, the King's metaphorical wife, the King's Siamese wives imitate Western fashion in a slavish manner and pay for their automatism just before the arrival of the British ambassador. In walks the King, and his wives, dressed in hoop skirts, prostrate themselves on the floor in a traditional act of obeisance. Anna, standing upstage of them, realizes that their Western dress is all outward show, lacking even undergarments. As the stage directions indicate, "Anna sees the naked truth" (45) and warns the King of the potential social impropriety. While the King occasionally acts in compulsive ways, total robotic conformity to the ways of tradition would render him unfit for the civilizing makeover that Anna must be able to perform on his character. To be effective, Anna's agency requires relative flexibility from other members of her metaphorical family.

Where the objectification of compulsive characters in *King and I* led to laughter, similar embodiments of compulsion in *Dark at the Top of the Stairs* evoked pathos. Whenever she is disappointed, sixteen-year-old Reenie Flood goes into the parlor to practice the piano. Her automatic rendition of the scales, pounded out several times during the play, reminded the audience of both her teenage desperation and the deadening of passion that has come to characterize the Flood's marriage. Like the King in the musical, however, Reenie must be reformable if Cora's agency is to be effective within her family. And it is; Reenie begins to grow out of her compulsiveness when Rubin returns. Cora's brother-in-law Morris, however, is outside of the Family Circle of the play and remains unregenerate. His compulsive fastidiousness contrasts with the boisterous physicality of the departed Rubin; it reminded both sisters (and the audience) that even rough sexuality is better than none at all. Other moments of objectification and compulsion occurred in the production of both plays, strategically placed as a foil to emphasize the relative freedom and agency of Mom in solving family problems.

In general, the possibilities for agency and the relegation of compulsive figures to minor type characters in Family Circle plays demonstrate that this rhetorically successful genre was less influenced by radiophony than were plays featuring Empty Boys. Of course the schema of containment massively informs Family Circle plays; and radio listening, as already discussed, did play a significant role in inducing Americans to construct much of their culture with containment at its center. *Allegoresis*, another mark of the radiophonic, also remains important in *King and I* and *Dark at the Top of the Stairs*. But the ur-narratives shaping both dramas, *Uncle Tom's Cabin* and the story of Oedipus (à la Freud), control less of the dramatic action than do the narratives of Adam and Eve and the Passion of Christ in *The Seven Year Itch* and *A Hatful of Rain*. This contrast between the genres suggests that as long as Americans believed that they could keep conflicts within a contracted or extended Family Circle, the rest of the world would be a less threatening place.

■ The question of agency in the theater (as in life) is linked directly to ethics; the ability to act is always informed by how one should act. The "mothered performances" of the 1950s embraced and proliferated a morality that was primarily utilitarian in orientation. This ethical theory, in turn, worked within what Lakoff and Johnson call the nurturant parent model of morality, a significant bulwark of containment liberalism. In the nineteenth century, when Jeremy Bentham and John Stuart Mill preached its virtues, utilitarianism advocated social policies that could produce what Mill called "the Greatest Happiness" for the greatest number of people. Within this conception, the citizens of a nation-state were understood as family members needing to cooperate to decrease their pain and maximize their pleasure. According to Mill: "Utility would enjoin that, first, the laws and social arrangements should place the happiness ... of every individual as nearly as possible in harmony with the interest of the whole; and secondly, that education and opinion, which have so vast a power over human character, should so use that power as to establish in the mind of every individual an indissoluble association between his own happiness and the good of the whole." Significantly, the part-whole schema gives coherence to this passage; in a perfect country, each citizen-part will embody the values of the nation-whole. To effect this harmony, Mill relies on empathy, what he later terms "the desire to be in unity with our fellow creatures," to help in constituting and legitimating the nation as a family. Sometimes, however, the state must act as a nurturant parent toward its willful children-citizens, helping them to realize their true interests and full potentials. This ethical position underwrote much of state socialism in Europe and influenced many U.S. liberals eager to shape a culture of caring during the 1950s.[39]

For most Americans, however, the bunkered family and the Family of Man limited the reach of utilitarian ethics. Within this constricted or inflated Family Circle, the containment version of utilitarianism elevated the primary nurturer, Mother, to a position of authority. Musicals, domestic plays, and other "mothered performances" from the 1950s located spectators as loving, fair-minded mothers who always put their family's welfare above their own. From that position, audience members were invited to empathize with "their" family on stage, celebrating their victories, weeping at their defeats, and occasionally withdrawing their sympathy from onstage mothers who did not live up to the expectations of containment culture. Spectators watching *King and I* and *Dark at the Top of the Stairs* learned through theatrical experience that teaching, loving, advising, encouraging, and even hectoring in the name of family "togetherness" (which might be redefined in utilitarian terms as "the Greatest Happiness" for the whole family) was a high moral calling. Putative mothers in the audience were also positioned to become the gatekeepers of the Family Circle. Were the performances of whiteness by groups of Outsiders sufficiently believable to allow them through the front door? Mothers eager to shape an international Family of Man were willing to overlook differences of coloration and invite them inside if the imitations of civilization were sincere. Thus Anna and the audience metaphorically became the mothers of Siam by the end of the musical. Assimilation to white ways might produce toleration and even sympathy from the bunkered family, but back in America keeping the Other outside the door seemed safest. Thus, in *Dark*, Sammy must die so that the Flood family may flourish.

This difference between the racial dynamics of Family of Man and bunkered-family plays goes a long way toward explaining the different valuation of social performance in *King and I* and *Dark at the Top of the Stairs*. While the proto-American insider, Anna (played by a white star), is the best performer in the musical, Sammy, proto-homosexual/black outsider and victim of suicide (played by a young man who might be a Jew), is the best actor in *Dark*. "Mothered" musicals can celebrate the naturalness of performing, while domestic plays underline its artificial, staged quality. This difference between the natural and the artificial, however, rested on the ideology of whiteness in cold war America. *Dark at the Top of the Stairs* raises the specter that whiteness, despite its essential invisibility, can be performed and that ethnic or racialized Others like Sammy may "pass" for white. Unless one were careful, the grownup Sammys of the era—homosexuals, Communists, and especially blacks—could infiltrate the bunkered family and influence its children. (Kazan made this problem less pressing through his casting and staging choices, but it remained.) Of course this difficulty of simulated whiteness did not arise in Family of Man musicals because skin color remained to mark the foreigners who had learned to imitate white ways. Further, by naturalizing and infantilizing the foreign Other, such musicals could contain the potential disruption of expert role-playing.

■ Naturalizing social performance to neutralize its danger was a liberal strategy that also shaped the scene designs of many stage productions during the 1950s. Ben Edwards's design for *Dark at the Top of the Stairs* featured a large window at the rear of the set through which the audience saw part of the front porch and the natural world beyond. Edwards also located nature in the upstairs hallway, hinting at the sexual fears behind adjacent bedroom doors—fears unresolved until Cora runs up the stairs to join Rubin's "naked feet." The vertical thrust of Edwards's huge stairs, which visually pointed directly at the hallway, kept audience members vaguely aware of the "possible threat" (as the stage directions specify) of the upstairs darkness. Nature as a secret dark place could be found in other areas of his masterly set as well. Walter Kerr opened his insightful review of the production with this observation: "It's a curious fact that almost the first thing you notice about designer Ben Edwards' long, rambling, old-fashioned Oklahoma living room is the alcoves: the dim recess where a swinging door opens and closes silently, the tiny back parlor where the player-piano lurks behind fringed drapes, the empty space that surrounds the front screen door and seems to lead off to nowhere." For Kerr, the darkened, improbable alcoves of Edwards's design (and Jean Rosenthal's lighting) established the atmosphere for "the kind of play that a child might have overheard as he passed, hastily or idly, through the back corners of his parents' lives."[40] In short, the setting suggested the psychoanalytic action to come. Illuminate the darkened hallways and alcoves of the mind, the design promised, and nature will provide.

The sets and lights for *Dark at the Top of the Stairs* followed the conventions of spatial order that Jo Mielziner and Tennessee Williams had already elaborated, initially in *Glass Menagerie* (1945) and later in *A Streetcar Named Desire, Summer and Smoke* (1948), and *Cat on a Hot Tin Roof*. Inge followed Williams's lead in depicting interiors that flowed into exteriors and in dividing up his playing areas into distinctive kinds of spaces. As Thomas Postlewait has noted, Williams generally established "three spatial realms that operate visibly and thematically in his plays: an enclosed space of retreat, entrapment, and defeat, a mediated or threshold space of confrontation and negotiation, and an exterior or distant space of hope, illusion, escape, or freedom."[41] In *Streetcar*, for instance, the stage-left bedroom where Stanley rapes Blanche is the space of entrapment; the center kitchen area for the poker night, the birthday party, and similar scenes is used for confrontation and negotiation; and the exterior of the apartment provides spaces for possible hope and escape. By linking space to psychology in these ways, Williams and Mielziner were able to help their spectators follow the shifting moods and meanings of their productions.

Mielziner, in fact, had already worked his psychologizing magic on an Inge play before Edwards and Rosenthal designed *Dark at the Top of the Stairs*. Mielziner's scenery and lighting for the 1953 production of *Picnic*, Inge's most popular play of the decade, derived from the spatial logic he had established in working with Williams. *Picnic* is a play about youthful sexuality bursting out of conventional repressions. The backyard facades of two small midwestern houses shaped most of the playable stage space. The interiors of both houses—viewed through open doors and windows and heard through short arguments among characters the audience cannot see—come to represent the defeated, entrapped world of midwestern conformity. Mielziner and Josh Logan, the director of *Picnic*, used the broad triangular space created by the two houses placed alongside each other and by the line of the proscenium as the general space for confrontation in the play. A practical open porch that wrapped around the two visible sides of the larger house became the threshold between its open exterior and confined interior, thus facilitating an easy flow between them. Mielziner, Logan, and Inge also incorporated a distant space of escape and freedom — an upstage panorama of a small town painted on an enormous backdrop that towered over the roofs of both houses.

As the two young people in *Picnic* fall in love, Mielziner's version of nature implicitly reinforces their rejection of small-town repression and their embrace of Dionysian release. It also naturalizes the elements of social performance in the comedy-drama. Inge's play occurs over the twenty-four hours of a late summer day, flowing from a bright morning sky, to a radiant orange sunset, to a harvest moon, and returning, again, to morning sunlight. Mielziner used the towering backdrop to bathe the setting and characters in this reassuring cycle of nature. His design carved out three areas in particular where characters could draw attention to themselves and others could watch their performances — the raised platform of the porch, the partly framed space between the two houses, and an upstairs window in the larger house. Both of the teenage girls in the play use the back porch as a stage. And in one scene the upstairs window provides a voyeuristic look for two of the male characters (and the audience) at the pretty older sister as she is dressing for the picnic. Within Mielziner's environment, such performative moments became a "natural" part of sexual interaction between men and women, not a seedy peep show. Nature was smiling when Inge's characters performed for each other.

In *Dark at the Top of the Stairs*, Inge, Edwards, and Rosenthal constructed a psychologized spatial order similar to that of Mielziner's *Picnic*. Edwards's set featured a tiny front parlor, placed upstage of the general living space, where Reenie practiced her piano and Sonny retreated to gaze at his collection of film star photos. Although not completely enclosed, this space localized the entrapment and defeat felt by the Flood children, which threatened to overtake the family. The downstage living room, the space in front of the stairs, and the stairway landing functioned as Inge's spaces for general dramatic conflict. Here characters confronted their personal and familial problems and eventually resolved them. The place of "hope, illusion, escape, and freedom" in the play, of course, was the space where nature rules, the dimly lit upstairs hallway. As had Mielziner in *Picnic*, Edwards used these spaces to underline those moments when the characters consciously perform for others within the world of the drama. For example, the front parlor in Edwards's design, framed by a mini-proscenium, showcased Reenie's piano performances and Sonny's recitation of a monologue from *Hamlet*. And the landing of the stairs helped Cora to stage her announcement to Sonny that he must no longer seek the kind of affection from his mother that he enjoyed as a little boy. Inge deployed a spatial grammar for both plays that had broad psychological legibility and appeal for business-class theatergoers.

Significantly, Edwards's setting for *Dark at the Top of the Stairs*, like Mielziner's for *Picnic*, also embodied the principle of family flow that shaped the suburban ideal of postwar America. Apart from the bedrooms, the typical ranch house of the period organized interior rooms to flow into one another to increase efficiency and family "togetherness." The ranch house had eliminated the small, semiprivate spaces of the larger Victorian home used for reading, music, and intimate conversations. Though Ben Edwards designed a turn-of-the-century house, its hallway, stairs, living room, and front parlor effectively suburbanized the interior space of the play. His design allowed for an easy flow among the major rooms of the setting; Sonny and Reenie never have to knock on a closed door before entering a room, even though a more thoroughly realistic treatment of the historical architecture would have mandated this. The upstage parlor, though equipped with sliding doors, is never closed off. Its player piano, placed along a side wall, looked as though it could be traded in for a television—as happened to many parlor pianos during the 1950s. The marital bedroom in ranch houses—often the only space for adult privacy—tended to accrete more mystery than did its Victorian predecessor because it was one of the few spaces closed to the curious eyes of children after they reached school age. Likewise, the dark at the top of Inge's stairs, the place of adult sexuality, carries all the ambiguous meanings of repression, release, and possible "togetherness" of marital bedrooms during the "Freudian fifties."

Jo Mielziner's design for *The King and I* carried the suburban ideal a step further. Not only did it suggest an easy flow among all the rooms of the King's palace, but it also merged interior and exterior space. Nestled close to the ground with picture windows and "window walls" opening to the outdoors, the suburban ranch house, as understood by its advocates, attempted to unify the family with nature. Belief in the restorative power of nature had played a significant role in earlier architectural home styles, but the ranch house could realize this desire more fully because, presumably, it opened into a controlled suburban environment, not noisy, dirty urban streets. Many ranch houses in the 1950s featured porches, patios, and breezeways designed to minimize the difference between inside and outside.

No doubt Mielziner's palace rooms for *The King and I* struck spectators as curiously exotic, but if they looked closely they might also have found similarities to Hollywood and magazine versions of suburbia. Most of Mielziner's settings for the musical virtually eliminated the distinction between inside and outside. The full-stage rooms of Act I, scenes 2 and 6, for instance, opened at the rear to a vista of Bangkok; these spaces seemed half balcony or patio and half roofed interior, separated at mid stage by columns and a ceiling facade. Decorative motifs of spiraling towers and twirling tree branches, both "outside" and "inside" in these spaces, unified the craftsmanship of humans with the work of nature. Even in recognizably interior spaces, such as Anna's classroom with a world map on its back wall, Mielziner merged exterior and interior motifs. The scrim drop for this scene featured an organic design of branches and leaves through which could be seen the painted spires and decorative gables of the Bangkok backdrop. Spectators looking at *The King and I* saw an exotic suburbia with natural and constructed forms harmoniously flowing together. As in *Picnic*, they could see that human actions and institutions operated within the larger container of nature.

The designs of Jo Mielziner, the single most productive and influential creator of stage environments in the postwar era, encouraged Broadway audiences to engage in *allegoresis* when they experienced his designs. Designing since the 1920s, Mielziner broke with the dominant conventions of realism for serious dramas with the production of *Winterset* in 1935. Although the author, Maxwell Anderson, wanted a naturalistic setting for his play, Mielziner convinced him and the director that Anderson's poetic tragedy would be better served by a more impressionistic setting that drew on the imaginations of its spectators. Photographic realism, noted Mielziner in his *Designing for the Theatre*, "would hem [*Winterset*] in and pull the audience earthward."[42] The result was a setting that

Jo Mielziner's set for the schoolroom scenes of The King and I. *Vandamm photo, courtesy New York Public Library.*

induced the audience to follow the upward sweep of the Brooklyn Bridge, emphasizing the hopefulness of the play.

Mielziner's interest in freeing spectators from the concrete trappings of realism into the more generalized realms of the imagination suited the abstracting and allegorizing tendencies of the early Cold War. It also aligned his work with the dematerializing cultural effects of radiophony. Nearly all of his post-*Winterset* designs, for instance, took the ceiling lid off of the typical box set. As design historian Orville K. Larson remarks, Mielziner led the charge against enclosed box settings, which rapidly disappeared after the war: "The upper edges of the interior walls now blended into the exterior surroundings of the setting's locality. Interiors now became but a small part of the universe."[43] Mielziner's setting for *Salesman* in 1949—the frame of a house with few walls and no ceilings, a high, painted backdrop, and a gauze scrim for the memory scenes— canonized his mix of scenic realism and expressionism. Mielziner relied on the same or similar design elements, which emphasized line over mass and the vertical over the horizontal, in some of the most influential productions of the early Cold War, including *Summer and Smoke* (1948), *Guys and Dolls* (1950), *A Tree Grows in Brooklyn* (1951), *The Lark* (1955), and *Look Homeward, Angel* (1957), as well as *A Streetcar Named Desire, Picnic, The King and I*, and *Cat on a Hot Tin Roof.*

As designer Howard Bay remarked ruefully in 1974, "The craze for gauze cum toothpick skeletons ruled the '50s and was deemed the only Genuine, Official type of 'Imaginative' Scenery—the only correct form of chic decor." Mielziner's gauze and toothpick settings also influenced the design work of Donald Oenslager, Lee Simonson, and David Hays during the decade. Even Howard Bay designed a light, flow-through, interior-exterior setting, including a room without a ceiling, for *Toys in the Attic* by Lillian Hellman, a thoroughly realist play in most respects, in 1960. But "something got mislaid in the switchover from the solid boxes [for interiors of realist plays] to the skeletons and distressed masonry," said Bay. "That something is the emotionally charged environment totally hemming in fictional characters." What theorist Bert States terms "naturalism's dense centripidal mass" gave way to the lighter design elements of color and line.[44]

As Bay recognized, the era of gauze and toothpicks took the spectators' minds off the material conditions that shaped dramatic characters and allowed more Platonic, universal considerations to influence their impressions; in short, away from materiality and history and toward abstraction and allegory—also toward metatheatricality. The painted scrim that Mielziner used to such effect in *The Glass Menagerie* (1945) and many subsequent productions drew specifically on the schema of containment, the cognitive logic that allows for the perception of metatheatricality. In *Menagerie*, the seeming solidity of the exterior setting for Tom's introductory monologue seemed to melt away to reveal an interior setting depicting his memory of life with his mother and sister several years before. Painted scrim and modern lighting allowed for the revelation of one world within another. Thomas Postlewait finds that this shift away from a mimetic and toward an "emblematic" mode of theater in the designs of Mielziner was particularly beneficial for the plays of Tennessee Williams,[45] who worked with the designer on seven productions before 1963. Certainly it deepened their psychological complexity, celebrated their expansive lyricism, and heightened their moments of metatheatricality. But it also detached Williams's plays from the actuality of their historical circumstances. For example, Williams had envisioned that the bedroom setting of *Cat* should appear still redolent of Straw and Ochello's homosexual love. Instead, Mielziner's setting, following strong advice from Kazan, slighted such concrete specifics to emphasize the potentially allegorical aspects of the play. His setting favored the dematerialized "grandeur" of Kazan's conception but also allowed for the performance of *discours* inherent in Williams's script.

Mielziner, like all professional designers during the 1950s, worked within the spatiality of the proscenium stage, a stage designed initially for grandeur and abstraction. Virtually all theater buildings in the Broadway area, most of which dated from the turn of the century through the 1920s, mandated that spectators watch a production that was framed and visually contained by a proscenium arch. Proscenium spatiality draws on the cognitive schemas of center-periphery and balance as well as containment for its visual legibility; the *mise en scène* of any good proscenium image allows for the dominance of center stage and the importance of visual balance for the audience. In this regard, it is unlike Elizabethan staging and theater-in-the-round, which also privilege the three-dimensional presence of the actor instead of flattening out the human form, another consequence of the picture frame stage. Given the cognitive logic of proscenium viewing, it is not surprising that this mode of theatrical architecture was initially adopted and came to be prized by the royalty and aristocracy of Europe. The proscenium stage provided an appropriate space for the theatrical realization of Renaissance and Baroque allegories of power.[46] Balance, center-periphery, and containment also facilitated the visual hierarchies of the bourgeoisie in the painterly pictorialism of the nineteenth century.

By the 1890s, when realism was becoming the dominant style of production, the separation of a darkened house from a lighted stage by a proscenium arch had become the conventional mode of theater lighting and architecture, and these technologies facilitated the transition to the new style. Photographic realism, however, emphasized visual masses that were not necessarily or ideally centered and balanced and drew attention to the shared material reality of both spectator and actor, qualities that proscenium staging could not emphasize. Even with sophisticated electric lighting, proscenium viewing flattened the dense materiality of real objects on the stage. By the 1950s directors and designers had been using the proscenium stage to depict apparent "slices of life" for several decades, but the proscenium had always been better suited for abstraction and allegory. In abandoning many of the conventions of realist design, Mielziner and other postwar designers returned spectators to modes of viewing more in keeping with the traditional cognitive possibilities of proscenium spatiality.

Several of Mielziner's designs effected this break from realism by accentuating the visual containment produced by the proscenium arch itself. The typical interior or exterior setting for realism encourages the illusion that other rooms or a similar outside environment continue offstage; the arch only happens to frame part of a much larger reality that is, finally, coextensive with the real world. In this convention of realism, the arch frames the illusion but does not implicitly contain it. Several of Mielziner's most distinctive cold war settings, however, place a unit set center stage and surround it with visual cues that cut it off from the presumably real world offstage. As a result, the arch, visually joined by the stage floor, creates the illusion of a contained world separated from the rest of reality rather than continuous with it. Stanley and Stella's New Orleans apartment, for example, floated visually against an expressionistic backdrop that emphasized the grotesque extremes of life in the Quarter. Similarly, the Lomans' house in *Salesman* had little visual connection to an offstage world; it was either overwhelmed by the threatening apartment buildings behind it or bathed by golden-green leaves, in the memory scenes, on the scrim in front of it. Mielziner used the barrier of the proscenium arch to effect the containment of the onstage worlds of *The King and I*, *Cat on a Hot Tin Roof*, and several scenes from many musical comedies as well. As if to compensate for visually separating the proscenium picture from the real world offstage, Mielziner naturalized many of his onstage abstractions by featuring painted trees, clouds, and even water as prominent elements in his designs.

The cold war interest in naturalizing spatial abstractions found its popular epitome in Disneyland. The "lands" of Disney's amusement park in Anaheim, California, leaned heavily on allegory. Ur-texts, many of them Disney films, stood behind all of the spaces of Frontierland and Fantasyland, but also of Adventureland, which was based on *The African Queen*, the Humphrey Bogart/Katharine Hepburn film (1951). Spectators strolling down Disney's Main Street in 1955 when the park opened were reminded of comfortable narratives of the American past. Tomorrowland thrust visitors into the future by recalling sci-fi stories and corporate advertising fictions. Disney's "imagineers," the Hollywood designers of the park, embedded their architecture, rides, and landscape in numerous familiar texts, most prominently fairy tales, famous American novels, and popular films — many of which the Disney Studios had already produced. Unless they performed *allegoresis* by linking their experience of Disneyland to prior texts, spectators could make little sense of the major "themes" of this theme park.

In his *New Yorker* review for *The King and I*, John Lardner noted "a touch of Walt Disney" in "I Whistle a Happy Tune." He was probably thinking of Disney's "Whistle While You Work" from the feature-length cartoon *Snow White and the Seven Dwarfs* (1937). The connections between Disney's version of family entertainment and the sunny vision of a Rodgers and Hammerstein musical were more numerous than this statement suggests, however. Like many musicals, Disneyland was another "mothered" (or, more specifically, "uncled") production of the Cold War. As cultural historian Karal Ann Marling relates, Disneyland, even more than the setting for *The King and I*, epitomized the suburban ideal of the postwar era. Emerging from Walt Disney's disgust with the amusement centers of dirty, noisy Los Angeles, Disneyland, says Marling, "was a kind of pre-EPCOT utopia, a better, cleaner, more pleasant and resonant American place than 1955 afforded the average urbanite who drove to Anaheim on the interstate and the Santa Ana freeway."[47]

Family Circles, Racial Others, and Suburbanization 175

Taking advantage of the nearly perpetual good weather of southern California, Disneyland allowed for a flow between the natural and the architectural that average suburbanites could only dream about. Unlike most suburbs of the '50s, Disneyland was not racially exclusive. By universalizing suburbia, however, Uncle Walt effectively whitened his utopia; signs of African American culture, if not of black Americans, were as invisible in Disneyland as in other areas of the United States beyond the inner cities. Once inside this suburban ideal, park-goers were treated just like family. In sharp contrast to the old amusement parks, the ambience of Disneyland was wholesome and restrained—no candy butchers, freak-show talkers, and ticket sellers to excite and cheat visitors.

Many of the rides in Disneyland extended the kind of empathetic projection that spectators experienced at a musical drama. In addition to offering the kinesthetic delights of all amusement park rides, Disney typically invited a willing suspension of disbelief from his participants in which they could temporarily share in the adventures of a star character from one of his films. As Uncle Walt put it, "What youngster hasn't dreamed of flying with Peter Pan over moonlit London? Here in the 'happiest kingdom of them all,' you can journey with Snow White through the dark forest to the diamond mines of the Seven Dwarfs; flee the clutches of Mr. Smee and Captain Hook with Peter Pan; and race with Mr. Toad in his wild auto ride through the streets of old London Town."[48] Likewise, in Frontierland, spectator-participants could "paddle" a canoe like Davy Crockett as flames engulfed a settler's cabin on a nearby island. As these examples illustrate, Disneyland usually erased the stars from the make-believe of these rides so that the children could become their own heroes, rerunning Disney films in their heads with themselves in the leading roles. For adults, the rhetoric of Disneyland alternately positioned them as nurturing parents and as coddled children, encouraging them both to facilitate their children's enjoyment of the park and to become kids again by immersing themselves in playful fantasy. As in musical drama, they could enjoy mothering and being mothered. Most of the friendly cartoon characters that peopled the park, like the Mickey Mouse played by female employees, were maternal, with rounded shapes and comforting dispositions.

With an innocence and arrogance typical of American liberalism in the 1950s, the makers of Disneyland assumed that their values were universal. The lands of Disney's magic kingdom purported to encompass the fantasies of humankind. "It's a Small World After All," a ride first built for the New York World's Fair in 1964 and later incorporated into a corner of Fantasyland, best exemplifies Disney's one-world universalism. Participants sat in small boats pulled through a spectacle of animated dolls with enlarged heads (like the heads of infants) and costumed in an international-style pastiche of colors to suggest different nationalities. The dolls danced to an ingratiating song with the refrain "It's a small world after all." Like the Family of Man exhibit at MOMA, the human face—in this case, a child's face—became the icon of commonality uniting humankind. More sentimentally than Edward Steichen, however, Disney suggested that childhood innocence and imagination were the keys to world peace and happiness. Significantly, "It's a Small World" nearly reprised a song from the 1959 musical *Gypsy*—"Small World"—which celebrated the universality of family love.

Disney's films and television programs during the 50s, like many family-centered plays and musicals, rested on the cold war assumption that family entertainment played a significant role in fighting international communism. A 1956 promotional film on Disneyland assured viewers that the park "could happen only in a country where freedom is a heritage and the pursuit of happiness a basic human right." Cultural historian Steven Watts aptly names the immense social resonance of Disney's cold war entertainments "the Disney Doctrine." At the center of this doctrine was the notion that "the nuclear family, with its attendant rituals of marriage, parenthood, emotional and spiritual instruction, and consumption, was the centerpiece of the American way of life. Illustrated through a long string of productions, this idea became a bulwark in America's defense against enemies, both foreign and domestic."[49] The Disney Doctrine had wide appeal, primarily because it idealized the mother-centered family that many Americans turned to for security, comfort, and morality during the 50s.

The same liberal, utilitarian morality found in most family-centered plays anchored the Disney Doctrine. Disney reassured white nuclear families that they were the source of empathic feelings and thus the potential saviors of uncivilized humanity. For the bunkered family, the Disney Doctrine taught that empathetic parenting ensured psychological independence, social responsibility, and democratic citizenship. Better than a Mielziner stage design, Disneyland combined the built and the natural, legitimating white suburban privilege. Like many musicals, Disneyland contained the threat of the performative by wrapping it in a sentimental notion of childhood fantasy. Children of all ages, for example, could temporarily set aside their essential identities to play the role of Peter Pan on one of Disney's rides and easily return to their individual selves after the ride was over. By joining commercial profit and white suburbia to the rhetoric of mothering, Disneyland became a kind of utilitarian utopia: the amusement park seemed to many to provide the Greatest Happiness for the greatest number of American families. Best of all, the Disney Doctrine in all its manifestations eliminated or infantilized the threat of Otherness.

■ There can be little doubt that Lorraine Hansberry despised Disneyland and all it stood for. A romantic socialist, Hansberry had little use for a liberal utilitarianism that proffered the oppressions of cold war capitalism and reassured white families that suburban living and mass-produced fantasies could secure the good life for all. Although critics and biographers of Hansberry have noted the radical nature of her political beliefs, these insights have not substantially reshaped the understanding of her most popular play, *A Raisin in the Sun*. As a Marxist, she rejected much of the dominant culture's analysis of relations between black and white Americans and its prescription for future interracial progress. After a decade of the Cold War, Broadway spectators, including most of the black bourgeoisie who attended *Raisin*, did not expect that a play centered on "the Negro problem," as American race relations were commonly termed, would draw on the racial politics of the Popular Front. For much of the mid 1930s through World War II, American Communists and progressives attempted to forge an interracial coalition to abolish racism by establishing socialism in the United States. *Raisin* is more indebted to the legacy of Hegelian Marxism current during the Popular Front years than to the Christian fervor, civil disobedience, and liberal agenda of the early Civil Rights movement, with which it is familiarly associated. Although Hansberry believed that she had depicted a slice of universal Marxist history in *Raisin*, her white audience in 1959 primarily saw it as an allegory about a universal family with many of the same hopes and frustrations as themselves.

Born in 1930, Hansberry matured in a social milieu that was thoroughly committed to fighting American racism through Popular Front socialism. W. E. B. Du Bois, Paul Robeson, and Langston Hughes visited the Hansberrys at their home in Chicago, where Lorraine's father ran a successful real estate business. Imagining herself one of Du Bois's "talented tenth," Hansberry joined the Communist Party and led the Young Progressives Association at the University of Wisconsin, which campaigned for Progressive candidate Henry Wallace in 1948. After studying directly with Du Bois at the New School for Social Research in New York, she went to work at Paul Robeson's magazine *Freedom* and became associate editor in 1952. At *Freedom*, Hansberry was influenced by Louis E. Burnham, the legendary organizer and hero of the Southern Negro Youth Congress from the 1930s. She participated in the campaigns defending the outspoken radicalism of Du Bois and Robeson from federal harassment during the early 1950s. When the State Department revoked Robeson's passport, Hansberry traveled to an international peace conference in Uruguay as his representative.

After the success of *Raisin* in 1959, followed by other play productions, essays, and fiction, Hansberry continued to affirm her debt to Marxism. In her 1963 "Tribute" to Du Bois, she stated that his life "teaches us to look forward and work for a socialist organization of society as the next great and dearly won universal condition of mankind." Steven Carter, author of the best critical work on Hansberry's drama, concludes that she "was unquestionably a Marxist but in the largest sense of this frequently narrowed and abused term, as unhindered by doctrine and as open to new ideas as was Marx himself. . . ."[50]

Despite Carter's knowledge of Hansberry's politics, his own treatment of *Raisin* does not deploy Marxist criticism to understand her play.[51] Alternatively, I suggest that the meanings that Hansberry hoped spectators would take away from *Raisin*—though not the reasons for its enormous popularity in 1959—can best be understood within the tradition of Popular Front socialism still very much alive among radicals in the 1950s, who were fighting what they took to be the intertwined evils of class- and race-based oppression. No doubt Hansberry learned much of her Hegelian Marxism directly from Du Bois, whose reading of both thinkers pushed his own politics to the left of most other progressives in the 1940s and 1950s. Among young black radicals of Hansberry's generation, the early work of Sidney Hook, the editorial efforts of Louis Adamic, and especially the postwar sociology of Oliver C. Cox were also influential. In *Towards the Understanding of Karl Marx* (1933), Hook downplayed Marxian determinism and emphasized the importance of ideas in animating historical action. Hook's Hegelian and pragmatic version of Marxism had wide influence within American socialism. As the founding editor of *Common Ground* in 1940, Louis Adamic urged that "race" be eliminated as a category in public discourse. Instead, Adamic favored the more neutral and encompassing term "ethnicity" and published authors who celebrated working-class commonalities among a variety of American ethnic groups (including African Americans) during the 1940s. The editorial position of *Common Ground* influenced several leftist magazines of the 1950s, including *New Challenge* and *New Foundations*, which published several of Hansberry's early essays. Oliver C. Cox's *Caste, Class, and Race* (1948) linked American racism to the rise of Western capitalism. With insights that anticipated much of the current scholarship on the social construction of whiteness, Cox stated that the dynamics of capitalism led the ruling class and others to racialize certain ethnic groups during specific historical periods.[52]

Cox's 1948 book directly challenged the methods and conclusions of Myrdal's *An American Dilemma*, the guide to racial reform favored by containment liberalism. Myrdal's underlying explanation for the enormous disparities in wealth, power, and living standards among blacks and whites was his notion that white Americans perpetuated a caste system to keep the races apart. This led Cox to complain that Myrdal had ignored economic forces and class oppression to lay "the whole meaning of racial exploitation" at "the altar of caste." One result of this caste system, according to Myrdal, was that every facet of black culture had become "a distorted development, or a pathological condition, of the general American culture."[53] Preferring more orthodox Marxist explanations, Cox refused to psychologize the situation of black families and identities.

Cox also disagreed with Myrdal about the solution to American racism. For Myrdal, the key to racial progress in the United States was simultaneously to play upon white guilt regarding past and present racial oppression and to encourage blacks to assimilate to white norms. Myrdal believed that U.S. citizens were united ideologically through an "American Creed" that stressed the equality of all citizens. When most white Americans came to understand themselves as racist sinners against this creed, they would change their ways and allow blacks greater freedom and equality. (Not coincidentally, the logic of civil disobedience and Christian brotherhood in the early Civil Rights movement followed Myrdal's suggested appeal to the conscience of white America.) Myrdal assumed that black assimilation to white norms would gradually reverse the pathological conditions of black culture and ensure a racially integrated "modern democracy" in America. For his part, Cox also believed that gradual assimilation was inevitable, but he utterly rejected as "mystical" the assumption that white guilt could help to transform the racial status quo.[54] For Cox, the establishment of democratic socialism in the United States was the only solution to American racism.

Like Cox's study, *A Raisin in the Sun* rejected Myrdal's analysis of and purported solutions to "the Negro problem" on every significant point.[55] The first two acts of the play make it clear that the Younger family in Hansberry's play suffers not from a general caste system in America but from the material conditions of poverty, racism, and class exploitation. Influenced by the socialist dramas of Sean O'Casey, *Raisin* details the degradations of ghetto existence for the Younger family in Chicago just as carefully as *Juno and the Paycock* observed the oppressions of slum life in Dublin. The first act shows a tired family waking up amidst threadbare furniture in a cramped kitchen–living room, with the adults fighting about bathroom rights and money while preparing for school or menial jobs. In this stifling environment, it is better for Walter to "eat your eggs" and "go to work" (33), as Ruth, his wife, advises — even to a dead-end job as a chauffeur — than to compound frustration by dreaming of economic success. Poverty and exploitation are slowly squeezing the life out of the Younger family. Indeed, these material conditions have already killed the family patriarch, Big Walter, and a third child, Claude, brother to Walter and his sister Beneatha, before the play begins. When Lena, the new matriarch of the family, announces to Ruth that she is considering using the insurance money from Big Walter's death to buy a new house, the imperative to move is achingly apparent.

By Act II, the poisonous influences of the ghetto are clearly taking their toll on the family. Walter desires the insurance money to become part-owner in a liquor store, Beneatha wants it to finish her schooling regardless of her brother's ambitions, and Ruth, in despair, has made an appointment to abort her pregnancy. These factors motivate Lena to purchase a house in a working-class white neighborhood: "I just seen my family falling apart today . . . just falling to pieces in front of my eyes. We couldn't have gone on like we was today. We was going backwards 'stead of forwards — talking 'bout killing babies and wishing each other was dead" (94). Lena purchases a house in Clybourne Park not to break out

Walter Lee Younger/Sidney Portier confronts Beneatha/Diana Sands as Mama/Claudia McNeil looks concerned in Act I of A Raisin in the Sun. *Friedman-Ables photo, courtesy New York Public Library.*

of a caste system and integrate a white neighborhood but to save her family from physical and spiritual strangulation. For much of the first two acts, Hansberry's focus on the material realities constraining the Younger family is unrelenting. Race and class dynamics based on concrete economic forces, not an abstract belief system, shape their lives. In his review of *Raisin* for the *Nation*, Harold Clurman called it an "old-fashioned play," because Hansberry's interest in the material realities of black life differed from the usual abstract and lyric "neo-realism" of most of her contemporaries.[56] He was right; with the romantic Marxism of Sean O'Casey as her model, Hansberry's play was much closer to Odets in the 1930s than to Miller in *Salesman* and his later plays.

In an essay written shortly before the opening of *Raisin*, "The Negro Writer and His Roots: Toward a New Romanticism," Hansberry decried "the villainous and often ridiculous money values that spill over from the dominant culture" into the black community.[57] While the primary target of her scorn for capitalist values in the play is George Murcheson, the spoiled son of a black real estate entrepreneur, Hansberry is more interested in analyzing the corrosive effects of capitalist "money values" on Beneatha and Walter. Despite her ambition to become a medical doctor, college student Beneatha "flits" among boyfriends, intellectual positions, and expensive fashions and hobbies; she denies her class position and family responsibilities. Walter desires to become the chief provider and moral leader of his extended family, but he also conspires behind their backs to profit from the pain of others by opening a liquor store, temporarily giving in to the American dream of status through material success. Both want to be "givers" like their father, but historical circumstances push them toward the role of "takers," in the language of the play. And both, especially Walter, threaten the integrity and strength of their family. Insofar as the Youngers are typical of other ghettoized blacks in postwar America, Hansberry, like Myrdal, notes the tendency of black culture to model itself on the white majority, often with pathological results. *Raisin*, however, lays the blame squarely on American capitalism. Beneatha and Walter must transcend their capitalist "illusions"—a term Hansberry regularly deployed in her journalistic essays—and both do so in the course of the play.

Several sociological studies in the 1950s based on the premises of Myrdal's *American Dilemma* concluded that matriarchal dominance within the black family was retarding the modernization of black culture and leading to widespread hostility and aggression in black males. Hansberry's portrait of Lena Younger was based on her knowledge of women's traditional roles in African tribal culture. Consequently, although it does demonstrate the repressive side of matriarchy, it also celebrates its potential for nurturance and progressive action in Marxist-Hegelian terms. In an interview with Studs Terkel, Hansberry admitted that Mama's control of her family during the play was, at different times, both tyrannical and loving. Out of these contradictions, however, came what Hansberry termed "the embodiment of the Negro will to transcendence": "It is she who, in the mind of the black poet, scrubs the floors of a nation in order to create Black diplomats and university professors. It is she who, while seeming to cling to traditional restraints, drives the young on into the fire hoses and one day simply refuses to move to the back of the bus in Montgomery."[58] Hansberry's allusions to the scrubwomen of Langston Hughes and the actions of Rosa Parks center her portrait of Lena Younger. Although Hansberry had no more practical use than Beneatha for Mama's Christian God, she understood that history often works in ironical, Hegelian ways. The synthesis of Mama's contradictions produces a "will to transcendence" that pushes universal history forward.

Hansberry had already struck the chord of Hegelian romanticism in her essay "The Negro Writer and His Roots." In this piece, initially delivered as a speech at a black writers' conference, Hansberry pitted Sean O'Casey, "warrior against despair and lover of mankind," against absurdist playwrights, beat poets, and others she felt had given up on the struggle against oppression. In classic Hegelian fashion, Hansberry explained how the best dramatic art must synthesize apparent opposites: community history with international history, political truth with aesthetic beauty, and what is with what can be. The most romantic Hegelian moment in her talk occurred at the conclusion, when she called on artists not simply to look for the meaning of the universe but to "*impose* the reason for life on life" (her emphasis).[59] Lena Younger, for all of her foolishness, recognizes that the survival of the family outweighs every other consideration, and she imposes "the reason for life" on her family.

Indeed, the clash of opposites and their eventual resolution in a new synthesis structure the general action of the play. Out of the problems created by capitalism and the family's fight against racial oppression emerges a new familial solidarity. Beneatha rejects the blandishments of George Murchison's capitalism and comes to understand her higher purpose as a "giver" of life through doctoring. Walter's recognition that self-respect and familial pride must transcend capitalist values eventually unifies his entire family. Realizing that her initial opposition to Walter's liquor store idea blocks his path to full maturity, Lena Younger gives him part of the insurance money, even though she remains opposed to his decision. When Walter loses the money to a crook, he bitterly concludes that he must give in to capitalism and racial oppression and arranges to sell the house his mother has just purchased to the Clybourne Park Improvement Association for the financial gain they offer. In the end, however, Walter's humanist values overcome the "money values" of an oppressive America, and he refuses to sell. "[He] come into his manhood today," says Mama (151) after this climactic scene, a recognition that Walter's choice of family solidarity over capitalism has elevated him into the position of head of the Younger family formerly held by his father. (For all of Hansberry's celebration of female power in *Raisin*, the play concludes like most socialist plays and novels of the 1930s; males, it seems, will lead the revolution.) Indeed, the Younger family is united as never before in anticipation of the racist degradations and possible violence that await them in Clybourne Park. As in Hegel's notion of the ideal drama, the conflicts of *Raisin* work toward "transcendence," a higher stage in history than was possible before the play began. More specifically, the synthesis at the end of *Raisin* produces family solidarity against racial and class oppression; the Younger family joins the larger social movement that Hansberry and other radicals were struggling to maintain in 1959.

From the socialist perspective of *Raisin*, the fight against capitalism is worldwide. Through the characterization and goals of Joseph Asagai, a Nigerian university student fond of Beneatha, the Youngers become representative historical types whose struggles to free themselves from the oppressions of capitalism are offered as instances of a general struggle for freedom. Beneatha and Walter come to understand what Asagai already knows—that all people are a part of larger wholes, including families, nations, and international classes. Part-whole relationships do not stop at the boundary of the Family Circle; human beings can effect change at the worldwide level. Asagai's lecture to Beneatha in Act III—perhaps Hansberry's most idealistic speech in the play—demonstrates the Hegelian function that individuals can play in the process of universal history. Despite the poverty, ignorance, and dangers in rural Nigeria, Asagai vows to return to his village: "I will teach and work and things will happen, slowly and swiftly. At times it will seem that nothing changes at all . . . and then again the sudden dramatic events which make history leap into the future. And then quiet again. Retrogression even. . . . Perhaps [for my work against illiteracy and disease] I will be butchered in my bed some night by the servants of empire. . . . They who might kill me even . . . actually replenish all that I was" (135–36). Here and elsewhere, Hansberry projects Asagai as a potential Hegelian hero of history, a world-historical individual who embodies History with a capital "H." Hence even Asagai's martyrdom would feed the fight for freedom.[60] Asagai's heroism shines less brightly after Beneatha decides not to marry him — she has a different role to play, Hansberry assures us, in the transformations to come — but this minor setback does not deflect him from his mission.

Like Asagai, the Younger family, in its own small way and mostly unwittingly, becomes a part of the historical process of liberation. Hansberry makes explicit the link between the fight for independence in Africa and the struggle for dignity and economic justice in the United States at the beginning of Act II when Walter imaginatively becomes an African warrior. "That's my man, Kenyatta," shouts Walter, referring to the Kenyan leader recently imprisoned by the British authorities for protesting colonialism (78). Although the primary action of the play focuses on the Youngers' struggle for familial unity and against segregated housing in the context of 1950s Chicago, Hansberry wants the audience to understand the potential ripple effect of their victory. The Younger family becomes a synecdoche for all families pushing for liberation. From a Marxist perspective, *Raisin* approaches allegory, with its ur-text as *The Communist Manifesto* and the Youngers as Everyfamily, marching toward the Revolution. Of course few Americans in 1959 were prepared to read it as Marxian *allegoresis*. Most probably saw the Youngers in romantic, not allegorical, terms as a general symbol of the fight for freedom. Indeed, the weight of materiality and the specificity of history in *Raisin*, as in *Juno and the Paycock*, pull the cognitive dynamics of "part-whole" in the play toward romantic Marxism rather than Platonic allegory.

In her own comments on *Raisin*, Hansberry relied on Hegelian imagery to describe the drama. In a piece originally published in the *Village Voice* in the midst of *Raisin*'s run, she compared Walter and the Younger family at the end of the play to Anne Frank, Joan of Arc, the black children who integrated the schools of Little Rock, and other historical heroes. These figures, marching for justice, were a part of "the golden thread of history," she stated. Hansberry also compared Walter to Willy Loman in the same article but noted the superiority of her character to Miller's in terms of progressive action. Unlike Willy, who kills himself, she wrote that "more sophisticated confusions do not yet bind [Walter] and he can make a small protest against the status quo." Hansberry also used *Raisin* to undermine conventional notions of racial assimilation. When asked by an interviewer why she had Beneatha looking to Africa for a sense of her identity, Hansberry stated: "[P]erhaps we must take a more respectful view of the fact that African leaders today say that with regard to Europe and European traditions in the world that we will take the best of what Europe has produced and the best of what we have produced and try to create a superior civilization out of the synthesis. I agree with them and I think that it commands respect for what will be inherently African in the contribution."[61] Here, as elsewhere in her public statements, Hansberry did not offer an authentic black culture as a superior alternative to assimilationism. Rather, in the tradition of the Popular Front and universal socialism, she looked forward to a new civilization that would synthesize the best of all world cultures. Like her play, Hansberry endorsed a romantic socialism in which history created possibilities for humans to join or get swept up in movements that might lead to a higher, deracialized culture. The path of progress led beyond racial pride and modest reform to cross-racial movements and the Hegelian utopia of a "superior civilization." Her sense of historical agency as a Marxist moved far beyond the confines of containment liberalism; a family might move history, but only if it were in accord with universal historical dialectics.

For Hansberry, relations of class could be more important than race in positioning people to march in the vanguard of change. The characterization of Karl Lindner, the representative of the Clybourne Park Improvement Association, is crucial in this regard. On the one hand, Lindner is an obvious rebuke to the assumption by Myrdal and others that white guilt would lead whites to reform themselves. Myrdal had written that the "ordinary white man," if given correct information, would alter his beliefs about blacks; "people want to be rational, to be honest and well informed," he stated.[62] Lindner, of course, believes that he is already rational and well informed. With no trace of hypocrisy or guilt, he justifies racial segregation on humanistic grounds, explaining that "our Negro families are happier when they live in their own communities" (118).

Lindner's justification also rests on a realistic understanding of property values and racism under capitalism. As presented in *Raisin*, the Clybourne Park Improvement Association is acting rationally to protect its homeowners' investments. Hansberry, who knew firsthand about real estate values and racial dynamics from her father's business in Chicago, signals her understanding of the dilemma of these working-class homeowners by characterizing Lindner as mild-mannered and friendly, not racist and threatening. He and his neighbors know that selling to black people will cause a steep decline in their property values. In short, she wants her audience to see that the Youngers face a structural obstacle in capitalism best solved through the abolition of private property; white guilt and humanitarian openness will not solve their problem. In the short term, she encourages her audience to foresee the same kind of massive resistance, race baiting, and harassment for the Youngers that she faced with her own family when they integrated a Chicago neighborhood during her childhood. In the long term, however, her portrait of Lindner does not rule out the possibility of cross-racial alliances based on a commonality of class position to fight the structural impediments of capitalism.[63]

Raisin, however, does not altogether live up to Hansberry's hopes to craft a metonymic image of the class dynamics powering universal history. The Hegelian structuring of the play suggests that a hardy new people—symbolized by Mama's still struggling plant throughout the drama—will transcend spiritual and material oppressions to continue the fight for freedom. On the spiritual side, the play plunges the family members into a near acceptance of racial inferiority before they conquer their fears and emerge with new self-respect and fighting spirit. Regarding the materialism of *Raisin*, Walter's loss of the $6,500 that his mother gave him to invest for Beneatha and to buy his liquor store inflicts no permanent damage on the family. In the end, the loss is simply written off, and the family resolves to work all the harder to pay the mortgage on the new house. This all too casual resolution of the problem implicitly contradicts Hansberry's sharp focus on the determining pressures of poverty during the first two acts of the play. It also points up a logical problem in Hansberry's plot. Walter could recoup some of the money he has lost by dealing with Lindner and selling the house back to the

Clybourne Park Improvement Association for a profit. The Youngers would then have more money for a down payment on another house and could perhaps finance some of the costs of Beneatha's medical school—an immense burden that the ending of the play ignores. Of course, given the rhetoric of the play, such a resolution is unthinkable. As Hansberry has structured audience response, the "money values" of capitalism are antithetical to the freedom of the Youngers. In her determination to damn capitalism, she ignored the material circumstances of her characters at the end of the drama. *Raisin* suffers from some of the same idealizing Platonism of other cold war productions.

Hansberry's rejection of "money values" also compromised her hopes for cross-racial cooperation. However mild-mannered Lindner may be, he remains a symbol of white money in conflict with family pride. When Walter rejects his offer, he expels the Other from the family circle. As in *Dark at the Top of the Stairs*, *Raisin* removes the threat of an "exotic" outsider so that a bunkered family may survive and flourish; it deploys the same dramatic narrative as in many other domestic plays, films, and television shows operating within containment liberalism. Business-class audiences comfortable with this formula would understand *Raisin* as yet another play arguing primarily for the protection of the family, thus marginalizing or ignoring Hansberry's political agenda. Once again, an intruder had pierced the container of the Family Circle and had to be expelled. The familiarity of *Raisin*'s narrative would have serious consequences for the play's reception. In its rejection of "money values" and its "othering" of a white outsider, the ending of *Raisin* is much more Hegelian than Marxist. Or, to put it in terms more relevant to the cold war 1950s, the dematerializing effects of the radiophonic, firmly rejected for two acts of the play, return in the end to claim a sentimental victory.

Of course a dramatic triumph of universal abstractions over the limitations of materialism presented no problem for Broadway audiences and mainstream critics. Insofar as they understood the play in universal terms at all, it was as Family of Man allegory, not Hegelian-Marxist metonym. Several writers misquoted Hansberry as stating that the characters in her play embodied such universal features that they could have been any race at all. Anxious to dispel this contention, she told Studs Terkel in a 1959 interview that good dramatists always "pay very great attention to the specific" in order "to create the universal." "In other words," Hansberry continued, "I've told people that not only is [the Younger family] a Negro family, specifically, and definitely, and culturally, but it's not even a New York family, or a southern Negro family. It is specifically about Southside Chicago." Like Odets and other socialist playwrights from the 1930s, Hansberry used the specific language, cultural habits, and social situations of a particular ethnic group to suggest the dilemma of many groups at a similar stage of history. From her Popular Front perspective, the African American experience of the Younger family could be both particular and universal.[64]

Not surprisingly, the reception of *Raisin* in 1959 ignored Hansberry's socialist history lesson to focus on what critics took to be the Family of Man values of the play. The drama opened on 11 March at the Ethel Barrymore Theatre with Claudia McNeil as Lena, Sidney Poitier as Walter, Diana Sands as Beneatha, and a cast that included Ruby Dee, Louis Gossett, and Douglas Turner. Lloyd Richards directed—his first Broadway job. The play ran into 1960 for a total of 530 performances. All of the principals, especially Poitier and McNeil (both of whom had enjoyed successful film careers before *Raisin*), won lavish praise from the Broadway reviewers. Completely misreading Hansberry's political intentions, however, most critics breathed a sigh of relief that *Raisin* did not agitate for radical change. Richard Watts, Jr., for instance, rejoiced to find "no special pleading in the play," and Robert Coleman complimented Hansberry for refusing to mount a "soapbox." Brooks Atkinson believed that the production "will destroy complacency" but noted that the author had no "axe to grind." In praising *Raisin* for refusing to indulge in any "abnormal exploitation of the current racial problems," John McClain spoke more overtly than other critics to the anxiety of his white readers.[65] Sadly, the critical reception of *Raisin*'s politics mostly mirrored the response of the FBI agent sent by Hoover to watch Hansberry's play. He concluded that it "contains no comments of any nature about Communism but deals essentially with negro [sic] aspirations, the problems inherent in their efforts to advance themselves, and varied attempts at arriving at solutions."[66]

Following their relief at what seemed to be the play's moderate politics, the Broadway critics relaxed to weep over a "beautiful, loveable play," in the words of John Chapman. "The number of tears shed by presumably worldly first-nighters must have set a new record at the Ethel Barrymore last evening," admitted Frank Aston in his review. The production "may rip you to shreds," he concluded, but "[i]t will make you proud of human beings."⁶⁷ The spectacle of white audience members in tears over the tribulations of a black family was hardly new in the American theater, of course. The primary effect of this outpouring at the production of *Raisin* in 1959, as it had been for *Uncle Tom's Cabin* more than a hundred years before, was to awaken white spectators to the possibility of common human feeling across racial lines. Once again, white folks were surprised and heartened to discover that they could share in the emotional problems of a black family struggling for freedom. While it is always difficult to account for spectators' emotional responses, it seems likely that a mix of guilt and self-congratulation powered the empathetic flood of tears among white audience members that greeted *Raisin* in 1959.

Writing in 1969 about viewing *Raisin* ten years before, James Baldwin stated: "I personally feel that it will demand a far less guilty and constricted people than present-day Americans to be able to assess [Hansberry's drama] at all." Baldwin was perhaps the most perceptive observer of white guilt during the Civil Rights era. In *Ebony* in 1965, Baldwin noted that whites, looking into his or other black faces, saw skin color before they saw anything else—a pigmentation signifying, for them, "an appallingly oppressive and bloody history . . . a disastrous, continuing present condition which menaces them, and for which they bear an inescapable responsibility." Because history has treated whites in the United States so much better than blacks, however, "white Americans tend to believe that they [i.e., white people] deserve their fate and their comparative safety and that black people, therefore, need only do as white people have done. . . . But this simply cannot be said, not only for reasons of politeness or charity, but because white people carry in them a carefully muffled fear that black people long to do to others what has been done to them." Consequently, stated Baldwin, many white people are "impaled" like butterflies on their guilt and anxiety, fearful of opening a dialogue with blacks, "which must, if it is honest, become a personal confession." "No curtain under heaven is heavier than that curtain of guilt and lies behind which white Americans hide," concluded Baldwin. "The curtain may prove to be yet more deadly to the lives of human beings than that Iron Curtain of which we speak so much and know so little."⁶⁸

This "curtain of guilt and lies" shrouded the critical establishment in the professional theater just as completely as it blanketed much of the rest of white America in the 1950s. One way of avoiding down-home truths about racial injustice in the United States was to climb up the ladder of universality and make Platonic pronouncements about the Family of Man. After *Raisin* won the New York Critics Circle Award for the 1958–1959 season, critics beyond Broadway also hailed the drama's universality. Henry Hewes in *Saturday Review*, for instance, wrote that the play "deals with real people. The fact that they are colored people, with all the special problems of their race, seems less important than that they are people with exactly the same problems everyone else has. . . . [The Youngers'] interfamily joys and anxieties are universal ones." Gerald Weales wrote in *Commentary* that the basic strength of the play "lies in the character and problem of Walter Lee, which transcends his being a Negro." Like Willy Loman, stated Weales, Walter was trapped by a "false dream." Consequently, he concluded, "Miss Hansberry has come as close as possible to what she intended—a play about Negroes which is not simply a Negro play." In a narrow sense, Weales was correct; *Raisin* did stretch toward universality, but not the bland humanism that he supposed. Weales had taken Hansberry's complaint that few critics thought of comparing Walter Younger to Willy Loman and unknowingly turned it back on her play. In his allegorizing view, *Raisin* could be just as universal, and just as white, as *Salesman*. To celebrate *Raisin* for its Family of Man universality was also, in white America, to celebrate the United States as a racially blind nation for the world to admire and emulate. A review of *Raisin*'s pre-Broadway, New Haven opening in late January in *Variety* connected the success of *Raisin* to the propaganda battles of the Cold War. After praising the moving portrayals of Poitier and McNeil, the *Variety* reviewer called the play "great dignity-of-man propaganda."[69]

One white newspaper critic did question the emotional outpouring among white spectators that greeted the production. John Hastings, in a *Village Voice* article entitled "White Guilt or Northern Hypocrisy," wondered whether the mostly rich white audience at the Barrymore "saw any discrepancy between their emotional partisanship for a Negro family . . . and the fact that most of them would return to their homes in apartment houses that are as segregated as streetcars in the South." "Something about the applause at the final curtain," Hastings concluded, "struck me as profoundly guilty and of uneasy conscience."[70]

Hansberry noted that white guilt impeded a full understanding of her play in her *Village Voice* article comparing Walter Younger and Willy Loman. Professing astonishment that many critics failed to perceive Walter's "class aspirations" because they continued to stereotype him as an American primitive, Hansberry lectured her readers that the "much-touted 'guilt' which allegedly haunts most middle-class white Americans with regard to the Negro question would really become unendurable" if the image of "the simple, loveable, and glandular 'Negro'" were shattered. Unlike Myrdal and many American liberals, Hansberry recognized that white guilt, by itself, was a poor ally in the fight against racial and class oppression because guilt created anxiety that led whites to flee rather than confront and expunge the stereotypes that populated their cultural memories. Consequently, when "a new character [like Walter] emerges," guilt impedes whites from moving past older stereotypes to see him as different from previous "glandular" Negroes.[71] But Hansberry's essay was also a tacit admission that *Raisin* had failed to penetrate the white guilt that washed her drama in cathartic tears. By writing an article whose purpose was to animate a very different response to *Raisin*, Hansberry conceded that the play had changed very few white liberals into radical activists. Empathy with a black family fighting for its freedom was not enough to change white America.

Several mainstream reviews inadvertently supported Hansberry's contention that Walter Younger had been infantilized by white critics. Walter Kerr, for instance, fixed on Poitier's pose after Walter learns he has lost the family's money through his liquor store speculation: "[H]is arms rise in a limp and helpless arc until they seem to embrace a whole defeated race."[72] Kerr's smugness aside, the image of racialized men acting like spoiled or defeated children was hardly unique to *Raisin*; Yul Brynner had many such moments as the King of Siam. For white Americans, Poitier's Walter, like Brynner's King, were Empty Boys in need of mothering. White Empty Boys might be just as infantile and dangerous, but their whiteness entitled them to bask in ethical egotism. Racialized Empty Boys, however, had to be taught a lesson—and the best place for learning civilization was within the family. Here was another American boy who needed the tough love of a powerful mother!

If the Youngers could be understood as "just like us" under the skin, white viewers could transform *Raisin* into yet another mother-centered performance of the 1950s. Hansberry's ironic hero, Lena Younger, could become the black matriarch of the white imagination, a bossy but loving "mammy" figure leading her children toward assimilation. In his review, Chapman evoked the timeworn image of the black mammy by commenting that McNeil gave a "warm, big performance." Black actor Ossie

Davis wrote insightfully in 1985 that the "color-ain't-got-nothing-to-do-with-it" assumption on the part of white spectators watching *Raisin* became "fixed in the character of the powerful mother with whom everybody could identify, immediately and completely. [This] made all other questions about the Youngers, and what living in the slums of Southside Chicago, had done to them, not only irrelevant and impertinent, but also disloyal . . . because everybody who walked into the theatre saw in Lena Younger . . . his own great American Mama. And that was decisive."[73] *Raisin*'s invitation to identify with Mama was certainly familiar to audiences who had empathized with Anna in *The King and I*, Cora Flood in *Dark at the Top of the Stairs*, and numerous other stage mothers as they corralled their families into line for their own good. *Raisin* offered white spectators the opportunity to merge Family of Man and bunkered-family tropes. The "we" of the white audience could define a black family as "just like us" and further erase class and racial differences by imagining a shared sense of embattlement.

Claudia McNeil's performance as Lena confirmed Ossie Davis's remarks about a "great American Mama" inducing white audiences to overlook skin color (and class position). In Hansberry's play, Lena Younger is fallible and sometimes foolish as well as nurturing and noble. She reprimands Beneatha too harshly about religion at the end of Act I, scene 1, badly misjudges Walter's desperation, and consults none of her family or friends before putting down money on a house in a white suburb. After the revelation of Walter's loss of the money, Lena momentarily gives up on the dream of moving and begins to unpack the family's belongings. *Raisin* as written does not reduce the family to the morality of Mama. There are moments and scenes when her part in the family can stand for the whole of it, but other times when she is clearly wrong. And at the end of the play, Walter, by deciding that the family must move into Clybourne Park, replaces Mama's temporary matriarchy with his own authority; he becomes his father's son. All of the adult family members exercise limited moral agency in the world of *Raisin*. Hansberry's Youngers are not Cora's Floods or Anna's metaphorical family in Siam.

McNeil, however, ignored the contradictions and weaknesses of Hansberry's character and the larger arc of the narrative to create a figure nearly monolithic in her rectitude and righteousness. First-night critics spoke of her as a figure of "magnitude" (Watts), a "solid rock" (Kerr), or simply "the matriarch" (Atkinson, Watts, Aston).[74] In the 1961 film of *Raisin*, closely modeled on the Broadway production, McNeil's bulldog forcefulness filled the screen and dominated nearly every scene. (Poitier reported in his autobiography that he struggled to wrest onstage control from McNeil but—if the film version accurately reflected their battle for focus and dominance in the theater—rarely succeeded.)[75] For white business-class audiences, long familiar with the moral probity of scolding mammies on screen and stage, McNeil's Lena Younger became the ethical center of the play. McNeil probably reminded many whites in the audience of Ethel Waters in *The Member of the Wedding* ten years before, or perhaps of a racialized version of Ethel Merman, performing in *Gypsy* during the run of *Raisin*.[76] All three of these actors could induce spectators to position themselves, alternately, as mothers and children during the performance. Given the flood of tears that greeted the performance, it is likely that Walter Younger was not the only person in the theatre infantilized by the production.

Hansberry probably hoped that empathetic projection would transform some whites in the audience of *Raisin* into advocates of radical change. She drew on the rhetorical-dramatic tradition of O'Casey and Odets, in which spectator identification with lower-class characters in a romantic-realist play seemed to have effected progressive change in the status quo in the past. Further, the socialist legacy of the Popular Front also taught her that ideas could make a difference, especially in altering class and racial consciousness. But the racialization of African Americans had hardened by the 1950s. Where earlier in the century it had been possible for some Americans to understand blacks as simply another ethnic group and all poor ethnics as "workers" or "the people," the cold war consensus required water-tight containers for racialized others. Myrdal and liberal sociologists in the 1950s helped white Americans to confirm that blacks were either radically Other or potentially assimilable within an implicitly white Family of Man. The culture of liberal containment had no place for an image of a Chicago black family that could stand in for oppressed peoples everywhere struggling for liberation against capitalism and imperialism. Instead, white guilt ensured that *Raisin* would be made to recycle old stereotypes or, at best, to serve the meliorative goals of the early Civil Rights movement. *Raisin* may be criticized for its rhetorical naiveté—even in better historical circumstances, the political reach of the play among whites would probably be modest—but not for its author's radical idealism.

For black playgoers, however, *Raisin* probably carried more progressive meanings. Although the percentage of African Americans attending *Raisin* on Broadway was likely low, the later success of the film and numerous college, church, and community theater productions ensured that *Raisin* would become the best-known African American play among blacks by the mid 1960s. Critics in the African American press in New York dissented from the Family of Man universalism of white reviewers and greeted the play as an occasion for racial pride. The editors of *New York Age*, for example, urged their readers to attend the production because there were too many "Negroes in American walking around and not knowing who they are, or what they think, or what they feel . . . because they haven't resolved the problem of being Negroes and being proud that they are." Similarly, Anna Arnold Hedgman of the *Amsterdam News* praised the play for correcting negative stereotypes about blacks and told her readers that *Raisin* would spur them to "capture the strength which is in [their] roots."[77]

While neither of these reviews explored the radical politics of Hansberry's play, they at least called for action, mobilizing African Americans for the marches and lunch-counter sit-ins of the early 1960s. Recalling the impact of the play many years later, both James Baldwin and Amiri Baraka, theatrical contemporaries of Hansberry, came to believe that *Raisin* did substantial political work after its opening. Baldwin reported that "I had never in my life seen so many blacks in the theatre" when he attended the tryout production in Philadelphia prior to the Broadway opening. The black spectators, he noted, "supplied the play with an interpretative element which could not be present in the minds of white people: a kind of claustrophobic terror, created not only by their knowledge of the house but by their knowledge of the streets."[78] Most white critics overlooked the slow strangulation of the Younger family and did not comment on the firestorm of hatred that awaited them when they moved to Clybourne Park. Business-class blacks who saw *Raisin*, however—and who, as Hansberry's play reports, were just as ghettoized in the 1950s as poor members of their race—knew firsthand the claustrophia within and the fear outside of the slums that contained their lives.

Baraka criticized the play in 1959 as politically conservative, but by 1986 he had reversed his opinion. "We missed the essence of the work," he admitted: "that Hansberry had created a family on the cutting edge of the same class and ideological struggles as existed in the movement itself, and within individuals. . . . The concerns I once dismissed as 'middle-class'—buying a house and moving into a 'white folks' neighborhood'—actually reflect the essence of black will to defeat segregation, discrimination, and oppression. The Younger family is our common ghetto Fanny Lou Hamers, Malcolm X's, and Angela Davis, etc." *Raisin*, Baraka concludes, "was political agitation."[79] Baraka may be generally correct with regard to the play's effect on many African Americans from 1959 through the early 1960s. By then, however, most American blacks regarded the kind of political agitation that Hansberry really had in mind—the Younger family as avatars of a worldwide revolution against capitalism and imperialism—as *passé*, if not unpatriotic. Even Baraka in 1986, after his own turn to Marxism, did not analyze *Raisin* in the kind of Hegelian socialist language that Hansberry might have recognized as her own. Nonetheless, his arguments, like the comments of Baldwin, underline crucial differences between the black and white receptions of *Raisin*.

■ As previously noted, the "mothered performances" of the 1950s helped white Americans to solve a crisis in historical agency. Concerns that social performance might be contradicting essential identity, caused in part by new media of communication, destabilized role models and undermined traditional notions of purposeful practice. "Let Mom do it" contained imaginative social action within the family. More successfully than Inge, Hansberry naturalized the disruptive potential of social role playing through the realist conventions of *Raisin*. Beneatha's and Walter's play-acting as an African drummer and warrior at the start of Act II, for example, grows out of their fantasies and what Hansberry would like us to believe is their African heritage. In both cases, temporarily playing the role of an "Other" expresses a part of themselves; it does not destabilize their identities or the general notion of normative identity put forth in the play. Indeed, there is even a tinge of antitheatricalism in *Raisin* that undermines the possibility of a politically effective metatheatricality. When Walter, in despair after losing the money, calls Lindner and demonstrates how he will grovel before "Captain, Mistah, Bossman" (144), he refers to this performance several times as putting on "a show." In *Raisin*, overt theatricality signals insincerity and ethical failure.

Unlike Hansberry, African American playwright Alice Childress recognized that metatheatricality had the potential to challenge the nearly invisible hegemony of American whiteness. The off-Broadway production of her *Trouble in Mind* in 1955 took a backstage look at a white producer-director's attempt to rehearse a mostly black cast in a purportedly humanistic drama about lynching in the South.[80] When a black actor refuses to portray the suffering-mammy figure of the script, the director angrily justifies his "humanitarian" point of view and then cancels the rehearsal, later sending a message that fires the upstart actor. Based on Childress's own experience as a performer, *Trouble in Mind* was a call for radical change in the power disparities between black actors and white producers and, implicitly, between blacks and whites in society. It was also a caustic analysis of the universalizing psychology of whiteness. Childress's director practices the techniques of the Method and assumes that they give him access to the inner truths of his black performers. Rather than change his Platonic beliefs, the white director simply closes his eyes to the reality of racial differences that emerge in the rehearsal process. The play takes metatheatrical aim at the denial and aggression caused by white guilt.

Trouble in Mind may be the closest that an American play during the early cold war theater ever got to Brechtian aesthetics and politics. The continual shifting between the "real" rehearsal situation and the melodrama-within-the-play underscores the problematics of agency for blacks in terms that cannot be accommodated by liberal values. Further, the utopian thrust of the comedy-drama—Childress invites the audience to compare African Americans with the Irish before independence from Great Britain—points to a future of revolutionary action. It is clear from *Trouble in Mind* that such Brechtian rhetoric focused on the realities of race in America might have engaged some white spectators to challenge their own racialized guilts and investments in ways that *Raisin* could not. Equally clear, however, is the fact that Broadway wanted nothing to do with this play. At a time when successful off-Broadway shows were often transferred to the Great White Way, Childress's drama, which enjoyed a modest run and won an Obie for playwriting, received no more professional productions in the 1950s.

Fragmented Heroes, Female Others, and the Bomb

Herbert Blau, looking back from 1964 at his twelve years with the San Francisco Actors Workshop, used a striking metaphor of containment to characterize the theater of the 1950s. It was, he said, "a carapace in which one secreted his fear and trembling, muffled his indignation, and relieved outrage by innocuous subjective ejaculations. If it wasn't therapy, it wasn't collective action either—which had gone out with the thirties." Blau primarily blamed the threat of nuclear war for making human beings in the theater tremble, muffle, and relieve themselves like armored bugs. "What do you do about the Bomb? All questions coagulate in that," he stated.[1] Like strontium 90, the radioactive material from nuclear tests that worked its way into the food chain, even altering cows' milk, the cultural fallout from nuclearism shaped significant components of the American theater of liberal containment in the early Cold War.

Soon after General Thomas Farrell witnessed the first explosion of an atomic bomb in the New Mexico desert on 16 July 1945, he wrote:

> The effects could well be called unprecedented, magnificent, beautiful, stupendous and terrifying. No man-made phenomenon of such tremendous power had ever occurred before. The lighting effects beggared description. The whole country was lighted by a searing light with the intensity many times that of the midday sun. It was golden, purple, violet, gray, and blue. . . . It was that beauty the great poets dream about but describe most poorly and inadequately. Thirty seconds after the explosion came first, the air pressing hard against the people and things, to be followed almost immediately by the strong, sustained, awesome roar which warned of doomsday and made us feel we puny things were blasphemous to dare tamper with

the forces heretofore reserved for The Almighty. Words are inadequate tools for the job of acquainting those not present with the physical, mental and psychological effects. It had to be witnessed to be realized.[2]

Many more would vicariously experience the majestic power and destructive force of the Bomb during the next twenty years, as newsreel coverage, magazine photos, sound recordings, film footage, and television broadcasts kept the threat of "doomsday" alive in the minds of cold war Americans. Farrell spoke of "witnessing" atomic power as others have spoken of witnessing divinity.

Historians and critics have blamed the Bomb for a wide variety of developments in the second half of the twentieth century, ranging from postwar gender roles to the rise of postmodernism.[3] While nuclear anxieties dislocated most cultural fields during the early Cold War and have maintained several tropes of cold war culture into the new millennium, adult male identity, national security, and American Christianity were the nearest to ground zero during the 1950s. The cultural impact of the nuclear blast on these fields derived from the paradoxical effects of the Bomb. General Farrell's account takes up two contradictory points of view about the explosion. On the one hand, the general identifies with the universal power that could create such beauty and terror, even granting critical approval to the "lighting effects" of the Almighty. On the other hand, the general fears for his life, identifying himself as a "puny thing" about to be obliterated by an angry God jealous of His power. At one moment, he became God; at the next, he sought refuge in divine protection. Put another way, the general experienced a crisis in agency, a sudden loss of power that could only be recuperated when he transferred his potential for action from himself to a higher power.

The American response to the nuclear destruction of Hiroshima echoed Farrell's deeply ambivalent reaction to the Bomb. Initial concern for the Japanese victims soon gave way to more universal, even theological awe and fear. "[One] forgets the effect on Japan," stated the *New York Herald Tribune*, "as one senses the foundations of one's own universe trembling." For cultural arbiter Norman Cousins, the threat of atomic power loosed "primitive fear . . . filling the mind with primordial apprehension." In the shadow of the Bomb, intoned *Time*, "all men were pygmies." *Life* magazine, in contrast, celebrated "our Promethean ingenuity"; and Philip Wylie in *Collier's* said that Americans "now own infinity and eternity." "We have become the people physically most powerful on earth," boasted Wylie.[4]

The cognitive ambivalence inspired by the Bomb played a significant role in the psychic fragmentation of many American males during the Cold War. On the one hand, adult men had just won World War II, sparked a postwar economic boom, and protected the "free world" from communism. Most stood guard at the border of their bunkered families, protecting them from societal incursions and attempting to secure their welfare. On the other hand, security—especially from the Bomb but also from devious Others—proved to be an impossible goal. The disparity between expectations of a secure life and the reality of insecurity at the familial, national, and international levels produced a deadening fatalism and a nagging guilt in many American males. Anxiety about security was nothing new for twentieth-century American males, of course; historians have noted a range of insecurities and general anxieties about masculinity among American males since the emergence of a modern middle class in the mid nineteenth century. Nuclearism may not have produced a new insecurity, but, as with General Farrell, it did exacerbate the distance between feelings of puniness and omnipotence in many business-class males.

Weird representations of impotence contrasted with images of supermasculinity on the movie and television screens of cold war America. In *The Incredible Shrinking Man* (1957), for instance, a man begins to shrink after an atomic cloud contaminates him. Finally less than an inch high, he comes to accept his new emasculated status after successfully defending himself from a spider in his basement. To compensate for their feelings of impotence, cold war males turned to stars with well-muscled biceps and chests, such as William Holden, Charlton Heston, and George Reeves, who played super-studs, super-patriarchs, and Superman on film and television. In 1958 humorist Richard Armour dubbed the decade "The Age of the Chest," for its fascination with the male torso.[5] Identifying with images of exaggerated virility may temporarily have reassured some adult males, but such representations no doubt left others feeling more vulnerable.

The psychic fragmentation of business-class men in the early Cold War was particularly evident in images of what R. W. Connell terms "hegemonic masculinity." A norm of masculine lifestyle that guarantees positions of wealth and power for some adult males, hegemonic masculinity sits at the top of a hierarchy of other images of manhood in every historical era. These images, notes Connell, include "conservative masculinities," which are complicit in preserving male power but not on the front lines of the struggle, and "subordinated masculinities," which model themselves on hegemonic images but—for racial, class, and/or economic reasons—cannot aspire to the authority of the hegemonic males.[6] Sloan Wilson's novel *The Man in the Gray Flannel Suit* (1955), for instance, positions white-collar businessman Tom Rath as the hegemonic model, while his boss represents conservative masculinity; and a former army pal, an Italian American now an elevator operator in the corporation that employs Rath, fulfills the subordinated role. The enormous popularity among the professional-managerial class of Wilson's story (both as a novel and as a film) about a prototypical American male suggests its centrality to the anxieties surrounding images of masculinity during the era. As did Willy Loman in the theater, Tom Rath epitomized the Fragmented Male of cold war novels and films.

The opening footage of the 1956 film links Rath's anxieties to the problem of simulation during the Cold War. Behind the printed credits a two-dimensional outline of a gray flannel man appears on the left side of the screen. This image is replicated, moving from left to right across the screen as the credits proceed. Each machine-made copy of the gray flannel man gets progressively smaller as the credits continue and finally run out. The initial footage encapsulates the challenge of *Gray Flannel* for American viewers: does the protagonist have an inner essence that will set him apart from the crowd of other white-collar execs and revive his shrinking virility? Or will corporate America turn him into an impotent hollow man, a mere suit of clothes? Tom Rath's situation appears to derive from the pressures of corporate America and his status as a hegemonic male, not directly from nuclearism. Nonetheless, the hopes and fears induced by the film for Rath—omnipotence in his personal and professional life or impotence in both—were the same as those generated by the Bomb. In effect, nuclearism shaped the expectations for cold war masculinity that *Gray Flannel Suit* worked within. Luckily for America, the role was played by Gregory Peck, whose charismatic stardom guaranteed that a real man of full representational presence would triumph over mass-produced simulations. But the film, like the book, made Rath's eventual victory a close call. Mentally fragmented between the present tensions of his family and job and past guilt deriving from the war, Tom Rath has difficulty taking positive action to secure his family's happiness. Memories of combat, which include the extremes of elation and despair, continue to intrude into his present circumstances. Only after his wife shames him into action can he begin to resolve the problems of his new position in a public relations firm, his feelings of responsibility for the death of his best friend during combat, and a wartime romance involving a secret love child. Gregory Peck's vocal abruptness and physical stiffness heightened the effect of Rath's repressions in the film, underlining his agonizing paralysis.

Jennifer Jones played Betsy Rath, a woman constricted by the norms of business-class wife and mother. Although Betsy goes into psychological freefall at the climax of the film when Tom finally confesses his past, her trauma opens no narrative space to examine the contradictions of her social role. Rather, as the story is constructed, her problems temporarily heap more difficulties on the shoulders of her husband, leaving him more isolated and alienated than before. In the end, they work through their problems, but not before Betsy Rath has been scapegoated as a major cause of her husband's distress. From the point of view of the book and film, however, Betsy's pain and Tom's despair put them in touch with their true selves and play a necessary role in the psychological healing and restoration of virility to a Fragmented Male.

Confined to passivity and dependent status when it came to the security and economic well-being of their families, business-class wives made easy targets for husbands wracked by guilt and impotence. A popular booklet written by the male editors of *Look* magazine and published in 1958 entitled *The Decline of the American Male* asked on its dust-jacket, "How is the American male to recover his fast-fading individuality and escape the growing domination of the distaff side?" The editors had no answers, but they drew on the Kinsey Report, Margaret Mead, and numerous psychologists to detail the increasing "fatigue," "passivity," "anxiety," and "impotency" of the average white-collar male, laying most of the blame on the sexual aggressiveness, psychological manipulation, and simple greed of his wife. As Elaine Tyler May and other scholars have demonstrated, the dominant culture put business-class wives in a box and then blamed them for struggling to get out of it.[7] Women, especially wives and mothers, were convenient whipping posts for male insecurities in the 50s.

Some critics linked pervasive feelings of guilt among adult American males directly to the witch hunts of the Red Scare. Playwright Arthur Miller noted that Americans who harbored "illicit, suppressed feelings of alienation and hostility toward standard, daylight society" felt disloyal and guilty about these attitudes. In reaction, they projected their "own vileness onto others in order to wipe it out," said Miller, effectively replicating the impotence they had initially experienced. Certainly the "degradation ceremonies" of McCarthyism, as historian Victor Navasky terms them, left the national terrain littered with guilty souls—people guilty about testifying, about not testifying, about profiting from the testimonies of others, even about enjoying the spectacle of national scapegoating and mortification.[8] Behind the Red Scare lurked the ever-present reality of the Bomb, which, as with cold war masculinity, structured its parameters and shadowed its guilts. Recalling his childhood in the late 1940s, writer Frank Conroy stated:

> It goes without saying that the effects of the bomb on the American mind were profound.... We felt exhilaration at the indisputable proof that America was the strongest power on earth, apprehension because the power was mysterious, and most significantly we felt guilt, secret guilt that verged on the traitorous, guilt we could not possibly talk about. Our political apathy, later, as college students in the Eisenhower years, seems to me to trace directly to our inability to reorganize those simple propagandistic concepts of democracy and political morality which had been our wartime heritage and which the bomb had rendered untenable.[9]

Guilt about the political morality of the Bomb and dread that it might be used against "us" fed the anxieties that fueled the Red Scare.

Belief in the need to contain nuclear "secrets" made security a matter of life and death in the minds of many postwar Americans. Nuclearism was an underlying condition of the Red Scare in the late 1940s and early 1950s, even though the Red Scare itself had more immediate causes. In part, citizens carried over concerns about espionage on the home front from World War II, when "loose lips" could "sink ships." International crises widely covered in the press—the Soviet occupation of Czechoslovakia and the Berlin blockade in 1948, the formation of NATO and the "loss" of China to communism in 1949, early Communist victories in the Korean War in 1950—heightened public fears that internal subversion might account for the nation's apparent loss of its international preeminence. Most importantly, pro-business and conservative groups desiring to undercut the effectiveness of labor unions and progressive politicians fanned these anxieties to carry out their agendas. The new reality of the Bomb and the belief that its secrets were vital to American national security increased the significance of these apparent threats. Previous Red Scares after World War I and during the 1930s did not grab and hold the imagination of the American public with the same intensity and longevity as postwar McCarthyism. The fear of Soviet spying and the occasional conviction of U.S. citizens such as Klaus Fuchs and Julius Rosenberg as nuclear spies kept the Bomb at the center of concern. After Russia exploded a nuclear device in 1949, the nascent security panic that had focused on the federal government and Hollywood escalated rapidly into a national anti-Communist crusade.

Thousands of citizens were caught up in the Red Scare. The Federal Employee Loyalty Program, mandated by Truman in 1947, fired some 300 government employees and forced nearly 3,000 more to resign by 1951. Despite rampant (and often frivolous) accusations of disloyalty, the Loyalty Program uncovered no spies or saboteurs. The Eisenhower administration continued the campaign, dismissing some 2,200 "security risks" by 1954, none of whom were ever convicted of subversion. Most state governments followed the trend; by 1953, thirty-nine of them had instituted their own loyalty boards and commissions. In Hollywood, the House Un-American Activities Committee (HUAC) held hearings that resulted in the dismissal of several writers, actors, and directors who refused to cooperate, plus the blacklisting of hundreds more in the entertainment industry. Librarians, bureaucrats, and secretaries were dismissed for reading the wrong books, admitting their homosexuality, professing atheism, even questioning the norms of female chastity. Those suspects who kept their positions often had to undergo degrading hearings where they confessed past political sins, named the names of other leftists, and affirmed their patriotism. The quest for total security—based on the false belief that containing nuclear secrets was the key to national survival—gutted political progressivism across America.

It also remodeled the federal government into a national security state. The imperial presidency inherited from World War II, the geopolitical realities of the Cold War, and the perception that the Bomb had ruptured history placed unprecedented moral authority in the hands of security experts. For example, despite purported civilian control, the Atomic Energy Commission, created in 1946, wrapped itself in the armor of national security and used secret hearings to banish dissenters and to ignore environmental and health hazards in pursuit of nuclear bomb testing. The Central Intelligence Agency, begun in 1947, fought to keep secret the details of its budget, and a cowed Congress obliged. The provisos of the National Security Council, fully empowered in 1950, established the United States armed forces as world police and allowed the NSC to conduct a truth campaign within the country to combat anti-American propaganda. These and other agencies within the stealth state operated within codes of "deniability," virtually unchanged for the next twenty-five years, that kept their secrets from public view. In effect, as Catherine Lutz contends, "the national security apparatus created 'inside' spaces where security experts generated both knowledge and national safety. Civilians became 'outsiders' defined as 'naïve' to the inverse extent that the military-political elites claimed the secret space of knowledge and the doctrinal position of 'realism.'"[10] The nuclearism fueling the Red Scare led to the contained spaces of the national security state.

Two related narratives, a melodrama of conspiracy and a comedy of restoration, helped Americans to accept and justify the Red Scare and the stealth state. Both containment narratives drew on the desire for omnipotence and the fears of compulsion and fragmentation generated by the Bomb. Newspaper, radio, and Hollywood versions of the conspiracy narrative warned Americans that nefarious forces sought to breach our defenses, gain our knowledge of ultimate power, and make us their slaves when they controlled the world. The conspiracy narrative ceded active agency to an outside power, often Russia, though any conspiring, alien force attempting to compel obedience would do. True patriots could jail or expel subversives and build stronger defenses, but these were inherently reactive positions. Alien conspirators attacked individuals as well as states, making the Fragmented Hero an inherent security risk. Further, narratives of conspiracy required a God-like perspective; to secure final victory, Americans had to see behind alien doors and into the minds of invisible enemies. As Alan Nadel concludes, "Internal security [under nuclearism] becomes synonymous with external, universal scrutiny." Because the enemy could be anyone anywhere, permanent alert was required to secure atomic secrets in this melodrama of compulsion and containment. The U.S. Defense Advisory Commission recognized as much in 1955 when it stated that "the battlefield of modern warfare is all-inclusive. Today there are no distant front lines, remote no-man's lands, far off rear areas. The home front is but an extension of the fighting front."[11]

This put the Fragmented Hero directly in the crosshairs of national concern. Could American men use their omnipotent power to read the intentions of our enemies and defend the nation or would guilt and impotence disable them at the crucial moment of battle? This was the underlying conflict in such films as *Above and Beyond* (1952) and *The Strategic Air Command* (1955). *Above and Beyond* focuses on Colonel Paul Tibbets, the pilot who dropped the bomb on Hiroshima, and his guilt over the extreme secrecy that separates him from his wife when he is training for his fateful mission. Eventually Tibbets, played by Robert Taylor, conquers his guilt and rage and fulfills his patriotic duty. "God," his single utterance when the Bomb explodes, moves him (and American power) from impotence to transcendence. *The Strategic Air Command* starred Jimmy Stewart as a SAC pilot who is torn between his patriotic duty to fly a dangerous mission and domestic concerns that threaten to soften and disarm him. Stewart's likeable image in the 1950s — a mix of charm and awkwardness, tenacity and good humor, hesitation and aggressiveness, plus (hetero)sex appeal — made him the obvious choice of many filmmakers for Mr. Hegemonic Male. In *The Man Who Knew Too Much* (1956), *Rear Window* (1954), and *Vertigo* (1958), Hitchcock used Stewart to embody a Fragmented Hero of superior knowledge and intelligence rendered temporarily impotent by physical or psychological problems.

Another Jimmy Stewart film, *The FBI Story* (1959), exemplifies the second kind of narrative to emerge from nuclearism and the Red Scare. The film glorified the work of J. Edgar Hoover's agency by depicting the life of a "typical" agent, Stewart, from the 1920s through the mid 1950s. As the Fragmented Hero, Stewart struggles to keep his worried wife happy while battling various national enemies, from the Ku Klux Klan to Communist spies. By depicting Stewart's growing film family through idealized moments of family history (childbirth, Easter-egg hunt, daughter's graduation, etc.), *The FBI Story* celebrates the traditional family that agent Stewart is defending. This fundamentally comic narrative restores agency to the Fragmented Hero, who now works to contain the depredations of dangerous Others so that the true roots of American virtue may sprout and blossom once again. Unlike the conspiracy narrative, which is fixated on a potentially disastrous future, the narrative of restoration looks to the values of an idealized past as a model for the present. Rather than centering on an image of compulsion, the restoration narrative derives its power from the schema of "restraint removal." In *The FBI Story*, Stewart's character works to remove the dangers that constrain his family so that their inherent goodness can be reborn. In a psychological sense, "restraint removal" is a kind of logical next step after containment that enhances agency: first contain the evils that are holding back utopia and then remove them. Restoring past virtues is never easy, however; Fragmented Hero Stewart may have the omnipotent power of the FBI at his fingertips, but domestic crises (almost more dangerous to the good life, oddly, than gangsters and commies) continue to challenge his restored family.

Just as General Farrell evoked the Almighty in his response to the Bomb, so nuclearism led many Americans to figure their containment narratives in religious terms. Narrative explanations about the Bomb that centered on conspiracy were easily translated into stories of apocalypse. Indeed, President Truman had coupled nuclear destruction with divine retribution at the beginning of the atomic age. "If [the Japanese leaders] do not now accept our terms," he warned, "they may expect a rain of ruin from the air, the like of which has never been seen on this earth." Although the bombs dropped on Hiroshima and Nagasaki actually wreaked less destruction than the previous firebombing of Dresden and Tokyo, American military and civilian leaders frequently likened the Bomb to the biblical apocalypse. As Frank Kermode notes, narratives of apocalypse continue to underlie "our ways of making sense of the world," specifically regarding our sense of the finitude and coherence of time.[12] If, as many cold war Americans supposed, some Almighty deity contained all of human history in a Divine Design, then citizens might identify with this God and His plans to bring time to an end. Like conspiratorial stories, apocalyptic narratives transferred agency from "us" to an outside force; in effect, divine compulsion would end the world. Both kinds of stories also underlined the need to take a God's-eye view of human events.

Apocalyptic narratives circulated widely in cold war America. Following the news in 1949 that the Soviets had tested an atomic bomb, revivalist Billy Graham held his first tent meeting in Los Angeles to warn of God's Final Judgment and the imminent division of the saved from the damned. During the next decade millions listened on radio and television to Graham's fulminations against the Godless Communists and to similar apocalyptic warnings from Monsignor Fulton Sheen and the Reverend Norman Vincent Peale. Fears of atomic destruction inspired several sci-fi films in the early 1950s, which often depicted extraterrestrials with nuclear capabilities, as in *The Day the Earth Stood Still* (1951), or mutant insects contaminated by atomic testing, such as *Them!* (1954). Near the test sites in the Southwest, thousands of Americans saw UFOs, avatars, many believed, of divine intervention in human affairs. As cultural historian James Gilbert explains, the debates about UFOs and much science-fiction literature and film in the 50s "reflected the transfer of apocalyptic speculation from its traditional place in Christian eschatology to imagination about the future. The sudden, terrible birth of atomic energy and then the anxieties of the Cold War made such plots inevitable and popular."[13] Not surprisingly, traditional religious tropes—prophecy, myths of origin, secret knowledge, and images of divine retribution and salvation—peppered the episodes of these stories.

Americans in the 1950s also looked to the biblical past for reassurance about God's future. In this regard, many popular biblical films, though chock full of melodrama, followed the general narrative pattern of comic restoration. *Quo Vadis?* (1951), *The Robe* (1953), *The Silver Chalice* (1954), *The Ten Commandments* (1956), and *Ben-Hur* (1959) dominated the box office during the decade. Typically, these Bible pics pitted Christians or proto-Christians (e.g., the Jews in Cecil B. DeMille's *Ten Commandments*) against a tyrannical empire and demonstrated that God's justice and the values of cold war Americanism—freedom, property, and faith—were synonymous. Their wide-screen format (beginning with *The Robe*) celebrated American technological supremacy and gave viewers the closest most would come to a God-like perspective on the religious past. These films often conflated the compulsive, destructive force of the Almighty with the power of the Bomb, as in images of the darkened sky at the crucifixion scene in *The Robe* and the tower of fire blocking Pharaoh's chariots in *The Ten Commandments*. Despite occasional apocalyptic destructions of past evil empires, however, the Bible epics primarily emphasized the historical continuity of God's people through time. The faithful became implicit models by which present-day Americans might restore their lives.

The primary narrative thread of the Bible epics was the jeremiad rather than apocalypse. Seventeenth-century Puritan ministers evoked the warnings of the prophet Jeremiah as a means of contrasting a relatively sin-free past to a sinful present. Meant to call back a Chosen People to their divine mission by arousing shame and guilt, the jeremiad evoked anxiety in the service of reform and restoration. According to historian Sacvan Bercovitch:

> The American Puritan jeremiad was the ritual of a culture on an errand—which is to say, a culture based on a faith in process. Substituting teleology for hierarchy, it discarded the Old World ideal of stasis for a New World vision of the future. Its function was to create a climate of anxiety that helped release the restless "progressivist" energies required for the success of the venture.... [The American jeremiad] made anxiety its end as well as its means. Crisis was the social norm it sought to inculcate. The very concept of errand, after all, implied a state of unfulfillment. The future, though divinely assured, was never quite there, and New England's Jeremiahs set out to provide the sense of insecurity that would ensure the outcome.[14]

The Jeremiahs of the 1950s used stories from the biblical past to attack the conformity and materialism of the decade. In this regard, the firm faith and simple lives of the early Christians and Jews in the Bible films stood as a potent rebuke to the consumerism of modern Americans. The proto-suburbanism of Baka and Dathan and the debauchery surrounding the worship of the golden calf in *The Ten Commandments*, for instance, point a wagging finger at the sinfulness of the present. The larger narrative of these films also echoed the Puritan call to heed God's prophet and forego the sins of the world. Put another way, the jeremiad of the Bible pics echoed the same structure and themes as the secular narrative of comic restoration seen in *The FBI Story* and similar fictions. Moses, Saul of Tarsus, Ben-Hur, and others touched by the Almighty are the religious counterparts of Jimmy Stewart in those films: Fragmented Heroes pushing to remove the restraints that keep the Chosen from aligning the values of the present world with divine revelation from the past—restraints that block the full flowering of God's plan for His People.

Most sci-fi disaster films, too, followed the jeremiad narrative of restoration; God's Judgment was a divine warning to return to true values, not a trope for the end of time. In *The War of the Worlds* (1954) and *Godzilla* (1954), for example, survivors remain to pick up the pieces of nuclear-derived destruction. Many of these movies first urge the wayward Fausts and Frankensteins of science and the military to repent of their pride and lust for power, but then the films typically embrace a mixture of scientific knowledge, military power, and religious faith as the answer to nuclear disaster. "When man entered the atomic age, he opened the door into a new world," says a scientist in *Them!* "What we eventually find in that new world, nobody can predict."[15] Despite the imminence of disaster evoked in these films, they affirm that there will be a future, an "eventually" in which scientific progress and teleological process ensure survival. As this quotation suggests, scientists often stand in as the voice of authority in sci-fi thrillers; the progress prophesied by scientists was often conflated with the power of God. The Bomb had elevated the status of science in the public imagination, allowing scientists an apparent peek at the ultimate power of the universe. Unlocking that power, removing those restraints, could lead past survival to a restoration of virtue on earth. Like the biblical epics, most sci-fi pics followed the restoration narrative of the jeremiad, not the finality of apocalypse.

Indeed, most Americans in the 1950s believed that they could survive nuclear warfare. For many, this dogged belief in a survivable future degraded what might have been a complex religious faith into what one critic called simple "religiousness." In *Protestant, Catholic, Jew* (1955), Will Herberg derided this vapid sentimentality in which "sociability or 'belonging'" mattered far more than the content of religious teaching. President Eisenhower's oft-quoted statement on the importance of faith regardless of theology—"Our government makes no sense unless it is founded on a deeply felt religious faith, and I don't care what it is"—sums up the nation's investment in what Herberg elsewhere termed "faith in faith."[16] Because the Bomb might fall at any moment, feeling close to God (whoever He might be) might guarantee a person's salvation, either earthly or eternal. In addition to serving as a kind of insurance policy in the nuclear age, "religiousness" also helped Americans to ascend to objectivity, to gain God's point of view on the world. As in many sci-fi films, Americans were anxious to reconcile science and religion, both recognized as keys to ultimate knowledge. The two discourses often converged in Sunday sermons, just as they did in such educational films such as *Our Mr. Sun*.

During the 1950s total church membership in the United States, in decline for most of the twentieth century, increased from 86.8 million to 114 million. For many Americans, the church or temple building became the container of the "religiousness" they sought and going to a place of worship became the single best way to get close to God. Religious historian Robert Wuthnow remarks that cold war religious leaders "had succeeded in rendering spirituality virtually equivalent to participating in a local congregation." Places of worship were understood "as homes, with all the cultural significance that this word implied." Churches, temples, and similar sites became centers for recreation, family-fun nights, teen get-togethers, and other nurturant activities. Following the domestic model, church members also saw their sanctuaries as "fortresses whose walls needed to be protected from exterior threats so that life inside could be kept under control." In his exploration of sanctuary-as-bunker, Wuthnow draws on the transitivity of containment metaphors to extend his insights to the nation as a whole: "And if the local enclaves in which people worshipped were sacred fortresses, the nation in which they lived was even more in need of being inviolable. It, too, was sacred space, a place in which spirituality and identity were forged together. Being a good American was a way of exhibiting faith, and both depended on keeping intruders out."[17] Communist intruders, of course, were the most feared, but sanctuary walls also excluded Others of different races and creeds. Numerous state practices buttressed the analogy that bonded church membership to national citizenship during the early Cold War. "God's Float," for instance, led Eisenhower's inaugural parade in 1953. Congress added "under God" to the pledge of allegiance in 1954 and "In God We Trust" to the currency in 1955. If the United States was God's Country, an enlarged sanctuary for His Chosen People, keeping it secure from domestic and foreign enemies became a divine mandate.

The anxieties of nuclearism even transformed theater buildings, normally houses of entertainment, into temporary sites for religious witness, as narratives of apocalypse and jeremiad played out on Broadway stages. As in other forms of popular culture, apocalyptic concerns structured nominally secular dramas centered on conspiracy, and the energies of the jeremiad shaped plays based on the hope for a restoration of traditional values. Most of these plays put a Fragmented Hero, torn between the expectation of justice and strength and the fear of impotence and evil, in the midst of their dramatic conflicts. Several courtroom dramas, for example, examined Fragmented Heroes unable to overcome the conspiracies that shaped their dramatic worlds — conspiracies that suggested divine purposes beyond human control. Louis Coxe and Robert Chapman's adaptation of Herman Melville's *Billy Budd* (1951), for example, foregrounds the impotence of Captain Vere, bound by the limitations of human law and unable to save Billy from Claggart's conspiracy. In *Darkness at Noon* (1950), the conspiratorial triumphs of the Communists in Russia leave the shattered hero hoping for judgment from God, since earthly justice seems impossible. The defense attorney in *The Caine Mutiny Court Martial* (1954), haunted by guilt about the Holocaust, struggles to preserve the readiness of the U.S. Navy, despite the cowardly conspiracies of the men who run it. Even *Inherit the Wind* (1955) by Jerome Lawrence and Robert E. Lee, perhaps the most liberal of the cold war courtroom dramas, suggests in the end that mundane justice, though it may eventually overturn the verdict of the Scopes "Monkey Trial," can never match the judgment of God. All of these plays stretch a Fragmented Hero between reluctant commitment to human law and a yearning for final justice that could only come through the intervention of an Almighty power.

Although Broadway lacked the special effects of Hollywood to dramatize apocalypse, New York producers could turn to ancient Greek and biblical myths for a similar glimpse at divine power shaping human fate. Greek tragedies had rarely been popular or profitable in commercial American theaters, but early cold war theatergoers had several to choose from. In Robinson Jeffers's adaptations, Medea, Cassandra, Phaedra, and other mythic figures from ancient times found their free will compromised by omnipotent forces. These plays included *Medea* (1947), *The Tower beyond Tragedy* (1950) — both starring Judith Anderson — and *The Cretan Woman* (1954). Anouilh's version of the myth of Antigone, performed as a star vehicle by Katharine Cornell in 1946, reminded business-class audiences of the disparity between human justice and divine justice. The power of the Almighty and the insignificance of humanity were also potent themes in two of Paddy Chayefsky's plays from late in the period, *The Tenth Man* (1959) and *Gideon* (1961). Not all of these plays evoked a divinely ordered end of time, but they did underline humanity's ultimate lack of control over its fate. Anxiety about the Bomb animated the search for a secure home in the mysteries of the universe.

As in the films of the era, however, most plays leaned on the restorative possibilities of the jeremiad rather than the final justice of a distant God in their response to nuclearism. Apocalypse could be averted, these plays promised, if we learned from the past and removed the restraints to God's will to secure our future. A few of the jeremiad plays, though not generally the most popular ones, commented directly on the nuclear situation. In *The Traitor* by Herman Wouk (1949), a nuclear scientist decides to give atomic secrets to the Soviets to prevent another war. "In the end, I found myself between conflicting loyalties," says the Fragmented Hero of the title. He was, he states, trapped between "loyalty to the United States and my oath of secrecy—loyalty to all mankind and my own reason. I decided that one was provincial and limited, and the other eternal and right."[18] A jeremiad against the depredations of capitalism and nationalism, Arch Obler's *Night of the Auk* (1956) depicts the nuclear destruction of the earth from the moon, which scientists deduce suffered an earlier nuclear apocalypse. Obler places a wise physicist at the center of the play who, like Albert Einstein, warns that the atom has changed everything except human thinking. In *The Highest Tree* by Dore Schary (1956), a nuclear scientist decides to break the silence that has muzzled his conscience and work for an end to atomic testing. The Fragmented Heroes of these plays struggle to free themselves from guilt and alienation in order to save the world or what little is left of it.

Jeremiad dramas at some remove from nuclear terror generally found a more appreciative audience. Clifford Odets based his comic allegorical warning about the end of the world on the story of the biblical Flood and Noah's ark. *The Flowering Peach* (1954), Odets's final bow on Broadway, demonstrated that God and humanity can work together to avert apocalypse. His comedy followed the success of *The Madwoman of Chaillot* during the 1948–1949 season, which showed common people saving the world from destruction by a conspiracy of greedy capitalists. The most popular jeremiad narrative of the postwar period with business-class spectators was the Joan of Arc tale, whose peasant-girl-gets-God's-call-and-saves-France story had clear links to cold war jeremiads about threatening disaster, saintly tenacity, and divine omnipotence, plus a young woman untainted by sexuality. Maxwell Anderson's *Joan of Lorraine* scored a hit in 1946; a revival of Shaw's *St. Joan* with Uta Hagen enjoyed a modest run in 1951–1952; and Lillian Hellman's *The Lark*, her adaptation of Anouilh's drama, flourished on Broadway in 1955. For Hellman, a medieval version of McCarthyism caused Joan's martyrdom;

her play thus tied the Red Scare to a hunger for divine guidance. All three plays provided several Fragmented Heroes struggling to understand Joan's saintly mission. Martha Graham also staged a St. Joan dance, *Seraphic Dialogue*, in 1955, which presented four overlapping versions of the Joan figure. A related drama warning of doom but carving out a hopeful ending if only humanity will heed its call was *The Diary of Anne Frank* (1956), also featuring a sexually innocent girl, in which the Holocaust figures as the end of the world for the characters of the drama. Many other plays of the early Cold War (including *The Member of the Wedding* [1949] by Carson McCullers; *Come Back, Little Sheba*; *A Hatful of Rain*; and *Raisin in the Sun*) allude to the possibility of nuclear destruction and provide jeremiad-like warnings without organizing their narratives as jeremiad stories.

■ Fragmented Heroes and nuclear narratives focused the energies of two productions that attracted widespread interest in the 1947–1962 period: Martha Graham's modern dance version of Jocasta's story in the Oedipus myth, *Night Journey*, and Archibald MacLeish's retelling of the story of Job from the Bible, *J.B.* Like many of the other performances deriving from cold war nuclearism, the schemas of containment, compulsion, and restraint removal shaped the rhetoric and form of *Night Journey* and *J.B.* on several levels. Both deployed type, even archetypal, characters, wove plots that leaned heavily on the determinism of compulsion or the enablement of restraint removal, elaborated metatheatrical layers that could be unpacked like Chinese boxes, and deployed containment metaphors to induce *allegoresis* in their audiences. The compulsion of a nuclear explosion, the anxiety to contain nuclear secrets, and the hunger to wrench universal meaning from nuclear fear pervaded these productions.

MacLeish's poetic drama opened on 11 December 1958 with a cast that included Pat Hingle in the title role, plus Raymond Massey as Mr. Zuss and Christopher Plummer as Nickles. They played two actors reduced to selling balloons and popcorn at the circus who become transformed when they put on the masks of God and Satan to tell the Job story. Kazan directed the production, which was set in a world-encompassing circus tent designed by Boris Aronson. The story of the play generally follows the biblical narrative, in which God tests J.B.'s faith by killing his children, taunting him with "Comforters," and finally restoring him to wealth and family. At the end of MacLeish's version, however, J.B. turns his back on an inscrutable and arbitrary Almighty to rejoice in the possibility of human love. *J.B.* won two Tony awards, one for Best Play and the other for Best Directing, and also the Pulitzer Prize, MacLeish's third. (His earlier two were for poetry.) Although a severe elevator accident necessitated Hingle's replacement in the title role only two months after the opening, the play ran for most of 1959 on Broadway and toured the country in 1960.[19]

Graham's *Night Journey* premiered before business-class Broadway spectators on 3 May 1947, with Graham in the role of Jocasta, Erick Hawkins as Oedipus, Mark Ryder as Tieresias, and a chorus of six women; all dancers were members of Graham's troupe. Isamu Noguchi designed the set, sculpted to resemble ancient forms, including a symbolic bed joining a male and female figure at center stage. The narrative of the dance begins at the moment when Jocasta, having learned that she is married to her son, is about to kill herself. Tieresias enters, propelled by an enormous walking stick, and forces her to review her life. Flashback scenes recount the entrance of Oedipus into Thebes, his success with the Sphinx, his formal marriage to Jocasta, and his sexual conquest of the Queen. Jocasta's seductive wooing softens the bullying of Oedipus into love, and the two become locked in embraces that sexualize Jocasta's maternal desire. Tieresias separates them from the rope in which they have become ensnared, a rope representing the umbilicus that once joined mother and son. After the blinding and departure of Oedipus, Jocasta, now returned to the present moment, hangs herself with the same rope. Graham and her troupe danced *Night Journey* frequently during the next twenty years, often coupling it with *Cave of the Heart, Errand into the Maze,* and/or *Clytemnestra,* three other postwar dances based in Greek myths with heroes chosen by fate.[20]

State Department funding also sent Graham's production of *Night Journey* to Southeast Asia. The Eisenhower administration, concerned about the spread of communism in the area after the departure of the French from Indochina in 1954, sponsored tours of renowned artists in the mid-1950s. Graham and her company performed several of her most popular dances in Burma, India, Pakistan, Japan, the Philippines, Thailand, Indonesia, Malaya, and Ceylon between 23 October 1955 and 12 February 1956. Her company's performances impressed her Asian hosts, many of whom had expected a kind of dance theater more akin to Hollywood musicals. *Night Journey* and *Cave of the Heart*, especially, won

Oedipus/Erick Hawkins dominates Jocasta/Martha Graham in a flashback to their marriage in Night Journey. *Bennett & Pleasant photo, courtesy New York Public Library.*

high praise from Asian critics for their rigorous aesthetics and what were assumed to be their universal truths. Graham understood the political goals of the tour and was proud to assist the cold war efforts of her county.[21]

By 1947, when *Night Journey* premiered, Graham had been dancing for over two decades and her work, together with her status as a celebrity, had gained her a popular following. In part to overcome the indifference of most Americans to modern dance, Graham had cultivated a public image that certified her as a high priestess of modernism. Her published statements — often aloof, elliptical, and cosmic — connected her to Eastern religions, Jungian psychology, and primitive mysteries. Most photographs of her dancing showed the same composed, almost masklike face: half-closed eyes under arched eyebrows, sensuous lips over a wide, protruding mouth and jutting jaw, high cheekbones accented by dark hair pulled back in a chignon. Graham's reputation for high seriousness and deep mystery made her the butt of several satirists. Among the best was Danny Kaye, whose "Marta Gra-ham"—he Russified her first name and elongated her last—parody of the dancer in *The Kid from Brooklyn* contorted in angular and convulsed spasms. Several articles about Graham and her troupe, often with photos, appeared in the late 1940s in popular magazines, including *Junior Bazaar*, *Life*, *Coronet*, and *Atlantic Monthly*. The *New Yorker* profiled Graham in 1947. So well known was she that *Truth or Consequences*, a nationally syndicated radio program, used rhymed clues to Graham's name in a mystery puzzler call-in contest to raise money for the March of Dimes. The two previous celebrities for the contest had been Jack Dempsey and Clara Bow.

Despite her popularity, even notoriety, audiences had difficulty understanding Graham's dances. In part, this had to do with her investment in the cultural capital of rarified mysticism. The poet Robert Horan criticized Graham's spectators in 1947 for trying to divine the stage properties of her dances "as obscure and calculated symbols." When not symbol-mongering, business-class audiences trained to appreciate the techniques of ballet found themselves confused by the apparent lack of conventional narratives and movements in Graham's dances. The press releases and program copy sent out by arts impresario Sol Hurok, who represented Graham's troupe for two seasons between 1946 and 1948, tried to anticipate and alleviate public confusion about her work. In addition to trumpeting Graham as a typically American artist and celebrating the war heroism of two of her male dancers, Hurok's publicity emphasized the dramatic form of her dances. One program in San Francisco, for instance, reassured its audience that Graham "created dances which are really drama.... Each dancer dances a role." "It may not be a specific realistic person, [however]," the program cautioned. Rather, "it is likely to be an element in human nature, a concept in the mind of the main character."[22] In addition, Graham's programs summarized the main plot and primary emotions of each dance for the audience. Apparently, Hurok reasoned that most spectators would read the dances as dramatic action.

Although Hurok's two national tours of Graham's company lost money, his strategic framing of Graham's dances as drama helped to sell her to a wider public. Indeed, most postwar theater artists already understood modern dance as a branch of dramatic theater. ANTA (the American National Theater Alliance) produced Graham's 1948 season in New York, and in 1950 the Women's National Press Club presented awards to Graham and Olivia de Havilland for their artistry in "the theater." In 1953 a Broadway concert program praised Graham as "perhaps our greatest and most profound dramatist" for creating "a form of dance-theater which is the essence of drama." Graham biographer Don McDonagh concludes that her postwar audience was "an adventurous and chic assembly that included many from the theater as well as other arts."[23] What began as a Hurok marketing strategy effectively broadened Graham's claim to be a mainstream theater artist. The core of spectators for *Night Journey*, then, was probably a more sophisticated version of the typical audience for a serious play on Broadway: professional-managerial couples generally conversant with modern dramatic, if not choreographic, conventions.

Night Journey and *J.B.* are modern allegories based on old myths. Graham and MacLeish, however, used the myths of Oedipus and Job without fully subscribing to the belief system implicit in the original stories. For them, as for many other modernists, a myth could be both religiously false and cognitively true; its narrative could harbor significant truths about humanity despite the fact that it was based on a world picture that modern understanding had rejected. As Martin Heidegger explained, the modern age was the first to understand its beliefs in relativistic terms: "The world picture does not change from an earlier medieval one into a modern one, but rather the fact that the world becomes a picture at all is what distinguishes the essence of the modern world." Hence, "modernist mythopoeia," according to literary critic Michael Bell, "is the recognition that this edifice of the human world is not a building resting on the ground, but a boat; and if all men dwell in one, it is not necessarily the same one. There is a multiplicity of possible human worlds."[24] Like James Joyce, William Faulkner, and Tennessee Williams, Graham and MacLeish moved old stories from ancient "buildings" into modern "boats" for *Night Journey* and *J.B.* Many members of their cold war audience, however, more familiar with the Platonic truths of containment liberalism, did not understand the relativistic truths of the artists' cargo. Looking for security in a threatening world, they wanted to build a universal faith on a firm foundation, not sail a relative belief around the world to compare its culture-bound truths to other faiths.

The problem of relativism was especially acute for the audience of *J.B.* MacLeish had modernized the story of Job to probe for a humanistic explanation of innocent suffering, which had recently occurred on a vast scale during the war and was threatened daily by the Bomb. In an article in the *New York Times*, reprinted in the souvenir program for *J.B*, MacLeish stated: "The poem of Job is the only one I know of which our modern history will fit. Job's search, like ours, was for the meaning of his afflictions.... The enormous, nameless disasters that have befallen whole cities, entire peoples, in two great wars and many small ones, have destroyed the innocent together with the guilty—and with no cause our minds can grasp.... Hiroshima, in its terrible retrospect, appalls us."[25] Seeking a humanistic rather than a Christian or Jewish understanding of Job's dilemma, MacLeish made several changes to the biblical story. Drawing on Jungian insights into the Book of Job, the author painted the deity as primitive and emotional, a God who could let loose the horrors of the nuclear age with little justification. In the end, MacLeish's J.B. rejects this amoral force and takes up life again on his own terms, despite his pain and ignorance. MacLeish also marginalized the Almighty in the final scene of his play. In contrast to the biblical story, J.B. and his wife, Sarah, discover a new basis for their love of each other in nature.

The popular response to *J.B.*, however, almost completely ignored MacLeish's changes to the old myth. The reviews—initially delivered orally on radio and television because of a newspaper strike, then published later—generally skipped over the humanistic alterations to emphasize the play's continuities with the biblical story. "The Book of Job is interpreted in literal terms," wrote John McClain, "[It asks] the eternal question, 'Why does God punish the innocent?'" Several reviewers conflated MacLeish's humanistic ending with an affirmation of religious faith. "God triumphs over evil as J.B. is restored, in mind and body, by love," noted John Chapman. Barked Walter Winchell: "Great simplicity of faith—which enables humans to defy the cruelties of fate—is eloquently conveyed." In part, these reviewers were simply following ads and press releases on the show that trumpeted the production as a "modern story of Job."[26]

Articles on *J.B.*, in fact, were as likely to appear in the religious as in the theater sections of the newsweeklies; *Time* even ran religiously slanted reports on the play in both places for its 22 December issue. Henry Luce's other mainstream journal, *Life*, also pumped the production. A fifteen-page spread featured an extensive review of the show, interviews with three theologians about the play's religious implications, and several pages that coupled photos from the production with nineteenth-century engravings by William Blake, "the famous English mystic" (according to *Life*), meant to illuminate the Bible story. Headlined by an appropriate quotation from the King James Book of Job, the photo and engraving series no doubt led readers to suppose that MacLeish's morality play had simply updated the biblical story but preserved intact its ancient religious truths. Even though the introductory review admitted that "the ending is too biological for good theodicy," the picture spread assured readers of *Life* that God's Word was still supreme, even on the Broadway stage.[27]

MacLeish was partly to blame for the play's overwhelmingly religious reception. Although he had tacked on a new ending, the main outline of the biblical narrative remained. Spectators who knew the general story but had not studied the Book of Job—probably most audience members—would have been hard pressed to tell the differences. More importantly, the Old Testament deity, though eventually sidelined, drives the action forward for much of the MacLeish drama. The playwright borrowed from his experience as a radio dramatist to characterize the Almighty. A sonorous presence emanating only from the theater's loudspeaker, MacLeish's "Distant Voice" prompts Zuss and Nickles to say their lines after they have donned the masks of God and Satan, controls the actions and speeches of one of the messengers who reports the calamities that kill J.B.'s five children, drops an atomic bomb to humble J.B., and shames the hero into repentance with a deafening roar of King James verse. For much of the allegory, this deus-ex-microphone functions like a master puppeteer, pulling the strings of many of MacLeish's characters to ensure that the plot follows its preordained path. A God of divine compulsion propels most of the action forward.

Several critics objected to the characters' apparent lack of agency. "The play itself is a mask," said Walter Kerr, "a matter of sounds projected from behind rigidly formed lips, of thoughts filtered through graven—though meaningful—images." Henry Hewes judged *J.B.* ineffective as drama, for "drama presupposes real characters doing real things for reasons discoverable by an audience." Likewise, Harold Clurman found the play abstract and lifeless: "No people, no true situations." Arguably, these critics misunderstood MacLeish's humanistic intentions, but MacLeish, for his part, did accord primary agency to the Almighty until near the end, and even there he botched J.B.'s decision to live his life without God. Instead of placing J.B.'s awakening to existential freedom at the emotional climax of the drama, the highpoint comes when the Voice commands J.B.'s obedience and he submits. J.B. and Sarah are given only the denouement to move beyond monotheism and remake their lives.[28]

Indeed, the power of Platonic abstraction, related to the general effects of radiophony on the culture of liberal containment, squeezed much of the life out of *J.B.* Not only does a disembodied voice propel most of the play, but two of the major characters, Zuss and Nickles, also lose much of their physicality when they put on their masks to become God and Satan in the frame play encompassing J.B.'s story. This metatheatrical device further abstracts the narrative of *J.B.* and, like all modes of metatheatricality, problematizes the dramatic agency of the hero. Boris Aronson's setting also emphasized the production's abstract, allegorical ambitions. He used a tattered circus tent to represent a *teatrum mundi*, a universal space in which Zuss and Nickles could logically become versions of God and Satan when they put on their masks and J.B. could become an Everyman to enact the timeless tale. Within the tent was a large center ring for the mortals of the play, a pole with an elevated trapeze platform stage right for Zuss/God, and steps descending from the ring on the left for Nickles/Satan to stand or sit on. Visually, J.B., his family, and his wife frequently stood between a God mask on high at stage right and a Satan figure below on the left. Ingenious though it was, the setting

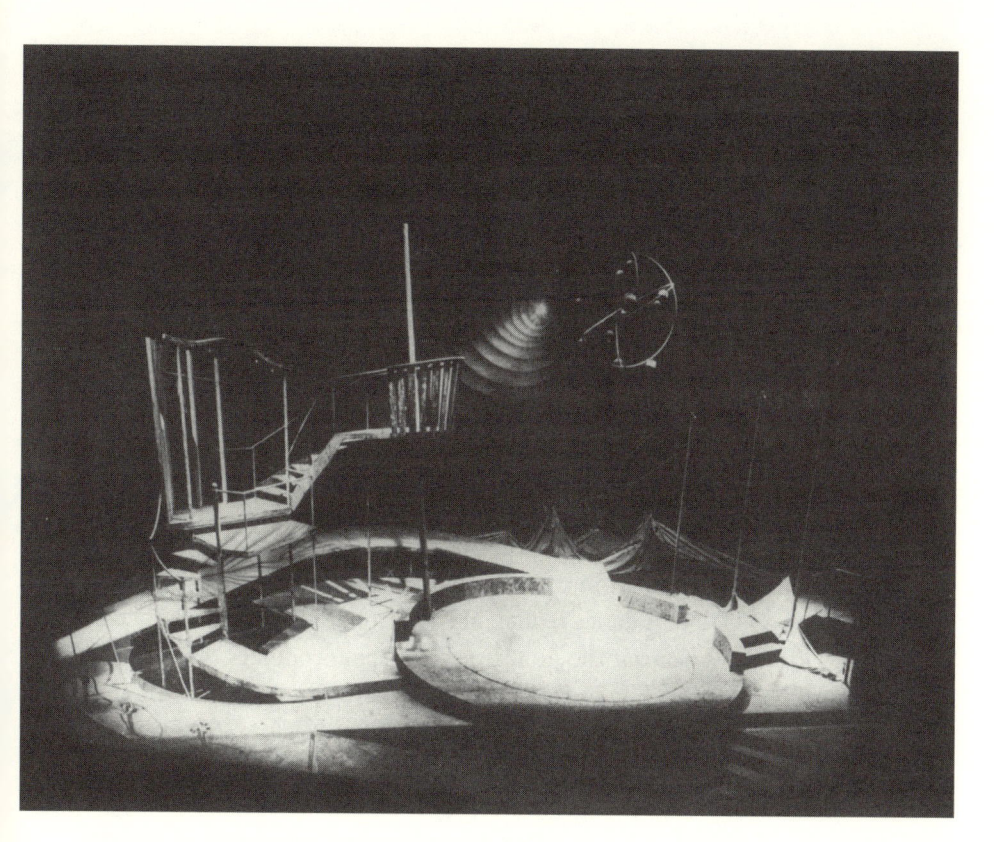

Boris Aronson's set for J.B. *Courtesy New York Public Library.*

promised a Sunday school lesson justifying the ways of God to man, not, as MacLeish apparently intended, a humanistic response to the problem of an amoral Almighty. More than Empty Boy or Family Circle plays did, *J.B.* climbed into a world of disembodied abstractions and, for some in the audience, never left it.

Night Journey also resorted to metatheatricality, but its framing device was less of an impediment to its spectators' enjoyment than in *J.B.* In part, *Night Journey's* greater tolerance for Platonic abstraction was due to its different genre; nearly all dance works at a further remove than most dramatic theater from the randomness of everyday reality. Like the play, however, the framing situation of the modern dance severely restricted the hero's agency. Graham set the present time of *Night Journey* at the moment just before Jocasta's suicide; all that is left for her character to do is to recognize the depths of her sin and kill herself. A 1948 program note began with a quotation from Sophocles' *Oedipus* about Jocasta's fate then continued: "This dance is a legend of recognition. The action takes place in Jocasta's heart at the moment when she recognizes the ultimate terms of her destiny. She enters her room where the precise fulfillment of its terms awaits her. Here the Daughters of the Night, Oedipus in his inescapable role, and the Seer pursue themselves across her heart in that instant of agony."[29] Thus the dance stretches the "moment when [Jocasta] recognizes" her fate, that "instant of agony," into a fifteen-minute flashback in which she remembers her courtship, marriage, and intimacy with her son.

In accord with the constricted agency of her hero, Graham's rendition of the Oedipus story is much more deterministic than Sophocles' tragedy. Unlike Sophocles, Graham allows no room for character interaction to shape dramatic outcome; not only are the figures of Jocasta and Oedipus doomed from the start, but their specific fates are sealed. In addition to the flashback structure, Graham alters the usual function of the Greek chorus to effect this change. Instead of setting the context for the action and expressing concern about the future of the polis, the Chorus of six, rendered omniscient in Graham's version, dances only the present anxiety and immediate doom awaiting Jocasta In fact, the Choral Leader sometimes doubles as a second Jocasta to represent the hero's immediate anguish. Even more than the story of Job structures most of *J.B.* and limits the hero's ability to alter his situation, the narrative of the Greek tragedy determines the fate of Jocasta. Compulsion combines with allegory to doom her to suicide.

The only question of agency in the dance is the extent of Jocasta's (and hence the audience's) recognition of the past actions that have brought her to her present agony. Graham used the conventions of expressionism to structure this interior journey toward gradual recognition — conventions her spectators had seen before. Dance critic Deborah Jowitt has drawn attention to the influence of Noh theater on the structure of Graham's narratives. Certainly Graham, like Noh artists, used memory as a narrative framework for several of her pieces, including *Night Journey*, which allowed her to extend or collapse time and to shift quickly from place to place. Few of her spectators had any experience of Noh; but they had watched numerous flashbacks in films and such dream dances on the stage as Agnes DeMille's piece for *Oklahoma*, all of which worked within the logic of expressionism. Graham's spectators, then, were prepared to look directly into the thoughts and feelings of a unified dramatic character. They understood that the images and sounds they found there expressed the interior truth of this character but might not mirror actual events. In line with these expectations, *Life* magazine assured spectators in 1947 that Graham's dances lie "in a subconscious world of poetic impulses, impressions, and symbols. To their audiences, they look like lucid and beautifully costumed dreams."[30]

Spectators eager to follow Jocasta's dreamlike journey toward recognition could not have missed the importance of Tieresias, whose three entrances mark significant turning points in the dance and suggest the implacability of a fate that dooms Jocasta. At each of his appearances, Tieresias methodically propels his body, draped in a cavernous costume, across the diagonal of the stage with a long walking stick whose evenly paced thuds on the stage floor seem to measure out the time remaining in Jocasta's life. On his first entrance, only moments after the dance has begun, he momentarily plants his stick between Jocasta's legs before thumping off, an action that awakens her memory. His second dance across the stage, which maintains the same methodical rhythm as before, is a series of pogo-stick–like hops with the walking stick. The movement, almost comical in its grotesquerie were it not also so forceful and threatening, culminates when Tieresias stops to untie the umbilicus–sexual knot that unites Oedipus and Jocasta with his stick. Finally, near the

Jocasta/Martha Graham strangles herself with the umbilicus rope at the climax of Night Journey. Bennett & Pleasant photo, courtesy New York Public Library.

end of the dance and again in the same rhythm, Tieresias places his stick once again between the legs of Jocasta, who collapses limply on her back. This action brings her back to present time, and she quickly hangs herself with the rope. In his three appearances, then, Tieresias sends Jocasta back into her past, points up her fatal confusion between mother love and sexual desire, and recalls her from her memories to kill herself. Much as the Distant Voice functions in *J.B.* to keep the narrative in line with the Book of Job, the entrances of Tieresias tie the actions of Jocasta to the fate of the character in Sophocles' play. Tieresias, like Zuss in *J.B.*, even wears a mask. Echoing the abstracting effects of radiophony, Tieresias and the Distant Voice are agents of dramatic Platonism, enforcers of allegories to stifle human agency.

In addition, Tieresias is also a figure of patriarchal power. His monolithic power and phallic stick of fate finally determine Jocasta's suicide and even structure the kind of recognition she gains from her journey into memory. Although *Night Journey* allowed female sexuality more complexity than male, Graham's investment in phallo-centrism drives the narrative of the dance. For Graham, womanhood involved both an outside container and an inside self. As dance critic-historian Susan Foster explains, "Among the most prominent of all dualities organizing Graham's world is that of the exterior body and the interior self. Residing inside the body, the self is composed of thinking and feeling functions, conscious and unconscious attitudes, and a spiritual aspect or soul. Influenced by the body's physical needs and affected by the outside world, the self nonetheless lives an autonomous existence as unitary and as bounded as the body it inhabits."[31] Because the self can only be known through the body, however, the body also becomes the boundary of conflict between the "body," in its distinctive sense as container, and the interior, contained self. The tension between inner self and outer body shapes the movements of individual dancers and motivates much of the kinesthetic action of an entire dance. Graham's use of the body and the self was much the same as the techniques of Method acting, which emphasized the conflict between an authentic, interior self and an exterior social mask; both embodied the kinesthetics of containment liberalism.

For Graham, ground zero of this ongoing conflict between self and body was the female pelvis. Graham's technique centered on alternations and variations of physical contraction and release rippling out from the sexual organs. The initial contraction typically turned the pelvis up and under against the bowed curve of the lower spine, sending out shock waves that would twist and contort the extremities of the body. Although release involved a countermovement, realigning the pelvis and spine, it rarely led to much muscular relaxation; the self vs. body agon kept many of the dancer's muscles in tension. As dance critic Graham Jackson observes, "The pubic bone . . . is the real center of movement [in Graham's choreography]."[32] Because sexual energy spiraled outward into the rest of the body, Graham's dances always carried more complex meanings than the bumps and grinds of erotic dancing in nightclubs. Nonetheless, the origin of that energy, before it was twisted by counter-impulses from the body and the self, was essentially the same.

With the pelvis as the natural site of sexuality in the human body, *Night Journey* radiated female eroticism. Pelvic contractions shaped the initial movements of the Chorus, as they marched on stage in profile foreshadowing Jocasta's incest. Later in the dance, an aroused Jocasta began contraction and release movements toward Oedipus, at first coyly, in a sitting position, and then with increasing abandon as she sought to win his affection. At different points in their erotic entanglements, Graham was standing with her feet on Hawkins's thighs, her pelvis turned toward his face; lying under him with her legs spread as their lips almost touched in a kiss; and later grabbing his torso with her legs around his hips and her head nearly touching the floor. Their mother-son relationship never lost its adult sexuality. When Jocasta cradled her son in her arms, with her pelvis turned in and up, for example, the context of their lovemaking gave their momentary Madonna-child pose a heightened erotic charge.

For all of its sexual gymnastics, however, the dance never paused for the moment of physical release and relaxation that normally follows the climax of sexual coupling. *Journey* demonstrated the conflict between the self and the body but the complete satisfaction of neither one. Thus the dance made clear the unsuccessful attempt of Jocasta's self to contain and channel the libidinal energy erupting from her physical needs and unconscious desires. The bias-cut, clinging jersey dresses that Graham used to costume herself and her female dancers, which reached from shoulder to mid-calf, emphasized the twisted, angular movements produced by this agon. The self-body conflict ravaged Jocasta, leaving her finally a limp rag doll in the hands of fate.

In contrast to the women on stage, Oedipus and Tieresias rarely motivated their movements from their pubic bones; in fact, both appeared to lack an internal self. As critic Jack Anderson notes, Graham's male characters have often been "muscular dimwits, undeniably virile, but possessing little emotional or moral complexity."[33] Their lack of internality, however, gave them less vulnerability and more power. Oedipus was forceful and bullying in his courtship—effectively a rape—of Jocasta. At one significant point in their duet, with her kneeling in front of him, he slapped his thigh and slowly lowered his calf over her shoulder, arrogantly placing her underfoot. Just as Oedipus had raped Jocasta in the past, Tieresias performed two symbolic rapes—the stick between her legs—in the present moments of the dance. Her initial domination by the hegemonic masculinity of Oedipus prefigured the fate that Tieresias would seal at the end of her life.

Several critics have taken Graham to task for her investment in phallo-centrism in *Journey* and other dances from this era. Hawkins's chest muscles rippled with as much beefcake as William Holden's, and Graham costumed him in what amounted to a Greek version of a jockstrap to emphasize his sexual power. Unlike many musclemen and most film stars, Hawkins did not shave his chest and legs for Oedipus, thus increasing his sexual threat. (Bertram Ross, who took over the role from Hawkins in 1950, was even hairier than Hawkins had been.)[34] Hawkins's movements as Oedipus frequently turned him into an erect phallus: tense, vertical poses, stiff-legged struts and bows, and arm and shoulder thrusts, for example. Graham's phallo-centrism worked in easy conjunction with her sexualized women; her male dancers could simultaneously be both flesh-and-blood musclemen and female wish-fulfillments.

In *Night Journey*, then, Jocasta's sexualized body defeats her contained, interior self. Biology is destiny here; Jocasta's sexual desire kills her. Graham's Jocasta joined a variety of postwar images of women who struggle vainly against their desiring bodies to express their inner selves. Elsewhere in the theater, Kazan's direction of *Streetcar* provided perhaps the best example. Like his treatment of Blanche, *Night Journey* justified the rape of a sexualized female by a hegemonic male. In both, the male was primarily a force of nature—hence guilt for the act rebounded to the female for inciting male desire. Similarly, predatory women seeking self-realization lurked in the shadows of *film noir* and usually deserved to die or go insane for their desires. Even more to be feared, however, Jocasta represented a mom on the prowl for her son, a nightmare of "Momism" in mythic form. These images of the sexualized woman as Other proliferated during World War II and were quickly linked to nuclear power after Hiroshima. Though appearing in a different cultural field, Graham was as much of a "bombshell" as Rita Hayworth or Marilyn Monroe. Yuriko Kikuchi, a Japanese American who achieved minor stardom in the 1950s dancing in Graham's troupe and elsewhere (including *The King and I*), later deployed a nuclear metaphor to recall her mentor's effectiveness: "Onstage, she was like the core of an atom bomb. She was like a hurricane that sucked us all into the dance."[35]

A similar dynamic joining hegemonic and conservative masculinities and marginalizing women as the Other occurs in *J.B.* A biblical man-in-a-gray-flannel-suit, J.B., though a banker, is "middle management" in terms of the hierarchy of males on stage. Zuss and Nickles are the conservative males; both older men represent a traditional approach to power and morality, especially when playing God and Satan. Positioned beneath J.B. are the two male messengers who relate the catastrophes that kill his children. MacLeish establishes J.B.'s hegemonic status early in the play. Sitting with his family at their Thanksgiving dinner, J.B. tells the "lucky story" that lies behind his success. A recent immigrant in town, an Irishman named Patrick Sullivan, asks J.B. why he gets "the best of the rest of us." J.B. replies that where others see only streets, he sees "roads" that are "going somewhere" and follows them. When Sullivan says that only "God knows" where such roads are going, J.B. replies, "He does. . . . That's why [I] get the best of you: It's God's country, Mr. Sullivan" (43). This smug J.B. may be ripe for a fall, but it is the fall of a hegemonic male, not of a recent immigrant whose problems could not be representative of American business-class culture.

The female characters in *J.B.* have little agency that matters. Much as Betsy Rath was relegated to the margins as a scold in *The Man in the Gray Flannel Suit*, Sarah, J.B's wife, carps at her husband from the sidelines but has little effect on the main action of the play. Against J.B., she takes a Calvinist position on God's covenant with humanity in the Thanksgiving scene, refuses to praise a God who slaughters her children, and even abandons her husband after the Bomb has ruined their lives. Shell-shocked and childlike, Sarah returns to him in the end holding a forsythia branch. In MacLeish's initial script for this final scene, Sarah advises J.B. to let their love for each other become the foundation for their renewal. "Blow on the coal of the heart / And we'll see by and by" (153), she tells him. J.B. agrees, and together they begin to put in order what remains of their house as the curtain falls. Director Kazan, however, advised MacLeish to downgrade Sarah's importance in this scene. Arguing that "in the theater you've got to end the play you've begun," Kazan urged MacLeish to give the "coal of the heart" speech to J.B.; the will of the hero, Kazan felt, must shape the end of the play.[36] MacLeish objected at first but bowed to Kazan's theatrical knowledge. Kazan's version, though arguably less believable in terms of American business-class marriages, does replicate the J.B-Sarah relationship in the rest of the play.

Woman as Other also characterizes the five women and a girl who appear as refugees from the bombed-out city—Miss Mabel, Mrs. Murphy, Mrs. Botticelli, Mrs. Lesure, Mrs. Adams, and her daughter Jolly. MacLeish uses their lower-class, ethnically accented voices to suggest the bleak conditions of post-Bomb living and to comment on J.B. and his Comforters. Significantly, they cannot hear the Distant Voice when it speaks to J.B.

In contrast to *Night Journey*, however, none of these women is demonized for her sexuality. Indeed, Sarah's fecundity in the post-Bomb world at the end of *J.B.* is one of the keys to the play's hopeful conclusion; it becomes a source of moral and spiritual regeneration. In line with the general narrative of *J.B.*, the ending caps the jeremiad pattern of the play. Human biology has been there all along, the play suggests; America has only to remove the restraints blocking the realization of love and desire—has only to "blow on the coal of the heart"—and nature will provide. Like Sarah, the Mrs. Murphys, Botticellis, and other women are not simply refugees from nuclear devastation. They are female survivors with the capability of repopulating the world.

After an initial scene setting up the Pirandellian framework of the drama, the dramatic action within the frame begins with J.B. and his family at Thanksgiving dinner. As J.B. carves the turkey, he explains his confidence that God will continue to reward him not because he deserves it (as his wife believes) but because bounty is in the nature of things and he is in tune with nature. J.B. is correct about the bounty of nature, as this jeremiad narrative eventually demonstrates, but he has much to learn about his place in the universe. The scene is a pastoral idyll, drawing on the myth of America as a garden of plenty and rejecting the Puritan notion of a covenant, a mutually binding relationship linking God with His Chosen People. Although MacLeish modifies the conventional notion of a Chosen People here, he does not discard it. Living in the abundance of the Almighty's cornucopia, Americans, suggests MacLeish, have been extraordinarily blessed. The ethnic joke of the "lucky story" underlines J.B.'s faith in God and nature, his belief, as he says, in "some mysterious certainty of opulence" (43).

MacLeish uses the Thanksgiving scene to suggest that the material abundance of the postwar era has lulled Americans into a false sense of themselves as God's Elect. The scene draws rhetorically on the common perception among business-class Americans that they were a "people of plenty," a term coined by historian David Potter in a 1954 book and widely quoted for the rest of the decade. According to Potter, American inquisitiveness, optimism, practicality, exuberance, and competitiveness — in short, the defining features of American individualism — derived from the widespread material abundance of American life. John Kenneth Galbraith repeated many of Potter's claims in his popular book *The Affluent Society* (1958).[37] *J.B.* accords with the conventional wisdom about nature's generosity to America but criticizes J.B.'s smugness for thinking it is his rightful due. Confident about his American future as God's Chosen, J.B. is ripe for a warning from the Almighty.

The Bomb annihilates J.B.'s confidence but not his faith. When his wife warns that "God rewards and God can punish" (39), J.B. reacts like most churchgoing Americans. The God of Judgment can be safely ignored, he assumes, because He is present in the love of his family and the bounty of nature. The next four scenes deliver a series of hammer blows to J.B.'s self-confidence. His five blond children and his bank are destroyed in increasingly grotesque calamities — an armistice, a car crash, a rape, and the fall of an atomic bomb. The explosion brings down the circus tent; returns J.B. to the stage in rags, with blistered skin; and leaves Sarah shell-shocked. One of the women temporarily outside the circle of hags who huddle around J.B.'s house for warmth in the aftermath of the blast asks to be included in "the ark" (51). Indeed, the audience is induced to interpret the nuclear catastrophe as a second Flood, and hence a suitable warning from the Almighty. Looking for allegorical connections, spectators might have supposed that J.B. was punished for his smugness and pride, if not for his wickedness. Although one of the main points of the biblical story was Job's innocence, the fit between the play production and the jeremiad narrative remained close. Spectators knew they were a "people of plenty" but worried that God might not continue to favor an affluent nation.

J.B., too, believes that some evil act on his part must have triggered his calamity. J.B.'s "Show me my guilt, O God," specified in the stage directions as a "great cry," ends Act I and begins Act II (54, 56). This plea sets up the scene with the Comforters, whom MacLeish has updated as a Marxist, a psychiatrist, and a clergyman. After the first two maintain that guilt is an illusion, J.B. counters that guilt is a reality that "matters." At this point in the argument, there is nothing in J.B.'s perspective on guilt to trouble an audience familiar with Judeo-Christian belief. In refuting Zophar, the clergyman, however, J.B. rejects the doctrine of original sin, the first significant sign in the play that MacLeish is pushing for a humanistic not a religious ending to his reworking of the Job myth. Belief in original sin is one of the restraints that J.B. must remove from his mind if he is to achieve self-knowledge. But no sooner has he announced that he will not admit to a sin he cannot know he has committed than the Distant Voice overwhelms him with its power, and J.B., still in ignorance of his sin but following the King James script, says, "Wherefore / I abhor myself . . . and repent" (60).

Kazan wanted a "recognition scene" to follow soon after this moment of abasement, when, he said, "J.B., having accepted his insignificance and impotence in the face of the scale and majesty of the universe, passes from dependence and humbleness to independence and dignity and pride in his own manliness." Following Kazan's advice, MacLeish rewrote the ending. J.B. kicks Zuss and Nickles off the stage and stands alone in triumph: "Neither the bowing nor the blood / Will make an end for me now! / Neither the / Yes in ignorance . . . / the No in spite . . . / Neither of them" (64). In his next scene with Sarah, J.B. convinces her to "blow on the coal" of their love for each other. Now that all restraints have been removed, the wonder and power of nature, briefly glimpsed in the Thanksgiving scene, can triumph in the end.[38]

Significantly, even though MacLeish discards the theological underpinnings of a conventional jeremiad tale, *J.B.* remains a story of moral regeneration. In the typical jeremiad, guilt powers repentance and reformation. The plot of the play, however, moves J.B. away from any link to God through guilt and toward an existential recognition of his human freedom. In the end, as biblical scholar W. D. White concludes, J.B.'s freedom from guilt abolishes God: "In the crisis of his life, [J.B.] protests (not his innocence as the Biblical Job) but his guilt. He must be guilty; otherwise his idea of God cannot stand; and since his idea of God is the only dramatically realized God in the play, the puncturing of his idea means the abolition of God." Probably few in the audience worked through the problem of God and guilt in this syllogistic manner, but the narrative of the play leads invariably to White's conclusion. MacLeish sets up God as the ultimate ontological justification for a guilty conscience only to knock Him down. Perhaps not wishing to accept this ending or simply annoyed at MacLeish's hesitations in arriving at it, most reviewers termed the conclusion weak and confusing. As critic Thomas Porter remarks, however, MacLeish's ending may have rejected one god, but it ushered in another: "The comic structure [of *J.B.*] is itself a denial of [MacLeish's humanism]. The 'sacred marriage' on which this structure is modeled is a celebration of an extrinsic power—the power of Nature. Dispatching the God of the theologians, of the Book of Job, of traditional Calvinism out the front door in the epiphany scene, MacLeish slips the 'strong' gods of fertility in through the kitchen."[39] Porter is right; all Western definitions of God, the final restraints holding humanity back from existential freedom, must be tossed out. The fertility gods might not be Christian or Jewish, but they could work through sexual love to induce moral regeneration, the necessary conclusion of a successful jeremiad. And spectators educated in the virtues of spousal "togetherness" would have had little difficulty with this business-class version of Dionysian theology.

Actually, MacLeish advanced three distinct notions of God in *J.B.*: Jungian, Judeo-Christian, and pantheistic. Regarding the first two, the drama distinguishes theologically between the Distant Voice and the deity of the God-mask worn by Mr. Zuss. The first is an arbitrary, demanding force—the essence of compulsion—deriving from MacLeish's reading of Carl Jung's interpretation of the Book of Job. The second, embodied on stage by an impassive, Michelangelo-inspired mask and the rich baritone of Raymond Massey, was the conventional God of wisdom and justice. This deity's Dantesque catch-phrase "His will, our peace" (1958 version of *J.B.*, 62) sums up his conventional Judeo-Christian relationship to humankind. The third is the Dionysian life force, expressed through external nature and human sexuality. Despite these different versions of God, there is little evidence that spectators ever moved beyond their Judeo-Christian assumptions in interpreting the play.

Significantly, only one of the contemporary reviewers questioned the cultural and religious preconceptions that conditioned the reception of

J.B. In his *New Yorker* review, Kenneth Tynan cited Asian scholar Alan Watts on the theological and psychological benefits of separating divine creation and earthly justice in imagining a God. If creation and justice are joined, said Tynan, quoting Watts, the believer gets "a sense of guilt so preposterous that it must issue either in denying one's own nature or in rejecting God."[40] Ironically, MacLeish would have agreed with Tynan, but the spectacular production of his overly complex and too subtle play suggested otherwise to playgoers unused to questioning conventional religious beliefs. Tynan's (and Watts's) warning to the contrary, all other reviewers and no doubt nearly all spectators assumed that MacLeish's God was One, and all the more omnipotent, for combining violence, creation, justice, and nature. For audiences during the Eisenhower era committed to moral regeneration but uninterested in theology, *J.B.* made no sense unless based upon some religion—and most, like their president, did not care what it was.

While *J.B.* generally fulfilled the narrative expectations of a jeremiad, *Night Journey* arrested spectators at the moment of nuclear apocalypse. As previously noted, Graham altered Sophocles' narrative to keep the audience focused on the "instant of agony" just preceding Jocasta's suicide. Time is ticking down to zero from the moment the dance begins. Noguchi's set design included several pedestals of different heights with a frozen hourglass design as well as a swag of curtain also twisted to resemble the point-to-point triangles of the hourglass shape. Like Salvador Dali's melting clocks, the stage picture told the audience forthrightly that this was an expressionistic dance about time. More importantly, perhaps, the movement and sound of Tieresias kept spectators mindful of Jocasta's present dilemma, the moment when her past memory and present recognition would come together in apocalyptic simultaneity. Like some implacable clock of fate, the walking stick of Tieresias counted down the remaining time in Jocasta's life.

Graham's interest in the fateful instant of apocalypse imitates a similar focus on the instantaneous nature of annihilation in nuclear narratives. In anticipating a nuclear attack, Americans imagined that the past and the future would become suddenly irrelevant, that all of life would collapse into an instant. News reports of Hiroshima stressed the immediacy of the obliteration; and John Hersey's novel of the same name, published the next year, reminded American readers of this fact. The first section of Hersey's book, entitled "A Noiseless Flash," resembles a series of photographs of survivors and victims frozen in the moment of their fate. For example: "At exactly fifteen minutes past eight in the morning, on August 6, 1945, Japanese time, at the moment when the atomic bomb flashed above Hiroshima, Miss Toshiko Sasaki, a clerk in the personnel department of the East Asia Tin Works, had just sat down in her place in the plant office and was turning her head to speak to the girl at the next desk."[41] Readers later learn more about Toshiko Sasaki's past and her recovery after the blast, but the immediate impression created by Hersey's prose is of a random person caught in the midst of action, her life suddenly summed up by a nuclear snapshot. Hersey underlined that instant—"exactly fifteen minutes past eight in the morning"—by invoking clock time. Time became a potent metaphor of nuclear apocalypse during the early Cold War. In 1946 the editors of the *Bulletin of Atomic Scientists* printed an "atomic clock" on the cover of their journal. For the next fourteen years of the journal, the hands of the atomic clock on the cover remained near midnight.

Night Journey attempts to capture the moment of life immediately before it is doomed by a fate similar to a nuclear explosion. It was a commonplace in the late 1940s that fear of the Bomb made people speechless. Near the beginning of *Journey*, Chorus members attempt to force sounds out of their mouths to warn Jocasta, but no words come forth. They know that apocalypse hovers on the instant but are powerless to stop it with language. The futile attempt to speak was only one of many gestures that may be read as an arrested moment in the shadow of the Bomb.

Graham approached much of her choreography as a series of snapshots, which partly accounts for the success of still photography in rendering the essentials of her work. In formal terms, the static pose and its full-stage counterpart, the tableau, are the opposite of flow, the fluidity of movement that links stage pictures together. Commenting on Graham's artistry in the early 1930s, Mark Franko noted that "weight, tension, and angularity" were the hallmarks of her dances, "to the virtual exclusion of flow." Flow figured more prominently in her postwar dances, but it remained what Rudolph von Laban, the systemizer of choreographic movement, would term "bound" flow because the muscles of her dancers were often pulling against, interrupting, and contradicting each other. Analyzing Graham's work in 1984, *New York Times* critic Anna Kisselgoff generalized that her images were "more jagged and filled with tension than even Picasso's forms." Stressing the angularity of her poses in 1947, Robert Horan wrote that Graham herself "is built like a series of diamonds joined at their points."[42] Graham rarely allowed herself or her dancers to "go with the flow."

Graham's arrested moments of jagged tension helped her dances to embody the snapshots of reality that haunted American nightmares of nuclearism after Hiroshima. Significantly, flow is the opposite of containment in kinesthetic terms. Spectators watching *Journey* saw her dancers producing moments of static poses by containing the flowing, sexualized energy of their bodies. The jump-cuts in Graham's dances, however, puzzled even some of her most insightful critics. In 1950 John Martin applauded the improvements he saw in *Errand into the Maze*, another of Graham's Greek pieces, but questioned the continuing lack of flow in the dance. "[Graham composes] in percussive clusters, so to speak, instead of in dynamic continuity," he noted. Horan wrote of an early version of *Cave of the Heart*, Graham's Medea dance, that "one is not engaged in the flow of the work from beginning to end, but intermittently, as if one had closed one's eyes for a moment between each section and opened them further along, having missed an essential link."[43]

Even more than *Night Journey*, *Cave of the Heart* (first performed in 1946 and repeated frequently during the 1950s) evoked nuclear fears. The program at its premiere, when it was entitled *Serpent Heart*, included these notes: "This is a dance of possessive and destroying love, a love which feeds upon itself, like the serpent heart, and when it is overthrown, is filled only with revenge. . . . Medea destroys that which she has been unable to possess and brings upon herself and her beloved the inhuman wrath of one who has been betrayed." Critic Walter Terry may have imagined a billowing mushroom cloud when he wrote of the dance as "flaming passion" and "violent destruction," adding, "the very chemistry of expanding hate is revealed." The image of a nuclear Salome seemed to hover above Robert Sabin's comments: "The trembling of her entire body, the sinuous movements of the hands and arms, the hypnotic intensity of her movement and facial expression suggest unholy power." Near the end of *Cave of the Heart*, Medea pulled on a corset-like apparatus radiating bronze spikes to celebrate her victory. For the poet Robert Horan, Graham's "coppery cage" appeared "to emphasize an insect-like inhumanity." Medea, he said, had been transformed into "a grasshopper in a desert."[44] Or, to extend the insect metaphor, she became one of the giant ants infected by radioactivity in *Them!* As in much *film noir*, a female "bombshell" could poison the world, leaving behind only insects in a wasteland. In both *Cave of the Heart* and *Night Journey*, the power of female sexuality mushrooms into apocalypse.

Graham's investment in choreographic brinkmanship, however, took its toll in formal and rhetorical coherence. At a fundamental level, spectators must be able to read narrative changes, especially those motivated by inner drives and tensions, in the shifting movements of the dancers' bodies. For Graham, however, the necessity of both involving her spectators in the flow of the narrative and analyzing the arrested moment of recognition was ultimately a double bind. Driven by a need for narrative, she looked to the Greek myths for stories that could involve her spectators in questions of human fate. Yet the finality of apocalypse cut against the choreographic usefulness of time and drove her toward space, toward an analysis and deployment of the spatial dynamics of her characters' last moments. Graham had bumped up against the ultimate contradiction of liberal containment culture: containment necessitated by nuclearism could stop narrative continuity and the necessary fluidity of human movement in its tracks. In the film *Dr. Strangelove or: How I Learned to Stop Worrying and Love the Bomb* (1964), Stanley Kubrick's comic meditation on nuclear apocalypse, the paranoiac commander who refuses to stop the Mutually Assured Destruction (MAD) of the USA and the USSR obsesses on a Communist conspiracy to control his "precious bodily fluids." The protocols of MAD contained the fluidity of life in order to save it. Similarly, Graham must arrest the flow of narrative to tell a story that ends all narrative. Her focus on the moment of Jocasta's death tied the usual flow of narrative into a Gordian knot.

Tellingly, in production *J.B.* had similar narrative problems following the explosion of the Bomb near the end of Act I. In his original poem, MacLeish continued his "all the world is a circus" metaphor throughout the play; only the Distant Voice comes from a space beyond the tent. When Kazan transferred *J.B.* to the stage, however, he evidently felt the need to literalize the nuclear blast, which is only hinted at in MacLeish's poem. Hence, the circus tent that had seemed to be the world collapses with the explosion, leaving only "a black sky streaked with smoldering light like the horizon of a stormy sunset or a burned-out city far away. There is a jangled sound of screaming sirens and falling walls; then dark and silence" (51). According to critic Thomas Porter, Kazan's change improved MacLeish's play: "[After the Bomb], performers and spectators are no longer sheltered even by the thin fabric of a circus tent. J.B. and Sarah, the bombed-out women, Zuss and Nickles are all unaccommodated; they share the same situation. The setting situates the action first in a man-made, make-believe world, then in a world of empty spaces behind the circus tent."[45] Porter's plausible explanation for the post-Bomb world of the play may have been what Kazan wanted to suggest through his elimination of MacLeish's framing metaphor.

The production's literalism regarding the effect of the nuclear blast, however, undermined the narrative coherence of the drama. Porter is right to suppose that annihilating the tent moved the reality of the play from a "make-believe" world to a more realistic one for theater spectators. But if make-believe has been destroyed, who are Zuss and Nickles and why do they continue to stand in as surrogates for God and the Devil? If all of the characters now share the same level of reality, is there a new relationship between the actors/circus vendors and J.B.? How could Zuss and Nickles continue to remain outside of the *J.B.* play-within-a-play?

This last question is particularly relevant to the inside/outside entailment of containment culture. In effect, the Bomb at the end of Act I collapsed the nesting blocks that kept the J.B. story safely inside the Zuss-Nickles narrative. The blast that brought down the circus tent seemed to level the playing field, leaving only the Distant Voice and, as Porter (alluding to *King Lear*) notes, "unaccommodated man," which now includes Zuss and Nickles along with the victims of the A-Bomb.[46] In this sense, Kazan and MacLeish may have been responding to the cognitive logic of nuclear war, which threatened to collapse all distinctions between inside and outside. That logic, however, radically destabilized the narrative frame and development of *J.B.* Contrary to Porter's conclusion, most of Act II maintains the convention established in the frame play that Zuss and Nickles can talk to each other without J.B. seeing or hearing them. If Zuss, Nickles, and J.B. were all on the same playing field, this convention could not hold. It breaks down at the end of Act II, however, when Nickles speaks directly to J.B. and he responds, even taking a swing at Zuss to chase him off the stage. In this instance, all three actors played on the "unaccommodated man" level of reality assumed by Porter. Yet only moments before, when J.B. complains of the boils and burns on his skin, Nickles tells him, "Oh come on! I know the look of grease paint!"

Fragmented Heroes, Female Others, and the Bomb

(62). This reference, of course, injected the "make believe" of the former frame play back into the action very soon after Nickles had violated it by speaking directly to J.B. In short, post-Bomb *J.B.* jumped between two theatrical levels of reality, one that insisted on the literal truth of J.B.'s experience of nuclearism and the other that treated that experience as so much "grease paint" to point up its universal significance. As in *Night Journey*, nuclearism scrambled the narrative coherence of *J.B.*

The attempt of both *Night Journey* and *J.B.* to incorporate the logic of the Bomb in their dramatic form moved both works away from the rhetoric and aesthetics of radiophony and back into the visual world of the photograph. When Jocasta kills herself in *Night Journey* and the nuclear blast levels the circus tent in *J.B.*, the metatheatrical games of both productions suddenly tumble to the ground. An instant in history, an arrested moment best captured in a photograph, brings Graham's convoluted flashbacks to an end and nearly destroys the boundaries separating MacLeish's carefully contrived nesting blocks of reality. It is as though neither artist could think beyond the snapshot of the Bomb imprinted on their minds.

This may have been because more than metaphor links photography to nuclearism. Both rest on natural realities that obstinately assert the primacy of the material world. Hence both resist the dematerializing processes of the radiophonic. As theorist Mary Price observes, "the photograph must be imprinted with what has been presented to the camera; it must literally receive something physical from out there." Because of the necessary causal connection linking the world of light and objects to the photograph, "there are no unicorns in the photograph," jokes Price, "and if one occurs disbelief is imperative." The optics and chemistry of the photographic process make snapshots fundamentally different from paintings and prints, despite the need for humans to point the camera and develop the film. Hence, again following Price, in a fundamental sense, a photograph does not represent reality at all; it transcribes it.[47] If thoughts of the Bomb dragged down the imaginations of both Graham and MacLeish to the dead-level literalism of a photograph, it may be because photography, whether moving or still, is the best mode for capturing the natural catastrophe that both believed nuclear warfare would entail.

The influence of photography on the imaginations of Graham and MacLeish is not surprising. Many Americans of the postwar era not only believed that the camera could transcribe reality but saw those transcriptions as natural and neutral. Art critic Clement Greenberg, for example, spoke of the camera's "glass eye" and noted its ability to "sense contemporary reality naively and express it directly." A photograph could be "clean of past and tradition," Greenberg stated in a 1946 review of one photographer's work.[48] Optimism about the potential neutrality of a photographic print sprang from the success of documentary photography in the 1930s, the era that witnessed the artistic and popular influence of Walker Evans and Paul Strand and saw the emergence of *Life* magazine in 1936. *Life*, which spawned many imitators and remained immensely popular through the 1950s, implicitly promised that its lavish picture spreads did not merely represent life; they were life.

The American faith that photographs objectively captured the material world had its origin in the scientific positivism of the nineteenth century. William Henry Fox Talbot, who claimed to have discovered (not invented) photography in 1839, wrote that photography imprints its images "by optical and chemical means alone"; the photograph, he said, is "impressed by Nature's hand," not humanity's. In the United States, Ralph Waldo Emerson, Henry David Thoreau, and Edgar Allan Poe celebrated photography as a form of natural, unmediated vision. Poe, for example, argued for a nearly "perfect identity of aspect" between an object and its photographic image.[49] By the 1940s Alfred Stieglitz and others had modified this initial optimism concerning the unmediated quality of photography to include the photographer's vision, but general belief in the superiority of photography over other forms of communication to transcribe the real remained high among Americans.

Consequently, when most Americans saw photos and films recording the destructiveness of the atomic bomb at Hiroshima and of later, larger bombs at test sites, they trusted that they had witnessed the literal truth of these events. Indeed, photography allowed them to believe that they had imaginatively experienced and survived these shocks. Although Americans knew that a nuclear catastrophe had never happened to them, photographic images encouraged them to respond to the Bomb as though it had. This paradox is best explained by Walter Benjamin's meditations on history and memory. For Benjamin, the discovery of photography encouraged people to think of memory as a series of snapshots. According to him, historians could only conceive of discrete past events by freezing them into photos. "The past can be seized only as an image which flashes up at the instant when it can be recognized and is never seen again."[50] This was especially true for past events that shocked the human imagination (and, for Benjamin, shock pervaded modern history). Following Freud, whose understanding of shock would be validated by later psychologists, Benjamin believed that shocks were never experienced directly but only latently, after the fact. Photographs can help the human mind to process a shocking event, not by recalling images from the shock—there is nothing to recollect—but by actualizing, bringing into conscious memory, the external photographic images.

Hence, because memory is only a series of mental photographs and shocking events leave no direct imprint on the mind, photographs of past shocks can momentarily trick the mind into believing that the body may actually have experienced that event. Thus photographs of nuclear obliteration gave Americans access to a memory of an experience they had never had. In this sense, Graham, MacLeish, and their co-creators were historians struggling to develop their own and other Americans' response to the shock of nuclearism from the negatives in their minds. By linking the flash of the photo to the flash of the Bomb, *Night Journey* and *J.B.* helped American spectators to recover from the ongoing shocks of Hiroshima and its awful legacy.

Like other nuclear narratives, *J.B.* produced a Fragmented Hero. Although J.B.'s love for Sarah heals the wounds of his fragmentation and allows the jeremiad arc of the play to end with wholeness and restoration, J.B. is a deeply divided soul for much of the action. Caught between his faith in God's justice and his fear that the Almighty may be amoral as his children die, between his certainty in his own guilt and the dawning realization that he has done nothing to deserve his calamities after the Bomb falls, and between his need to placate an angry God and his knowledge that he must reject this voice of anarchy near the end of the play, J.B. struggles to pull himself together, to search his soul for coherent and authentic selfhood. Several reviewers of the production emphasized J.B.'s agony and praised Pat Hingle's tormented performance. Atkinson, for instance, noted that "Hingle gives an almost unbearable, moving performance of a man of fortitude who is almost overwhelmed but never yields to the evil of his time."[51] As he had done with *Death of a Salesman*, Kazan spread signs of the protagonist's fragmentation around the stage, locating J.B./Hingle in the midst of the debris of his home, his family, his city, and his theology. Surrounding J.B. in his post-Bomb world were fragments of furniture, the chorus of homeless women, and the religious "Comforters," dressed in rags.

While these stage images suggested J.B.'s impotence in the face of nuclear destruction, others later in the play underlined his sudden escalation to near omnipotence. Kazan, in fact, used the sexualized language of nuclearism to describe J.B.'s final transformation when he kicks Zuss and Nickles off the stage: "J.B., having accepted his insignificance and impotence in the face of the scale and majesty of the universe [when the Distant Voice demands his obedience], passes from dependence and humbleness to independence and dignity and pride in his own manliness." In the *Life* magazine article that interviewed three theologians about *J.B.*, Reinhold Niebuhr remarked that the story of Job shows "the sharp contrast between man's greatness and his insignificance." This contrast, he added, is "more poignantly relevant to an atomic age which has the greatness to discover nuclear energy, but lacks the wisdom to avoid nuclear war."[52] The views of Niebuhr, who was more attuned to the intertwining of history, theology, and guilt than most theologians of the era, were widely reported and respected. Like Jimmy Stewart and Gregory Peck in their own Fragmented Hero roles from the 1950s, the meltdown in Hingle/J.B.'s character produced the extremes of impotence and omnipotence, a radical shift resting on the dynamics of nuclear culture and containment liberalism.

Similar dynamics shadowed *Night Journey*. Graham's *Errand into the Maze*, however, which also premiered in 1947, more closely paralleled the narrative transformation from impotence to omnipotence experienced by J.B. In this two-person dance, a woman journeys "into the maze of the heart in order to do battle with the Creature of Fear," according to Graham's 1947 program. The woman finally defeats this modern Minotaur and emerges in triumph from the containment of her self-created maze by confronting her own sexual fears. The dance critic for the *New York Herald Tribune*, alluding to fears sparked by cold war anxieties, noted the "particular appropriateness" of the dance "in these times when fear attacks us all."[53]

Unlike the Ariadne figure in *Errand*, of course, Jocasta cannot pull herself together to defeat her antagonist; her fate is beyond her control, resting on events from an ur-text that, at the start of the dance, have already fragmented her irreparably between mother love and sexual desire. The logic of the dance suggests that once Jocasta becomes fully aware of this fragmentation, her guilt overwhelms her and she must kill herself. *Night Journey* explores various facets of this hard-edged fate through the movements of the Chorus as well as those of Jocasta and Oedipus. In general, Jocasta's motherliness and queenliness move her toward omnipotence, while her sexuality disables and defeats her, though these positions are sometimes reversed and even intentionally confused. At one point, following danced action that the audience would have understood as lovemaking between the couple, Jocasta's remembered past seems to flash back to an earlier moment when she was a young mother caressing her infant son, Oedipus. The moment is purposefully ambiguous; is it a wife/husband scene in a marriage bed or a mother/son one in a nursery? The audience cannot know, but neither, of course, can Jocasta — and that is the point. Knowledge of her double desire taints all of her memories and dooms her. Her fragmentation is her fate.

The productions of *Night Journey* and *J.B.* provided audiences with no obvious or easy positions from which to view and judge the unfolding of their actions. The reviews suggest that J.B. and Jocasta evoked sympathy and awe from spectators for their mental and physical torments, but audiences were understandably reluctant to project themselves onto figures that experienced so much pain. Further, the fragmentation of both characters made it difficult for spectators to step into their shoes and even harder to adopt their point of view; the shifting, extreme, and contradictory positions of these protagonists foiled consistent identification. The Distant Voice and Tieresias did offer spectators another vantage point for interpretation, a godlike perspective that remained consistent throughout both performances. Both figures, however, were too mysterious, inhuman, and threatening to induce much identification. Not surprisingly, the critics of *J.B.* who saw the play through the allegorical lens of the Distant Voice dismissed the production as abstract and lifeless. While identifying with the Fragmented Hero threatened too much pain and incoherence, positioning oneself as the figure of fate could leave the spectator cold and indifferent.

In his research into Japanese A-bomb literature, John Whittier Treat notes a similar dualism in the fiction of Ota Yoko, a victim of the Hiroshima blast. "Her immediate project in authoring the most complete body of atomic-bomb literature we have today," writes Treat, "was devising the right calculus of mediated reception in her representation of Hiroshima." Ota's first work, *City of Corpses*, positioned her readers as empathizers in response to her first-person, testimonial narrative. Rejecting this point of view, she attempted an omniscient, third-person narrative for *Human Rags*, her second work, which kept her readers at a distance. In her third novel, *Half-Human*, the problem of narrative point of view collapsed upon itself; "[it] is very much about a writer trying to write," notes Treat. Treat concludes that her third book demonstrates "skeptical relations between her readers and everyone else, including author, narrator, and characters." Commenting on Treat's findings, critic Peter Schwenger states: "We see that what has been said of the narrator may apply as well to the reader, who occupies an equally uneasy place in atomic-bomb literature: the place of an understanding that is relinquished at our moral peril but that can never be achieved." In his analysis of Hersey's novel *Hiroshima*, Alan Nadel finds a similar ambivalence in the novel's rhetoric between inducing a desire for empathy and a desire for distance and omniscience. *Hiroshima* attempts both to put readers inside the experience of the victims and to maintain an outside distance from them.[54]

As Ota's and Hersey's work exemplifies, the inside/outside problem of rhetorical identification, endemic to containment culture and exacerbated by nuclearism, can have no final solution. If stories and characters are understood as containers, the reader must be positioned either inside or outside of them; she or he cannot occupy two positions at the same time. A third position is possible, though precarious, however, if the reader/spectator abandons the hope of fully inhabiting the inside or the outside and attempts to balance, as it were, on the border between them. This is the position of the witness, a figure who has survived the catastrophe experienced by the protagonist and has some knowledge of the ways of fate in the narrative. As Freddie Rokem recognizes in *Performing History*, the survivor-witness is a recurrent figure of identification for spectators in plays dealing with large-scale historical disasters, such as the French Revolution and the Holocaust. "The theater can seduce us to believe that it is possible for the actor to become a witness for the now dead witnesses," states Rokem.[55] Survivors of a catastrophe can never fully encompass its enormity, but they can bear witness to a part of its personal pain and general significance. Their position on the cusp of nuclear experience provides spectators who would identify with them a partial window both into and out from the characters and story of destructive historical events.

While Rokem is particularly interested in actors playing survivor-witnesses in Holocaust plays, an onstage witness in dramas centered on nuclear war can function as a site for spectator identification and projection. Many in the audience probably experienced empathetic projection with the figure of the Second Messenger in *J.B.*, for example. This survivor-witness reports the calamities that befall each of J.B.'s children in Act I. With increasing stammering and pain, the Messenger utters, "I only am escaped alone to tell thee," in each of these short scenes, a line of King James verse that signals his function as a mouthpiece of the Distant Voice. The witness's increasing distress, however, suggests that he has been profoundly disturbed by the mounting deaths of the children and resents his puppetlike role in reporting them. In his original poem, MacLeish envisioned what was essentially a photographic stage effect for these scenes. His stage directions for the first scene with the two messengers, for example, have the Second Messenger slowly turning to J.B., "his face drunken white, his eyes a blank," before speaking his line (1958 version of *J.B.*, 60). Even before he opens his mouth, then, his white face of trauma signals to the audience members what they need to know. Wriggling between empathetic involvement and transcendent distance, the Second Messenger struggles to resolve this dual position, but MacLeish does not let him off the hook. His position, of course, is close to that of most spectators; and, because his scenes occur early in the action, the Messenger's point of view provides a way into the drama for members of the audience.

The Chorus and Chorus Leader of *Night Journey* fulfill a similar function. Cursed like Cassandras with omniscient knowledge of Jocasta's imminent suicide, they nonetheless attempt to warn her of the fateful journey that lies ahead. Though outside of Jocasta's quest into the past, they also participate in it, often mirroring the queen's jagged, sensual movements. Probably most spectators of Graham's dance projected themselves into the Chorus in an advisory mode; without omniscient knowledge themselves, they could not fully share in the Chorus's point of view. (Although some spectators, remembering the Oedipus story, did know Jocasta's fate.) The Messenger and the Chorus, then, provided spectators with a position from which they could both distance themselves from the pain of the Fragmented Hero and humanize the workings of fate. The position of these survivor-witnesses did not exempt audiences from pain—nor did it guarantee them full understanding—but it did allow them to mediate between the nuclear polarities of the performative experience.

The Messenger and the Chorus also pulled the audience back to the authority of the ur-text on which both productions were based. The Messenger's key line cited the Book of Job, and Graham's Chorus could not help but remind the audience of the conventions of Greek tragedy, specifically *Oedipus the King*. Imaginatively taking up these positions, spectators became not only survivor-witnesses but classic or biblical survivor-witnesses. This positioning of spectators in both performances consequently empowered the rhetorical dynamics of *allegoresis*. Spectators were implicitly invited to draw parallels between the dramas they witnessed on stage and the original stories and characters on which they were based. Probably for many in the audience, the conservative bias of *allegoresis* was enhanced by their knowledge of the typical position of a witness in most Hollywood films dealing with classic or biblical material. Many business-class spectators at *J.B.* and *Night Journey* knew the conventional mixture of pain and knowledge that was expected of them because they had identified with a witness at the death of Socrates or the crucifixion of Jesus at the movies. This is not to equate all of the meanings generated by Graham's and MacLeish's dramas with a typical Bible epic but simply to note that the mainstream cultural construction of the witness position probably limited the imaginative reach of many Broadway spectators.

■ Drawn back to the logocentric authority of an ur-text by *allegoresis*, spectators at both productions embraced a rationalist ethics close to the patriarchal power of traditional Christian belief. According to Lakoff and Johnson, rationalist ethics work within the general system of a "Strict Father" model of morality.[56] As the name implies, this model projects the notion of a strong male presence able to protect his family from external dangers onto other ethical realms in which order, hierarchy, and abstract authority are prized. If this is carried to an extreme, Strict Fathers may become rigidly authoritarian.

Generally speaking, containment liberalism in the 1950s adhered to a Strict Father morality for geopolitics, economics, and other fields in which authority and rationality were prized. Most Americans believed that a powerful international presence was necessary to preserve order and contain communism in the world; they elected a former army general as president and supported strong leaders in diplomatic affairs, such as John Foster Dulles. Powerful men sat atop the hierarchies of Big Business and Big Labor in the postwar economy, like Charles Wilson of General Motors and George Meany of the American Federation of Labor and Congress of Industrial Organizations (AFL-CIO), and few citizens questioned the justice of that arrangement. These leaders generally believed that the workings of the economy were "rational"; modest tinkering with welfare provisions and massive subsidies for defense industries might be necessary, but most believed that the "free enterprise system," if generally left to itself, would produce abundance. Strict Fathers were especially necessary in the Atomic Age; the secular commandment of reason could mandate moral strength and calculated restraint in a world filled with evil. The rewards and punishments of rationality were primarily internal—feelings of self-esteem and self-respect—while failure to live up to this ethic produced shame and guilt.

Clearly, rationalist ethics provides the moral compass of *J.B.* and *Night Journey*. MacLeish's and Graham's world was an evil place, with atomic bombs slaying innocents and sexuality overwhelming moral restraint. Both Fragmented Heroes also broke moral guidelines that carried the force of commandments and paid with shame and guilt: Jocasta violated the incest taboo and J.B. placed the wrong God before him, seeking grace from the Distant Voice instead of nature. In the moral order of both performances, an omnipotent and mysterious male authority could justly demand death or promise life. Audiences at both productions were warned that they must act in accordance with this theological power or they would suffer unknown consequences. Further, the position of survivor-witnesses occupied by the audience members did not entitle them to intervene in this closed world; the Messenger and the Chorus Leader are passive before the dictates of fate. Although *Night Journey* and *J.B.* are modernist works set at a distance from traditional religion, both, ironically, rely on a form of belief that puts a "Strict Father" in command and control.

This ethical orientation implicated both productions in perpetuating the theological beliefs that underwrote the legitimacy of the stealth state. In situations when nuclear war threatened national security, *Night Journey* and *J.B.* suggested that Americans were to be passive witnesses, not active citizens. In fact, very few citizens questioned the nuclear policies of the United States during the 1950s. What Robert Jay Lifton and Richard Falk term "psychic numbing" cast a pall over nuclear debate that led to a kind of fatalism about the possibility of nuclear destruction. A 1950 article in *Life*, for example, asked "How U.S. Cities Can Prepare for Atomic War" and offered several suggestions (including rapid suburbanization) to alleviate total annihilation. Later in the decade, following the development of intercontinental ballistic missiles and the realization that nuclear attack would leave Americans with no time to evacuate cities or run to public shelters, thousands of citizens built shelters in their backyards rather than challenge the morality of nuclear policy. Even during the Cuban Missile Crisis, experts discussed probable rates of survivability while companies like Surviv-All, Inc., and Peace-O-Mind Shelter helped Americans to dig in. As Margot Henriksen points out in *Dr. Strangelove's America: Society and Culture in the Atomic Age*, "A sort of cultural accommodation to the probability of thermonuclear warfare and an accompanying acceptance of the need for both an activist civil defense and a sanguine fatalism about the death of millions underlay much of this outspoken survivalist sensibility."[57] If God the Father or classic fate decreed that it was time for a nuclear warning or apocalypse, the proper position of the witness was on the sidelines, watching with humility and fear.

In the late 1950s and early 1960s some citizens did protest current nuclear policies, although very few of them questioned the protocols of the national security state itself. Margaret Mead and others, for instance, attacked the morality of "gun-thy-neighbor" survivalists. In *The Day They H-Bombed Los Angeles* (1961), novelist Robert Moore Williams suggested that the real enemy was the U.S. government. A group of theologians, ministers, and rabbis published *God and the H-Bomb* in 1961 to protest the immorality of U.S. nuclear policies and project a more humane vision of society. Significantly, one essay from this collection leaned on a God-as-Strict-Father theology but specifically attacked the kind of fatalism implicit in *Night Journey* and *J.B.* In "Man, God, and Atomic War," Rabbi Samuel Dresner began in Job-like fashion by asserting that humanity could not know the will of God; hence it was foolish to try to predict His response in the event of a nuclear war. The best humans could do, said Dresner, was "to choose the good way, to love the Lord and walk in His ways." For Dresner, however, this conventional idea had radical implications: "Either there will be a change in man's heart or there will be no man nor heart to change." Dresner ended his article by asserting that "only the creation of a new society can prevent the use of the bomb and outlaw war," and this new society "requires a new man who can only become so by revering God and walking in his ways."[58]

Night Journey and *J.B.* were a part of the nuclear consensus of the 1950s. Dresner's essay, however, demonstrated how fragile the fatalistic part of that consensus had become by the early 1960s. A simple reemphasis within the same morality could turn some Jews and Christians against it. At the same time, Dresner's radical call for change did not directly challenge the deification of the stealth state. Nor did his Strict Father morality attempt to counter the feelings of omnipotence and guilt induced by nuclear culture. It would take a different kind of morality to escape from the thrall of the Bomb.

■ The directorial work of Elia Kazan occupied several significant positions at the intersection of popular entertainment, containment liberalism, and nuclear culture during the early Cold War. Kazan's successes dominated the 1947–1962 era on Broadway, beginning with *A Streetcar Named Desire* and *Death of a Salesman* in 1947 and 1949, including *Tea and Sympathy* and *Cat on a Hot Tin Roof* in 1953 and 1955, and culminating with *Dark at the Top of the Stairs* and *J. B.* in 1957 and 1958. During these years Kazan also directed several Hollywood hits, most famously *Streetcar* (1951), *On the Waterfront* (1954), and *East of Eden* (1955). In 1952 Kazan "named names" before HUAC, an action that influenced his subsequent work in Hollywood and New York. Perhaps the most obvious of Kazan's ties to nuclearism was his fear of impotence and his desire for omnipotence, sexual anxieties that expressed themselves in his career as well as in his attempts to control his theatrical and filmic images through *allegoresis*. Second, Kazan's kinesthetic sensibility, evident in the rhythms of his films and plays, was close to Martha Graham's; both centered their work on actors whose movements of "bound flow," in Laban's terminology, were arrested in emblematic snapshots that revealed their essence and their fate. Finally, and related to the other two points, Kazan's plays and films after 1952 explored the psychological dynamics of innocence and guilt. Following Kazan's appearance before HUAC, his most notable male figures on stage and screen struggle to reject unjustifiable feelings of guilt and proclaim their innocence, despite public opprobrium. For an American generation of anxious males, Kazan's images of innocent Empty Boys and Fragmented Heroes provided welcome relief during a guilt-plagued era.⁵⁹

The arc of Kazan's career shows a man increasingly determined to neutralize others who, from his perspective, threatened to compromise his artistic projects. As early as 1947 Kazan won name-above-the-title billing plus 20 percent of the profits from Irene Selznick for his direction of *Streetcar*, a condition he continued to insist on from Broadway producers during the 1950s. Kazan rarely cast established stars; his power struggles with big names like Tallulah Bankhead, whom he had directed early in his career in *The Skin of Our Teeth*, led him to prefer actors who would not challenge his authority. The Method actors he generally cast focused their energies on the internal dynamics of their characters, leaving much of their theatrical effectiveness in his hands as director. In his treatment of playwrights, Kazan became increasingly demanding. As discussed in chapter 2, Williams's disagreements with Kazan over the revisions of *Cat* finally led the playwright to publish separate versions of the drama's last act. In 1959 Kazan came to the conclusion that his own needs for self-expression were making it difficult for him to stage plays written by others, and he stopped directing on Broadway. When Kazan accepted the position of artistic director in the short-lived Lincoln Center Repertory Theater project of the early 1960s, he stated that if he could not do what he wanted he would quit. He quit after the first season. Kazan found more autonomy as a director and co-writer in Hollywood than on Broadway, even gaining authority for the "final cut" version of *Eden* and other films, but it was not enough. He stopped directing films in 1976 and, after several fallow years, turned exclusively to writing. In writing, Kazan seems to have found the control he desired; unlike people, typewriters and paper do not push back.

A passage from his autobiography, published in 1988, provides a clue to Kazan's lifelong pursuit of autonomy and control. "Since art is the product of a single vision," he wrote, "the director must, at all costs, maintain his grip on what he wants. Compromise is a trap, always ready to spring." In his autobiography, Kazan often portrayed the compromises of his life and his occasional victories over compromising situations in frankly sexual terms. This was especially true of his understanding of the events between his testimony before HUAC in 1952 and the release of *On the Waterfront* in 1954, arguably the most revealing period of his life. Kazan reported that in his first appearance before the congressmen he had felt "humiliated" by the power they exerted over him. "Humiliation" also haunted the memories of his dealings with the Communist Party in 1936 when they forced him to resign, threatened his negotiations with Hollywood producer Darryl Zanuck in the early 1950s when the two of them discussed film projects, and dogged him after his second testimony before HUAC when naming names lost him many old friends. "Wilt, scoundrel!" he imagined his former friends saying to him. To prove to himself that he had not "wilted," Kazan reported with some pride in his autobiography that he took two German women to bed with him while directing *Man on a Tightrope* (1953) in Europe. Making *On the Waterfront*, however, more fully avenged his humiliation: "Everyday I worked on that film I was telling the world where I stood and my critics to go and fuck themselves."[60] For Kazan in these difficult times and at many other moments in his stressful life, compromise threatened the humiliation of impotence. Autonomy and control allowed him to remain erect and on top.

Given Kazan's sexual aggressiveness and desire for omnipotence in the face of possible defeat, it is not surprising that he pushed his theatrical and filmic projects toward allegory. As Gordon Teskey argues in *Allegory and Violence*, allegories, by mandating a single, "true" reading of their narratives, conceal their aggressiveness through Platonic abstraction: "The very word *allegory* evokes a schism in consciousness—between a life and a mystery, between the real and the ideal, between a literal tale and its moral—which is repaired or at least concealed by imagining a hierarchy on which we ascend toward truth." When readers and spectators perform *allegoresis*, they believe they are moving "inward and upward," as Teskey notes, toward a transcendental truth that folds all variety and diversity into the container of a Platonic form. The oneness of this container, however, hides the violence that produces it. For Teskey, writers—and, by extension, play directors—who induce readers or spectators to allegorize involve them in their own will-to-power, a desire for Platonic totality "that subjects what it does not understand, the realm of physis or growth, to a knowledge it imagines it already has." Hence allegory works to stabilize knowledge, power, and sexual relations. "Allegory is more than the literary representation of this ideological order," concludes Teskey: "As the basis of the social practice of interpretation, allegory actively sustains that order. The integrity of the hierarchy is repeatedly affirmed while everything else is reduced to the status of a substance imprinted by form."[61] For writers and directors like Kazan, producing allegories kept the fears of impotence at bay and promised control over spectatorial interpretation. For spectators, witnessing allegories spoke to similar fears and desires animated by the cultural dynamics of nuclearism and containment liberalism.

"The only genuinely good and original films I've made, I made after my testimony," stated Kazan in his autobiography.[62] These films, like Kazan's theater projects of the middle and late 1950s, were also the most allegorical of his career. His earlier directorial efforts, such as *Gentleman's Agreement* (1947) and *All My Sons* (1947), had rarely strayed beyond the photographically influenced style and rhetoric of realism. In *Waterfront*, Terry Malone, played by Marlon Brando, learns that he must oppose the mobster in control of the longshoremen's union by naming names to federal investigators in order to maintain his self-respect. Kazan's climactic scene shows Brando/Malone sacrificing himself to the blows of the gangster's thugs to save his fellow workers. The Platonic ur-text of *Waterfront* comes clear at this point: Brando/Malone has been transformed from lost soul into Christ figure, martyred for naming names. *Eden* invoked a similar kind of *allegoresis*. Steinbeck's novel modernized the Cain and Abel narrative from the Bible; and Kazan's directing, together with Paul Osborn's script, heightened the allegorical links even as it altered the ethical dynamics of the old story. In Kazan's film, Cal Trask—the Cain figure, played by James Dean—gains audience sympathy through his revolt against the narrow moralism of his father and older brother. Nonetheless, he fulfills his allegorical role at the climax of the film by confronting his brother with the reality of their mother, who owns the town brothel—an action that drives his brother to enlist in the army during World War I for future death at the front.

As previously discussed, *Dark at the Top of the Stairs* invited the audience to read domestic melodrama as Freudian narrative, fitting the everyday actions of its characters into universal patterns. And audiences at *J.B.* witnessed a story even more closely aligned to the ur-text of the Bible than was *Eden*. In his critique of Kazan's direction of *Cat*, Eric Bentley complained of the production's yearning for "grandeur."[63] Big Daddy passing the life force into Maggie was one of several moments that arched toward allegory. This moment—like similar ones involving J.B. and the Distant Voice, Cora and her son in *Dark*, and the walk of a crucified Terry Malone staggering toward transfiguration—drew audiences, in Teskey's words, "inward and upward" toward Platonic meanings whose universal, typological significance left no room for further interpretation. Kazan had already moved toward allegory in his direction of *Salesman* in 1949. The itch for allegorical "grandeur" marked most of Kazan's projects during the 1950s.

The desire to control audience response through *allegoresis* also shaped the dances of Martha Graham, of course. Graham and Kazan shared another similarity—their love of the photograph. Both merged the dematerializing, Platonic effects of radiophony with an emphasis on the material particularity of the photograph in their art. Part of the aesthetic excitement of their work springs from the tensions between the universal and the particular; rhetorically, between the drive for allegorical control and the desire to explore unique psychological events. In a revealing paragraph of his autobiography, Kazan states: "The walls of my office in New York are covered with photographs—snapshots, mostly—of my family and my close friends.... The photographs of the people in my life fill me with memory and emotion. So do many news photographs. I clip them and collect them. I am part of the picture era."[64] In an adjacent paragraph, Kazan mentions his love of Sergei Eisenstein and his trust in pictures over words to convey meaning. Much like Martha Graham, Kazan structured the rhythmic style of his productions around "pictures," alternating between periods of flow and moments of tableau, to focus on an often emblematic "snapshot." Graham and Kazan both deployed "bound flow" in their choreography of dancers and actors, movement constricted by muscular tension rather than flowing from relaxation and release. Both artists swept their spectators toward moments of "grandeur" and pulled them in the opposite direction, toward the interior self of their protagonists—toward an escape from containment and a retreat within it. In this sense, nuclearism not only animated the allegorical thrust of Kazan's projects but also modified it through its insistent, photolike materialism.

Kazan was the first American director to sustain a successful career in Hollywood and New York for over twenty years. (Orson Welles preceded him but burned out sooner on both coasts.) Kazan's cold war critics generally agreed that the key to his popular success was his combination of filmic and theatrical techniques in both media, but they disagreed on the actual effectiveness of the mix. Film critic Eugene Archer, for example, praised Kazan's ability to shoot psychologically intense scenes in his early films, even though Archer recognized that "such scenes are inherently theatrical, their ultimate effect deriving from acting and dialogue rather than from any basically cinematic qualities." In a 1964 article, theater critic Gordon Rogoff decried the overlap between Kazan's stage and the screen efforts. "Kazan stands, finally, for several confusions," he stated. "The play as screenplay, the screen as stage, both supported by running soundtracks designed to underscore emotions, point moments, bridge scenes."[65] While Rogoff's summary was accurate, most of the public saw these points of overlap as advantages, not confusions. Other filmic influences on Kazan's stage work included his use of lighting specials to draw audiences into a "close-up" (e.g., Rubin's naked feet at the end of *Dark*), a quick "pan" across the stage that momentarily alters audience focus (effected near the start of Act II of *Cat* by Brick's spatial isolation), and occasional "over the shoulder shots" that turn a downstage actor's back to the audience to focus on the response of the actor above him/her (e.g., Stella's response to Stanley's ripped-T-shirt anguish in *Streetcar*). Kazan's major carryover from stage to screen, of course, was Method acting, which contributed both an edginess and an emotional coherence to the scenes of his films. Character psychology, following the Method emphasis on the outward constriction of inner emotion, typically dictated the rhythmic flow of timing and movement in Kazan's films.

Archer recognized that the flow of Kazan's films during the 1950s was often the key to their success:

> The visual style concentrates on continuous movement, with actors steadily in motion and a camera movement which is equally fluid, alternately panning and employing elliptical cross-cutting to keep the viewer's eyes in action. . . . The flow of movement is so regular that any sudden pause achieves the effect of an exclamation point, and Kazan employs this type of punctuation at frequent intervals. Occasionally he reverses the process, by keeping actors and camera in a stationary position which is eventually interrupted by a movement or gesture so unexpected that it immediately connotes violence.[66]

In *Eden*, for example, the opening sequence of shots uses a series of pans to follow a mysterious woman as she walks down the streets of a small California town in 1917. At the edge of most of the frames is a teenage boy, who jumps up, walks behind her, runs, stops, darts, and ducks to avoid her seeing him. The rhythmic flow of the sequence alternates between the woman's methodical pace and the boy's conflicted skittishness. It ends with the woman's abrupt closing of her front door. This opening sequence set up Cal's search for his mother, the rich madam of a whorehouse, and the conflicts that characterize their relationship. Another signature sequence emphasizing flow was Kazan's ending of *Waterfront*, when Brando/Malone must walk from the beating by the gangster's thugs to lead the longshoremen to work in defiance of the mobster who runs their union. Here, as in scenes of *Eden*, the camera works expressionistically to suggest the pain, exhaustion, and dizziness of Malone by its jittery movements, too-quick pans, and occasional out-of-focus lolling. The flow is constant yet "bound" by the character's emotional and physical condition.

Without videotapes of the stage productions, it is more difficult to track the "bound flow" of Kazan's theatrical work, but the dialogue and stage directions (usually copied from the stage manager's prompt book) of the Broadway scripts do provide much suggestive evidence. In the middle of Act II of *Cat*, for example, Brick is hobbling across stage with his crutch when Big Daddy abruptly jerks it from under his arm. Brick steps on the injured ankle then clutches a chair to catch his fall, pulling it "over on top of him on the floor."[67] Near the end of Act I in *Dark at the Top of the Stairs*, a flowing action, parallel to the one in *Cat* though primarily verbal rather than physical, climaxes in a similar "exclamation point." Rubin's and Cora's argument carries them into a hallway and out of sight of the audience, where the flow of the dialogue is abruptly stopped by the sound of Rubin's hand slapping Cora's face. In *J.B.*, Kazan used the chorus of five women and a child who appear after the bomb blast to provide a mostly lulling rhythm of motherly crankiness and concern to counterpoint the anguished cries of J.B. and Sarah at the end of Act I. MacLeish wrote this scene, which does not appear in his original poem, to Kazan's specifications. At one point, the women are singing a sad, sardonic version of "Good Night, Ladies," when "Sarah's shriek breaks it off" (53). After Sarah has abandoned J.B., the women, again humming a tune, clamber around the Hero to keep him warm; and J.B., with "a great cry," demands, "Show me my guilt, O God" (54). This curtain line—significantly centered on guilt with a chorus of mothers attempting to quiet the Fragmented Hero's fears—ends the act. Again, as in the signature sequences of his films, the bound flow of movement and/or sound ends abruptly in an exclamation point.

To some extent, Kazan's staging choices in the above examples were simply evidence of good directing. All directors since Stanislavski and Max Reinhardt have worked with rhythm and picturization to underline specific images for the audience. Several factors taken together, however, distinguished Kazan's work from that of his predecessors. First, he chose to emphasize certain kinds of moments — moments of violence, anguish, impotent guilt, and omnipotent triumph. Second, as previously noted, Kazan used filmic techniques to underline his stage pictures. Third, and more difficult to pin down, he apparently deployed many more climactic moments in a scene than most other directors would have. For Gordon Rogoff, Kazan created a kind of life on stage that exhibited "constant climax." Robert Brustein also criticized Kazan's productions for their obsessive busyness and eruptions. In his review of *Dark*, for example, Brustein complained: "Over the placid lake of this play, Elia Kazan hurled thunderbolts. His production was in a state of constantly controlled frenzy.... Inge proposes calm and lassitude, Kazan imposes theatrical hijinks. What with all the nut-cracking, chicken-eating, behind-patting, jewelry-fingering, shoe-shining, sewing, crying, stuttering and yawning that went on, his characters were rarely empty-handed or empty-mouthed — and in a play almost devoid of climaxes we are served up a climax every five minutes." Likewise, film critic Thomas Morgan spoke of Kazan's "supercharged" directing and related it to his desire for control over the spectator — Kazan's need "to grip the viewer at every moment."[68]

Others appreciated the nervous energy of Kazan's productions and recognized it as a distinctive mark of his genius. Despite their many differences, Tennessee Williams continued to seek Kazan to direct his plays during the 1950s. When a reporter asked him about Kazan's range of directorial interests on the eve of the Lincoln Center project, however, Williams wisely noted: "It is unthinkable that Kazan would ever direct a *Waiting for Godot*."[69] For a play in which "nothing happens," Kazan's sequences of "bound flow" topped by abrupt climaxes would have been badly out of place.

As a director of popular films and stage plays, Kazan could not push the rhythms and pictures of his projects toward the same levels of abstraction as could Martha Graham with her dances. Nonetheless, many of the same general dynamics are evident in the kinesthetics of the work of the director and the choreographer, similarities that mark both as artists of the nuclear age. As in *Night Journey*, "bound flow"—repetitive, directional movement working against jagged, eruptive emotions—characterized most of Kazan's films and plays. In their work with individual actors or dancers, both explored tensions between interior, often sexualized, desires and the external constrictions of the body. Graham was able to focus audience attention on arrested moments of time by freezing the forward narrative movement of her dances as well as through choreographic techniques, while Kazan also showed an interest in stopping time through abrupt and frequent climaxes frozen into emblematic snapshots. Although both worked toward moments of mythic "grandeur" indebted to the Platonic dynamics of radiophony, both were also members of the "picture era." Shadowed by the Bomb, artists and spectators needed photos of arrested reality that also served as emblems to transcend its pain. Bound flow provided both.

Kazan's partial allegories of nuclearism took as their ur-text a variation on the jeremiad tale. Jeremiads typically chart a journey from sinfulness to redemption that hinges on a moment of epiphany, when the Everyman of the plot sees the errors of his ways, digs deep within himself, and removes the final restraints to his regeneration. Secondary characters can assist the protagonist in his quest for rebirth and wholeness. In Kazan's version of the jeremiad tale, the protagonist is mired in the sins of despair and alienation; he often suffers from the fragmentation of a guilty conscience, even though he has done very little to deserve his guilt. Kazan's allegories from the middle and late 1950s also deploy a motherly woman to facilitate the protagonist's epiphany by leading him to a recognition of his inherent innocence and helping him to a renewed life through sexual love. As in *J.B.*, female sexuality represents a naturalized life force that can rejuvenate a male hero and spark his quest for ego integrity and moral authenticity. Though instrumental in helping an Empty Boy toward manhood or returning a Fragmented Hero to wholeness, Kazan's sexualized servers exercise no other agency of interest in the narratives of these allegories. Hence most of Kazan's film and theater projects from the middle and late 1950s position spectators to embrace some version of a Strict Father morality; they stabilize sex and gender roles in conventionally patriarchal terms.

While the female facilitator of male epiphanies is most evident in the scripts of *Waterfront* and *Eden*, which Kazan helped to shape, the director probably got his idea for this figure from a Broadway play he directed in 1953, *Tea and Sympathy*. In this melodrama set in a private boys' school, a frustrated woman decides to abandon her husband to make love with a student, Tom Lee, who is deeply confused about his sexual identity. Playwright Robert Anderson encouraged his audience to embrace Laura's life-giving action as a matter of sexual charity, a move motivated by motherly concern, not erotic desire. For Laura Reynolds, Kazan cast Deborah Kerr, a woman, he notes in his autobiography, of "immaculate delicacy," whose final action of opening her blouse to Tom Lee as the lights fade seemed to spring from "the most decent and honorable" intentions.[70] Kazan's use of "immaculate" to describe Kerr is telling; a secularized St. Joan, Laura Reynolds/Deborah Kerr could save souls by denying her own desires and placing her sexuality at the service of a higher cause.

Waterfront and *Eden* resembled *Tea* in significant ways, "most notably in the tortured confusion of the male protagonist and the crucial help he receives from a compassionate, understanding woman," states Kazan's biographer Thomas H. Pauly. In effect, she and a working-class priest pass on the life force to Terry Malone, another innocent Empty Boy, and their salvific grace helps him to oppose the mobster in control of the union. According to 1950s film critic Eugene Archer, the Cal Trask/ James Dean figure in *East of Eden* "presented the embodiment of the Life Force," energized by an understanding girlfriend who helps him to work through his misplaced guilt.[71] In *Eden*, Cal's epiphany comes late in the film, when the girlfriend, played with motherly tenderness by Julie Harris, effects a reconciliation between the misguided hero and his stern father, which allows Cal/Jimmy to overcome his Oedipal rage and move to maturity. Both Eva-Marie Saint, the girlfriend in *Waterfront*, and Julie Harris are cut from the same cloth as Laura Reynolds/Deborah Kerr. "Will these characters be able to overcome their own doubts and offer their natural maternal affection to the Empty Boy who so desperately needs their sexual compassion?" is the only real question about them posed by each film. As in *The Man in the Gray Flannel Suit*, the wife-mother figure must deny her own needs to serve as helpmate to her partner or be branded as irresponsible and neurotic. Likewise, the overriding concern of these Kazan films is to ensure that his Empty Boys mature into hegemonic men.

Presenting a woman who could offer salvific grace to a confused male on his journey toward rebirth also shaped Kazan's theatrical work in *Cat on a Hot Tin Roof*, *Dark at the Top of the Stairs*, and *J.B.*, although he had less direct control over the scripting of these female roles than in Hollywood. Significantly, Kazan had considered Barbara Bel Geddes, who played Maggie-the-cat, for the role of Laura Reynolds in *Tea and Sympathy*. Commenting on the revisions Kazan requested for the ending of *Cat*, Williams wrote to his director: "Do you think it contains an echo of *Tea and Sympathy*? The other, harder ending [of *Cat*] didn't. Here is another case of a woman giving a man back his manhood, while in the original conception, it was about a vital, strong woman dominating a weak man and achieving her will."[72] Williams was right to ask. Kazan's recent work had embraced the necessities of cold war, hegemonic masculinity through their emphasis on male potency; any dramatic resolution centered on female domination of a weak male was unthinkable. As Kazan conceived of *Cat*, Big Daddy pressed the life force into Maggie in Act III, who then used it much as Laura Reynolds had in *Tea* to revive Brick at the end of the play. In *Cat*, as in *Tea*, *Waterfront*, and *Eden* before it, a woman can be the carrier of life-giving energy, but she is only a vehicle, not the natural home of such power.

Kazan's ending of *Dark at the Top of the Stairs* also emphasized the need for women to serve as helpmates in reviving male potency. Having already saved her son from the unhealthy illusions of Momism, Cora Flood turns her attention to her husband, Rubin, who feels that his masculinity is now in question because he has been fired from his job as a traveling harness salesman. As Cora starts up the stairs toward "Rubin's naked feet standing in the warm light at the top" (304), the implication is clear: it is Cora's responsibility to forgive Rubin for his past dalliance and revive their marriage through sexual compassion. Lighting Rubin's naked feet was Kazan's idea, recalling a similar "special" that he used to illuminate Laura's unbuttoning of her blouse at the end of *Tea and Sympathy*. Again, a secular St. Joan passes on the life force to her man through sexual coupling so that the man will regain his potency. This same resolution, of course, shaped the ending of *J.B.* Sarah brings the branch of life to J.B., and their love rekindles his will to live.

In all six of these vehicles, Kazan heightened the guilt of his primary male characters while downplaying their justification for feeling guilty. Again, *Tea and Sympathy* set the pattern for later developments. Tom Lee is caught up in a McCarthyite witch hunt for homosexuals in a New England boys' school. Although "straight" himself, Tom comes to believe that he may harbor the cold war cancer of homosexuality and feels guilty for his presumed sexual deviance. While Anderson provided a teenage victim who was completely innocent in *Tea*, Kazan had to work carefully with scriptwriters and casting choices to emphasize the guilty feelings of his male characters but undercut their justification for feeling guilty in subsequent projects during the decade. In *Eden*, for example, Kazan and writer Paul Osborn created a crafty brother and an overbearing father to ensure that the guilt James Dean/Cal Trask feels for his missteps is completely out of proportion to the blame that is rightly his. Likewise, Kazan influenced Williams to downplay the rationale for Brick's guilt in *Cat* by trying to make it clear that Brick, though partly responsible for Skipper's suicide, had never committed homosexual acts with his friend. Following Kazan's suggestions, Inge revised *Dark* to deemphasize Rubin's infidelity; for some reviewers, it disappeared completely. MacLeish had already determined that J.B. should not, in the end, feel guilty before God, but Kazan's "recognition scene" ensured that spectators would be in no doubt of the protagonist's theological innocence. Although Kazan cast actors with strikingly masculine personas in these roles, the performers also suggested a vulnerability that laid their characters open to the ravages of guilt. In short, many of Kazan's projects for stage and screen in the middle and late 1950s dealt sympathetically with the problem of a guilty conscience. While his male protagonists and victims might feel guilty, their accusers were wrong to believe that they deserved condemnation.

Tea and Sympathy may have set the pattern, but *On the Waterfront* provided the best example of a male character who must learn to embrace his innocence before he can regain his manhood. Terry Malone, as co-written with Budd Schulberg, discovers that the guilt he feels for ratting on his gangster acquaintances is completely unjustified. This film, which many critics have called Kazan's apologia for his testimony before HUAC, created "a context in which the naming of names is the only honorable thing to do," states Victor Navasky. In his *Director's Notebook* for *Streetcar*, Kazan jotted down the "thought" that "directing finally consists in turning Psychology into Behavior."[73] Kazan had in mind the "psychology" of his actors and their characters, but the phrase might also be applied to the "psychology" of the director. Regardless of formal artistic intentions, most directors stage their desires and concerns; and Kazan has freely admitted that his personal problems have always been a part of his work. No doubt Kazan could cite several reasons for his decision to underline the innocence of his primary male figures and dismiss the guilt-mongering of their accusers in his films and plays of the 1950s. Several concerns, as well, may have shaped Kazan's need to create sexualized mother figures who could help his Empty Boys and Fragmented Heroes toward maturity and wholeness by relieving their guilt. But anxiety about his own bad faith, as Jean-Paul Sartre would call it, during the HUAC hearings probably played a significant part in Kazan's fixation on this nexus of compulsion, guilt, sex, and justification.

What is striking about Kazan's behavior in 1952 was less his naming of names—hundreds of cooperative witnesses in front of numerous investigating committees did that—than his need to seek public vindication for his action. Preceding his testimony in April 1952, Kazan provided the committee with a list of the plays and films he had directed, each annotated to plead their anti-Communist correctness. Under carefully planned questioning, Kazan named eight members of the Party he had known in the mid 1930s when he participated in a Communist cell in the Group Theater. Following the public release of his testimony and annotated list, Kazan placed an ad in the *New York Times* explaining the reasons for his testimony and exhorting other liberals to follow his example. It read, in part:

> Firsthand experience of dictatorship and thought control left me with an abiding hatred of . . . Communist philosophy and methods and the conviction that these must be resisted always. It also left me with the passionate conviction that we must never let the Communists get away with the pretense that they stand for the very things which they kill in their own countries. I am talking about free speech, a free press, the rights of property, the rights of labor, racial equality and, above all, individual rights. . . . I believe these things must be fought for wherever they are not fully honored and protected, whenever they are threatened.[74]

A month later, Kazan delivered a major address at Harvard about the influence of communism in Hollywood, further justifying his HUAC testimony. He even sought the publication in book form of all his anti-Communist statements, but Viking Press backed out of the deal.

Since 1952 Kazan has admitted his contradictory feelings about naming names, but he has also continued to justify his action. In perhaps his most revealing interview, given in 1971, Kazan stated:

> I don't think there's anything in my life toward which I have more ambivalence, because, obviously, there's something disgusting about giving other people's names. On the other hand, ... at that time I was convinced that the Soviet empire was monolithic.... Since then I've had two feelings. One feeling is that what I did was repulsive, and the opposite feeling, when I see what the Soviet Union has done to its writers, and their death camps, and the Nazi pact and the Polish and Czech repression.... I also have to admit and I've never denied, that there was a personal element in it, which is that I was angry, humiliated, and disturbed — furious, I guess — at the way they booted me out of the Party [in 1936].

A truculent Kazan styled himself less guilty and more unrepentant in his 1988 autobiography. In a section directly addressed to the "Reader," Kazan states that he does not seek to curry favor then adds: "If you expect an apology now [for naming names], you've misjudged my character. The 'horrible, immoral thing' I [did], I did out of my true self. Everything before [i.e., his refusal to inform on his comrades] was seventeen years of posturing."[75] Clearly, Kazan's anguish about his testimony continued to haunt him for years. He lost many friends over the issue and also some work, an ironic comeuppance since part of his reason for testifying was to protect his future as a Hollywood director.

Kazan was not alone in his confused and contradictory response to his part in the HUAC hearings. Anger, guilt, compulsion, revenge, humiliation, and vindication came with the nuclear territory of all Fragmented Heroes during the early Cold War, and Kazan qualified as a prime example of the type — certainly in his own eyes if not in those of his critics like Navasky. Insofar as Kazan was able to explore the fragmentation of his own life through his work, his directing projects spoke eloquently to other hegemonic males in the 1950s also pulled apart by the contradictions of the era and trapped in bad faith. "Attention must be paid" to Kazan because his post-HUAC work so dominated the 50s. "There is only one trend in the Broadway theater and its name is Kazan," wrote Kenneth Tynan in 1959.[76] Among their other virtues, *Tea, Waterfront, Eden, Cat, Dark,* and *J.B.* reassured guilty men of their innocence; the plays and films provided a saving balm, smoothed on by an understanding woman, that hegemonic men needed to dress their cold war wounds.

All of this is not to reduce Kazan's directing to his personal problems and spectator response to his vehicles to a response to him. But insofar as Kazan's projects did concretize his anxieties and desires, they touched on what Frank Conroy has called the "secret guilt" of many cold war American males. While growing up in the 50s, Conroy vaguely realized that the legacy of the Bomb—HUAC, the national security state, the conflation of God and nation—made it impossible "to reorganize those simple propagandistic concepts of democracy and political morality which had been our wartime heritage."[77] Kazan's projects made obligatory bows to the values of grassroots democracy and cross-racial solidarity popular in the late 1930s and during the war, but a passion for progressive change no longer fired his directing. In *Eden* and *Dark*, for instance, Kazan underlined instances of good Americans protecting the rights of minorities. Similarly, *Tea* and *Waterfront* advocated individual rights against blind conformity.

The compulsion to transcend guilt and the itch for allegorical grandeur, however, undercut these values in his projects. Commenting on Kazan's films of the 1950s and early 1960s, critic Robin Wood noted that his tendency to simplify problems of social morality "has the effect of placing him and us too squarely on the right side, so that the end result is complacency rather than disturbance."[78] Kazan's post-HUAC projects, when they focus on social issues at all, stress the psychological effects of injustice on individuals; they do not model a kind of agency that might correct social injustices themselves. Rather, the rhetoric of these plays and films encouraged identification with an Empty Boy or with a witness to the situation of a Fragmented Hero. And their allegorizing privileged a prior narrative, not present action, as the source of meaning. Products of nuclear culture and containment liberalism, Kazan's plays and films of the 50s were too wrapped up in the ethics of patriarchy and the psychology of guilt to push for progressive reform.

■ No stranger to the psychology of guilt himself, Arthur Miller struggled for several months in 1959–1960 to write a play about a remorseful atomic scientist. As he relates in *Timebends* (his autobiography): "Ever since Hiroshima I had been thinking about a play that would deal with the atomic bomb. Now, fifteen years later, it was less a feeling of guilt than of wonder at my having approved the catastrophe that moved me to investigate firsthand how the scientists themselves felt about what they had created." After interviewing J. Robert Oppenheimer and another atomic physicist from the Los Alamos project, Miller wrote several scenes about an Oppenheimer-like character preparing to test the first experimental bomb. "The scenes had a certain elegance, but would not bleed," writes Miller. The play was turning out to be "interesting when it should have been horrifying."[79] It seems that Miller may have run up against the same problem as John Hersey and Ota Yoko did in writing about nuclear catastrophe — how to maintain some aesthetic distance from the horror while also inducing spectator empathy. Miller abandoned the project.

In a certain sense, however, Miller had already written a play about the effects of nuclearism on American culture. Two years after *The Crucible* premiered, William Carlos Williams directly linked the subject of Miller's play, which he likely saw or read, to the ongoing devastations of the Bomb in his poem "Asphodel, That Greeny Flower" (1955): "The bomb speaks, / All suppressions, / From the witchcraft trials at Salem / to the latest / book burnings, / are confessions / that the bomb / has entered our lives / to destroy us. . . ."[80] As he understood, the root cause of most public "suppressions" in the 1950s was the Bomb. When Miller denounced "the witchcraft trials at Salem" in *Crucible*, he was not simply attacking McCarthyism; behind the success of the junior senator from Wisconsin was the secrecy, guilt, and paranoia of nuclearism.

Nuclearism imprinted itself on many of the plays of Arthur Miller, beginning with *Salesman* in 1949 and continuing into the present. Unlike Tennessee Williams's and Lorraine Hansberry's, however, Miller's opposition to the dominant culture of the 1950s drew little from the romanticism and radicalism of the 1930s. Rather, Miller's chief inheritance from the past, the realist well-made play, pushed his dramas toward the conventional pieties of containment liberalism. In tension with these views, however, was an existential humanism driven by guilt to renounce the authority of God, the state, or any higher power that threatened to compromise individual conscience. Recognizing the inevitability of guilt in a fragmenting age, Miller's plays move toward a rationalist ethics undercut by the tragic recognition that there is very little reasonable basis for any ethical judgment. Outcast by themselves as much as by the public and their friends, Miller's Fragmented Heroes assert an absurd agency that positions them in opposition to societal norms. This is as true for the compromised heroes Biff Loman in *Salesman* and Eddie Carbone in *A View from the Bridge* (1956) as it is for John Proctor, the idealized hero of *The Crucible*. Although radically individualistic, Miller's plays ironically provide little basis for the role of public intellectual, a role Miller himself played in the 1950s. Partly a product of the anxieties of nuclearism, *Crucible* nonetheless defuses the extremes of impotence and omnipotence induced by nuclear culture, although it does not challenge the prerogatives of the stealth state.[81]

Crucible opened in New York in January 1953 to mixed reviews. Arthur Kennedy and Walter Hampden won praise for their moving and forceful portrayals of John Proctor and Judge Danforth, the stolid farmer who dies for refusing to "name names" in the witch trials and the chief judge and prosecutor of the Salem witches. Jed Harris directed the production as a period piece, with formal blocking and presentational acting that impressed the critics but left most of them unmoved. As Miller later remarked of the production: "It was not condemned, it was set aside. A cold thing, mainly; to lay to one side of entertainment, to say nothing of art."[82] Despite its cool reception and modest run (197 performances), *Crucible* won the Antoinette Perry and Donaldson Awards in 1953. New York audiences got another look at the play in 1957, when an off-Broadway company revived it with a more emotionally charged production that ran for 571 performances. Since then, *Crucible* has become Miller's most frequently produced play.

In January 1953 the critics and probably many spectators responded first to the play's relationship to the McCarthyism of the period. The security panic of the early Cold War—the investigations of government employees, the blacklisting of entertainers, the hundreds of un-American committees probing citizens for disloyalty, and McCarthy himself, still uncensored, railing against Communists in Washington—shaped the initial response to *Crucible*. By 1953 many opposed to the excesses of McCarthyism had used the term "witch hunt" to characterize the panic. Several of the Broadway critics commented on the parallels Miller had drawn between seventeenth-century Salem and contemporary witch hunts in the United States. Walter Kerr was the most pointed: "As a man of independent thought, [Miller] is profoundly, angrily concerned with the immediate issues of our society—with the irresponsible pressures which are being brought to bear on free men, with the self-seeking which blinds whole segments of our civilization to justice, with the evasions and dishonesties into which cowardly men are daily slipping." In her review in the *Nation*, Freda Kirchwey noted her sense of "having experienced simultaneously the anguish and heroism of Salem's witch hunt and of today's" when she saw the play. And a critic for the *San Francisco Chronicle* observed that "the parallel between unintelligent men of Old Salem and unintelligent men in contemporary America, who hurl accusations of 'witchcraft' indiscriminately, is unmistakable."[83]

Certainly Miller intended to point out these parallels. His 1987 autobiography sums up his main concerns at the time he was writing the play:

> Gradually, over weeks, a living connection between myself and Salem, and between Salem and Washington, was made in my mind—for whatever else they might be, I saw that the hearings in Washington were profoundly and even avowedly ritualistic. . . . The main point of the hearings, precisely as in seventeenth-century Salem, was that the accused make public confession, damn his confederates as well as his Devil master, and guarantee his sterling new allegiance by breaking disgusting old vows—whereupon he was let loose to rejoin the society of extremely decent people. . . . In effect, it came down to a governmental decree of moral guilt that could easily be made to disappear by ritual speech: intoning names of fellow sinners and recanting former beliefs.[84]

Insofar as Miller translated the analogy between the historical and the contemporary witch trials into dramatic narrative, *Crucible* probably induced some *allegoresis* in many of its spectators. Parts of Act III and IV in the play do indeed invite the audience to read the earlier witch trials as a model for the rituals of McCarthyism. The public pressure to recant, the judges' desire for more names, and the relief generated by confession are all a potent part of the dramatic action.

Building on these parallels, some critics read the play as a full-blown allegory and then berated Miller for his imprecision in aligning Salem history with analogous events in the early 1950s. For them, the primary sticking point undercutting Miller's presumed allegory was the difference between the unreal witches of the seventeenth century and real Communists in the twentieth. John Mason Brown in the *Saturday Review of Literature* said: "This time the Devil is all too real, so are his disciples, and they are threats to our national survival. Witches never existed . . .

but today there are traitors who have wormed their way into positions where they can do great harm." According to Eric Bentley, Miller made the mistake of assuming that communism was "merely a chimera: The analogy between 'red baiting' and witch hunting can seem complete only to communists, for only to them is the menace of communism as fictitious as the menace of witches." Brown and Bentley, both liberals, were foes of McCarthyism, but their need to distance themselves from any taint of Communist sympathy—all the more so because of their liberalism—clouded their judgment. To attack the play because witchcraft, unlike communism, cannot cause any harm is to reduce Miller's narrative to a one-to-one, allegorical linkage to a historical event, as occurs in the relationship between George Orwell's *Animal Farm* and the Russian Revolution, for example. Miller had warned against such a misreading even before the play opened. "I am not pressing an historical allegory here," he said. "And I have even eliminated certain striking similarities from *Crucible* which started the audience to drawing such an allegory."[85]

While *Crucible* hints at some specific connections between the Salem witch trials and McCarthyism, the general relationship between the historical events and the play probably remained more analogical than allegorical for most in the audience. Several of the initial Broadway critics understood this distinction. John Chapman pointed to the similarities but noted that the play was not a "political parable," and William Hawkins stated that the play "attempts no blatant modern comparisons." For Brooks Atkinson, "*The Crucible*, despite its current implications, [was] a self-contained play about a terrible period in American history."[86] Further, apart from the critical response, there is too much in the drama (especially in the first two acts, which occur in domestic settings) that cannot fit into a reading of the play as political allegory. Unless prompted to make allegorical connections early in the action, most spectators are unlikely to link a play's narrative to a specific ur-text later on. Thus few in the audience probably quibbled about the differences between Communists and witches, an occupation more central to the concerns of critics eager to maintain their anti-Communist credentials. *The Crucible* as an allegory of McCarthyism is largely a red herring.

Though not an allegory on the order of *J.B.* or *Night Journey*, *Crucible* does draw on the pattern of a jeremiad. By the end of the tragedy, Miller has singled out a small nucleus of Salemites and their symbolic representative, John Proctor, as his Chosen People, most of whom are destined to die for refusing to hand over their consciences to the witch hunters. These include Elizabeth Proctor (saved from hanging by her pregnancy), Rebecca Nurse, Giles Corey (already dead), and a few others who refuse to confess. On the margin of this band of heroes is the Reverend John Hale, who recognizes the witch hunt as a sham but cannot yet conceive of sacrificing his life to assure his ethical authenticity. John Proctor, of course, embodies the conscience of them all; his simple desire to preserve his "good name," both for his own self-respect and for the future of his children, finally sweeps aside other restraints, and Proctor realizes he must die. His death puts iron in the resistance of others. In opposition to HUAC's definition of true Americans, Miller positions Proctor and other courageous nonconformists as a genuine Chosen People, singled out not by God but by history and their own morality.

Although Miller secularized the jeremiad narrative, its general outline remained to challenge Broadway audiences in 1953. Like the jeremiad sermons of seventeenth-century Puritanism, *Crucible* implicitly contrasts the corruption of sinners in the McCarthyite present to the morality of good people faced with similar burdens and temptations in the past. As C. W. E. Bigsby has remarked, many of Miller's plays evidence a "desire to reach back [to a past] before corruption." *Crucible*, in particular, "expresses a longing for a time in which moral issues seemed clear and the language of moral debate had not been ironized. . . ."[87] A modern Jeremiah, Miller creates a climate of anxiety in *Crucible* to exhort his Broadway congregation to learn from this example in the past and fulfill the true promise of America.

Miller's model of an ethical community, his secularized Chosen People, emerges slowly during the action of the play, primarily in contrast to the other communities that populate *Crucible*. The rhetoric of the drama, through both advisory and empathetic projection, encourages the audience to identify with this group of witnesses to Proctor's martyrdom and to oppose the corrupt members of the other groups. Acts I and II demonstrate the greed, hypocrisy, indifference, and envy of the local congregation, with the cowardly Reverend Parris as its chief symbol. Deputy Governor Danforth stands in for the Puritan theocracy of Massachusetts; his chief concern is perpetuating his political power. By the end of Act III, Miller has indicted the legal and religious rulers of the entire colony. Abigail Williams represents the third community, a group of girls bound together through fear, despair, adolescent sexuality, and the mesmerizing power of its leader. This protofascist *Bund* builds upon the moral ruin of the other two and vanishes when it can destroy no more.

Through specific character types and social dynamics, Miller distills out the Chosen Few from the irrational villagers, the benighted judges, and the fear-mongering girls. Unlike those in the other groups, Miller's witnesses are honest, rational, humble, forthright, and strong-willed. None, however, is without some taint of sin. Giles Corey is stubborn and easily angered, Elizabeth Proctor is emotionally cold, and even Rebecca Nurse is a bit smug in her righteousness. Significantly, none is guilty of sexual excess except John Proctor, who admits to "lechery" with Abigail. Proctor, however, more than atones for his adultery during the play's action; by the conclusion, his martyrdom has cleansed him of this misstep. Miller's point in tarnishing the ethical lives of his Chosen People is clear: ordinary human beings can aspire to membership in this community. Moral courage, not perfection, is the chief requisite that distinguishes this group from others; even Broadway playgoers might join this ethical band to shape the future of the republic.

In this regard, Proctor learns that his sinful past is less important than standing up for an ethical future, though it costs him his life. *Crucible* fulfills its purpose of moral exhortation primarily by instructing the audience to watch John Proctor's gradual conversion from guilty bystander to active opponent of injustice. All of us are guilty, this cold war play affirms, but we must work through the anxieties and fragmentations caused by guilt to take purposeful action. Unlike Kazan's handling of guilt, Miller neither minimizes nor conveniently exorcises Proctor's guilty conscience. By the end of Act II, it is evident that Proctor's guilt over his adultery with Abigail has led him to delay his testimony at the trials and hence endangered his wife. Even at the end of his life, after his wife has forgiven him and after he realizes that his adultery pales in comparison to the mountain of sin that has created the witch hunts, Proctor goes to his death a guilty man. Guilt cannot be removed, the play suggests, but the paralysis caused by guilt can be sufficiently eased to allow for moral action.

Although *Crucible* underlines the disabling effects of a guilty conscience, it also points to positive uses of guilt. As Bigsby states, "there are in fact two different forms of guilt in the play — one destructive, one creative."[88] If guilt is understood as a recognition of social responsibility toward others, Proctor's guilt about delaying his exposure of Abigail's conspiracy and saving his wife—the guilt that finally drives him to court in Act III—must be counted as a positive force. His guilty concern that his children will suffer from his compliance with the court's demand that he name names also leads Proctor to protect his own "good name." Further, the rhetorical force of Miller's jeremiad hinges on a creative deployment of guilt. From Miller's point of view, an audience driven at least partly by guilt might take a stand against McCarthyism.

Miller's jeremiad narrative and his depiction of a Chosen People, symbolized in the journey of his Fragmented Hero, qualify the individualism inherent in his formal embrace of liberal tragedy. In the Ibsen tradition of liberal tragedy, according to Raymond Williams, an alienated individual rebels against the conventions and mores of a destructive social order that cannot accommodate his—the protagonist is typically male—ideals. For Ibsen and his followers, the form allowed for biting social critique but also blunted the possibility of collective action to alter social oppression. Most heroes of liberal tragedy found that the masses were unwilling to follow their leadership and also discovered that the corruptions they had uncovered festered within themselves. Hence their rebellion typically led to tragic, rather than liberating, consequences. In his "Tragedy and the Common Man," an essay published soon after the success of *Salesman* in 1949, Miller modified Aristotelian precepts about tragedy to embrace a tragic form close indeed to Williams's notion of liberal tragedy. While most men passively "accept their lot without active retaliation," wrote Miller, the tragic hero, spurred by his conscience, will actively oppose society to demand freedom and dignity. Such action, which finally pits a human life against an oppressive society, "demonstrates the indestructible will of man to achieve his humanity," according to Miller.[89] While Miller's tragic hero is generally less mired in the corruptions of his time than Ibsen's, the tragic outcome of the hero vs. society conflict is the same in both cases.

Miller wrote "Tragedy and the Common Man" with Willy Loman in mind; but, as critic Thomas Adler suggests, *Crucible* may be a better example than *Salesman* for his theory: "Proctor, because he finally 'refuses to remain passive' in the face of a 'threat to his personal dignity' that would rob him of his name and his self-respect and innocence, fulfills Miller's criteria for the tragic hero even more unquestioningly than does Willy Loman."[90] In addition to protecting his "good name," however, Proctor also dies a martyr and empowers his witnesses to oppose the status quo in Salem. While it is true that many of "the people" in the play have turned against the hero, *Crucible*, unlike most liberal tragedy, has not wholly given up on the idea of rebellion from below. After Proctor tears the paper documenting his confession, Elizabeth, realizing his action means his death, rushes to her husband in fear. "Show honor now, show a stony heart and sink them with it!" (133), Proctor tells her. Proctor's admonition purposefully recalls the heroism of Giles Corey, pressed to death by heavy stones for refusing to confess, who mocked his tormentors by calling for "more weight" while dying. A minute later, Hale enjoins Elizabeth to plead with her husband to save his life; but Elizabeth, now understanding that Proctor's dignity and freedom are more important than life itself, refuses. And Rebecca Nurse reassures Proctor, "Let you fear nothing! Another judgment waits us all!" (133). Proctor may die a tragic hero, in the sense of that term in "Tragedy and the Common Man," but his tragedy empowers others to continue the fight against oppression. His martyrdom consolidates the oppositional force of Miller's Chosen People.

"Another judgment waits us all," the energizing insecurity of Miller's jeremiad, is also the historiographical battle cry of *Crucible*. Rebecca Nurse, of course, refers to God's final judgment, but Miller has in mind the secular judgment of history. The play attempted to remind the 1953 audience that future generations would likely judge the current sins of McCarthyism in much the same way that they judged the Puritan witch hunts. Historian Edmund S. Morgan points out that *Crucible* significantly alters the actual culture of the seventeenth-century Puritans so that it can damn Miller's very twentieth-century notion of Puritanism.[91] While Morgan's observations about the many disparities between the historical Puritans and Miller's version of them are generally true, the historian misses the point. Despite his claim of historical accuracy, Miller was no more interested, finally, in historical reportage than was G. B. Shaw when he wrote *St. Joan*, a play that uses historical materials for similar rhetorical advantage. Just as Shaw beats up on the Catholics to argue that a rational understanding of historical martyrdom can energize contemporary forces of change, so Miller flays the Puritans to oppose McCarthyism. Both playwrights are fundamentally "presentist" in their orientation toward historical sources, using the past to make a case about present concerns, not to attempt to explore it on its own terms. Proctor, like Shaw's St. Joan, stands in for rational people throughout history. (Proctor's journey to martyrdom, in fact, parallels Joan's in many of its details, including an initial decision to confess.) Like Shaw, Miller uses history primarily to transcend it; both position the spectator as a rational human witness who can stand above the fray of the present time to envision a better humanity.

Miller's Shavian inheritance also shows up in the rationalist ethics that undergird his play, a version of the Strict Father model of morality but crucially different from the God-the-Father morality of *J.B.* and *Night Journey*. This ethical orientation supports Miller's secular jeremiad. According to Lakoff and Johnson, "moral rationalism conceives of the Father as Universal Reason, possessed by all people and telling each person what is morally required of him or her." Further, the internal, judgmental Father of rationalist ethics rewards its duty-bound adherents with self-respect and punishes its wrongdoers with guilt and shame. "Moral strength takes top priority," state Lakoff and Johnson, "since it is the essential condition for our being able to do what Reason morally commands."[92] The commands of moral rationalism echo through all of Miller's plays, resounding more insistently, perhaps, in *Crucible* than in others. More than any other attribute, moral strength separates the Chosen People and Fragmented Hero of this play from the other benighted Puritans. Like Shaw in *St. Joan*, Miller would hold his characters and his audience up to the bar of Universal Reason. Mystery and supernaturalism carry no weight in this court, even though this rationalist version of Strict Father ethics derives from religious authority. Like all Strict Father codes, the morality of *Crucible* views the world as a dangerous place, rife with evil and temptation, requiring masculine restraint and control.

There can be little doubt that many in Miller's predominately business-class audience in 1953 understood *Crucible* as a principled, progressive objection to the nightmares of McCarthyism. Miller reports in *Timebends* that the *Crucible* cast continued to perform on reduced pay when the producers gave notice that they were about to close its run. In one performance, notes Miller, "the audience, upon John Proctor's execution, stood up and remained silent for a couple of minutes with heads bowed. The Rosenbergs were at that moment being electrocuted in Sing Sing. Some of the cast had no idea what was happening as they faced rows of bowed and silent people, and were informed in whispers by their fellows. The play then became an act of resistance for them. . . ." Perhaps the best evidence of the influence of the play was its effect on other progressive authors. As critic Brenda Murphy states: "A number of writers took their hint from Miller's strategy of historical analogy to create their own statements about the issues it raised through historical analogs. Others who had been working along these lines became bolder and more overt."[93] These included Lillian Hellman in *The Lark* (1955), Louis Coxe in *The Witchfinders* (1956), and a series of anti-McCarthyite *You Are There* television programs in 1953 written by several blacklisted authors (among others) and centering on such historical martyrs as Galileo Galilei, Socrates, and St. Joan.

The popularity of St. Joan as a symbol of resistance to McCarthyism in the mid 50s throws into sharp relief Miller's demonizing of female sexuality in *Crucible*. The threat of sexually aggressive women—clear opposites to the saintly, virginal Joan in those plays—brands the desiring female as "the Other" in the rhetoric of Miller's play, as it does in many other Fragmented Hero plays, films, and TV shows of containment liberalism, including several of Kazan's directorial projects. Miller does not label all the women in *Crucible* as dangerous, sexualized Others, of course. Free from impetuous sexual desire, Elizabeth Proctor learns charity and understanding with her husband, and Rebecca Nurse is a paragon of rational restraint and moral courage throughout the play. As critic Iska Alter explains, these and similar women in Miller's dramas from the 1950s and early 1960s escape his censure because of their primary role as nurturers.[94] Their ability to forgive and bless Miller's male protagonists, including Proctor, gives them a stabilizing function and some limited power within the patriarchal world of his plays.

In sharp contrast to the nurturers in *Crucible* are the betrayers, led by Abigail, who personifies insurgent, amoral, and devouring sexual energy. Driven to revenge herself on Proctor, his wife, and all the Puritans if she cannot regain him as a sexual partner, Abigail preys on the inchoate adolescent sexuality and marginal social status of the other young girls to achieve her villainous ends. Like the handling of *femme fatales* in *film noir*, *Crucible* strictly segregates good wives and mothers from sensual single women. The plays and films of Kazan and others took some of the misogynist sting out of sexualized women by combining the type with the nurturing girlfriend in *Tea and Sympathy* and later dramas, but this new combination simply ensured the perpetuation of patriarchal privilege on the back of a new stereotype.

While *Crucible* perpetuates the *femme fatale* stereotype, the main problem with Abigail is less her characterization than the dominance of unbridled sexuality, both her own and others', in the architecture of the play. In principle, there is little common ground linking Proctor's unfortunate infidelity to the monstrous injustice of the witch trials; offending against marital vows and social mores lacks the substance and magnitude of a crime that leads to numerous hangings. Although *Crucible* never actually equates these sins, it gives more weight than necessary to the Proctor-Abigail coupling as both the initiating cause of the witch hunt and the reason for its murderous excesses. Like those of the villains of many melodramas, Abigail's desires drive much of the main action of the play, from the initial outbreak of witch naming in Act I through Proctor's imprisonment at the end of Act III. Bigsby rightly complains that other evils contributing to the witch hunt—the scapegoating of poor women, the land greed of several villagers, the status-seeking and hunger for power evident in Parris, Danforth, and others—get little attention at Miller's hands.[95]

Toward the end of Act II, the Reverend Hale tells Proctor and his wife that we must "look to cause proportionate" for the evils that have befallen the people of Salem. "Think on cause, man, and let you help me to discover it" (75). While Hale believes that the single cause of witchcraft explains all, Miller wants his audience to understand that there were many reasons for the witch hunt in Salem. Although he partly succeeds in linking the cause of Abigail's campaign and the town's fury to several historical circumstances, his complex historical analysis finally bows to a single prime mover: the sexual lust in one woman, an omnivorous desire that seems beyond the capacity of any history to contain or explain. In short, Miller has not provided a "cause proportionate" for his witch hunt.

As several cultural historians have noted, narrative dislocations caused by "disproportionate" sexuality were often a mark of nuclearism in the early Cold War. Abigail's sexuality is another nuclear "bombshell" of containment culture, and it disrupts the narrative structure of Miller's play. Her moral opposites, Miller's Chosen People, have many minor sins but are innocent of sexual desire. These temporary survivors from the witch trials remain, like the short-term survivors chronicled by Hersey, as witnesses to the blast, guarantors that a band of ethical beings will pick up the pieces of civilization and start anew. When some badly scarred female victims of Hiroshima traveled to the United States in 1955 for plastic surgery, the press dubbed them the "Hiroshima Maidens," despite their various ages and marital statuses. The Chosen Few of *Crucible* are Miller's "Hiroshima Maidens," their combination of moral courage and sexual innocence recalling the numerous St. Joans in circulation throughout the culture.

Similarly, female desire inflames and enervates Proctor in *Crucible* much as it nearly immolates Mike Hammer, Mickey Spillane's detective, in the film version of *Kiss Me Deadly* (1955). At the climax of this cold war thriller, a *femme fatale* shoots Hammer in the side then opens a lead box containing radioactive material. As the babe burns up, shrieking in pain, Hammer crawls and stumbles out of the beach house, finally looking back to watch it explode in a nuclear fireball. In forms of drama at some distance from ground zero in the culture of containment liberalism, such as the Empty Boy comedy of *The Seven Year Itch*, a play could accommodate a bombshell with little disturbance to its conventional structure. Because *Crucible*, like the "Hiroshima Maidens" and *Kiss Me Deadly*, deals metaphorically with a problem of national security, however, its narrative is more fragile, its contradictions more apparent.

Insofar as sexual desire dominates the plotting of *Crucible*, the play ironically mirrors the conspiracy theory narrative imagined by McCarthy, Richard Nixon, and the witch hunters of HUAC. Miller was seeking to challenge McCarthyism, of course, but the play ends up by replicating one of the deepest fears of the anti-Communist crazies—that a vast conspiracy rooted in sexual anarchy and controlled by a tyrant could overturn established authority. While Abigail's compulsive conspiracy has none of the institutional power that the witch hunters associated with international communism, it does possess the imagined influence of Communist propaganda to infiltrate and control the lives of the simple people of Salem. A few reviewers questioned the believability of Abigail's persuasive power. "Fact or not," said John McClain, for example, "I found it constantly incredible that four malicious maidens in Salem, 1692, could have corrupted the courts and brought about the horror and execution of so many obviously innocent folk."[96] Significantly, neither McClain nor others questioned Miller's construction of Salem history. Miller's interpretation was "fact," even though these facts were stranger than fiction.

Abigail's conspiracy at the center of *Crucible* poses a different version of history and agency than the narrative of jeremiad that structures the ending and much of the rest of the play. This contradiction in the narrative structure of the drama is a further indication of its involvement in nuclear culture. As in most melodramas of conspiracy, active agency passes to Abigail in *Crucible*, and her victims can only react to her depredations. Proctor's guilt and his own sexuality, of course, contribute to his passivity. Like the McCarthyites, Miller believes that the conspirators in *Crucible*, like Communists everywhere, may be successful in appealing to the baser instincts of their victims; indeed, even the crusty Danforth falls before Abigail's charms. In general, conspiratorial history undercuts the possibility of revolt from below because "the people," easily duped by villainy, rarely have enough foresight, analytical acumen, and political power to fight compulsive conspirators and push for radical reform. Neither the people nor the elite can stop Abigail and her girls in *Crucible*. The small group of rational dissenters led by Proctor may win a moral victory, but history crushes them. Miller wants jeremiad morality to triumph over the steamroller of conspiratorial history, but some spectators may have wondered about the future effectiveness of a Chosen People and their Hero, given the power of sexualized persuasion.

The version of history and agency evident in Miller's conspiracy narrative was close to the conclusions about American history reached by Richard Hofstadter, the most influential U.S. historian during the early Cold War. Hofstadter believed that corporate elites and popular demagogues had misled the American people for much of their history and urged that apolitical experts, with ties to no faction, should guide America toward a better future. In *The Age of Reform* (1955), for example, Hofstadter painted the populists of the 1890s as "paranoid" fanatics and the progressives of the 1900s as old-fashioned moralists out of touch with the realities of the new century. Historian David W. Noble concludes that Hofstadter's point of view led to the implication that "for progress and order to be restored, the majority should shed their older emotional commitment to widespread participatory democracy and turn civic and economic power over to experts better qualified to direct the nation through dangerous waters."[97] Hofstadter's commitment to rational experts over compulsive democrats accords with the conspiratorial narrative of *Crucible* and one side of Miller's rationalist ethics. Hofstadter's and Miller's pessimism about democratic historical agency also mirrors the general impotence felt by many people as a result of nuclear culture; better to let experts with technical know-how, like the scientists who built the Bomb, manage the United States. On the other side, however, is

Miller's belief that simple people unschooled in science and technology can awaken from their guilt and confusion and take a stand for a rational and courageous public morality.

Miller built both of the narratives that inform his play, the jeremiad and the conspiratorial, out of primary and secondary historical sources. The documents available to him in the Salem library and elsewhere (court records, diaries, reports, etc.) plus Marion Starkey's popular history, *The Devil in Massachusetts* (1949), were almost entirely textual in nature. Yet one of the most curious aspects of *Crucible*, and another mark of its relation to nuclear culture, is Miller's disparagement of the written word during the course of the drama. In part, Miller undermines the legitimacy of texts to attack his version of Puritanism. As a people of "the Book," the Puritans relied on printing and its apparent black-and-white truths much more than did many Westerners in the seventeenth century. When the Reverend Hale arrives in Salem, he brings with him several "heavy" tomes on demonology, "weighted," as he says, "with authority" (34). The printed and written texts of laws and depositions become the focus of substantial concern during the trial scene of Act III; at one point, all other stage action stops entirely so that four characters can read Mary Warren's deposition. And *Crucible* climaxes at the moment when Proctor refuses to sign his name to the text of his confession. Hale, in despair by Act IV, completely reverses his earlier reliance on the written word. "We cannot read His will" (122), he admits. Written knowledge apparently holds little validity in Miller's rational morality.

Knowledge based on oral performance is equally suspect in *Crucible*. Much of the dialogue of the play consists of legalistic questions and answers, a mode that predominates among parents and children, ministers and parishioners, and even husbands and wives as well as in the more formal courtroom relationships of Act III. While these close questionings and careful responses reveal substantial reliable knowledge for characters and spectators during the course of the play, Abigail's oral performances can trump this legalistic oral mode at any time. The audience may recognize Abigail's feigned visions as "pretense," a term repeated often in the drama, but her pretense succeeds in the world of the play. In Act III, Abigail's improvisations, coordinated by her stage management of the semihysterical girls, overwhelm Proctor's testimony against her and strike such fear into Mary Warren that she retracts her deposition. Abigail achieves most of her effects through orality, but she and her girls finally succeed by reducing the spoken word to nonsense by repeating, verbatim, what Mary Warren has said. Ironically, Proctor himself mounts another performance in Act IV that also undercuts the validity of oral testimony when he pretends to confess his witchcraft before Danforth to save his life. By the end of the play, both oral and written modes of communication have taken a beating. If neither can be trusted, if both can hide "pretense," how may the truth be represented?

The problem is potentially acute for an avowedly public playwright like Arthur Miller. His numerous interviews, essays, and plays throughout the 1950s suggest that Miller rarely questioned the validity of oral or written communication per se. And he certainly hoped that *Crucible*, both as oral performance and as published text, would influence the public debate on McCarthyism. Nonetheless, *Crucible* betrays the pessimistic understanding that the media of speaking and writing, by their nature, cannot be trusted as neutral channels of communication. Rather, the mode of communication validated in the play is visual. Like Kazan and Graham, Miller lived in "the picture era," an era in which the Bomb confounded spoken and printed language even as its cultural fallout multiplied photographic images.

The climax of *Crucible* is a picture of Proctor ripping up his written confession, a gesture that undercuts writing and orality at the same time as it elevates the visual. Instead of answering Danforth's question, "Which way do you go, Mister?" (133), with words, he replies with action: "His breast heaving, his eyes staring, Proctor tears the paper and crumples it, and he is weeping in fury but erect" (133). In effect, Proctor has countered the arousing picture of Abigail, the visual truth that predominates for most of the play, with a higher visual image. Proctor's gesture seems to proclaim the superiority of Miller's jeremiad tale over his conspiracy narrative. In the moment of existential truth, neither written nor spoken words are necessary; only action fit for a photo matters.

Proctor's ultimate gesture, however, compromises what he has just said about his name: "How may I live without my name? I have given you my soul; leave me my name" (133). Names must be spoken or written before they are understood; mute action—unless it stands in for writing or speaking, as in signing among the hearing impaired—cannot communicate a name. A name is necessary for authorship, and Miller's own life is testimony to the importance of a public life anchored in authorship. Like Proctor, Miller could not separate his name from the oral testimony he

John Proctor/Arthur Kennedy, his torn, crumpled confession in his right hand, refuses to give his name to the prosecution. Others on stage, from left to right: Elizabeth Proctor/Beatrice Straight (seated), Rev. John Hale/E. G. Marshall, Deputy Governor Danforth/Walter Hampden, and Rebecca Nurse/Jean Adair. Fred Fehl photo, courtesy Fred Fehl.

gave before HUAC in 1956, when he refused to "name names" and was cited and fined for contempt of Congress. And for essentially the same reason, because his name was synonymous with the authorship of *Crucible*, Miller felt he could not allow the Wooster Group to perform a radically altered version of "his" play in New York in 1984. Yet, in the face of a security panic linked to nuclear culture, *Crucible* retreats to a mode of communication closer to the photograph than to orality or print.

In the Western tradition from Socrates to Shaw, rationalist ethics has traditionally stood on the legitimacy of oral testimony or written authorship, and frequently on both. Typically, the right words have been worth a thousand pictures in constructing a morality that could withstand the tests of reason. By radically undercutting this tradition to embrace the visual, Miller's play leaves his hero with nothing but mute individual conscience to clothe his ethics, a nearly untenable position for an ethical rationalist. *Crucible* was closer to the "theater of the absurd" than Miller or his critics ever suspected. Like an Ionesco play, it assaults the notion that language can fully comprehend and represent reality.

Again, the natural ties binding the Bomb to the photograph are relevant here. Embedded in the material effects of nuclearism, *Crucible* sidesteps most of the Platonic pressures of radiophony by denigrating the potential truthfulness of orality and the idealizing tendencies of language. A modern history play, *Crucible* may be understood as an attempt to replace the lost memory of a shocking event with snapshots from the past. The play climaxes in a "photo opportunity" from history. Walter Benjamin would have understood.

■ Unlike *Crucible*, *What Use Are Flowers* (1962) by Lorraine Hansberry drew back from the abyss of the absurd to assert a small hope for rational, progressive action in the face of possible nuclear obliteration.[98] Where *Crucible*'s politics stop with its objection to McCarthyism, Hansberry's antiwar "fable," as she termed it, takes on the legacy of the Enlightenment and its partial culmination in the stealth state. Published posthumously, *What Use Are Flowers* begins in a postapocalyptic world in which only a gang of children and a Hermit, newly emerging from self-exile, remain alive several years after a nuclear war. Once the old Hermit realizes that these predatory, feral children have no knowledge of Western civilization, he begins to teach them art, music, and science. When the leader of the gang wrecks a miniature water wheel fashioned by one of the Hermit's pupils and the children revert to their former savagery, the frustrated teacher gives up. Near death, he berates himself for believing he could save the human race. As he is dying, however, the children and eventually their leader gather around the pupil as he begins to reconstruct his water wheel, curious about this new invention.

Like Brecht's *Galileo*, another drama of the atomic age, *What Use Are Flowers* affirms the power of curiosity and reason in the face of mass destruction. Both recognize that science may be harnessed to political repression; both know that Enlightenment rationalism can serve inhuman ends. But both also insist that human reason can eventually overcome the worst that humanity can inflict on itself. Nonetheless, Hansberry's play is too sentimental to support its ambitious goals. The trope of a dying teacher finally vindicated by his pupil (which also occurs in *Galileo*), offers meager support for utopian hopes. More importantly, the reduction of humanity to a skeptical Hermit and unruly children avoids the larger political problems of disarmament that Hansberry wants to engage. For all of its bite, *What Use Are Flowers* ends up closer to the universalizing humanism of the "Family of Man" than to Brecht's narrative of the nuclear age. Even *Galileo*, however, struggled (arguably without success) to position its spectators to take action against the enormities of nuclearism.

It may be that the Bomb and its cultural fallout ultimately defy successful stage representation, at least within the rhetorics and aesthetics of modernism.[99] Nonetheless, Hansberry takes the rationalist ethics of *Crucible* to the next logical step. If further Red Scares are to be avoided, her fable affirms, nuclear disarmament must diffuse the power of the stealth state.

Epilogue, 1962-1992

Cold war theater in the United States did not end in the early 1960s, of course. Although new modes of theatrical production proliferated after 1962 — with the success of off- then off-off-Broadway, the rise of festival and regional theaters, the growing professionalism of educational theater, and the continuation of road companies — the Empty Boys, Family Circles, and Fragmented Heroes that had dominated the Broadway theater of the 1950s continued to people the American stage for the next thirty years. Likewise, the cognitive dynamics of containment and compulsion, plus the other primary metaphors that organized the narratives of containment culture, endured to attract audiences to the rhetoric and aesthetics of similar representations in fiction, films, and television programming. From a cognitive perspective, it is not surprising that modes of theater popular during the early Cold War should persist in the culture; the near universality of cognitive processes and the generally conservative nature of cultural perception make continuity more likely than change in any culture. Rather, the persistence of cold war theater after 1962 throws into sharper relief the formative alterations that had already occurred between the mid 1930s and 1950. The conjunction of photography, radio, political paranoia, capitalistic consumerism, and the Bomb in the late 1940s had produced a geologic shift in the plate tectonics of American culture; its structural effects would outlast the political Cold War that ended in 1989.

At the same time, significant structural changes were occurring in the 1962-1992 period that altered some of the cognitive dynamics of the era. As before, it was primarily new modes of communication that powered these changes. The generation that had dominated the culture of the 1950s had grown up with photographs and radio; their historicist and materialist or Platonic and metonymic effects had shaped that generation's understanding of the real. By the mid 1960s the first television generation came to maturity; and the cognitive dynamics of TV, which was already reshaping the culture faster than had any earlier media, challenged older perceptions of reality.

In brief, television induced viewers to activate and privilege three primary metaphors of cognition that had not been a major part of the containment liberalism before the 1960s: "iteration," "surface," and "link." Similar to radio but more so, commercial television was and remains enormously repetitious. Viewers become comfortable with the same faces, the same advertisements, and the same program genres while also looking for and taking pleasure in small changes that vary but rarely break the iterative quality of nearly all broadcasts. Somewhat like photographs, television emphasized the different surfaces of its images, a necessity for legibility in the early black-and-white days of the medium, but one that continues to be important because of the small size of the screen. Unlike still and moving photography, the television camera has more difficulty creating illusions of depth; hence the proliferation of medium shots and close-ups on TV, which rely on contrasts in surface and the pleasure viewers take in reading those differences, especially differences in facial expressions. Finally, the diagetic flow of television linked numerous images in webs of causation and similitude. Television advertisers take advantage of the ontology of the medium when they rely on viewers' ability to create links between juxtaposed images—between, say, a sexy smile or a rippling brook and the toothpaste they are selling. Earlier visual modes of communication also educated the public in such associations; but television, through its fragmentation of viewing and proliferation of programming genre, offers greater complexity and a wider range of linking conventions than any previous medium. As with photography and radio, television requires and rewards modes of cognition that have played a part in the biological and ecological situation of humankind for centuries. But TV's dominance in the late twentieth century elevated these modes over others to structural prominence in the culture of the period.[1]

The primacy of "iteration," "surface," and "link" in television viewing played out in the 1962–1992 culture in several of the ways that many commentators have identified as postmodernist. Because the perception of the speed of historical change is always relative for a spectator, television viewers, inured to the repetitive sameness of TV images, exaggerated minor changes in their everyday lives and came to believe that American history and culture were in constant flux. Attuned to the surface qualities of phenomena rather than looking for depth and essence, Americans became even more conscious of glamour, packaging, and skin color than during the 1950s. Trained to discover links of similitude and causation by television viewing, Americans in the 1962–1992 period embraced both hard-edged conspiracy theories and vague notions of universal oneness. As the cultural implications of the cognitive schema "link" suggest, TV culture was rife with structural contradictions. Notions of historical flux, even impending chaos, might be just as believable as historical conspiracy. Skin color could be a reason for celebrating universality, a cause for alarm, or a fashion statement. Television helped to produce a culture that inflated the value of change, collage, conspiracy, and celebrity.[2]

In the United States, television culture modified, though it did not wholly displace, notions of the real embedded in the culture of the Cold War. Under pressure from TV-induced cognitive modes, some of the old containers that separated Platonic essences during the early Cold War began to crumble after 1962: white/black, private enterprise/public government, public image/private life, among others. Significant economic and political changes (including the domestic response to the Vietnam War, the globalization of corporate power, the Watergate political scandal, and the election of a movie star as president) also undermined the legitimacy of these older containers. Because perceiving and thinking about relations among phenomena in terms of links is very different than imaging that apparently different phenomena fit into a single, larger container, the typifications and allegorizing that had sustained much of containment liberalism also lost some of their credibility and allure. Universal heroes and allegorical stories that felt right at home on the radio or film screen seemed too large for the tube. At the same time, there were some commonalities and continuities linking the 1950s to the adult education induced by TV, with the believability of conspiracy perhaps the most salient. Moreover, television culture did little to challenge the dominance of "compulsion" from the cold war era. This cognitive mode, reinforced by the ongoing militarization of U.S. culture, remained a central structural component of American experience during the last third of the century.

Given the pervasive, enveloping nature of televised communication after 1962, it may seem surprising that the Empty Boys, Family Circles, and Fragmented Heroes of the cold war theater survived on stage at all into the early 1990s. By tracing their durability from 1962 to 1992, this epilogue also suggests the tenacity of containment liberalism and cold war thinking during the period. As before, I focus on popular and representative productions on the New York stage, still the center of the American commercial theater for these thirty years, but here I broaden my concerns to include those productions from off-Broadway that enjoyed substantial success in New York and throughout the country. (As a site for alternative, nonmainstream theater, off-Broadway, with its greater financial flexibility and increasing prestige, was already losing its distinctiveness by the late 1950s.) Many of the following plays and musicals and their authors gained cultural prestige as well as popular success; several won Tony and Drama Desk Awards, Pulitzer Prizes, and Drama Critics Circle honors. In part because of the complexity of several of these plays and their production on many stages around the country, I focus on the cognitive dynamics of the scripts and say little about their productions and receptions. This epilogue also excludes dance from consideration, both for reasons of space and because modern dance in 1962 was emerging from under the culture's general conception of theater that had encompassed the work of Martha Graham and most earlier dancers and choreographers. Finally, I have less to say, proportionally, than before about productions that substantially contested the culture of containment. This is because containment liberalism, fully constituted by 1962, did not stand still for the next thirty years but shifted to adjust to the new cognitive realities. The story of these changes, consequently, involves too many complexities for the scope of this epilogue. My focus, then, is on the continuities linking the theater of the early Cold War to developments over the next thirty years. And these continuities are stronger than many current surveys of American theater might lead one to suppose.[3]

From 1961 through 1992 Neil Simon provided American theatergoers with a continuous supply of Empty Boys. In his first Broadway success, *Come Blow Your Horn* (1961), Simon hails the hijinks of two playboys: Alan Baker, the oldest son of a middle-class couple who finally settles into marriage and adult responsibilities, and his younger brother, who learns the tricks of the trade from Alan and will continue the playboy lifestyle after the curtain falls. *The Odd Couple* (1965) comically explores the moral vacuity of two heterosexual misfits who have been tossed out by their wives and are struggling to live together in the same apartment while searching for some solid ground in their lives. In *The Last of the Red Hot Lovers* (1969), Barney Cashman is thrown back into boyhood by a midlife crisis. After twenty-three years of a safe marriage and an uneventful life, he is seeking a romantic affair but comically fails to find it with three women in each of the play's three acts. In 1972 Simon demonstrated that Empty Boyhood could last into old age; *The Sunshine Boys* shows two aging vaudevillians squabbling like teenagers. In the 1980s Simon returned to his own boyhood to trace his gradual coming of age as a playwright over the course of three autobiographically based plays, *Brighton Beach Memoirs* (teenage years, 1983), *Biloxi Blues* (in the service, 1984), and *Broadway Bound* (gag writing for radio, 1986). *Broadway Bound* featured Eugene Jerome, Simon's alter ego for all of these plays, finding maturity and his comic voice in the midst of an Odets-like family melodrama. With nearly a hit a year since 1961—mostly comedies and a few musicals—Simon has had more success than any other American playwright. And many of his most memorable characters are Empty Boys.

Musical comedies persisted in boosting traditional family values and the figure of the Family Circle that anchored them from the 1960s through the 1980s. With the enormous success of *Hello, Dolly!* (1964) and *Mame* (1966), starring Carol Channing and Angela Lansbury, the mother-centered musical dominated the decade. Like *Mame*, two musicals celebrating marriage, *I Do! I Do!* (1966) and *Two by Two* (1970), also derived from popular mainstream plays of the 1950s—*The Fourposter* and *The Flowering Peach*. Narratives and songs about single women who strive for success but also want a family perpetuated the ideology of the Family Circle, too. These included *Funny Girl* (1964), *Cabaret* (1966), *Sweet Charity* (1966), and, taking an African American angle on the same theme, *Hallelujah Baby* (1967) and *Dreamgirls* (1981).

At the same time, the musicals of the 1962–1992 period found new ways of perpetuating the cold war family. In *The Fantasticks* (1960), the longest-running show in off-Broadway history, two fathers hire some actors to trick their son and daughter into giving up their romantic notions for the realities of a conventional marriage and family. Keeping the bunkered family together in the midst of marriage, the breakdown of "Tradition," and anti-Semitic pogroms in turn-of-the-century Russia was the comic and melodramatic burden of *Fiddler on the Roof*, which opened in 1964 and ran for nine years. Dorothy's creation of a pseudo-family in Oz and her struggle to return home to her real one in Kansas recurred in *The Wiz* (1975), as it had in the original stage version of *The Wizard of Oz* nearly seventy-five years before. Annie-finds-a-safe-family was the plot line of *Annie* (1977), based on the "Little Orphan Annie" cartoon strip. *The Best Little Whorehouse in Texas* (1978) and *La Cage aux Folles* (1983) demonstrated the durability and flexibility of the Family Circle, though neither production could have succeeded in the 1950s. In the first, a power-hungry broadcaster traps a Texas politician into closing his favorite brothel, a contained and contented little family with a mother figure who helps her girls to grow up and corrals her johns into good manners. *La Cage* presented a gay version of *Guess Who's Coming to Dinner*: Boy wants to marry Girl but cannot introduce the "parents" to each other because Mom and Dad are actually Dad and Dad and the Girl's parents are homophobic. The musical managed to endorse both a Mom-centered (well, drag-centered) family and the continuance of the closet for homosexuality.

The nuclear dilemmas of Fragmented Heroes persisted but took a different turn than the Empty Boys and Family Circles of the Cold War after 1970. During the 1960s, *The Man of La Mancha* (1965), like *Camelot* before it, presented a doomed hero who is caught between dreams of omnipotence and fears of death and fragmentation. Both musicals, however, sentimentalized the hero's idealism and eliminated all but minor reasons for his guilt. Not surprisingly, perhaps, the chief dramatic explorer of the Fragmented Hero in the 1960s continued to be Arthur Miller, whose new plays drew wide audiences during the decade but decreased in popularity in the 1970s and 1980s. In *After the Fall* (1964), Miller's hero, Quentin, reaches for power in his relationship with Maggie but must settle for guilt and self-awareness after her suicide. Struggling to control his memories and to discover his psychological essence, this modern Adam also comes to recognize his complicity in the Holocaust and the other horrors of the twentieth century. *Incident at Vichy* (1965), set in France during World War II, extends the morality of *After the Fall* by setting up a situation in which the hero can sacrifice himself to save another human being from the death camps. Both plays relied on the inducements of containment, compulsion, and restraint removal that had organized earlier Fragmented Hero plays. *The Price* (1968) balanced a guilty Fragmented Hero (Walter Franz), who has achieved success, against his brother (Victor), who suffers from envy and disillusionment because he rates himself a failure. In this play, Miller suggests that the price of valuing economic success results in one form of psychological fragmentation or another; American males must pay in either envy or guilt. The shadow of the Bomb continued to haunt these plays (especially *After the Fall*), but female sexuality no longer provided the necessary Otherness to define the fragmented male in Miller's later plays of the decade.

Few other white playwrights won popular fame by exploring the decimated psychological landscape of Fragmented Heroes after 1970. (One exception was Jason Miller—no relation to Arthur—whose *That Championship Season* in 1972 contrasted the present empty lives of former basketball champions and their coach with their past glory.) Instead, the primary inheritors of Miller's moral and psychological concerns were African American playwrights Charles Fuller and August Wilson. Miller's link to Fuller and Wilson is grounded in a significant similarity: all three playwrights continue to draw their dramatic energy and focus from a past disaster in world history—the Great Depression (and secondarily the Holocaust) for Miller and chattel slavery and its legacy of racism for Fuller and Wilson. Echoing Miller's adaptation of *An Enemy of the People* (1950) and *A View from the Bridge*, Fuller's *Zooman and the Sign* (1980) pits an isolated hero, Ruben Tate, against community cowardice after an arrogant teenager accidentally kills his daughter in a gang shootout. Ruben's attempt to invoke the rational morality of the law ironically backfires, however, when his brother shoots the teenager (nicknamed Zooman) for destroying Ruben's sign that condemned the neighborhood for its silence after the initial slaying. More ironies trapped the Fragmented Heroes of *A Soldier's Play* (1981), Fuller's next hit, which won the Pulitzer Prize as well as the Drama Critics Circle Award. Transposing the dramatic situation of Melville's *Billy Budd* into an "all-Negro" unit of the U.S. army in 1944, Fuller explored the psychology of the Claggart figure, a Sergeant Waters, whose racial mix of pride, envy, and self-hatred led to the suicide of the Billy Budd figure and, finally, to his own killing at the hands of an enraged black soldier. After the initially self-assured black officer and lawyer, Captain Davenport, investigates these deaths in the Louisiana army camp, his own confidence is destroyed, and he comes to recognize the madness of American racism. As in *Zooman* (and many of Miller's plays), the law remains a necessary though a radically insufficient instrument for discerning and containing the bewildering fallout from slavery.

Several of the popular plays of August Wilson demonstrate an affinity with the major images of containment from the 1950s. *Ma Rainey's Black*

Bottom (1984) puts a strong woman at the center of a protofamily of musicians in 1920s Chicago and focuses on the growing rage of an Empty Boy, Levee, who finally kills one of the musicians after Ma Rainey fires him and the white owner of the recording company exploits him. In *Fences* (1985), a play set in the 1950s with striking similarities to *Death of a Salesman*, a Fragmented Hero struggles to dominate his son while the disclosure of his affair (and illegitimate son) with an Other Woman tears apart his nuclear family. On stage, the fence-as-container that Troy Maxon is building around his backyard stands as a potent reminder of the confinement he enforces, the security his wife seeks, and the pressure cooker that locks down family emotions until his death near the end of the play. *The Piano Lesson* (1988) focuses on the conflict between an Empty Boy brother and a strong woman sister in a Pittsburgh family in the 1930s as they struggle with each other over the legacy of slavery, embodied in an intricately carved piano that depicts family members during slave times. The problem of what to do with this microcosm of the past—sell it for farmland or keep it to honor one's ancestors—is finally resolved when the strong woman of the family plays the piano to exorcise a ghost representing white oppression from the South. Like his other plays, Wilson's *Joe Turner's Come and Gone* (1986) and *Two Trains Running* (1990) also appealed to white and black audiences through their jeremiadlike warnings about American racism. If a time machine dropped spectators from the 1950s into a theater producing a Wilson play in the late 1980s, they might have resented Wilson's racial politics (despite similarities in racial essentialism), but they would have understood his psychological realism and the Empty Boys, Family Circles, and Fragmented Heroes populating his stage.

Despite these and other continuities that demonstrate the direct influence of containment liberalism on the production and reception of mainstream theater in the 1962–1992 period, television culture—especially when linked to parallel pressures from social, economic, and political developments—was gradually shifting the structural components of the American theater. Alternative productions inducing spectators to experience performances through the image schemas of "iteration," "link," and "surface" proliferated in New York after the mid 1960s. These included *Viet Rock* (1966), *America Hurrah* (1966), and *The Serpent* (1967) at the Open Theatre, *Slave Ship* (1967) at the Black Arts Repertory Theatre in Harlem, *The Cry of the People for Meat* (1969) at the Bread and Puppet Theatre, and *Dionysus in '69* by the Performance Group. *America Hurrah*, for example, engaged audiences with the surfaces of American consumerism; *Dionysus in '69* explored the iterative qualities of ritual; and *The Slave Ship* deployed a web of associations to link American racism to the history of slavery. Several of these productions also engaged their audiences through metatheater and *allegoresis*; not surprisingly, these theatrical experimenters found it necessary to reinforce some traditional devices of containment culture in the midst of overthrowing others in order to preserve the legibility of their shows. Nonetheless, by opposing conventional dramatic structures, conventional relations among actors and audiences, and conventional theatrical spaces, the late 60s avant-garde explored its own notions of freedom in opposition to the constrictions of containment liberalism.[4]

The initial impact of the avant-garde on mainstream theater was innocuous. The "counterculture" musical *Hair* opened off-Broadway in 1967 and moved to the Great White Way in 1968 for a five-year run. It celebrated the iterative qualities of rock and roll and gloried in the surface similarities of dress, language, and music that appeared to link a group of hedonistic youngsters in tribal solidarity. *Hair*'s gratuitous, fleeting nudity at the end of the first act, which capitalized on more serious investigations of nude bodies and spectators in the avant-garde, delighted a voyeuristic public. The success of *Hair* spawned several trends that continued on Broadway into the 1970s. *Oh! Calcutta!* (1969) and its several spinoffs exploited the popularity of watching nude bodies in suggestive relationships, while *Stomp* and *Sambo* (both 1969) amplified the rock musical's anger at conventional values. Soft-rock musicals like *Godspell* (1971) and *Pippen* (1972) had greater staying power, both running over three years on Broadway with numerous later productions around the nation. Although continuing the homage of *Hair* to the surface, iterative, and linkage inducements of television culture, both musicals also engaged audiences through many of the conventional devices of containment. The metatheatrical device of an acting troupe performing a story framed both shows, and their allegorical involvements—*Godspell* traces the final days of Jesus and *Pippen* is an Everyman tale—encouraged spectators to wallow in Platonic essentials and universals. Both productions sprinkled the surfaces of magic shows, circus gimmicks, burlesque turns, and television programs onto the stage primarily to perpetuate the pieties and cognitive modes of containment liberalism.

By the late 1970s the mainstream plays of Sam Shepard were exhibiting more substantial influences from the avant-garde than *Hair* and its spinoffs. Several of Shepard's plays focus on figures that the culture of the 1950s understood as Empty Boys; but in Shepard's less contained, more postmodern world these figures tend to be character types representing specific attributes and impulses—fragments that could never attain psychological and ethical wholeness. Although Shepard is committed to a dramaturgy that explores the problems and induces experiences that hinge on the image schemas of surface and link, the major characters and deterministic plots of many of his plays nonetheless share the schema of compulsion with earlier Empty Boy dramas.

The Tooth of Crime (1972), an early play that achieved modest popularity and durability, demonstrates the method that would shape Shepard's later, more realistic successes. In some weird parallel universe set in a future driven by the compulsions of rock fans, a young rock star challenges and finally murders an older one in a ritualized contest that has all the surface trappings of gang warfare. Although Shepard invites the audience to explain what has happened by mapping the action onto a mythological narrative, the inducement of *allegoresis* is only a tease; Shepard links the action to a larger world of myth, and this mythological world does predetermine the outcome, but the linkage only provides causes and similitudes, not the containment figuration of allegory. Likewise, myths of the old West drive the action of *True West* (1980), in which two brothers play out their rivalry in a suburban kitchen that comes to represent an arena for a gunfight in a Hollywood western. And in *Fool for Love* (1983), myths of forbidden passion and two generations of obsessive desire prefigure the final conflagration that engulfs an offstage Cadillac. Myth-driven rather than character-driven, Shepard's plays nevertheless suggest the legacy of the Empty Boy on the post-1962 stage. In effect, his major plays assume that the world of the Empty Boy—compulsive, amoral, fascinated with surfaces, and battered by powers beyond human agency—is the actual, normal world of America.

From this perspective, other Shepard plays savage the myth of "togetherness" that ostended the Family Circle of the 1950s as the home of bunkered security and international asylum. In *Buried Child* (1978), Shepard evokes the myth of regeneration through the soil to tell a Gothic tale about three generations on a family farm caught up in alienation, violence, and incest between mother and son that has resulted in a child killed and buried in the back yard. The working out of the myth of rebirth, however, finally overrides the compulsions of several of Shepard's monstrous type characters when the dead baby is revealed and a new son takes over the farm. An even bleaker family drama, *A Lie of the Mind* (1985), injects the ritual of the hunt into two overlapping Family Circles and witnesses family members hunting, stalking, and savagely beating one other—their primitive drives actually facilitated by the isolation of the American family from other social institutions. Shepard destroys any basis for family togetherness in this play, not only affection and security but even the possibility of communicating across the chasms of solipsism that isolate his obsessive characters. The grim, ironic ending of the drama seals the doom of the 50s family: as a suburban ranch house burns, an older couple folds an American flag.

Several women playwrights after the mid 1970s also attacked the constraints and hypocrisies of the Family Circle, but without, like Shepard, abandoning a notion of family altogether. Among the most successful of these were *Crimes of the Heart* (1981) by Beth Henley and, more relentlessly, *'Night, Mother* (1982) by Marsha Norman. Henley's comedy explores the misfortunes of three sisters who have attempted to live within the hopes and dreams of their absent Old Granddaddy, only to discover that he is leading them to self-destruction. By the end of the play, the sisters take their lives in their own hands and celebrate their sisterly affection for each other. Like parts of *Getting Out* (1977), Norman's earlier play about a woman's self-discovery and gradual liberation, *'Night, Mother* explores the constraints of traditional family ties on a woman's freedom. In this case, Jessie, the daughter, has chosen to kill herself and must convince her manipulative mother both that suicide is right for her and that her mother is not to blame for her decision. In the process of justifying her choice, Jessie redefines family relations. More conventional in their dramaturgy than Shepard's dramatic riffs, Henley's and Norman's plays show little affiliation with the inducements of surface, iteration, and link proffered by television culture. Drawing (like Williams and Hansberry) on the residual theatrical culture of photographic realism, both playwrights reject the containment of the 50s family for the possibilities of self-realization through history.

Several playwrights mixed traditional realism with other styles to fashion intentional families as an alternative to the nuclear, biological model of family togetherness. In part, this optimism about reshaping the family sprang from numerous television programs suggesting that surface similarities could facilitate family ties among people at work and at play. Edward Albee foreshadowed this development, as well as critiquing it, in *A Delicate Balance* (1966), a play that stretches the affectional boundaries of the Family Circle to the breaking point. When two friends, haunted by a nameless (perhaps nuclear) fear, appear at the home of Agnes and Tobias and ask to be taken in, they threaten the bunkered security of family relations. Tobias wants to oblige his friends, but Claire, the live-in sister-in-law, recognizes that Americans, though sometimes generous, are not inherently communal, and her point of view is proven correct.

Hair and its descendants suggested that generational friendships could easily become tribal families, but several playwrights were more skeptical. In Lanford Wilson's *The Hot L Baltimore* (1973), many of the transients living in a run-down hotel scheduled for demolition find a kind of family among themselves, more caring and resilient than the family relationships that haunt or encumber several of the residents. *The Heidi Chronicles* (1988) by Wendy Wasserstein traced the romantic and professional career over two decades of Heidi Holland, who despairs of relying on feminist sisterhood for familial support but deepens her friendship with a gay man over the years and finally adopts a child. Though the forms of both of their plays are grounded in realism, Wilson and Wasserstein pepper their content with numerous acknowledgments of the allures of television culture.

The new prevalence of the schemas of link, surface, and iteration in the culture allowed the form of musicals to shift from the "book" show, dominant since *Oklahoma*, back to the revue structure and to emphasize significant family relationships instead of a complete Family Circle. Although several musicals helped in the transition to the new-old form, *Company* (1970) by George Furth and Stephen Sondheim was the first "revusical" to succeed on a large scale. Lacking an overarching narrative, *Company* is linked together by a central character, Bobby, and a chorus of married New York couples who make him a part of their lives. The couples are individuated and all have their own scenes, but because they share in the same hopes, hypocrisies, guilts, and longings about marriage they can easily join in singing each other's songs. Sondheim repeated the formula with *Follies* in 1971 but focused on the different lives and similar problems of only two couples to dig deeper into their nastiness and narcissism. *Sunday in the Park with George* (1984) extended Sondheim's experimentation with links and surfaces; in this piece, he and James Lapine celebrated the artistic creativity of Georges Seurat by introducing the audience to the soldiers, boatmen, girls, and others whose only link to each other is their surface impression in Seurat's pointillist painting. The musical also leans on the cognitive mode of iteration to suggest the similarities between Seurat and his mistress in Act I and their biological counterparts several generations later in Act II.

Michael Bennett, who worked with Sondheim on *Company* and *Follies*, deployed the revusical form to build (with others) *A Chorus Line*, which opened in 1975 and ran for fifteen years. Framed as a series of auditions by Broadway chorus dancers, the structure of the show and its individual "spots" were driven by the compulsions of the choreographer, Zach, whose desire to get to know each dancer (and his or her desire for a place in the chorus line) set up the dancers' stories. Given the framework of the piece, surface and iterative delights (e.g., "Tits 'n Ass" and "I Can Do That") dominated the show; one number, "Nothing," even denigrated the desire for depth in Method acting. Although competing with each other, the dancers discover their commonalities, even a kind of family togetherness, but *A Chorus Line* also recognizes that these bonds of affection and concern are as temporary and as tied to economics as a family role on a television soap opera. Familial interactions were as important to the aesthetic and rhetorical appeal of *A Chorus Line* as to the success of several of Sondheim's musicals, but the idea of family had changed from a contained and natural circle to a porous and intentional work-in-progress.

Similarly, the popular plays of David Rabe and David Mamet altered and attenuated the Fragmented Heroes of the 1950s. While the memory and future threat of calamity continue to motivate the dramatic world of both playwrights and the hope of omnipotence and the fear of fragmentation haunt some of their characters, neither playwright puts a dramatic hero on the stage who struggles to contain these tensions. In a different kind of play, Ozzie, the father in Rabe's *Sticks and Bones* (1969), might have become a Fragmented Hero; he retains his youthful dreams of conquering the world as a runner and fears the debilitating realities that his son David has brought back with him from fighting in Vietnam. Rabe's grotesque surrealism, however, keeps Ozzie from becoming much more than his TV sit-com role as the suburban dad in *Ozzie and Harriet*, on which the figure is based. The meaningless violence of Vietnam also informs Rabe's *Streamers* (1976), in which desperation, homophobia, and racism, plus blind chance, combine to kill two soldiers in a U.S. Army barracks. Rabe paints a chilling picture of America as a contained "spider hole," a small tunnel with a trap door to hide a single Korean soldier—fate has thrown a hand grenade into it and is sitting on the lid. Both plays begin as jeremiads but, lacking a heroic central figure, end in the irresolution of grotesquerie.

The physical and emotional catastrophe awaiting American males in several of the plays of David Mamet is lack of economic success. Not surprisingly, the anxiety, fear, and self-loathing that animate the mature males of Mamet's world in the grip of this potential but minor catastrophe turn his plays toward ironic comedy rather than tragedy. The lowlifes of *American Buffalo* (1975), for example, comically turn on each other when their half-baked plans for the robbery of a coin collection fall apart. *Glengarry Glen Ross* (1983) is more melodramatic, but in performance none of the compulsive salesmen who populated this who-done-it, also based on a robbery, induced more than fleeting identification from the audience. As in Rabe's plays, potential Fragmented Heroes emerge—Donny Dubrow in *Buffalo* and Levene in *Glengarry*, for example—but they are not accorded the weight or self-awareness that might have saved them from comic objectification. They do, however, share with the contained figures of the 50s a fascination with and fear of female sexuality. It is the surface, especially the expletives, iteratives, and confusions in their language, that allows Mamet's characters to fascinate and repel. Though partly tied to the psychology of containment, they vomit forth comic brilliance.

As the fate of Fragmented Heroes in the plays of Rabe and Mamet suggests, few successful plays in the 1962–1992 period delved directly into the ramifications of nuclearism. But there were exceptions—*Angels Fall* (1982) by Lanford Wilson and *Wings* (1978) by Arthur Kopit, for example. An escaped cloud of uranium dust and loudspeaker orders from a hovering police helicopter strand some travelers inside a mission church on a New Mexico Indian reservation in *Angels Fall*. Facing human failure and possible apocalypse, several of Wilson's fragmented characters try to pull themselves back together around some central purpose for their lives. Wilson resolves his problem play with a guarded affirmation of religious faith and hope for progress. Kopit's *Wings* expressionistically explores a patient's recovery and then fatal relapse from the catastrophe of a stroke. After initial sounds and images that suggest the explosion of an inner atomic bomb, the drama explores Mrs. Stilson's subjective perceptions and follows her gradual return back to reality. With her second stroke, the character achieves transcendence in the midst of death as she recalls her youth as a stunt wing-walker on an airplane. Although neither play features a Fragmented Hero on the earlier model, Wilson's jeremiad and Kopit's narrative of inner apocalypse testified to the resilience of nuclear anxieties.

In retrospect, the themes and imagery of *Angels Fall* and *Wings* prefigured parts 1 and 2 of Tony Kushner's *Angels in America*, initially staged in 1991 and 1992. This "Gay Fantasia on National Themes," Kushner's subtitle for both *Millennium Approaches* and *Perestroika*, attacks and exorcises the cultural fallout of the Cold War, especially its nuclearism. Although set in the mid 1980s, at the height of Ronald Reagan's rekindling of cold war paranoia, references to the culture of the 1950s dot the varied landscapes of the play, and two prominent characters from that era, Roy Cohn and the ghost of Ethel Rosenberg—Senator Joseph McCarthy's vicious anti-Communist lawyer and one of his chief victims—figure prominently in the action. Aware, as well, of the Platonic pieties of cold war culture, Kushner levels specific barbs at the metatheatrical and allegorical thrust of much 1950s theater. *Perestroika*, for example, features a sendup of the microcosm/macrocosm trope in a diorama scene on the history of Mormonism. And Kushner's bureaucratic angels, haplessly stuck in ahistorical abstraction, inhabit a Heaven in which their chief means of communication with the world is an aging radio. More significantly, perhaps, Kushner subverts metaphors of containment that shape personal identity and human interaction. Whereas the cold warriors of *Angels* act on their belief that identity is evident in the reality of either skin (Joe Pitt) or innards (Roy Cohn)—the boundary or the essence of a contained self—other characters come to understand that such Platonic metaphors avoid the messy complexities of identity and change. Instead of grounding the self and possibilities for progressive politics in the cold war options of melting-pot assimilation or identity politics, Kushner suggests that intentional families of like-minded souls can become a nucleus for change.

Only at the end of *Perestroika*, however, does such a family emerge, survivors of a celestial visitation and a plague that are similar to a nuclear blast. Like *The Crucible* and a few other plays embedded in nuclear culture, *Angels* is a jeremiad based in a rationalist ethics intended as a warning for American democracy. Through its harrowing process, the play gradually separates the saved (Prior, Louis, Belize, Hannah) from the damned (Roy Cohn) and—again like *Crucible*—allows other characters (Joe and Harper) to remain in a kind of limbo, eager though not yet ready for transformation. Unlike Miller's tragedy, however, the general form of Kushner's play is finally comic, with the distillation of an affectionate family and the downsizing of potential Fragmented Heroes from martyrs to witnesses. Significantly, though, Prior's moment of epiphany is much the same as the response of many in the 1940s and 1950s to a nuclear explosion: he feels both sexually omnipotent and ridiculously small. At this level of the play's meaning, the plague of AIDS functions ironically as both a blessing and a curse, singling out those who are ready to work for the end of cold war culture but testing them, at the same time, with life-threatening infections. Like the Reds, gays, and nuclear victims of the 1950s, AIDS victims seem at first to be dangerous incubators of disease who might infect others. *Angels* moves beyond this containment metaphor, however, to suggest both that the complexity of the disease defies Platonic paranoia and that AIDS endows its victims with the symbolic efficacy (though not the innocence) of the Hiroshima Maidens, imagined by cold war Americans as survivors touched by divinity. Like *The Crucible*, but with a rhetoric and aesthetics more attuned to television culture, Kushner calls for the rebirth of democratic citizenship based on Enlightenment principles.[5]

As in 1953 when Miller's *Crucible* appeared, the theater of the early 1990s was ripe for Kushner's jeremiad. Most New York theater from the mid 1980s into the early 1990s wallowed in spectacles and revivals, both redolent of nostalgia for an imagined "morning in America"—often set in a never-never-1950s land—that Reagan's presidency had energized. Significantly, progressive treatments of homosexuality and the AIDS panic vanished on the commercial stage after the moderate success of *As Is* in 1985. Instead, New Yorkers thrilled to the sentimental and surface enchantments of Andrew Lloyd Webber's *Cats* (1982), *Starlight Express* (1987), and *The Phantom of the Opera* (1988). Broadway theater has often welcomed revivals, but the iterative qualities of television culture in conjunction with Reaganism's evocation of a pristine past made revivals and pseudo-revivals based on popular films especially profitable in the mid and late 1980s. These included *You Can't Take It With You* (1983), *Seven Brides for Seven Brothers* (1983), *Zorba* (1984), *The Wiz* (1984), *The King and I* (still starring Yul Brynner in 1985), *Singin' in the Rain* (1987), and *Our Town* (1988). In addition, high-cultural-capital productions of O'Neill masterpieces, often with aging stars—*A Moon for the Misbegotten* (1984), *The Iceman Cometh* (1985), and *Long Day's Journey into Night* (1986)—reminded Americans of their glorious theatrical history.

Although several of these shows induced audience enjoyment through the cognitive modes of television viewing, none of them substantially challenged the truisms of containment liberalism, unless it was to bring spectators back to a vision of the social polity even more conservative than the dominant culture of the 1950s. Looking at the successful productions on the New York stage in the late 1980s, a historian might be excused for believing that the experiments of the late 1960s and the innovations of Albee, Rabe, Shepard, Sondheim, Fuller, and Kopit in the 1970s and early 1980s had been completely disarmed or incorporated by Reaganism.[6] In the midst of such theatrical nostalgia, the moderate success of *Angels in America* on Broadway and across the nation was all the more surprising.

Despite ongoing shifts in the major forms of cultural communication, the culture of containment continues to adapt and flourish on the American stage in the twenty-first century. The success of *Angels* signaled a small rebirth of commercially viable oppositional theater in the 1990s. Its long-term survival, however, is now threatened by the renewal of cold war fears in the wake of "9/11," Big Oil imperialism, and the Empty Boy presidency of George W. Bush.

Notes

1. A Theater of Containment Liberalism

1. See Thomas Gale Moore, *The Economics of the American Theatre* (Durham, N.C.: Duke Univ. Press, 1968), 69–70. Also William J. Baumol and William G. Bowen, *Performing Arts—The Economic Dilemma* (New York: Twentieth Century Fund, 1966). Francis Fergusson, "Broadway," in *The Modern American Theater: A Collection of Critical Essays*, ed. Alvin B. Kernan (Englewood Cliffs, N.J.: Prentice-Hall, 1967), 109. The playbill for *Hatful* is located in the program file for *A Hatful of Rain* at the New York Library of Performing Arts.
2. Kerr quoted by Paul A. Carter, *Another Part of the Fifties* (New York: Columbia Univ. Press, 1983), 201.
3. Moore, *Economics*, 3–22, 69–89.
4. Ibid., 71–74.
5. See Barbara Ehrenreich and John Ehrenreich, "The Professional-Managerial Class," in *Between Labor and Capital* (Boston: South End Press, 1979), 5–45.
6. T. J. Jackson Lears, "A Matter of Taste: Corporate Cultural Hegemony in a Mass-Consumption Society," in *Recasting America: Culture and Politics in the Age of the Cold War*, ed. Lary May (Chicago: Univ. of Chicago Press, 1989), 51.
7. Moore, *Economics*, 82.
8. Ibid., 75–76.
9. On working-class culture in the late 1940s and 1950s, see George Lipsitz, *Rainbow at Midnight: Labor and Culture in the 1940s* (Urbana and Chicago: Univ. of Chicago Press, 1994), 229–335. One musical comedy that did manage to reflect and embody working-class values was *Sandhog*, which ran for forty-eight performances off-Broadway in 1954. See Mark Farrelly, "Rising from the Ashes of the Blacklist: Earl Robinson and Waldo Salt's *Sandhog*, A Worker's Musical," *American Drama* 7 (Spring 1998): 73–91.
10. Quoted in Lipsitz, *Rainbow*, 336.
11. Ibid., 256.
12. Ibid., 264.
13. The major critical and historical books that survey American theater during the period, listed in order of publication date, include Gerald Weales, *American Drama since World War II* (New York: Harcourt, Brace, 1962); Jean Gould, *Modern American Playwrights* (New York: Dodd, Mead, 1965); Morris Freedman, *American Drama in Social Context* (Carbondale: Southern Illinois Univ. Press, 1971); Tom Scanlan, *Family, Drama, and American Dreams* (Westport, Conn.: Greenwood, 1978); C. W. E. Bigsby, *Modern American Drama, 1945–1990* (Cambridge: Cambridge Univ. Press, 1992); and Thomas P. Adler, *American Drama, 1940–1960: A Critical History* (New York: Twayne, 1994). To my knowledge, only two book-length studies attempt to understand the 1947–1962

period from a cold war perspective, Brenda Murphy's *Congressional Theatre: Dramatizing McCarthyism on Stage, Film, and Television* (Cambridge: Cambridge Univ. Press, 1999) and David Savran's *Cowboys, Communists, and Queers: The Politics of Masculinity in the Works of Arthur Miller and Tennessee Williams* (Minneapolis: Univ. of Minnesota Press, 1992). Both are excellent; but Murphy is focused solely on the culture's response to McCarthyism, and Savran limits his investigation to the dramas, not the productions, of two canonical playwrights.

14 Immanuel Wallerstein, *After Liberalism* (New York: New Press, 1995), 1. For a materialist view of liberalism that mostly complements Wallerstein's arguments, see Ellen Meiksins Wood, *Democracy against Capitalism: Renewing Historical Materialism* (Cambridge: Cambridge Univ. Press, 1995), 225–37. Mary Sperling McAuliffe's *Crisis on the Left: Cold War Politics and American Liberals, 1947–1954* (Amherst: Univ. of Massachusetts Press, 1978) remains a solid summary of the difficulties of keeping New Deal liberalism alive after the war.

15 Michael S. Sherry, *In the Shadow of War: The United States since the 1930s* (New Haven and London: Yale Univ. Press, 1995), 138; Frederick M. Dolan, *Allegories of America: Narratives, Metaphysics, Politics* (Ithaca and London: Cornell Univ. Press, 1994), 60; and Catherine Lutz, "Epistemology of the Bunker: The Brainwashed and Other New Subjects of the Permanent War," in *Inventing the Psychological: Toward a Cultural History of Emotional Life in America*, ed. Joel Pfister and Nancy Schnog (New Haven and London: Yale Univ. Press, 1997), 252. Lutz borrows the term "ignorance effects" from Eve Kosofsky Sedgwick's *Epistemology of the Closet* (Berkeley: Univ. of California Press, 1990), 5.

16 Elizabeth Fox-Genovese, "Literary Criticism and the Politics of New Historicism," in *The New Historicism*, ed. H. Aram Veeser (New York and London: Routledge, 1989), 217–18. For a more complete discussion of the implications of synthesizing Fox-Genovese's call for structural history and the cognitive psychology of Lakoff and Johnson, see my essay "Doing Things with Image Schemas: The Cognitive Turn in Theatre Studies and the Problem of Experience for Historians," *Theatre Journal* 53 (December 2001): 569–94; as well as my "Metaphors We Act By: Kinesthetics, Cognitive Psychology, and Historical Structures," *Journal of Dramatic Theory and Criticism* 7 (Spring 1993): 25–45; and "Approaching Performance History through Cognitive Psychology," *Assaph* 10 (1994): 113–22. Also relevant are Mary Thomas Crane and Alan Richardson, "Literary Studies and Cognitive Science: Toward a New Interdisciplinarity," *Mosaic* 32:2 (June 1999): 123–40; and F. Elizabeth Hart, "Matter, System, and Early Modern Studies: Outlines for a Materialist Linguistics," *Configurations* 6:3 (1998): 311–43.

17 Mark Johnson, *The Body in the Mind: The Bodily Basis of Meaning, Imagination, and Reason* (Chicago: Univ. of Chicago Press, 1987), 22. On the cultural functions of cognitive metaphors, see Mary Thomas Crane, *Shakespeare's Brain: Reading with Cognitive Theory* (Princeton: Princeton Univ. Press, 2001); Raymond W. Gibbs, *The Poetics of Mind: Figurative Thought, Language, and Understanding* (Cambridge: Cambridge Univ. Press, 1994); Gerald Steen, *Under-*

standing Metaphor in Literature: An Empirical Approach (London and New York: Longman, 1994); and George Lakoff and Mark Johnson, *Metaphors We Live By* (Chicago: Univ. of Chicago Press, 1980).

18 George Lakoff and Mark Johnson, *Philosophy in the Flesh: The Embodied Mind and Its Challenge to Western Thought* (New York: Basic Books, 1999), 15, et passim. *Philosophy in the Flesh* is their most comprehensive and up-to-date statement of the significance of cognitive research and its relevance to other fields of scholarship. A postmodern and poststructuralist critique of embodied realism would find ample evidence of Lakoff and Johnson's "scientism" and "humanism." Regarding the former, they reject the Kuhnian argument that science is simply one of several philosophical positions with no privileged status. In *Philosophy in the Flesh* (88–93), they support the truth claims of science and their own results on the basis of "the methodology of convergent evidence" (89). Later in the same book (463–68), the authors demonstrate that four major claims of poststructuralist philosophy are "empirically incorrect": "1. The complete arbitrariness of the sign; that is, the utter arbitrariness of the pairing between signifiers (signs) and signifieds (concepts); 2. The locus of meanings in systems of binary oppositions among free floating signifiers (differance); 3. The purely historical contingency of meaning; 4. The strong relativity of concepts" (464). I find these arguments compelling and persuasive.

For further discussions of the epistemological implications of cognitive science for scholarship in the humanities, see Nancy Esterlin, "Making Knowledge: Bioepistemology and the Foundations of Literary Theory," *Mosaic* 32 (1999): 131–47; F. Elizabeth Hart, "The Epistemology of Cognitive Literary Studies," *Philosophy and Literature* 25:2 (October 2001): 314–44; N. Katherine Hayles, "Constrained Constructivism: Locating Scientific Inquiry in the Theater of Representation," in *Realism and Representation: Essays on the Problem of Realism in Relation to Science, Literature, and Culture*, ed. George Levine (Madison: Univ. of Wisconsin Press, 1993), 27–43; and Ellen Spolsky, "Darwin and Derrida: Cognitive Literary Theory as a Species of Post-Structuralism," *Poetics Today* 23:1 (Spring 2002): 43–62.

19 Lakoff and Johnson, *Philosophy in the Flesh*, 13. Along with others working in the field, Lakoff and Johnson continue to fine-tune their lists of image schemas and primary metaphors. Johnson's 1987 book *The Body in the Mind* contains the most inclusive listing of image schemas. His "partial list" includes twenty-seven different schemas.

20 Lakoff and Johnson, *Philosophy in the Flesh*, 6, 511, 97.

21 Ibid., 90.

22 On philosophical realism and its epistemology, see Roy Bhaskar, *A Realist Theory of Knowledge* (Sussex: Harvester Press; Atlantic Highlands, N.J.: Humanities Press, 1978). For an application of critical realism to theater history, see Tobin Nellhaus, "Science, History, Theater: Theorizing in Two Alternatives to Positivism," *Theatre Journal* 45 (1993): 505–27.

23 On cultural hegemony, see Antonio Gramsci, *Selections from the Prison Notebooks*

of *Antonio Gramsci*, ed. Quinton Hoare and Geoffrey Nowell-Smith (New York: International Publishers, 1971); Raymond Williams, "Base and Superstructure in Marxist Cultural Theory," in *Problems in Materialism and Culture* (London: Verso, 1980), 31–49; and Raymond Williams, *Marxism and Literature* (Oxford: Oxford Univ. Press, 1977). For useful interpretations of Gramsci and Williams, see Ernesto Laclau and Chantel Mouffe, *Hegemony and Socialist Strategy: Towards a Radical Democratic Politics* (London: New Left Books, 1985); T. J. Jackson Lears, "The Concept of Cultural Hegemony: Problems and Possibilities," *American Historical Review* 90 (June 1985): 567–93; and my essay "Using the Concept of Cultural Hegemony to Write Theatre History," in *Interpreting the Theatrical Past: Essays in Historiography and Performance*, ed. Thomas Postlewait and Bruce A. McConachie (Iowa City: Univ. of Iowa Press, 1989), 37–58. Slavoj Zizek, in his "Lacan between Cultural Studies and Cognitivism," in *Umbr(a): A Journal of the Unconscious* (2000): 9–32, has recently posed what he calls "cognitivism" and hegemony theory as opposites. For a critique of Zizek's "caricature" of cognitive studies and a refutation of his position, see Hart, "The Epistemology of Cognitive Literary Studies," 316–21.

As I indicate, cognitive psychology and hegemony theory can be fitted together primarily on the basis of their mutual investment in materialism and philosophical realism. But with regard to a notion of social totality, the fit pinches. In Raymond Williams's social theory, the totality of social-cultural processes—the combination of all residual, hegemonic, and emergent cultures within a larger culture—is always greater than the sum of its parts. As a totality, culture exerts structural pressure and effects historical change. My altered notion of hegemonic dynamics, however, relies on a particulate theory of culture. As cognitive anthropologist Roy Andrade notes, the central feature of cognitive anthropology in the 1990s is "the breaking up of culture in parts ... cognitively formed units—features, prototypes, schemas, propositions, theories, etc. This makes possible a particulate theory of culture; that is, a theory about the 'pieces' of culture, their compositions and relations to other things" (*The Development of Cognitive Anthropology* [Cambridge: Cambridge Univ. Press, 1995], 247). A particulate theory of culture is necessarily less historically deterministic than a totalizing one.

24 Johnson, *Body in the Mind*, 39; Lakoff and Johnson, *Philosophy in the Flesh*, 363, 364–90.
25 T. J. Jackson Lears, "A Matter of Taste: Corporate Cultural Hegemony in a Mass-Consumption Society," in *Recasting America: Culture and Politics in the Age of the Cold War*, 42.
26 Dolan, *Allegories of America: Narratives, Metaphysics, Politics*, 67–68, 68–69.
27 David Campbell, "Cold Wars: Securing Identity, Identifying Danger," in *Rhetorical Republic: Governing Representations in American Politics*, ed. Frederick M. Dolan and Thomas Dumm (Amherst: Univ. of Massachusetts Press, 1993), 43, 48.
28 Lakoff and Johnson, *Philosophy in the Flesh*, 93.

29 David Saltz, "Infiction and Outfiction: The Role of Fiction in Theatrical Performance," in *Staging Philosophy: New Approaches to Theater and Performance*, ed. David Krasner and David Z. Saltz (forthcoming), 170, 180 n. 30, 176.

30 Lakoff and Johnson, *Philosophy in the Flesh*, 281.

31 Alan Read, *Theatre and Everyday Life: An Ethics of Performance* (London: Routledge, 1993), 10.

32 Jon Erickson, *The Fate of the Object: From Modern Object to Postmodern Sign in Performance, Art, and Poetry* (Ann Arbor: Univ. of Michigan Press, 1995), 62. Significantly, Lakoff and Johnson recognize that certain insights of phenomenology and materialism coincide closely with embodied realism (*Philosophy in the Flesh*, 108–9).

33 Mark Turner, *The Literary Mind* (New York: Oxford Univ. Press, 1996), 12, 25.

34 Peter Brooks, "Freud's Master Plot," in *Literature and Psychoanalysis: The Question of Reading Otherwise*, ed. S. Felman (London: Yale Univ. Press, 1982), 283.

35 See Judith Butler, *Bodies That Matter: On the Discursive Limits of "Sex"* (New York: Routledge, 1993). In general, Lakoff and Johnson would agree with Butler that humans learn to perform sexuality, although they would disagree with the Lacanian premises of her argument. Much of this learning occurs at an earlier age and happens through processes that Freud and Lacan did not recognize.

36 See Kenneth Burke, *A Rhetoric of Motives*, 3rd ed. (Berkeley: Univ. of California Press, 1969); also Robert Wess, *Kenneth Burke: Rhetoric, Subjectivity, Postmodernism* (Cambridge: Cambridge Univ. Press, 1996).

37 The term "condensational event" is Joseph Roach's. See *Cities of the Dead: Circum-Atlantic Performance* (New York: Columbia Univ. Press, 1996), 28–30 et passim.

38 See my "Doing Things with Image Schemas," 591.

39 For semiotic and conventional ways of understanding spectatorship, see Susan Bennett, *Theatre Audiences: A Theory of Production and Reception*, 2nd ed. (London: Routledge, 1997); and the "Introduction" by Tracy C. Davis and Bruce McConachie and essays by Stacy Wolf, Lynn Dirks, Mary Trotter, Jim Davis, Victor Emiljanow, Henk Gras, and Philip Hans Franses in *Theatre Survey* 39:2 (November 1998): 1–98.

40 See Stanley Cavell, *The Claim of Reason: Wittgenstein, Skepticism, Morality, and Tragedy* (1979; rpt., Oxford: Oxford Univ. Press, 1999), 225–43 et passim. In "Darwin and Derrida," Spolsky merges Cavell's insights with cognitive literary theory. Also important for understanding spectatorial response is what Dan Sperber and Deirdre Wilson have termed "the principle of relevance." Given their experiments, it is likely that audience members will generally process new information in the theater only if it contributes to their understanding of the dramatic/theatrical context and if the processing effort is small. Otherwise they will ignore it. See *Relevance: Communication and Cognition* (Oxford: Basil Blackwell, 1986).

41 In writing about the past, theorists and critics oriented to cognitive studies generally distinguish between the enormous stretch of evolutionary time over

which *Homo sapiens* evolved and the brief period of historical time beginning with the advent of writing, when the human mind/brain and its cognitive structures have evolved very little, if at all. For a recent overview of cognitive evolution and its relationship to what would become "literature," see Paul Hernadi, "Why Is Literature: A Coevolutionary Perspective on Imaginative Worldmaking," *Poetics Today* 23:1 (Spring 2002): 21–42.

42 Walter J. Ong, *Orality and Literacy: The Technologizing of the Word* (New York: Routledge, 1988), 136; Julie Stone Peters, *Congreve, the Drama, and the Printed Word* (Stanford: Stanford Univ. Press, 1990), 4.

43 Harold Clurman, *The Collected Works of Harold Clurman*, ed. Marjorie Loggia and Glenn Young (New York: Applause Books, 1994), 645, 646.

44 Tobin Nellhaus, "Social Ontology and (Meta)theatricality: Reflections on Performance and Communication in History," *Journal of Dramatic Theory and Criticism* (Spring 2000): 3–39.

45 Jennifer Wise, *Dionysus Writes: The Invention of Theatre in Ancient Greece* (Ithaca: Cornell Univ. Press, 1998), 6.

46 On Benjamin and photography, see Eduardo Cadava, *Words of Light: Theses on the Photography of History* (Princeton, N.J.: Princeton Univ. Press, 1997). Susan Sontag's notable book is *On Photography* (New York: Delta Books, 1977). Roland Barthes, *Mythologies* (New York: Hill and Wang, 1983), 93. See also Mary Price, *The Photograph: A Strange Confined Space* (Stanford: Stanford Univ. Press, 1994); and Mary Warner Marien, *Photography and Its Critics: A Cultural History, 1839–1900* (Cambridge: Cambridge Univ. Press, 1997).

47 See W. B. Worthen, *Modern Drama and the Rhetoric of Theater* (Berkeley: Univ. of California Press, 1992), 12–98, for a general investigation of the significance of photography for realist theater.

48 See the essays in *Film Sound: Theory and Practice*, ed. E. Weis and J. Belton (New York: Columbia Univ. Press, 1985). In her "Image/Music/Voice: Song Dubbing in Hollywood Musicals," *Journal of Communication* 45:2 (1995): 44–64, however, Marsha Siefert demonstrates that sound was occasionally the co-equal of image in the production and reception of films.

49 Walter J. Ong, *The Presence of the Word: Some Prolegomena for Religious and Cultural History* (Minneapolis: Univ. of Minnesota Press, 1981), 128, 129–30.

50 Citations and quotations from Friedrich Kittler, *Gramophone, Film, Typewriter*, trans. Geoffrey Winthrop-Young and Michael Wirtz (Stanford: Stanford Univ. Press, 1999), 36, 88, 16.

51 Richard Butsch, *The Making of American Audiences: From Stage to Television, 1750–1990* (Cambridge: Cambridge Univ. Press, 2000), 207; and Rene Farabet, "From One Head to Another," *TDR (The Drama Review)* 40:3 (Fall 1996): 61. For a history of broadcasting in the United States, see also Michelle Hilmes, *Radio Voices: American Broadcasting, 1922–1952* (Minneapolis: Univ. of Minnesota Press, 1997).

52 Ray Barfield, *Listening to Radio, 1920–1950* (Westport, Conn.: Praeger, 1996),

50; and Joe Milutis, "Radiophonic Ontologies and the Avantgarde," *TDR* 40:3 (Fall 1996): 72.
53 Kipling statement noted by John Durham Peters in *Speaking into the Air: A History of the Idea of Communication* (Chicago: Univ. of Chicago Press, 1999), 211; Barfield, *Listening to Radio*, 17, 28, 65.
54 Quoted in Sherry, *Shadow of War*, 40.
55 Peters, *Speaking into the Air*, 213.
56 Critic Joe Milutis notes that "Beckett's plays are uniquely oral plays; if they do not explicitly engage with the radiophonic (for example, *All That Fall*, *Embers* [1959], *Cascando* [1964]), they limit the multimedia possibilities of the traditional stage in order to direct the visual and aural attention of the audience to something like the radiophonic" ("Radiophonic Ontologies and the Avantgarde," 73). Milutis calls Beckett's aurality a "nightmare space of schizophrenia and melancholy" (73).
57 Johnson, *Body in the Mind*, 45.
58 Gordon Teskey, *Allegory and Violence* (Ithaca: Cornell Univ. Press, 1996), 2. Maureen Quilligan, *The Language of Allegory: Defining the Genre* (Ithaca: Cornell Univ. Press, 1979); and Carolynn Van Dyke, *The Fiction of Truth: Structures of Meaning in Narrative and Dramatic Allegory* (Ithaca: Cornell Univ. Press, 1985) agree with Teskey. Sayre N. Greenfield, in his *The Ends of Allegory* (Newark: Univ. of Delaware Press, 1998), usefully complicates the allegory/*allegoresis* distinction. See especially 53–60 and 73–76. Theresa Kelley, *Reinventing Allegory* (Cambridge: Cambridge Univ. Press, 1997); and Deborah Madsen, *Rereading Allegory: A Narrative Approach to Genre* (New York: St. Martin's Press, 1994), have also been helpful. Greenfield's definition of *allegoresis*, upon which I have built my discussion, differs crucially from notions of intertextuality and more inclusive concepts of allegory (e.g., Frederic Jameson's in *The Political Unconscious* [Ithaca: Cornell Univ. Press, 1981]) because its activation requires the agency of readers or spectators. *Allegoresis* also differs from analogizing, in which spectators find similarities among narratives but do not map an entire prior narrative onto a present one. Analogizing occurs often in the theater. As I discuss in some detail in chapter 4, Miller's *The Crucible* involved spectators in frequent analogizing; but because there was no familiar master narrative through which they could understand the major events of the play, it probably did not evoke much *allegoresis*.
59 Greenfield, *Ends of Allegory*, 16.
60 For a year-by-year overview of the Broadway stage, see *The Burns Mantle Theater Yearbook [1945–1965]* (New York: Applause Theatre Book Publishers, 1946–66). On musicals during the era, see Ethan Mordden's *Coming Up Roses: The Broadway Musical of the 1950s* (New York: Oxford Univ. Press, 1998). For plays evoking Freudian or political readings, see Wieder David Sievers, *Freud on Broadway* (New York: Hermitage House, 1955); and Albert Wertheim, "The McCarthy Era and the American Theatre," *Theatre Journal* 34 (May 1982): 211–22. Clurman, *The Collected Works*, 645–46.

61 Madsen's discussion in *Rereading Allegory*, 109–29, of the allegory/symbolism dichotomy in Samuel Taylor Coleridge and its legacy in modern criticism is excellent.

62 On O'Neill and Wilder, see Joel Pfister, *Staging Depth: Eugene O'Neill and the Politics of Psychological Discourse* (Chapel Hill and London: Univ. of North Carolina Press, 1995); and Paul Lifton, *"Vast Encyclopedia": The Theatre of Thornton Wilder* (Westport, Conn.: Greenwood, 1995). C. W. E. Bigsby, *A Critical Introduction to Twentieth-Century American Drama*, vol. 1 (Cambridge: Cambridge Univ. Press, 1984), has useful sections on both playwrights.

63 For discussions of the production, see Brenda Murphy, *Miller: Death of a Salesman*, Plays in Production Series, ed. Michael Robinson (Cambridge: Cambridge Univ. Press, 1995); and Andrew B. Harris, *Broadway Theatre* (London and New York: Routledge, 1994), 48–64. Elia Kazan's memoir *Elia Kazan: A Life* (New York: Knopf, 1988) is also useful, as is Miller's *Timebends: A Life* (New York: Grove, 1987). The literature on the play both as a "tragedy" and as a psychoanalytic allegory, of course, is immense. See the bibliography in Murphy, *Miller: Death of a Salesman*, 208–39. One recent essay that speaks persuasively about Miller's debt to Platonism is Matthew C. Roudane, "*Death of a Salesman* and the Poetics of Arthur Miller," in *The Cambridge Companion to Arthur Miller*, ed. Christopher Bigsby (Cambridge: Cambridge Univ. Press, 1997), 60–85. See also Fred Ribkof, "Shame, Guilt, Empathy, and the Search for Identity in Arthur Miller's *Death of a Salesman*," *Modern Drama* 43 : 1 (Spring 2000): 48–55.

64 Reviews in *The New York Theatre Critics' Reviews*, vol. 19, *1949* (New York: Theatre Critics' Reviews, 1950): Ward Morehouse, "Triumph at the Morosco" (*Sun*), 360; Robert Coleman, "Death of a Salesman is Emotional Dynamite" (*Daily Mirror*), 360; Brooks Atkinson, "Death of a Salesman, a New Drama by Arthur Miller, Has Premiere at Morosco" (*New York Times*), 361; Howard Barnes, "A Great Play Is Born" (*New York Herald Tribune*), 358; William Hawkins, "Death of a Salesman Powerful Tragedy" (*New York World Telegram*), 359.

65 See *Six Plays of Clifford Odets* (1945; New York: Grove Press, 1979); and William W. Demastes, *Clifford Odets: A Research and Production Sourcebook* (New York: Greenwood, 1991).

66 Atkinson, "Death of a Salesman," 361.

67 Robert Garland, "Audience Spellbound by Prize Play of 1949" (*New York Journal American*), in *New York Theatre Critics' Reviews, 1949*, 358; one of Miller's earliest academic critics, Henry Popkin, also wrote persuasively about Miller's interest in allegorical narratives and characters in 1960: "The plays are dramatic parables or fables; their characters are as typical as the prodigal son or Aesop's lambs and wolves. They are as unattached and as nonsectarian as the medieval Everyman, and that is why they cannot be individuals" ("Arthur Miller: The Strange Encounter," *Sewanee Review* 68 [1960]: 39). It may be that early cold war critics of Miller, more caught up in the inducements of *allegoresis* proffered by the culture, were more likely than later ones to read *Salesman* as a fable or an allegory.

68 Murphy, *Miller: Death of a Salesman*, 5–6.
69 On the "abject Other," see Judith Butler, *Gender Trouble: Feminism and the Subversion of Identity* (London: Routledge, 1990), 133–34; and *Bodies That Matter*, 3, 15–19. Tellingly, Butler uses the container metaphor of inside/outside to describe the process of abjection: "In this sense, then, the subject is constituted through the force of exclusion and abjection, one which produces a constitutive outside to the subject, an abjected outside, which is, after all, 'inside' the subject as its own founding repudiation" (*Bodies*, 3). Contra Butler, however, Lakoff and Johnson offer persuasive evidence that all subjects are not constituted through an "abject Other." Containment culture, which induced its subjects to understand their bodies and minds as containers, did constitute selves in this way. But Lakoff and Johnson's cognitive psychology discusses several other cognitive orientations that can provide a foundation for the self. See *Philosophy in the Flesh*, 267–89.

2. Empty Boys, Queer Others, and Consumerism

1 I am indebted to Frederick M. Dolan, *Allegories of America: Narratives, Metaphysics, Politics* (Ithaca and London: Cornell Univ. Press, 1994), 70–71, for his discussion of these films.
2 Rupert Wilkinson, *The Pursuit of the American Character* (New York: Harper and Row, 1988), 2.
3 Wilkinson, in ibid., 16–19, 21–24, 33–35, usefully summarizes Riesman's and Potter's positions on the American character. See also David Riesman, with Nathan Glazer and Reuel Denny, *The Lonely Crowd: A Study of the Changing American Character* (New Haven: Yale Univ. Press, 1950); David M. Potter, *People of Plenty: Economic Abundance and the American Character* (Chicago: Univ. of Chicago Press, 1954); David M. Potter, "The Quest for National Character," in *The Reconstruction of American History*, ed. John Higham (New York: New York Univ. Press, 1962); and "American Individualism in the Twentieth Century," rpt. in *Innocence and Power: Individualism in Twentieth-Century America* (Austin: Univ. of Texas Press, 1964), 23–40. R. W. B. Lewis, *The American Adam* (Chicago: Univ. of Chicago Press, 1955), 196.
4 Quoted by Michael S. Sherry, *In the Shadow of War: The United States since the 1930s* (New Haven and London: Yale Univ. Press, 1995), 128.
5 Ibid., 144.
6 Kinsey Report and Senate Committee quoted in Robert J. Corber, *In the Name of National Security: Hitchcock, Homophobia, and the Political Construction of Gender in Postwar America* (Durham and London: Duke Univ. Press, 1993), 63, 64. On the popular response to the Kinsey Report, see also John D'Emilio, *Sexual Politics, Sexual Communities: The Making of a Homosexual Minority in the United States, 1940–1970* (Chicago: Univ. of Chicago Press, 1983). Corber's second book, *Homosexuality in Cold War America: Resistance and the Crisis of Masculinity* (Durham and London: Duke Univ. Press, 1997), is also useful.
7 See Ellen Herman, *The Romance of American Psychology: Political Culture in the*

Age of Experts (Berkeley: Univ. of California Press, 1995), 108-9. Bergler quoted in Sherry, *Shadow of War*, 152.
8 See Herman, *Romance of American Psychology*, 48-123.
9 See Catherine Lutz, "The Epistemology of the Bunker: The Brainwashed and Other New Subjects of Permanent War," in *Inventing the Psychological: Toward a Cultural History of Emotional Life in America*, ed. Joel Pfister and Nancy Schnog (New Haven and London: Yale Univ. Press, 1997), 247; also Herman, *Romance of American Psychology*, 124-52.
10 Regarding psychotherapy in the United States, see Nathan G. Hale, Jr., *The Rise and Crisis of Psychoanalysis in America: Freud and the Americans, 1917-1985* (New York: Oxford Univ. Press, 1995); and Elizabeth Lunbeck, *The Psychiatric Persuasion: Knowledge, Gender, and Power in Modern America* (Princeton: Princeton Univ. Press, 1994).
11 See Philip Rieff, *The Triumph of the Therapeutic: Uses of Faith after Freud* (New York: Harper and Row, 1966); Christopher Lasch, *The Culture of Narcissism: American Life in an Age of Diminishing Expectations* (New York: Warner, 1975); T. J. Jackson Lears, *No Place of Grace: Antimodernism and the Transformation of American Culture, 1880-1920* (New York: Pantheon, 1981); and Richard Wightman Fox, *So Far Disordered in Mind: Insanity in California, 1870-1930* (Berkeley: Univ. of California Press, 1978). See also the two collections of essays edited by Fox and Lears: *The Culture of Consumption: Critical Essays in American History, 1880-1980* (New York: Pantheon, 1983) and *The Power of Culture: Critical Essays in American History* (Chicago: Univ. of Chicago Press, 1993).
12 Kovel quoted by Joel Pfister, "On Conceptualizing the Cultural History of Emotional and Psychological Life in America," in *Inventing the Psychological*, 23.
13 Joel Pfister, "Glamorizing the Psychological: The Politics of the Performances of Modern Psychological Identities," in *Inventing the Psychological*, 179. Pfister has applied these ideas to the plays and popularity of Eugene O'Neill in *Staging Depth: Eugene O'Neill and the Politics of Psychological Discourse* (Durham: Univ. of North Carolina Press, 1995). In this regard, Pfister notes that the eminent psychoanalyst Karl Menninger estimated in 1938 that O'Neill had exposed more Americans to psychoanalytic ideas "than all the scientific books put together" (quoted in "Glamorizing," 173).
14 Steven Cohan, *Masked Men: Masculinity and the Movies in the Fifties* (Bloomington: Indiana Univ. Press, 1997), 201-37 (quotation on 228).
15 I have used the script for *Hatful* in *Famous American Plays of the 1950s*, ed. Lee Strasberg (1962; rpt., New York: Dell, 1988), 313-84. Subsequent citations from this script appear in the text. Strasberg's "Introduction" to the anthology provides a brief production history. See also Michael V. Gazzo, "A Playwright's Point of View," *Theatre Arts* 42 (December 1958): 20-22; and the clipping file for *A Hatful of Rain* at the New York Public Library of Performing Arts.
16 *The Seven Year Itch* is anthologized in *New Voices in the American Theatre* (New York: Random House, 1955), 301-75. Subsequent citations from this script ap-

pear in the text. See the clipping file for *The Seven Year Itch* at the New York Library of Performing Arts for a production history.
17 Elaine Tyler May, "Explosive Issues: Sex, Women, and the Bomb," in *Recasting America: Culture and Politics in the Age of Cold War*, ed. Lary May (Chicago: Univ. of Chicago Press, 1989), 154–70.
18 Brooks Atkinson, "A Play of Substance" (*New York Times*), in *New York Theatre Critics' Reviews*, vol. 16, *1955*, ed. Rachel Coffin (New York: Critics' Theatre Reviews, 1956), 216. Norton's review is in the clipping file for "Gazzara, Ben" at the New York Library of Performing Arts.
19 Barbara Ehrenreich, *The Hearts of Men: American Dreams and the Flight from Commitment* (Garden City, N.Y.: Doubleday, 1983), 20.
20 Reviews in *New York Theatre Critics' Reviews*, *1955*: John Chapman, "*A Hatful of Rain* an Impressive, Excellently Acted Social Drama" (*Daily News*), 213; Robert Coleman, "*A Hatful of Rain* Drizzles at Lyceum" (*Daily Mirror*), 216; and Richard Watts, Jr., "The Misfortunes of a Dope Addict" (*New York Post*), 215; see also Walter Kerr's review, "*A Hatful of Rain*" (*New York Herald Tribune*), 214, for similar views.
21 Spellman quoted by Stephen J. Whitfield, *The Culture of the Cold War*, 2nd ed. (Baltimore: Johns Hopkins Univ. Press, 1996), 96; McCarthy quoted in Lawrence Wittner, *Cold War America: From Hiroshima to Watergate* (New York: Praeger Publishers, 1974), 95; Spillane quoted in Whitfield, *Culture*, 36; Schlesinger quoted in Elaine Tyler May, *Homeward Bound: American Families in the Cold War Era* (New York: Basic Books, 1988), 98.
22 Quoted in Lutz, "Epistemology of the Bunker," 256.
23 Braitberg quoted in ibid., 254. Lutz's conclusion is on the same page.
24 Lee Mortimer, "*Seven Year Itch* Is Full of Delightful Dizziness" (*New York Times*), in *New York Theatre Critics' Reviews*, vol. 13, *1952* (New York: Critics' Theatre Reviews, 1953), 187.
25 See George Lakoff and Mark Johnson, *Philosophy in the Flesh: The Embodied Mind and Its Challenge to Western Thought* (New York: Basic Books, 1999), 290–334.
26 Ibid., 320–26.
27 Heinz Kohut, the major theorist of narcissism in the cold war era, did not begin to publish his findings until the mid 1960s. See Charles B. Strozier, *Heinz Kohut: The Making of a Psychoanalyst* (New York: Farrar, Straus & Giroux, 2001).
28 Lasch, *Culture of Narcissism*, 389–90.
29 Richard Butsch, *The Making of American Audiences: From Stage to Television, 1750–1990* (Cambridge: Cambridge Univ. Press, 2000), 24.
30 Reviews by Chapman, Watts, and McClain in *New York Theatre Critics' Reviews*, *1955*, 213–15; *Cue* (March 13, 1955), 13, in the "Gazzara, Ben" clipping file, New York Library of Performing Arts.
31 Kerr's review in *New York Theatre Critics' Reviews*, *1955*, 214.
32 Undated article in unknown journal by Dilys Powell in the "Gazzara, Ben" clip-

ping file, New York Library of Performing Arts. Steven Vineberg, *Method Actors: Three Generations of an American Acting Style* (New York: Macmillan, 1991), also lists Gazzara as a typical Method actor of the era and notes that *Hatful* was one of "the most celebrated of the Studio-initiated projects" (139–41). On Gazzara, see also Foster Hirsch, *A Method to Their Madness: The History of the Actors Studio* (New York: W. W. Norton, 1984), 251–56, 274.

33 Hoffman quoted in Vineberg, *Method Actors*, 102–3.
34 Mailer quoted in Hirsch, *Method to Their Madness*, 112.
35 On Strasberg, see Cindy Adams, *Lee Strasberg: The Imperfect Genius of the Actors Studio* (Garden City, N.Y.: Doubleday, 1980); David Garfield, *A Players Place: The Story of the Actors Studio* (New York: Macmillan, 1980); Foster Hirsch, *Method to Their Madness*; David Krasner, ed., *Method Acting Reconsidered: Theory, Practice, Future* (New York: St. Martin's, 2000); and Vineberg, *Method Actors*; plus Lee Strasberg, *A Dream of Passion: The Development of The Method* (New York: New American Library, 1987); Robert Hethmon, ed., *Strasberg at the Actors Studio* (New York: Viking Press, 1965); and the "Strasberg, Lee" clipping file, New York Library of Performing Arts.
36 Strasberg quoted in Vineberg, *Method Actors*, 104; Garfein quoted in Hirsch, *Method to Their Madness*, 167; Strasberg, *Dream of Passion*, 19.
37 See Burnet M. Hobgood, "Central Conceptions in Stanislavski's System," *Educational Theatre Journal* 25 (1973): 149–50, for Stanislavski's belief in the actor's ability to experience both self and character. For a full description of Stanislavski's acting process and the changes that resulted in the ideas attributed to him in the United States due to the vagaries of their oral and written transmission, see Sharon Marie Carnicke, *Stanislavsky in Focus* (Amsterdam: Harwood, 1998), 55–91. Stanislavski did not consistently hold to the view that actors could separate themselves from their characters. See, for example, W. B. Worthen's comments on Stanislavski in *The Idea of the Actor: Drama and the Ethics of Performance* (Princeton, N.J.: Princeton Univ. Press, 1984), 145–53. Natalie Crohn Schmitt, *Actors and Onlookers: Theater and Twentieth-Century Scientific Views of Nature* (Evanston, Ill.: Northwestern Univ. Press, 1990), in contrast, emphasizes Stanislavski's allegiance to the playwright's authority as the source of representation. So, too, does Carnicke, *Stanislavsky in Focus*, 35–91.
38 Strasberg and Penn quoted in Hirsch, *Method to Their Madness*, 133, 223.
39 Roberts quoted in ibid., 227; Robert Brustein, "The Keynes of Times Square," *New Republic* (1 December 1962): 28.
40 Carnicke, *Stanislavsky in Focus*, 165.
41 Richard Dyer, "'A Star Is Born' and the Construction of Authenticity," in *Stardom: Industry of Desire*, ed. Christine Gledhill (London: Routledge, 1991), 133.
42 Elia Kazan, "[Excerpts from] the Director's Notebook," in *Drama on Stage*, ed. Randolph Goodman (New York: Holt, Rinehart, 1961), 303. See also Brenda Murphy, *Tennessee Williams and Elia Kazan: A Collaboration in the Theatre* (Cambridge: Cambridge Univ. Press, 1992), 16–63.
43 John Gronbeck-Tedesco, "Absence and the Actor's Body: Marlon Brando's Per-

formance in *A Streetcar Named Desire* on Stage and in Film," *Studies in American Drama, 1945–Present* 7 (1993): 120.

44 Harold Clurman, *The Collected Works*, ed. Marjorie Loggia and Glenn Young (New York: Applause, 1994), 134.

45 Reviews of *Streetcar* in *New York Theatre Critics' Reviews*, vol. 8, *1947* (New York: Critics' Theatre Reviews, 1948): Ward Morehouse, "New Hit Named Desire" (*Sun*), 250; Robert Garland, "Williams' New Play Exciting Theatre" (*Journal American*), 251; Louis Kronenberger, "A Sharp Southern Drama by Tennessee Williams" (*PM Exclusive*), 250; John Chapman, "*Streetcar Named Desire* Sets Season's High in Acting, Writing" (*Daily News*), 249; William Hawkins, "Streetcar a Fine Play of Clashing Emotions" (*New York World-Telegram*), 251; Brooks Atkinson, "At the Theatre" (*New York Times*), 252; Robert Coleman, "Desire Streetcar in for Long Run" (*Daily Mirror*), 252; Howard Barnes, "A Long-Run Trolley" (*New York Herald Tribune*), 252; and Richard Watts, Jr., "*Streetcar Named Desire* Is Striking Drama" (*New York Post*), 249.

46 See reviews in note 45 above.

47 Williams, letter to Joe [Breen], 29 October 1950, cited in Cohan, *Masked Men*, 318. In her study of the collaboration between Williams and the director, Brenda Murphy agrees with Kazan's assessment: "[He] gradually came to realize that the audience's conflict, the division in sympathies, was the essence of the play as Williams had written it" (62). But this conclusion may be kinder to the director than the evidence warrants. Marlon Brando, *Songs My Mother Taught Me* (New York: Random House, 1994), 122–24. On the "imbalance" of audience response to Stanley and Blanche in the original production, see also Susan Spector, "Alternative Visions of Blanche Dubois: Uta Hagen and Jessica Tandy in *A Streetcar Named Desire*," *Modern Drama* 32 (1989): 545–60; and Philip C. Kolin, *Williams: A Streetcar Named Desire* (Cambridge: Cambridge Univ. Press, 2000), 1–30.

48 Hawkins, "Streetcar a Fine Play," 251.

49 Cohan, *Masked Men*, 249. Harold Brodky, "Translating Brando," *New Yorker* (24 October 1994), 82. See Cohan, *Masked Men*, 241–52, for the narcissistic effects of Brando's other film roles in the 1950s. Significantly, Hollywood columnist Hedda Hopper once summed up Brando's appeal when she called him "a grubby Peter Pan" (Cohan, *Masked Men*, 243).

50 Colin Counsell, *Signs of Performance: An Introduction to Twentieth-Century Theatre* (London and New York: Routledge, 1996), 59.

51 Ibid., 66, 67.

52 Philip Cushman, *Constructing the Self, Constructing America: A Cultural History of Psychotherapy* (Boston: Addison-Wesley, 1995), 79.

53 Motivational researcher Dr. Ernest Dichter and sociologist Martha Wolfenstein quoted in Barbara Ehrenreich, *The Hearts of Men: American Dreams and the Flight from Commitment* (Garden City, N.Y.: Doubleday, 1983), 45. Ehrenreich devotes an entire chapter to the *Playboy* phenomenon, 42–51.

54 Tennessee Williams, *Cat on a Hot Tin Roof* (1955; rpt. New York: Penguin,

1985), xiii–xiv. This edition of the play has two versions of Act III, Williams's preferred version and the "Broadway Version, as played in New York Production" (126), along with Williams's "Note of Explanation" for the inclusion of both versions. Subsequent citations in the text are from this edition of the play.

55 Mark Fearnow, *The American Stage and the Great Depression: A Cultural History of the Grotesque* (Cambridge: Cambridge Univ. Press, 1997), 9. Many critics, of course, have discussed Williams's interest in grotesquerie but no one, to my knowledge, has analyzed his plays as examples of a rhetorical genre of the grotesque. Probably the first to note the generically mixed nature of the play was Mary Hivor, "Theatre Letter," *Kenyon Review* 18 (1956), who asked, "If the battle for inheritance be the core of the plot, how could we have anything but comedy?" (126). See also Thomas M. Inge, "The South, Tragedy, and Comedy in Tennessee Williams's *Cat on a Hot Tin Roof*," in *The United States South: Regionalism and Identity*, ed. Valeria Lerda and Tjebbe Westendorp (Rome: Bulzoni, 1991), 157–65. Williams's attraction to the grotesque fundamentally has to do with his romanticism. See Esther Merle Jackson in *The Broken World of Tennessee Williams* (Madison: Univ. of Wisconsin Press, 1966); and, more recently, Nancy M. Tischler, "Romantic Textures in Tennessee Williams's Plays and Short Stories," in *The Cambridge Companion to Tennessee Williams*, ed. Matthew Roudane (Cambridge: Cambridge Univ. Press, 1997), 147–66.

56 Tennessee Williams, *Where I Live: Selected Essays*, ed. Christine R. Day and Bob Woods (New York: New Directions, 1978), 54.

57 Albert J. Devlin, "Writing in 'A Place of Stone': *Cat on a Hot Tin Roof*," in *The Cambridge Companion to Tennessee Williams*, 95–113. Flannery O'Connor, "Some Aspects of the Grotesque in Southern Fiction," in *Mystery and Manners: Occasional Prose*, ed. Sally Fitzgerald and Robert Fitzgerald (New York: Farrar, Straus & Giroux, 1961), 40.

58 Williams quoted in Devlin, "Writing in 'A Place of Stone,'" 100. Helen Gilbert, "De-Scribing Orality: Performance and the Recuperation of Voice," *Post-Colonial Drama: Theory, Practice, Politics* (London: Routledge, 1996), 9.

59 Like many other critics, Christopher Bigsby calls "mendacity" the major theme of *Cat* but cannot resolve the major contradiction centered on this theme: "Maggie is as involved in this process [what Bigsby earlier termed 'hypocrisy, cant, greed, and self-interest'] as anyone. She genuinely cares for Brick but her urgency and her energy seem to derive precisely from a refusal to let go of the inheritance which she believes to be hers by right. And she, too, is capable of lying. To [critic] Benjamin Nelson hers is a 'life-lie told in the face of death,' and yet the precise distinction between those lies which generate life and those which do not is never clearly established, the more so since Maggie's lie is a desperate bid to forestall Gooper's bid for the estate" (*A Critical Introduction to Twentieth-Century American Drama*, vol. 2 [Cambridge: Cambridge Univ. Press, 1984], 82–83). Other critics who discuss the play as an examination of "mendacity" include John V. Hagopian, "*Cat on a Hot Tin Roof*," in *Insight: Analyses of Modern British and American Drama*, vol. 4, ed. Hermann J. Weiand (Frankfurt:

Hirschgraben, 1975), 269–75; Philip C. Kolin, "Obstacles to Communication in *Cat on a Hot Tin Roof*," *Western Speech Communication* 39 (1975): 74–80; and Kenneth Tynan, *Curtains: Selections from the Drama Criticism and Related Writings* (New York: Atheneum, 1961).

More generally, critics' attempts to make meaning out of *Cat* have led in several contradictory directions. In his overview of criticism on the play, George W. Crandell states: "Williams's ambiguity regarding both the theme of the play and Brick's sexual identity continues to puzzle critics who debate what the play is really about. Not surprisingly, the focus of critical attention also shifts among various relationships. Is *Cat* primarily a story about a troubled marriage (Maggie and Brick), a possibly homosexual relationship (Brick and Skipper), a father and son's inability to communicate (Big Daddy and Brick), or a family squabble over an inheritance (Brick and Maggie versus Gooper and Mae)?" See Crandell's essay on *Cat* in *Tennessee Williams: A Guide to Research and Performance*, ed. Philip C. Kolin (Westport, Conn.: Greenwood Press, 1998), 117. Of course the play is "really about" all of these relationships, but I would suggest that none of them, individually or together, yield a coherent meaning.

60 Most published versions of the script continue to include both third acts. See George W. Crandell, *Tennessee Williams: A Descriptive Bibliography* (Pittsburgh: Univ. of Pittsburgh Press, 1995) for the publication history of *Cat*.

61 See Murphy, *Tennessee Williams and Elia Kazan*, 97–130. While my interpretation differs from some of Murphy's conclusions about the Williams-Kazan collaboration on *Cat*, I am deeply indebted to her original scholarly work on the 1955 production.

62 See David Savran, *Communists, Cowboys, and Queers: The Politics of Masculinity in the Work of Arthur Miller and Tennessee Williams* (Minneapolis: Univ. of Minnesota Press, 1992), 88–95. Savran, of course, relies on Raymond Williams's discussion of liberal tragedy in *Modern Tragedy* (Stanford: Stanford Univ. Press, 1966), 87–105.

63 See Kazan's discussion in *A Life* (New York: Doubleday, 1988), 543–44.

64 Eric Bentley, "Theatre," *New Republic* 132 (4 April 1955): 22. Maurice Zolotow, "The Season on and Off Broadway," *Theatre Arts* 39:6 (1955): 93, also commented on the "failure of artistic control" in *Cat*.

65 Reviews in *New York Theatre Critics' Reviews, 1955*: William Hawkins, "Cat Yowls High on 'Hot Tin Roof'" (*New York World Telegram and Sun*), 342; John McClain, "Drama Shocks and Socks" (*Journal American*), 344; and Richard Watts, Jr., "The Impact of Tennessee Williams" (*New York Post*), 343.

66 Reviews in *New York Theatre Critics' Reviews, 1955*: Robert Coleman, "'Cat on a Hot Tin Roof' Is Likely to Be a Hit" (*Daily Mirror*), 343; John Chapman, "'Cat on a Hot Tin Roof' Beautifully Acted, But a Frustrating Drama" (*Daily News*), 343; and Brooks Atkinson, "Theatre: Tennessee Williams' 'Cat'" (*New York Times*), 344.

67 Bentley, "Theatre," 22.

68 The published play acknowledged this epigraph on its title page as a quotation

from "Do Not Go Gentle into That Good Night," from *The Collected Poems of Dylan Thomas* (New York: New Directions, 1952).

69 Hawkins, "Cat Yowls High on 'Hot Tin Roof,'" 342.
70 McClain, "Drama Shocks and Socks," 344; Atkinson, "Theatre: Tennessee Williams' 'Cat,'" 344; Walter F. Kerr, "Theater: 'Cat on a Hot Tin Roof'" (*New York Herald Tribune*), in *New York Theatre Critics' Reviews, 1955*, 342; Chapman, "'Cat on a Hot Tin Roof' Beautifully Acted," 343.
71 Bentley, "Theatre," 22.
72 Robert J. Corber, *Homosexuality in Cold War America: Resistance and the Crisis of Masculinity* (Durham and London: Duke Univ. Press, 1997), 4.
73 Kerr, "Theater," 342. Walter F. Kerr, "Theater: A Secret Is Half-Told in Fountains of Words," *New York Herald Tribune* (3 April 1955); review in the clipping file "Cat on A Hot Tin Roof," New York Library of Performing Arts.
74 Chapman, "'Cat on a Hot Tin Roof' Beautifully Acted," 343.
75 Savran, *Communists, Cowboys, and Queers*.
76 For Miller's critique of *Cat*, see Arthur Miller, "The Shadows of the Gods," in *The Theatre Essays of Arthur Miller*, ed. Robert A. Martin (New York: Viking, 1978), 189–93. The term "ignorance effects" is from Eve Kosofsky Sedgwick, *Epistemology of the Closet* (Berkeley: Univ. of California Press, 1990), 8. As she points out, the closeting of homosexuality generates "ignorance effects" that have been "harnessed, licensed, and regulated on a mass scale for striking enforcements" (5).
77 See Emile Benveniste, *Problems in General Linguistics* (Miami: Univ. of Miami Press, 1966). As Helen Gilbert notes in "De-Scribing Orality: Performance and the Recuperation of Voice," in *Post-Colonial Drama: Theory, Practice, Politics* (London: Routledge, 1996), Benveniste's *histoire/discours* "should not be set up as absolute binaries" (126).
78 On orality in general, see Richard Bauman, *Story, Performance, and Event: Contextual Studies of Oral Narrative* (Cambridge: Cambridge Univ. Press, 1986); R. Finnegan, *Oral Poetry: Its Nature, Significance, and Social Context*, 2nd ed. (Bloomington: Indiana Univ. Press, 1991); and Walter Ong, *Orality and Literacy: The Technologizing of the Word* (London and New York: Methuen, 1982). On personal narratives, see Kristin M. Langellier, "Personal Narratives: Perspectives on Theory and Research," *Text and Performance Quarterly* 9 (1989): 243–76; and Carol Simpson Stern and Bruce Henderson, *Performance: Texts and Contexts* (White Plains, N.Y.: Longman, 1993), 35–71.
79 Gilbert, "De-Scribing Orality," 2, 4.
80 George Jean Nathan, "Theatre Week," *New York Journal American* (9 June 1956), no page. See the clipping file on *Cat on a Hot Tin Roof* at the New York Library of Performing Arts for a copy of the review.
81 Edward Albee, *The American Dream and The Zoo Story: Two Plays by Edward Albee* (New York: NAL, 1961), 53–54. Subsequent citations in the text are from this edition.

82 See Bigsby, *Critical Introduction*, 271–79, for his estimation of the play and the Broadway audience's response.

3. Family Circles, Racial Others, and Suburbanization

1 Margot Henriksen, *Dr. Strangelove's America: Society and Culture in the Atomic Age* (Berkeley and Los Angeles: Univ. of California Press, 1997), 189. Mead quoted in Henriksen, 217.
2 Eric J. Sandeen, *Picturing an Exhibition: The Family of Man and 1950s America* (Albuquerque: Univ. of New Mexico Press, 1995), 39. Barthes quoted in Sandeen, 54. See also *The Family of Man* (New York: Maco Magazine Co., 1955).
3 Stevenson quoted in Michael S. Sherry, *In the Shadow of War: The United States since the 1930s* (New Haven: Yale Univ. Press, 1995), 151. Betty Friedan, *The Feminine Mystique* (New York: Dell, 1963). "Progressive Dehumanization: The Comfortable Concentration Camp" is the title of her chapter 12, 271–98.
4 Elaine Tyler May, *Homeward Bound: American Families in the Cold War Era* (New York: Basic Books, 1988), 14.
5 Arlene Skolnick, *Embattled Paradise: The American Family in an Age of Uncertainty* (New York: Basic Books, 1991), 64.
6 See Talcott Parsons, *The Social System* (Glencoe, Ill.: Free Press, 1951). Ferdinand Lundberg and Marynia Farnham, *Modern Women: The Lost Sex* (New York: Grosset & Dunlap, 1947), 235.
7 Quoted in May, *Homeward Bound*, 27.
8 Clifford E. Clark, Jr., "Ranch-House Suburbia: Ideals and Realities," in *Recasting America: Culture and Politics in the Age of Cold War*, ed. Lary May (Chicago: Univ. of Chicago Press, 1989), 171.
9 Skolnick, *Embattled Paradise*, 72–73; and May, *Homeward Bound*, 184.
10 Matthew Frye Jacobson, *Whiteness of a Different Color: European Immigrants and the Alchemy of Race* (Cambridge, Mass.: Harvard Univ. Press, 1998), 271.
11 Eleanor Roosevelt quoted in Sherry, *Shadow of War*, 146; Mary L. Dudziak, *Cold War Civil Rights: Race and the Image of American Democracy* (Princeton: Princeton Univ. Press, 2000), 252.
12 Ellen Herman, *The Romance of American Psychology: Political Culture in the Age of Experts* (Berkeley: Univ. of California Press, 1995), 193.
13 Doob discussed by Herman in ibid., 136–38. See Jonathan Nashel, "The Road to Vietnam: Modernization Theory in Fact and Fiction," in *Cold War Constructions: The Political Culture of United States Imperialism, 1945–1966*, ed. Christian G. Appy (Amherst: Univ. of Massachusetts Press, 2000), 132–54.
14 Emily S. Rosenberg, "Gender," *Journal of American History* 77 (June 1990): 119.
15 Geoffrey Perrett, *Days of Sadness, Years of Triumph: The American People, 1939–1945* (New York: Coward, McCann & Geoghegan, 1973), 418. See also Mark Bradley, "Slouching toward Bethlehem: Culture, Diplomacy, and the Origins of the Cold War in Vietnam," in *Cold War Constructions*, 11–34.

16 Joanne Stang, "The R&H Brand on a Musical," *New York Times Magazine* (30 November 1958): 16. For general criticism of Rodgers and Hammerstein, see David Ewen, *Richard Rodgers* (New York: Henry Holt, 1957); Hugh Fordin, *Getting to Know Him: A Biography of Oscar Hammerstein II* (New York: Random House, 1977); William G. Hyland, *Richard Rodgers* (New Haven: Yale Univ. Press, 1998); Abe Laufe, *Broadway's Greatest Musicals* (New York: Funk & Wagnalls, 1973); Ethan Mordden, *Rodgers and Hammerstein* (1992; rpt., New York: Harry N. Abrams, Inc., 1995); and Richard Rodgers, *Musical Stages: An Autobiography* (New York: Random House, 1975). I published a piece on their three "Oriental" musicals (*South Pacific* and *The Flower Drum Song* as well as *The King and I*): "The 'Oriental' Musicals of Rodgers and Hammerstein and the U.S. War in Southeast Asia," *Theatre Journal* 46 (1994): 385–98. This essay was reprinted in *Staging Difference: Cultural Pluralism in American Theatre and Drama*, ed. Marc Maufort (New York: Peter Lang, 1995), 57–74. On *South Pacific* and cold war ideology, see, in addition, Philip Biedler, "South Pacific and American Remembering; or, Josh, We're Going to Buy This Son of a Bitch," *Journal of American Studies* 27 (1993): 207–22; Christina Klein, "Cold War Orientalism: Musicals, Travel Narratives, and Middlebrow Culture in Postwar America" (Ph.D. diss., Yale Univ., 1997); and Andrea Most, "You've Got to Be Carefully Taught: The Politics of Race in Rodgers and Hammerstein's *South Pacific*," *Theatre Journal* 52:3 (October 2000): 307–38.

17 Rodgers and Hammerstein's *The King and I* (London: Chappell & Co, 1955), 11. Subsequent citations in the text are from this edition.

18 Horace Morton, ["Review of *The King and I*,"] *San Francisco Examiner* (13 July 1954), clipping file on *The King and I*, New York Public Library of Performing Arts.

19 John Mason Brown, ["Review of *The King and I*,"] *Saturday Review* 34 (14 April 1951): 46; Albert Goldberg, ["Review of *The King and I*,"] *Los Angeles Times* (30 May 1954), and Elliott Norton, ["Review of *The King and I*,"] *Boston Sunday Post* (11 March 1951), both in the clipping file on *The King and I*, New York Library of Performing Arts.

20 Arthur Pollock, ["Review of *The King and I*,"] *Daily Compass* (24 July 1951): 20; and Harold Clurman, ["Review of *The King and I*,"] *New Republic* 124 (16 April 1951): 29. I found only one review of *The King and I* that commented on the condescending attitude of the musical toward the King or the people of Siam. Claudia Cassidy, ["Review of *The King and I*,"] *Chicago Tribune* (10 June 1951), gave the road show in Chicago a favorable notice but added that "it would be a stronger show with less patronizing treatment of the king" (clipping file on *The King and I*, New York Library of Performing Arts).

21 John McClain, "Another Great Hit for Dick and Oscar" (*New York Journal American*), in *The New York Theatre Critics' Reviews*, vol. 12, *1951*, ed. Rachel Coffin (New York: Critics' Theatre Reviews, 1952), 304. Other reviewers entranced and tickled by the King's kids included Brooks Atkinson, Robert Coleman, Otis Guernsey, and Richard Watts. See *New York Theatre Critics' Reviews*,

1951, 304–7. Robert Coleman, "*King and I* Has Heart, Comedy, Top Lyrics" (*New York Daily Mirror*), in ibid., 307. The New York Library of Performing Arts clipping file on the musical contains a revealing report (in an unidentified newspaper) about a radio play produced by the BBC in August 1970 dealing with the life of Anna Leonowens. Written by historian Ian Grimble, it depicts her as a "shrill woman whose religious prejudices and pretentiousness made her disdainful of the King of Siam and his subjects." According to Grimble, "She was one of those awful little English governesses, a sex-starved widow" (no page). The King, in contrast, "was a remarkable ruler," who subsidized the building of several Christian churches and welcomed the advice of many European friends and diplomats, said Grimble.

22 Christina Klein, "Family Ties and Political Obligation: The Discourse of Adoption and the Cold War Commitment to Asia," in *Cold War Constructions*, 46. Kennedy quoted by Klein, 65.

23 D. A. Miller, *Place for Us: [Essay on the Broadway Musical]* (Cambridge, Mass.: Harvard Univ. Press, 1998), 83. See also John Clum, *Something for the Boys: Musical Theatre and Gay Culture* (New York: St. Martin's Press, 1999).

24 Bert States, *Great Reckonings in Little Rooms: On the Phenomenology of Theater* (Berkeley: Univ. of California Press, 1985), 157–70.

25 Miller, *Place for Us*, 86, 7. See also Carey Wall, "There's No Business Like Show Business: A Speculative Reading of the Broadway Musical," in *Approaches to the American Musical*, ed. Robert Lawson-Peebles (Exeter, UK: Univ. of Exeter Press, 1996), 24–43. On empathy, see George Lakoff and Mark Johnson, *Philosophy in the Flesh: The Embodied Mind and its Challenge to Western Thought* (New York: Basic Books, 1999); also J. Brooks Bouson, *The Empathetic Reader: A Study of the Narcissistic Character and the Drama of the Self* (Amherst: Univ. of Massachusetts Press, 1989); Karl F. Morrison, *"I Am You": The Hermeneutics of Empathy in Western Literature, Theology, and Art* (Princeton, N.J.: Princeton Univ. Press, 1988); Janet L. Surrey et al., *Work in Progress: Empathy Revisited* (Wellesley, Mass.: Stone Center, 1990); and Arne Johan Vetlesen, *Perception, Empathy, and Judgment* (University Park: Pennsylvania State Univ. Press, 1994).

26 See *Four Plays by William Inge* (1979; rpt., New York: Grove, Weidenfeld, 1990) for a recent edition of Inge's major dramas. *Dark at the Top of the Stairs* is on 223–304 in this edition. Subsequent citations in the text are from this edition. Of the numerous essays and several books on Inge, I have found the following the most helpful: Thomas P. Adler, "The School of Bill: An Inquiry into Literary Kinship (William Inge, Robert Anderson, and Arthur Laurents)," *Kansas Quarterly* 18:4 (Fall 1986): 113–19; Thomas P. Adler, "William Inge: The Terms of Diminishment," in *American Drama, 1940–1960: A Critical History* (New York: Twayne, 1994), 84–104; Shuman R. Baird, *William Inge* (New York: Twayne, 1965); Janet Juhnke, "Inge's Women: Robert Brustein and the Feminine Mystique," *Kansas Quarterly* 18:4 (Fall 1986): 103–11; Richard M. Leeson, *William Inge: A Research and Production Sourcebook* (Westport, Conn.: Greenwood, 1994); Ralph F. Voss, *A Life of William Inge: The Strains of Triumph* (Law-

rence: Univ. Press of Kansas, 1989); Michael Wentworth, "The Convergence of Fairy Tale and Myth In William Inge's *Picnic*," *Kansas Quarterly* 18:4 (Fall 1986): 57–63; and Tennessee Williams, "Introduction" to *The Dark at the Top of the Stairs* in *Six American Plays for Today*, ed. Bennett Cerf (New York: Random House, 1961), 117–20.

27 Henry Hewes, ["Theatre,"] *Saturday Review* (21 December 1957): 27.

28 Benjamin Spock, *Baby and Child Care* (New York: Meredith Press, 1963), 388. On Spock's ideas and influence, see Michael Zuckerman, "Dr. Spock: The Confidence Man," in *The Family in History*, ed. Charles E. Rosenberg (Philadelphia: Univ. of Pennsylvania Press, 1975), 179–207.

29 William Inge, "From 'Front Porch' to Broadway," *Theatre Arts* 38:4 (April 1954): 32.

30 *Cue* (14 December 1957), no page, clipping file for *Dark at the Top of the Stairs*, New York Library of Performing Arts.

31 W. David Sievers, *Freud on Broadway* (New York: Hermitage House, 1955), 451.

32 Henry A. Kissinger, *American Foreign Policy* (New York: W. W. Norton, 1974), 48.

33 James William Gibson, "Technowar," in *To Reason Why: The Debate about the Causes of U.S. Involvement in the Vietnam War*, ed. Jeffrey P. Kimball (New York: McGraw Hill, 1990), 342.

34 Thomas Haskell, "Capitalism and the Origins of the Humanitarian Sensibility," *American Historical Review* 90 (April–June 1985): 339–61, 547–66.

35 Frank Rich, *Playbill* 19:5 (May 1991): 74. According to his son Rock and his biographer Jhan Robbins, Brynner was Russian-born, although he usually claimed to be Mongolian. See Rock Brynner, *The Man Who Would Be King* (New York: Berkeley, 1991), 11; and Jhan Robbins, *Yul Brynner: The Inscrutable King* (New York: Dodd, 1987), 2. To link his erotic and exotic appeal to a mysterious background and defuse cold war anxieties, Brynner did not reveal his ties to the arch enemy of the United States during the 1950s.

36 James Poling, "Gertie and the King of Siam," *Collier's* (7 April 1951): 71.

37 Jane Feuer, *The Hollywood Musical*, 2nd ed. (Bloomington: Indiana Univ. Press, 1993), 3.

38 Richard Dyer, *White* (London and New York: Routledge, 1997), 44. See also Dwight Conquergood, "Rethinking Ethnography: Towards a Critical Cultural Politics," *Communication Monographs* 58 (1991): 179–94. Conquergood reminds readers that in the Western tradition of whiteness "mental abstractions and rational thought are taken as both epistemologically and morally superior to sensual experience, bodily sensations, and passions" (180).

39 John Stuart Mill, *On Liberty and Other Essays* (Oxford: Oxford Univ. Press, 1991), 137, 148, 164.

40 Walter Kerr, "First Night Report" (*New York Herald Tribune*), in *New York Theatre Critics' Reviews*, vol. 18, *1957*, ed. Rachel Coffin (New York: Critics' Theatre Reviews, 1958), 161.

41 Thomas Postlewait, "Spatial Order and Meaning in the Theatre: The Case of Tennessee Williams," *Assaph: Studies in the Theatre* 10 (1994): 49.
42 Jo Mielziner, *Designing for the Theatre: A Memoir and a Portfolio* (New York: Bramhall House, 1965), 88. See also Harry W. Smith, "An Air of the Dream: Jo Mielziner, Innovation and Influence, 1935–1955," *Journal of American Drama and Theatre* 5:3 (Fall 1993): 42–54.
43 Orville K. Larson, *Scene Design in the American Theatre* (Fayetteville: Univ. of Arkansas Press, 1989), 151. See also Mary C. Henderson, *Mielziner: Master of Modern Stage Design* (New York: Back Stage Books, 2001).
44 Howard Bay, *Stage Design* (New York: Drama Book Publishers, 1974), 17; States, *Great Reckonings*, 89.
45 Postlewait, "Spatial Order and Meaning," 54.
46 Proscenium viewing also draws on what Neil Smith and Cindi Katz term the "absolute space" of Euclidian geometry and Cartesian philosophy. See "Grounding Metaphor: Towards a Spatialized Politics," in *Place and the Politics of Identity*, ed. M. Keith and S. Pile (London: Routledge, 1993), 75. As Daniel Dennett has noted, René Descartes conceived of thinking as a mental theater in which a single, silent spectator observed metaphorical objects illuminated by the inner light of reason. Hence, abstract human understanding could arrive at objective insight secure in the knowledge that "his" (*sic*) mental representations were a true picture of the external world. See Dennett, *Consciousness Explained* (Boston: Little, Brown, 1991). The cognitive science case against Cartesian thinking is also well argued by Antonio R. Damasio in *Descartes' Error: Emotion, Reason, and the Human Brain* (New York: Putnam, 1994).
47 John Lardner, "The Surefire Boys in Siam," *New Yorker* 27 (7 April 1951): 70; Karal Ann Marling, "Imagineering the Disney Theme Parks," *Designing Disney's Theme Parks: The Architecture of Reasurance*, ed. Karal Ann Marling (New York: Flammarion, 1997), 31.
48 Disney quoted in Marling, "Imagineering the Disney Theme Parks," 181.
49 Steven Watts, *The Magic Kingdom; Walt Disney and the American Way of Life* (New York: Houghton Mifflin, 1997), 392, 326.
50 Hansberry quoted in Steven R. Carter, *Hansberry's Drama: Commitment amid Complexity* (Urbana: Univ. of Illinois Press, 1991), 12; Carter, *Hansberry's Drama*, 190–91.
51 Thomas P. Adler's treatment of *Raisin* also overlooks Hansberry's radical politics. Although he understands the "revolutionary commitment" of her later play, *Les Blancs*, Adler finds convincing similarities between *Raisin* and the plays of that "other great social dramatist of the American theater during the 1950s, Arthur Miller" (194). See *American Drama, 1940–1960*, 181–200.
52 See Michael Denning, *The Cultural Front: The Laboring of American Culture in the Twentieth Century* (London and New York: Verso, 1996), 423–62, for a general discussion of the discursive legacy of Popular Front thinking. Also Oliver Cromwell Cox, *Caste, Class, and Race: A Study in Social Dynamics* (New York:

Doubleday, 1948). On the history of African American Marxism, see Cedric J. Robinson, *Black Marxism: The Making of the Black Radical Tradition* (Chapel Hill: Univ. of North Carolina Press, 1983); and William J. Maxwell, *New Negro, Old Left: African-American Writing and Communism between the Wars* (New York: Columbia Univ. Press, 1999).

53 Cox, *Caste, Class, and Race*, 519; Myrdal quoted in Ellen Herman, *The Romance of American Psychology: Political Culture in the Age of Experts* (Berkeley and London: Univ. of California Press, 1995), 179.

54 Cox, *Caste, Class, and Race*, 509.

55 I have used Robert Nemiroff's "complete original version" (cover) of *A Raisin in the Sun* (1958; rpt., New York: Signet Classics, 1987). For the text of the Broadway production, which cuts one character and some dialogue from Hansberry's original play, see *A Raisin in the Sun* in *Six American Plays for Today*, ed. Bennett Cerf (New York: Modern Library, 1961), 299–403.

56 Harold Clurman, *The Collected Works of Harold Clurman*, ed. Marjorie Loggia and Glenn Young (New York: Applause Books, 1994), 385.

57 Lorraine Hansberry, "The Negro Writer and His Roots: Toward a New Romanticism," *Black Scholar* 12:2 (March–April 1981): 8. Hansberry's former husband and the executor of her estate, Robert Nemiroff, arranged for the publication of this 1959 speech in 1981.

58 Hansberry quoted in Carter, *Hansberry's Drama*, 52–53.

59 Hansberry, "The Negro Writer and His Roots," 2, 11.

60 Hansberry's idealism about Africa was influenced by Julian Mayfield, who, with other black ex-patriots from the United States, settled in Ghana after its independence in 1957 and contributed reports about emerging African nationalism in the late 1950s to left-wing journals and newspapers. See Kevin Gaines, "From Black Power to Civil Rights: Julian Mayfield and African American Ex-patriots in Nkrumah's Ghana, 1957–1966," in *Cold War Constructions*, 257–69.

61 Lorraine Hansberry, "Willy Loman, Walter Younger, and He Who Must Live," *Village Voice* (12 August 1959): 7–8. Hansberry quoted in Carter, *Hansberry's Drama*, 39.

62 Myrdal, *American Dilemma*, 109.

63 One of Hansberry's comments about her drama effectively paraphrased Cox's socialism in *Caste, Class, and Race*: "I don't think there is anything more universal in the world than man's oppression of man. That is what most great dramas have been about, no matter what the device of telling it is. . . . To the extent that my work is a successful piece of drama it makes the reality of this oppression true" (quoted in Carter, *Hansberry's Drama*, 65).

64 Quoted in Carter, *Hansberry's Drama*, 26. For another perspective on the play as both universal and particular, see Robin Bernstein, "Inventing a Fishbowl: White Supremacy and the Critical Reception of Lorraine Hansberry's *A Raisin in the Sun*," *Modern Drama* 42:1 (Spring 1999): 16–27.

65 Reviews in *The New York Theatre Critics' Reviews*, vol. 20, *1959*, ed. Rachel

Coffin (New York: Critics' Theatre Reviews, 1960): Richard Watts, Jr., "Honest Drama of a Negro Family" (*New York Post*), 344; Robert Coleman, "*Raisin in Sun* Superior Play" (*Daily Mirror*), 347; Brooks Atkinson, "The Theatre: *A Raisin in the Sun*" (*New York Times*), 345; and John McClain, "Gives a 'Wonderful Emotional Evening'" (*Journal American*), 345.

66 Hansberry's FBI file cited by Margaret B. Wilkerson, "Political Radicalism and Artistic Innovation in the Works of Lorraine Hansberry," in *African American Performance and Theater History; A Critical Reader*, ed. Harry J. Elam and David Krasner (New York: Oxford Univ. Press, 2001), 46.

67 John Chapman, "*A Raisin in the Sun* A Glowingly Lovely and Touching Little Play" (*Daily News*), in *New York Theatre Critics' Reviews, 1959*, 344; and Frank Aston, "*Raisin in Sun* Is Moving Tale" (*New York World Telegram* and *Sun*), in ibid., 346.

68 James Baldwin, "Sweet Lorraine," *Esquire* 72:5 (November 1969): 139; and "White Man's Guilt," reprinted from *Ebony* in *Black on White: Black Writers on What It Means to Be White*, ed. David Roediger (New York: Schocken Books, 1998), 320, 322–23, 323.

69 Henry Hewes, "A Plant Grows in Chicago," *Saturday Review* (4 April 1959): 28; Gerald Weales, "Thoughts on *A Raisin in the Sun*: A Critical Review," *Commentary* 27: 6 (June 1959): 529; and *Variety* (28 January 1959): 56, in the clipping file for *Raisin in the Sun*, New York Library of Performing Arts.

70 John Hastings, "White Guilt or Northern Hypocrisy," *Village Voice* (29 July 1959): *Raisin in the Sun* clipping file, New York Library of Performing Arts.

71 Hansberry, "Willy Loman, Walter Younger, and He Who Must Live," 8.

72 Walter Kerr, "*A Raisin in the Sun*" (*New York Herald Tribune*), in *New York Theatre Critics' Reviews, 1959*, 346.

73 Davis quoted by Robert Nemiroff, "Introduction," in *A Raisin in the Sun*, xiii.

74 Watts, "Honest Drama," 344; Kerr, "A Raisin in the Sun," 346; Atkinson, "Theatre," 345; and Aston, "*Raisin in Sun*," 346.

75 See Sidney Poitier, *The Measure of a Man: A Spiritual Autobiography* (San Francisco: Harper, 1999), 150–58.

76 I am indebted to a discussion I had with Davies King at the University of California, Santa Barbara, about the film and the 1959 production of *Raisin* for his insights into the performance of Claudia McNeil and her competition with Poitier.

77 *New York Age* (21 March 1959) and Anna Arnold Hedgman, *Amsterdam News* (March 1959), both in the *Raisin in the Sun* clipping file at the New York Library of Performing Arts.

78 Baldwin, "Sweet Lorraine," 139.

79 Amiri Baraka, "*Raisin in the Sun*'s Enduring Passion," *Washington Post* (16 November 1986): F1:3.

80 Alice Childress, *Trouble in Mind: A Comedy Drama in Two Acts*, in *Black Theater: A 20th Century Collection of the Work of Its Best Playwrights*, ed. Lindsay Patterson (New York: Dodd, Mead & Co., 1971), 137–74. For recent criticism on

Childress, see Patricia Schroeder, "Re-Reading Alice Childress," in *Staging Difference: Cultural Pluralism in American Theatre and Drama*, ed. Marc Maufort (New York: Peter Lang, 1995), 323–38.

4. Fragmented Heroes, Female Others, and the Bomb

1. Herbert Blau, *The Impossible Theater: A Manifesto* (New York: Macmillan, 1964), 88, 19.
2. Farrell quoted by Margot Henriksen, *Dr. Strangelove's America: Society and Culture in the Atomic Age* (Berkeley: Univ. of California Press, 1997), xv.
3. See William Chaloupka, *Knowing Nukes: The Politics and Culture of the Atom* (Minneapolis: Univ. of Minnesota Press, 1993); Jacqueline Foertsch, *Enemies Within: The Cold War and the AIDS Crisis in Literature, Film, and Culture* (Chicago: Univ. of Illinois Press, 2001); Alan Nadel, *Containment Culture* (Durham, N.C.: Duke Univ. Press, 1995); Peter Schwenger, *Letter Bomb: Nuclear Holocaust and the Exploding Word* (Baltimore: Johns Hopkins Univ. Press, 1993); and J. Fisher Solomon, *Discourse and Reference in the Nuclear Age* (Norman: Univ. of Oklahoma Press, 1988).
4. *New York Herald Tribune*, Cousins, *Time*, and *Life* quoted in Paul Boyer, *By the Bomb's Early Light: American Thought and Culture at the Dawn of the Atomic Age* (New York: Pantheon, 1985), 3, 8, 21, 10; Wylie quoted in Nadel, *Containment Culture*, 20. See also Boyer's later book, *Fallout: A Historian Reflects on America's Half-Century Encounter with Nuclear Weapons* (Columbus: Ohio State Univ. Press, 1998); and Allan M. Winkler, *Life under a Cloud: American Anxiety about the Atom* (Urbana and Chicago: Univ. of Illinois Press, 1999).
5. Quoted in Steven Cohan, *Masked Men* (Bloomington: Indiana Univ. Press, 1997), 167.
6. R. W. Connell, *Masculinities* (Oxford: Polity, 1995), 77; and R. W. Connell, *Gender and Power: Society, the Person, and Sexual Politics* (Oxford: Polity, 1987), 110.
7. William Attwood, George B. Leonard, Jr., and J. Robert Moskin, *The Decline of the American Male* (New York: Random House, 1958), dust-jacket, 11–14. See Elaine Tyler May, *Homeward Bound: American Families in the Cold War Era* (New York: Basic Books, 1988).
8. Miller quoted by Dale Carter, *Cracking the Ike Age: Aspects of Fifties America* (Aarhus, Denmark: Aarhus University, 1992), 51. See Victor Navasky, *Naming Names* (New York: Viking, 1980).
9. Conroy quoted in Henriksen, *Dr. Strangelove's America*, 39.
10. Catherine Lutz, "Epistemology of the Bunker: The Brainwashed and Other New Subjects of Permanent War," in *Inventing the Psychological: Toward a Cultural History of Emotional Life in America*, ed. Joel Pfister and Nancy Schnog (New Haven, Conn.: Yale Univ. Press, 1997), 352.
11. Nadel, *Containment Culture*, 34; Defense Advisory Commission quoted in Carter, *Cracking the Ike Age*, 48.
12. Truman quoted in Nadel, *Containment Culture*, 14; Frank Kermode, *The Sense*

of an Ending: Studies in the Theory of Fiction (New York: Oxford Univ. Press, 1967), 28.
13 James Gilbert, *Redeeming Culture: American Religion in an Age of Science* (Chicago: Univ. of Chicago Press, 1997), 239.
14 Sacvan Bercovitch, *The American Jeremiad* (Madison: Univ. of Wisconsin Press, 1978), 28.
15 *Them!* quoted in Henriksen, *Dr. Strangelove's America*, 58.
16 Herberg quoted in Robert W. Wuthnow, *After Heaven: Spirituality in America since the 1950s* (Berkeley: Univ. of California Press, 1998), 40; Eisenhower quoted by Stephen J. Whitfield, *The Culture of the Cold War*, 2nd ed. (Baltimore: Johns Hopkins Univ. Press, 1996), 88; Carter, *Cracking the Ike Age*, 46, cites Herberg's "faith in faith" conclusion.
17 Wuthnow, *After Heaven*, 30, 33, 38, 39.
18 Wouk's drama quoted by Charles A. Carpenter, *Dramatists and the Bomb: American and British Playwrights Confront the Nuclear Age, 1945–1964* (Westport, Conn.: Greenwood Press, 1999), 44. Carpenter's book is the best single discussion of American playwrights' response to nuclearism.
19 For useful criticism of *J.B.*, see Richard Calhoun, "Archibald MacLeish's *J.B.*— A Retrospective Look," *Pembroke Magazine* 7 (1976): 74–77; Scott Donaldson, *Archibald MacLeish: An American Life* (New York: Houghton Mifflin, 1992); Robert Downing, "J.B. Journeys," *Theatre Arts* (February 1960): 29–32; Bernard A. Drabeck, Helen E. Ellis, and Seymour Rudin, eds., *The Proceedings of the Archibald MacLeish Symposium, May 7–8, 1982* (Washington, D.C.: University Press of America, 1988); Jerome Ellison, *God on Broadway* (Richmond, Va.: John Knox Press, 1971); Theodore E. Fleischer, "Suffering Reclaimed: Medicine According to Job," *Perspectives in Biology and Medicine* 42:4 (Summer 1999): 475–88; Haruko Fuwa, "Human Survival and J.B.," in *American Literature in the 1950s: Annual Report 1976* (Tokyo: American Literature Society of Japan, 1976), 191–98; Allan Lewis, *American Plays and Playwrights of the Contemporary Theatre* (New York: Crown Publishers, 1970), 116–28; Thomas E. Porter, *Myth and Modern American Drama* (Detroit: Wayne State Univ. Press, 1969), 77–101; and Janis P. Stout, "Re-Visions of Job: *J.B.* and 'A Masque of Reason,'" *Essays in Literature* 14:2 (1987): 225–39.
  Less useful, but still relevant, is the theologically oriented scholarship on the play, which includes Elizabeth Bieman, "Faithful to the Bible in Its Fashion: MacLeish's *J.B.*," *Studies in Religion* 4:1 (1974/75): 25–30; John H. Stroupe, "The Masks of MacLeish's *J.B.*," *Tennessee Studies in Literature* 15 (1970): 75–83; and W. D. White, "MacLeish's *J.B.*—Is It a Modern Job?" *Mosaic* 4:1 (1970): 13–20. For MacLeish's comments on his play and other relevant discussion, see *Archibald MacLeish: Reflections*, ed. Bernard A. Drabeck and Helen Ellis (Amherst: Univ. of Massachusetts Press, 1986); "The Poet's Three Comforters: *J.B.* and the Critics," *Modern Drama* 2 (1959): 228–29; and "Trespass on a Monument," *New York Times* (7 December 1958): section 2:1. In addition,

there are useful clipping and program files on *J.B.* at the New York Library of Performing Arts.

The standard published version of the play, *J.B.: A Play in Verse* (New York: Houghton Mifflin, 1958), precedes the version of the play presented on Broadway. The closest the critic may come to the version used in Kazan's production is the initial script by the stage manager (Robert Downing), published in *Theatre Arts* (February 1960): 34–62. Yet even this version omits the "recognition scene" at the end of the play, added later by MacLeish and Kazan. All citations in my text are from the *Theatre Arts* version, except where otherwise noted.

20 For useful criticism of *Night Journey*, see Evan Alderson, "Metaphor in Dance: The Example of Graham," *Dance History Scholars Proceedings* 6 (1983): 111–18; Jack Anderson, "Some Personal Grumbles about Martha Graham," *Ballet Review* 2 (1967): 25–30; Jill Antonides, "Night Journey and the Reconfiguration of Narrative," in *Society of Dance History Scholars: Proceedings, 1998* (Riverside, Calif.: Society of Dance History Scholars, 1998); Arlene Croce, "Tell Me, Doctor," *Ballet Review* 2:4 (1968): 12–18; Susan Leigh Foster, *Reading Dancing: Bodies and Subjects in Contemporary American Dance* (Berkeley: Univ. of California Press, 1986); Mark Franko, *Dancing Modernism / Performing Politics* (Bloomington: Indiana Univ. Press, 1995), 38–74; Russell Freedman, *Martha Graham: A Dancer's Life* (New York: Clarion, 1998); Robert Horan, "The Recent Theater of Martha Graham," *Dance Index* 6:1 (January 1947): 4–22; Graham Jackson, "The Roots of Heaven: Sexuality in the Work of Martha Graham," in *Dance Spectrum: Critical and Philosophical Enquiry*, ed. Diana T. Taplin (Waterloo: Univ. of Waterloo Press, 1982), 50–59; Jill Johnston, "Martha Graham: An Irresponsible Study," *Ballet Review* 2:4 (1968): 6–12; Deborah Jowitt, "In Memory: Martha Graham, 1894–1991," *TDR* 35 (Winter 1991): 14–16; Deborah Jowitt, *Time and the Dancing Image* (Berkeley: Univ. of California Press, 1988), 149–233; Valentina Litvinoff, *The Use of Stanislavsky within Modern Dance* (New York: American Dance Guild, 1972); Joseph H. Mazo, "Martha Remembered," *Dance Magazine* 65 (July 1991): 35–44; Don McDonagh, *Martha Graham: A Biography* (New York: Praeger, 1973); Genevieve Oswald, "Myth and Legend in Martha Graham's *Night Journey*," *Dance Research Annual* 14 (1983): 42–49; Stephen Polcari, "Martha Graham and Abstract Expressionism," *Smithsonian Studies in American Art* 4:1 (Winter 1990): 3–27; Suzanne Shelton, "Jungian Roots of Martha Graham's Dance Imagery," *Dance History Scholars Proceedings* 6 (1983): 119–32; Marcia B. Siegel, "American Dance and World War II," *Southern Humanities Review* 27:3 (Summer 1993): 219–30; Ernestine Stodelle, *Deep Song: The Dance Story of Martha Graham* (New York: Macmillan, 1984); Robert Tracy, *Goddess: Martha Graham's Dancers Remember* (New York: Limelight Editions, 1997); Tim Wengard, "Martha's Men," *Dance Magazine* 65 (July 1991): 48–52; and Martha Ullman West, "Frontier of Design: Isamu Noguchi, 1904–1988," *Dance Magazine* (May 1989): 58–60.

In addition, see the clipping file "Martha Graham, 1945–1949" and the program file "Martha Graham" at the New York Library of Performing Arts. I also used a 1957 black-and-white video of *Night Journey* included in *Martha Graham: An American Original in Performance*, Library of Master Performers Series (New York: Home Video Exclusives, 1957), featuring Graham, Bertram Ross, and Paul Taylor.

21 See Naima Prevots, *Dance for Export: Cultural Diplomacy and the Cold War* (Hanover, N.H.: Wesleyan University Press, 1998), 37–52.

22 Horan, "Recent Theatre of Martha Graham," 6; "Martha Graham in Concert (San Francisco, 9–10 April 1946)," "Martha Graham" program file, New York Library of Performing Arts.

23 "Martha Graham (1953)" program file, New York Library of Performing Arts; and McDonagh, *Martha Graham*, 199.

24 Martin Heidegger, *The Question Concerning Technology and Other Essays*, ed. and trans. William Lovitt (New York: Harper and Row, 1977), 130; and Michael Bell, *Literature, Modernism and Myth: Belief and Responsibility in the Twentieth Century* (Cambridge: Cambridge Univ. Press, 1997), 37.

25 MacLeish, "Trespass on a Monument," 1.

26 John McClain, "*J.B.*" (*Journal American*), in *The New York Theatre Critics' Reviews*, vol. 19, *1958*, ed. Rachel Coffin (New York: Critics' Theatre Reviews, 1959), 169; John Chapman, "*J.B.* Inspiring Poetic Drama" (*Daily News*), in ibid., 168; for Walter Winchell's review and the newspaper advertisements for the production, see the clipping file on *J.B.*, New York Library of Performing Arts.

27 *Life* (18 May 1959): 124–38, in clipping file on *J.B.*

28 See the Winchell review and Henry Hewes's review, *Saturday Review* (3 January 1959): no page, in the clipping file on *J.B.*, New York Library of Performing Arts; Harold Clurman's notice in *Nation* (3 January 1959), reprinted in *The Collected Works of Harold Clurman*, ed. Marjorie Loggia and Glenn Young (New York: Applause Books, 1994), 373–74. See Bieman, "Faithful to the Bible"; Stroupe, "The Masks of MacLeish's *J.B.*"; Stout, "Re-Visions of Job"; and White, "MacLeish's *J.B.*," for different responses to the play's faithfulness to the Bible.

29 "Martha Graham (21 February 1948)" program file, New York Library of Performing Arts.

30 *Life* (17 March 1947): 104.

31 Foster, *Reading Dancing*, 50.

32 Jackson, "The Roots of Heaven," 53.

33 Anderson, "Some Personal Grumbles," 26.

34 According to Kenneth R. Dutton, *The Perfectible Body: The Western Ideal of Male Development* (New York: Continuum, 1995), a shaved body presents less of a sexual threat than a hairy one: the shaved body cancels out "the aggressive or intimidating message of the super-normal adult male body shape, [demonstrating] that this is not a body to be feared on account of its dominance, but rather to be looked at or touched . . ." (306).

35 Yuriko Kikuchi quoted in Mazo, "Martha Remembered," 43.

36 Kazan quoted in Donaldson, *Archibald MacLeish*, 455.

37 See David M. Potter, *People of Plenty: Economic Abundance and the American Character* (Chicago: Univ. of Chicago Press, 1954); and John Kenneth Galbraith, *The Affluent Society* (Boston: Houghton, Mifflin, 1958).
38 Kazan quoted in Porter, *Myth and Modern American Drama*, 98. In this, as in much else, I agree with Porter's interpretation of the play.
39 White, "MacLeish's *J.B.*," 18–19; and Porter, *Myth and Modern American Drama*, 101.
40 Kenneth Tynan, *Curtains: Selections from the Drama Criticism and Related Writings* (New York: Atheneum, 1961), 70–72.
41 John Hersey, *Hiroshima* (New York: Bantam, 1946), 1. See Alan Nadel's commentary on *Hiroshima* in *Containment Culture*, 38–67.
42 Franko, *Dancing Modernism*, 45; Kisselgoff quoted in Polcari, "Martha Graham and Abstract Expressionism," 26; Horan, "Recent Theatre of Martha Graham," 18.
43 John Martin, *New York Times* (5 February 1950): Section 2:7; and Robert Horan, "The Recent Theatre of Martha Graham," in *Chronicles of the American Dance* (1948; rpt., New York: Da Capo Press, 1978), 249.
44 "Martha Graham (*Serpent Heart*, 1946)" program file, New York Library of Performing Arts; Walter Terry, "Cave of the Heart," *New York Herald Tribune* (28 February 1947); and Robert Sabin, "Martha Graham Presents New Work," *Dance Observer* 13:6 (June–July 1946): 73 (both reviews are in the "Martha Graham" clipping file at the New York Library of Performing Arts); Horan, "Recent Theatre of Martha Graham," 14.
45 Porter, *Myth and Modern American Drama*, 87.
46 Ibid.
47 Mary Price, *The Photograph: A Strange Confined Space* (Stanford: Stanford Univ. Press, 1994), 175, 7.
48 Greenberg quoted in Mary Warner Marien, *Photography and Its Critics: A Cultural History, 1839–1900* (Cambridge: Cambridge Univ. Press, 1997), 7.
49 Talbot and Poe quoted in ibid., 3, 5.
50 Benjamin quoted in Eduardo Cadava, *Words of Light: Theses on the Photography of History* (Princeton, N.J.: Princeton Univ. Press, 1997), 3.
51 Atkinson, "Theatre: MacLeish's *J.B.*" (*New York Times*), in *New York Theatre Critics' Reviews, 1958*, 170.
52 Kazan quoted in Porter, *Myth and Modern American Drama*, 98; Niebuhr quoted in *Life* (18 May 1959): 137.
53 "Martha Graham (*Errand into the Maze*, 1947)" program file, New York Library of Performing Arts; Walter Terry, "[Review of *Errand into the Maze*]," *New York Herald Tribune* (1 March 1947), in the "Martha Graham" clipping file, New York Library of Performing Arts.
54 Treat quoted in Schwenger, *Letter Bomb*, 54, 43, 46. Schwenger's conclusion is on 55. On *Hiroshima*, see Nadel, *Containment Culture*, 38–67.
55 Freddie Rokem, *Performing History: Theatrical Representations of the Past in Contemporary Theatre* (Iowa City: Univ. of Iowa Press, 2000), xii.

56 George Lakoff and Mark Johnson, *Philosophy in the Flesh: The Embodied Mind and Its Challenge to Western Thought* (New York: Basic Books, 1999), 318.
57 Robert Jay Lifton and Richard Falk, *Indefensible Weapons: The Political and Psychological Case against Nuclearism* (New York: Basic Books, 1982), 100–110. The *Emergency Plans Book*, generated by the Defense Department in 1958 and recently declassified, makes it clear that the federal government understood the futility of all public and most backyard shelters for protecting the American people in the event of a nuclear attack. This information was not shared with the public. See L. Douglas Keeney, *The Doomsday Scenario* (Beijing: MBI Publishing, 2002). The *Life* article and bomb shelter craze are noted in Henriksen, *Dr. Strangelove's America*, 200–203; ibid., 203.
58 See Henriksen, *Dr. Strangelove's America*, 203–18, for a discussion of survivalism. Dresner quoted in ibid., 226.
59 For an overview of scholarship on Kazan before 1985, see Lloyd Michaels, *Elia Kazan: A Guide to References and Resources* (Boston: G. K. Hall, 1985). I have found the following works particularly helpful: Eugene Archer, "Elia Kazan — The Genius of Style," *Film Culture* 2:2 (1956): 4–7, 21–24; David Arthur Jones, *Great Directors at Work: Stanislavsky, Brecht, Kazan, Brook* (Berkeley: Univ. of California Press, 1986); Jim Kitses, "Elia Kazan: A Structural Analysis," *Cinema* 7:3 (Winter 1972–1973): 25–36; Thomas B. Morgan, "Elia Kazan's Great Expectations," *Harper's Magazine* 225 (September 1962): 66–75; Brenda Murphy, *Tennessee Williams and Elia Kazan: A Collaboration in the Theatre* (Cambridge: Cambridge Univ. Press, 1992); John J. O'Connor, "The Great God Gadg," *Audience* 7 (Winter 1960): 25–31; Thomas H. Pauly, *An American Odyssey: Elia Kazan and American Culture* (Philadelphia: Temple Univ. Press, 1983); Gordon Rogoff, "A Streetcar Named Kazan," *Reporter* 31:11 (17 December 1964): 38–40; Richard Schechner, "New York: Sentimentalist Kazan," *Tulane Drama Review* 9 (Spring 1965): 194–98; Lewis Shelton, "Elia Kazan and the Psychological Perspective of Directing," *Journal of American Drama and Theatre* 14:3 (Fall 2002): 60–88; Roger Tailleur, "Elia Kazan and the House Un-American Activities Committee," trans. Alvah Bessie, *Film Comment* 4:1 (Fall 1966): 43–59; and Robin Wood, "The Kazan Problem," *Movie* 19 (1971): 29–31. In addition, I have relied on Navasky's *Naming Names* and Kazan's autobiography, *Elia Kazan: A Life* (New York: Knopf, 1988).
60 Kazan, *A Life*, 339, 448, 467–529, 529.
61 Gordon Teskey, *Allegory and Violence* (Ithaca: Cornell Univ. Press, 1996), 2, 4, 17.
62 Kazan, *A Life*, 465.
63 Eric Bentley, "Theatre," *New Republic* 132 (4 April 1955): 22.
64 Kazan, *A Life*, 583.
65 Archer, "Elia Kazan — The Genius of Style," 6; and Rogoff, "Streetcar Named Kazan," 40.
66 Archer, "Elia Kazan — The Genius of Style," 24.

67 Tennessee Williams, *Cat on a Hot Tin Roof* (1955; rpt., New York: Penguin, 1985), 77.
68 Rogoff, "Streetcar Named Kazan," 38; Brustein quoted in Pauly, *American Odyssey*, 223; Morgan, "Elia Kazan's Great Expectations," 68.
69 Williams quoted in Morgan, "Elia Kazan's Great Expectations," 75.
70 Kazan, *A Life*, 504.
71 Pauly, *American Odyssey*, 179; Archer, "Elia Kazan—The Genius of Style," 24.
72 Williams quoted in Pauly, *American Odyssey*, 209.
73 Navasky, *Naming Names*, 210; Elia Kazan, "[Excerpts from] the Director's Notebook," in *Drama on Stage*, ed. Randolph Goodman (New York: Holt, Rinehart and Winston, 1961), 295.
74 Kazan quoted in Navasky, *Naming Names*, 205–6.
75 Ibid., 208; Kazan, *A Life*, 460.
76 Tynan quoted by William Stott in Fred Fehl, *On Broadway: Performance Photographs by Fred Fehl, Text by William Stott with Jane Stott* (Austin: Univ. of Texas Press, 1978), 334.
77 Conroy quoted in Henriksen, *Dr. Strangelove's America*, 39.
78 Wood, "The Kazan Problem," 31.
79 Arthur Miller, *Timebends: A Life* (New York: Grove Press, 1987), 516, 520.
80 This selection from "Asphodel" quoted by Edward Brunner, *Cold War Poetry* (Urbana and Chicago: Univ. of Illinois Press, 2001), 186.
81 The scholarship on *The Crucible* is immense. For bibliographic guides, see the essays by James J. Martine in *Critical Essays on Arthur Miller* (Boston: G. K. Hall, 1979) and Alvin Goldfarb in *American Playwrights since 1945: A Guide to Scholarship, Criticism, and Performance* (Westport, Conn.: Greenwood, 1989). I have found the following sources particularly helpful: Thomas P. Adler, *American Drama, 1940–1960* (New York: Twayne, 1994), 62–83; Thomas P. Adler, "Conscience and Community in an Enemy of the People and The Crucible," in *The Cambridge Companion to Arthur Miller*, ed. Christopher Bigsby (Cambridge: Cambridge Univ. Press, 1997); Iska Alter, "Betrayal and Blessedness: Explorations of Feminine Power in *The Crucible, A View from the Bridge*, and *After the Fall*," in *Feminist Rereadings of Modern American Drama*, ed. June Schlueter (Cranbury, N.J.: Fairleigh Dickenson Univ. Press, 1989), 116–45; C. W. E. Bigsby, *A Critical Introduction to Twentieth-Century American Drama*, vol. 2 (Cambridge: Cambridge Univ. Press, 1984), 135–248; E. Miller Budick, "History and Other Spectres in Arthur Miller's *The Crucible*," *Modern Drama* 28:4 (1985): 535–52; Stephen Fender, "Precision and Pseudo Precision in *The Crucible*," *Journal of American Studies* 1 (April 1967): 87–98; Gary Hendrickson, "The Last Analogy: Arthur Miller's Witches and America's Domestic Communists," *Midwest Quarterly* 33:4 (1992): 447–55; James J. Martine, *The Crucible: Politics, Property, and Pretense* (New York: Twayne, 1993); Edmund S. Morgan, "Arthur Miller's *The Crucible* and the Salem Witch Trials," in *The Golden and Brazen World*, ed. John M. Wallace (Berkeley: Univ. of California Press, 1985), 171–86; Brenda Murphy, "Arthur Miller: Revisioning Realism," in *Realism and*

the *American Dramatic Tradition*, ed. William W. Demastes (Tuscaloosa: Univ. of Alabama Press, 1996), 189–202; Brenda Murphy, *Congressional Theatre: Dramatizing McCarthyism on Stage, Film, and Television* (Cambridge: Cambridge Univ. Press, 1999); David Savran, *Communists, Cowboys, and Queers: The Politics of Masculinity in the Work of Arthur Miller and Tennessee Williams* (Minneapolis: Univ. of Minnesota Press, 1992); Wendy Schissel, "Re(dis)covering the Witches in Arthur Miller's *The Crucible*: A Feminist Reading," *Modern Drama* 37 (1994): 461–73; and Gerald Weales, *The Crucible: Text and Criticism* (1971; rpt., New York: Viking, 1982).

I have also relied on Miller's *Timebends* and his essays in *The Theater Essays of Arthur Miller*, ed. Robert A. Martin (New York: Viking, 1978); and the clipping file and program file on *The Crucible* at the New York Library of Performing Arts. For a script of the play, I have used *The Crucible: A Play in Four Acts* (1952; rpt., New York: Penguin, 1982). Subsequent references in the text are from this version.

82 Reviews in *The New York Theatre Critics' Reviews*, vol. 14, *1953*, ed. Rachel Coffin (New York: Critics' Theatre Reviews, 1954): Brooks Atkinson, "At the Theatre" (*New York Times*), 386; John Chapman, "Miller's *The Crucible* Terrifying Tragedy about Puritan Bigotry" (*Daily News*), 383; Robert Coleman, "*The Crucible* a Stirring, Well-Acted Melodrama" (*Daily Mirror*), 385; William Hawkins, "Witchcraft Boiled in *The Crucible*" (*New York World Telegram and Sun*), 384; Walter Kerr, "The Crucible" (*New York Herald Tribune*), 385; John McClain, "Play of Enormous Strength and Depth" (*New York Journal American*), 383; and Richard Watts, Jr., "Mr. Miller Looks at Witch-Hunting" (*New York Post*), 384. Miller, *Timebends*, 347.
83 Walter Kerr, "The Crucible," in *New York Theatre Critics' Reviews, 1953*, 385; reviews in *Nation* and the *San Francisco Chronicle* quoted in Henriksen, *Dr. Strangelove's America*, 448.
84 Miller, *Timebends*, 331.
85 Brown, Bentley, and Miller quoted in Henriksen, *Dr. Strangelove's America*, 448, 449.
86 Chapman, "Miller's *The Crucible*," 383; Hawkins, "Witchcraft Boiled in *The Crucible*," 384; and Atkinson, "At the Theatre," 386.
87 Bigsby, *Critical Introduction*, 136.
88 Ibid., 198.
89 Raymond Williams, *Modern Tragedy* (Stanford: Stanford Univ. Press, 1966), 87–105; Miller, *Theater Essays*, 3–7.
90 Adler, *American Drama*, 79.
91 Morgan, "Arthur Miller's *The Crucible* and the Salem Witch Trials," 171–86.
92 Lakoff and Johnson, *Philosophy in the Flesh*, 321.
93 Miller, *Timebends*, 347; and Murphy, *Congressional Theatre*, 158.
94 Alter, "Betrayal and Blessedness," 137–44.
95 Bigsby, *Critical Introduction*, 195–97.
96 McClain, "Play of Enormous Strength and Depth," 383.

97 David W. Noble, "The Reconstruction of Progress: Charles Beard, Richard Hofstadter, and Postwar Historical Thought," in *Recasting America: Culture and Politics in the Age of the Cold War*, ed. Lary May (Chicago: Univ. of Chicago Press, 1989), 74.

98 See *What Use Are Flowers* in *Les Blancs: The Collected Last Plays*, ed. Robert Nemiroff (New York: New American Library, 1983). According to Nemiroff in his introduction, Hansberry conceived of *Flowers* initially as a television drama then rewrote it for the stage. Unsatisfied with her revision, she set it aside in 1962 and died (in 1965) before returning to it. For criticism of the play, see Steven R. Carter, *Hansberry's Drama: Commitment amid Complexity* (Urbana: Univ. of Illinois Press, 1991), 141–54; and Carpenter, *Dramatists and the Bomb*, 88–92.

99 Nadel's *Containment Culture*, in fact, following Chaloupka and Schwenger, argues that nuclearism pushed American culture into postmodernism.

Epilogue, 1962–1992

1 To my knowledge, no theorist or historian has read television viewing through the lens of cognitive psychology. I have drawn my observations and conclusions from the following sources: Richard Butsch, *The Making of American Audiences: From Stage to Television, 1750–1990* (Cambridge: Cambridge Univ. Press, 2000), 235–94; E. Ann Kaplan, ed., *Regarding Television: Critical Approaches—An Anthology* (Frederick, Md.: Univ. Publications of America, 1983); Sonia Livingstone, *Making Sense of Television: The Psychology of Audience Interpretation* (New York: Pergamon, 1990); Joshua Meyrowitz, *No Sense of Place: The Impact of Electronic Media on Social Behavior* (New York: Oxford Univ. Press, 1989); Lynn Spigel, *Make Room for TV: Television and the Family Ideal in Postwar America* (Chicago: Univ. of Chicago Press, 1992); and Cecelia Tichi, *Electronic Hearth: Creating an American Television Culture* (New York: Oxford Univ. Press, 1991).

2 See Joshua Gamson, *Claims to Fame: Celebrity in Contemporary America* (Berkeley and Los Angeles: Univ. of California Press, 1994); Linda Hutcheon, *A Poetics of Postmodernism: History, Theory, Fiction* (New York: Routledge, 1988); Jean-François Lyotard, *The Postmodern Conditon: A Report on Knowledge*, trans. Geoff Bennington and Brian Massumi (Minneapolis: Univ. of Minnesota Press, 1984); and Gianni Vattimo, *The End of Modernity: Nihilism and Hermeneutics in Postmodern Culture*, trans. J. R. Snyder (Baltimore: Johns Hopkins Univ. Press, 1988).

3 See, for example, Arnold Aronson, "American Theatre in Context: 1945–Present," in *The Cambridge History of American Theatre*, vol 3, ed. Don B. Wilmeth and Christopher Bigsby (Cambridge: Cambridge Univ. Press, 2000), 87–162. The recent emphasis in U.S. theater studies on cultural nationalism and identity politics also obscures the continuities between the early cold war era and the next thirty years, even though the cultural essentialism driving much of this theater derives from containment thinking.

The literature on the 1962–1992 period of the American theater is vast. I have found the following sources helpful: Gerald M. Berkowitz, *American Drama of the Twentieth Century* (London and New York: Longman, 1992); C. W. E. Bigsby, *Modern American Drama, 1945-1990* (Cambridge and New York: Cambridge Univ. Press, 1992); *Cambridge Guide to American Theater*, ed. Don B. Wilmeth with Tice L. Miller (Cambridge and New York: Cambridge Univ. Press, 1996); Ruby Cohn, *American Drama, 1960-1990* (New York: St. Martin's Press, 1991); John Degan, "Musical Theatre since W W II," in *The Cambridge History of American Theatre*, vol. 3, 419-65; William W. Demastes, *Beyond Naturalism: A New Realism in American Theatre* (Westport, Conn.: Greenwood Press, 1988); Lehman Engel, *The American Musical Theatre: A Consideration*, rev. ed. (New York: Collier Books, 1975); Stanley Green, *The World of Musical Comedy*, 4th ed. (San Diego: A. S. Barnes, 1980); Ethan Mordden, *Broadway Babies: The People Who Made the American Musical* (New York: Oxford, 1983); Matthew Roudane, "Plays and Playwrights since 1970," in *The Cambridge History of the American Theatre*, vol. 3, 331-418; Matthew Roudane, *Public Issues, Private Tensions: Contemporary American Drama* (New York: AMS Press, 1993); and June Schlueter, *Modern American Drama: The Female Canon* (Canbury N.J.: Fairleigh Dickinson Press, 1990).

4 In addition to several of the sources I have listed above, for insight into the theatrical avant-garde of the late 1960s, see also Marvin Carlson's helpful overview, "Alternative Theatre," in *The Cambridge History of the American Theatre*, vol. 3, 249-93.

5 My discussion of *Angels in America* has been informed by several of the essays in *Approaching the Millennium: Essays on Angels in America*, ed. Deborah R. Geis and Steven F. Kruger (Ann Arbor: Univ. of Michigan Press, 1997), especially the essays by David Savran, "Ambivalence, Utopia, and a Queer Sort of Materialism: How *Angels in America* Reconstructs the Nation," 13-39; David Roman, "November 1, 1992: AIDS/*Angels in America*," 40-55; and Steven F. Kruger, "Identity and Conversion in *Angels in America*," 151-69.

6 On the commercial theater of the 1980s, see Alan Woods, "Consuming the Past: Commercial American Theatre in the Reagan Era," in *The American Stage: Social and Economic Issues from the Colonial Period to the Present*, ed. Ron Engle and Tice L. Miller (Cambridge: Cambridge Univ. Press, 1993), 252-66.

Index

Above and Beyond, 207
Actors Studio, 51, 67, 87, 89–92
Actors' Workshop, 8
Adamic, Louis, 179–80
Adding Machine, The, 49
Adler, Stella, 91
Adler, Thomas, 271
Advise and Consent, 37
African Americans, 5–6, 60, 132–35, 138–40, 158, 166, 176, 178–81, 183–84, 186–98, 287, 289–90
African Queen, The, 175
After the Fall, 288–89
AIDS, 298
Albee, Edward, 7, 53, 55, 124–25, 294, 299
Albert, Eddie, 67
All My Sons, 53, 66, 253
allegoresis, 39–42, 47–50, 54, 81, 105, 110, 123, 152–153, 155, 164, 170, 175, 186, 215, 247, 250, 252–253, 267, 285, 291–92, 307
allegory, xi, 28, 22, 39–40, 42, 51–52, 56, 74, 78–80, 104, 122, 152–53, 162, 173–75, 178, 186, 189, 192, 214, 222, 225, 227, 232, 244, 252–54, 258, 264, 267–68, 292, 307
America Hurrah, 290–91
American Adam, The, 59
American Buffalo, 296
American Dilemma: The Negro Problem and Modern Democracy, An, 134
American Dream, The, 7, 124–25
American National Theater Alliance, 219
Anderson, Jack, 229
Anderson, Judith, 38, 213
Anderson, Maxwell, 66, 170, 214
Anderson, Robert, 113, 259, 261
Andrews, Julie, 145
Angels Fall, 296–97
Angels in America, 297–99

Annie, 145, 288
Annie Get Your Gun, 146
Anouilh, Jean, 53, 213–14
apocalypse, 208, 210–14, 235–36, 238, 249, 281, 296–97
Arena Stage, 8
Aristotle, 16
Armour, Richard, 201
Aronson, Boris, 215, 222–23
As Is, 298
assimilation, 60, 84, 133–38, 140, 162–63, 165, 180–81, 187, 193, 195, 297
Aston, Frank, 190–91, 194
Atkinson, Brooks, 47–48, 72–73, 95, 108, 113, 190, 194, 242, 268
Atomic Energy Commission, 206
audience demographics, 1–8
audiophony, x–xi, 29–31, 43
Auntie Mame, 140
authenticity, 50–51, 56, 58–59, 64, 74, 78, 82, 87–89, 91–93, 99, 258, 269
Autumn Garden, 139
Awake and Sing, 43–44, 46–47, 53, 65
Axelrod, George, xi, 50, 66–67, 71–72, 78, 80–82, 86, 102

Bad Seed, The, 38, 138
Balcony, The, 7
Bald Soprano, The, 124
Baldwin, James, 114, 191, 196
Bankhead, Tallulah, 52, 251
Baraka, Amiri, 55, 196–97
Barefoot in Athens, 41
Barry, Phillip, 42
Barthes, Roland, 30, 128
Bay, Howard, 172–73
Beck, Julian, 7
Beckett, Samuel, 35, 307
Behrman, S.N., 42
Bel Geddes, Barbara, 110, 113, 118, 121, 260
Bell, Michael, 220

Ben-Hur, 209–10
Benjamin, Walter, 30, 241–42, 281
Bennett, Michael, 295
Benny, Jack, 36
Bentley, Eric, 107–8, 110, 114, 253, 268
Bergler, Edmund, 61
Berkey, Ralph, 66
Berlin blockade, 59, 204
Best Little Whorehouse in Texas, The, 288
Big Business, 9, 248
Billy Budd, 39, 66, 213, 289
Biloxi Blues, 287
black assimilation, 181
black culture, 180–81, 183, 187
Blackboard Jungle, 58
Blacks, The, 7
Blake, William, 221
Blau, Herbert, 199
Blob, The, 56
Body in the Mind, The, 10–11
Bomb, the, v, 51, 71, 126, 132, 199–209, 211, 213, 220, 222, 230–32, 236, 238–42, 244, 250, 258, 264–65, 277, 279, 281–83, 289
bombshell, 71, 230, 238, 275–76
Book of Job, 52, 215, 219–21, 224, 227, 234, 247
brainwashing, 62, 66, 75, 78–79
Brando, Marlon, 18, 57, 86–87, 93–100, 137, 253, 256
Brecht, Bertolt, 21, 29, 198, 282
Brecht on Brecht, 7
Breuer, Bessie, 66
Brigadoon, 40
Brighton Beach Memoirs, 287
Broadway Bound, 287
Brodky, Harold, 98
Brooks, Peter, 22
Brown, John Mason, 142, 267–68
Brown v. Board of Education, 133–34
Brown, Vanessa, 67, 69, 71, 102
Brustein, Robert, 91, 257
Brynner, Yul, 141–42, 158, 162, 193, 299, 320
Buck, Pearl, 144
Bulletin of Atomic Scientists, The, 236
Buried Child, 292–93

Burke, Kenneth, 23
Burnham, Louis E., 179
Burns and Allen Show, 35
Bus Stop, 139, 146, 160
Bush, George W., 299
Bye Bye Birdie, 5, 145

Cabaret, 287
Cage aux Follies, La, 288
Caine Mutiny Court Martial, The, 38, 213
Camelot, 40, 139, 288
Camino Real, 37, 104, 106
capitalism, 3–9, 14, 30, 102, 134–36, 156–57, 178, 180, 183–85, 188–89, 195, 197, 214
Capra, Frank, 57
Cardner, Abraham, 62
Carousel, 140
Cat on a Hot Tin Roof, xi, 50, 53–54, 67, 86, 103–25, 167, 172–73, 175, 250–53, 255, 260–61, 263, 314–15
Catholicism, 81
Cats, 298
Cave Dwellers, The, 39, 138
Cave of the Heart, 216, 237–38
Central Intelligence Agency (CIA), 9, 56, 77, 206
Channing, Carol, 145, 287
Chapman, John, 74, 86, 95, 97, 108, 113, 115–16, 190, 193, 221, 268
Chapman, Robert, 213
Chayefsky, Paddy, 213
Chekhov, Anton, 106, 118
Childress, Alice, 7, 138, 197–98
China, 136, 155–56, 204
Chorus Line, A, 295
Christian Children's Fund, 144
Circle in the Square, 7
City of Corpses, 244–45
Civil Rights Movement, 177, 180, 195
Clark, Clifford, Jr., 131
class, x, 1–6, 10, 15, 38, 42–43, 54, 63–64, 84, 114, 127, 132, 134, 179–81, 183, 185, 187–89, 192–94, 202; business, 4, 7–8, 12, 24, 38, 42, 58, 63, 85, 126, 129, 133, 136, 143, 157, 163, 169, 195–96, 201, 203, 213–14,

216, 218, 230–32, 234, 273; middle, 1, 3, 5, 43, 47, 66, 132, 193, 197, 201, 297; professional-managerial, 3–4, 63, 202, 219; upper, 1, 3–5, 63, 75, 180; working, 1, 3, 5–7, 42, 63–64, 180–81, 188, 259
Clift, Montgomery, 64–65, 87
Clurman, Harold, 27–28, 41, 94, 142, 183, 222
Clytemnestra, 38, 216
Cobb, Lee J., 45–46
Cocktail Party, The, 40
Cohn, Roy, 297–98
Cold War, vii, x–xi, 4–5, 8–9, 11–12, 16–18, 27, 36, 50–52, 54–58, 60, 62–65, 77, 81, 98, 102, 114, 126–29, 132–36, 144, 146, 156, 172, 175, 178, 192, 195, 199–202, 205, 209, 212, 215, 236, 250, 263, 266, 275, 277, 283, 285–86, 288, 297
Coleman, Robert, 48, 74, 95, 108, 143, 190
Come Back, Little Sheba, 38, 139, 146, 160, 215
Come Blow Your Horn, 286
Command Decision, 39
communication media, x–xi, 27–30, 32, 34, 37–38, 43, 197, 279, 281, 283–84. See also film; radio; television; telephone
communism, xi, 6, 9, 34, 56, 59–60, 62, 74–75, 77–78, 81–82, 131, 133, 136, 144, 156–57, 166, 177–78, 190, 201, 204–5, 207, 209, 212–13, 216, 238, 248, 262, 266–68, 276–77, 297
Communist Manifesto, The, 186
Communist Party, 179, 252
Company, 294–95
Compass Theatre, 8
conformity, 58–59, 62–63, 66, 101, 124, 131, 163, 168, 210, 264
Connection, The, 7
Conroy, Frank, 264
consumerism, 5, 30, 51, 86, 100–3, 105, 124–25, 177, 210, 283, 291
containment liberalism, 9, 18–19, 52–54, 57, 63, 83, 105, 123, 128, 140, 164, 180, 187, 189, 220, 222, 227, 243, 247, 250, 253, 264–65, 274, 276, 284–86, 290–91, 299
Coogan, Jackie, 161
Cornell, Katharine, 52, 213
corporate liberalism, 7–9
Cousins, Norman, 200
Cox, Oliver C., 179–81
Coxe, Louis, 213, 274
Crawford, Cheryl, 89
Cretan Woman, The, 213
Crimes of the Heart, 298
Crothers, Rachel, 42
Crucible, The, xi, 50, 53–54, 265–82, 298
Cry of the People for Meat, The, 290
Cuban Missile Crisis, 249
Cushman, Philip, 100

Damn Yankees, 40, 66
Dark at the Top of the Stairs, The, xi, 18, 50–51, 139–40, 146–53, 160–69, 189, 194, 250, 253, 255, 257, 260–61, 263, 264
Darkness at Noon, 41, 213
Davis, Angela, 197
Davis, Ossie, 138, 193–94
Day the Earth Stood Still, The, 56, 209
Dean, James, 57, 87, 253, 259, 261
Death of a Salesman, 43–50, 53, 66, 68, 70, 80, 172, 174–75, 183, 187, 192, 202, 242, 250, 254, 265–66, 271, 290
Decline of the American Male, The, 203
Dee, Ruby, 190
Deep Are the Roots, 138
Delicate Balance, A, 294
DeMille, Agnes, 209, 225
democratic socialism, 181
Denker, Harry, 66
Depression Era, 3, 32, 42, 47, 129, 189
Design for a Stained Glass Window, 40
Designing for the Theatre, 170
Dewey, John, 15, 149
Diary of Anne Frank, The, 37, 139, 215
Dionysus in '69, 291
Disenchanted, The, 38
Disney Doctrine, 177–78
Disneyland, 175–78

divorce, 130
domesticity, 6, 102, 128–32, 149
dominant culture, xii, 1, 5, 7, 9, 12, 15–16, 18–19, 29, 31, 36–38, 53–54, 57, 61, 64, 123, 178, 183, 203, 265, 299
Donaldson Award, 124, 266
Doob, Leonard, 135
Dr. Strangelove or: How I Learned to Stop Worrying and Love the Bomb, 238
Dragnet, 35, 122–23
Dreamgirls, 287
Drunkard, The, 78
Dubois, W.E.B., 133, 178–79
Dullea, Keir, 90
Dulles, John Foster, 136, 248

East of Eden, 250–51, 253, 255–56, 259–61, 263–64
Edwards, Ben, 166–69
Ehrenreich, Barbara, 3, 73
Ehrenreich, John, 3
Einstein, Albert, 254
Eisenhower, Dwight D., 60, 77, 136, 204–5, 216, 235, 211–12
Eliot, T. S., 40
Ellison, Ralph, 133
Emhardt, Robert, 67
Emperor Jones, The, 42, 49
Empty Boys, v, xi, 22, 49–54, 57–58, 60, 65–68, 71–72, 75, 81–82, 94, 99, 102, 107–8, 113, 117, 122, 124–25, 140, 164, 193, 224, 251, 258–59, 262, 264, 276, 283, 285–88, 290, 292, 299
Enemy of the People, An, 289
Enlightenment, 41, 281, 282, 298
Errand into the Maze, 216, 237, 243
essentialism, 16, 40, 116, 159, 162, 290
ethics: ethical egoism, 51, 84, 102, 125; liberal rationalist, 52; liberal utilitarian, 51; nurturant parent morality, 83–84; rationalist, 247–48, 265, 273, 277, 281–82, 298; Strict Father model of morality, 83, 247–48, 250, 258, 273; utilitarian, 51, 84, 164–65, 178

Evans, Walker, 241
Everett, Timmy, 151
Everyman, 48
Everyman figure, 47–49, 78, 222, 258, 291
Ewell, Tom, 67, 69, 80
expressionism, 48–49, 171, 225

Faithfully Yours, 66
Family Circle, v, xi, 22, 50–51, 53–54, 126–28, 130, 132, 137–40, 143–45, 148, 161, 163–64, 189, 224, 283, 285, 287–88, 290, 292–94
Family of Man, 51, 126–27, 136–37, 142–44, 157, 160, 163, 165–66, 189–90, 192, 194–96
Family of Man exhibit, 127, 177, 282
Fantasticks, The, 138, 287
Farnham, Marynia, 130
Farrell, General Thomas, 199–201, 208
Faulkner, William, 220
FBI Story, The, 207–10
Federal Bureau of Investigation (FBI), 56, 81, 190
Federal Employee Loyalty Program, 205
Feminine Mystique, The, 128
femme fatale, 274, 276,
Fences, 290
Fiddler on the Roof, 287
film, 5, 27, 29–30, 32, 35, 39, 56, 58, 65, 67, 87–89, 91–93, 98, 103, 113, 137, 139, 144, 146, 159, 175–77, 189–90, 195–96, 200–2, 207, 225, 229, 240, 250, 254–59, 262, 264, 276, 283, 285
film gris, 5
film noir, 5, 35–36, 46, 95, 144, 229, 238, 274
Finian's Rainbow, 37
Fiorello!, 66
Flower Drum Song, The, 140
Flowering Peach, The, 40, 141, 214, 287
folk theory of essences, 16–17
Follies, 294–95
Fontaine, Lynne, 52
Fool for Love, 292

football, 14, 24–25, 115
Forward the Heart, 138
Fourposter, The, 287
Fragmented Hero, v, xi–xii, 22, 50–54, 199, 202–3, 206–10, 212–15, 242–46, 248, 251, 256, 258, 262–65, 271, 273–74, 283, 285, 288–90, 295–98
Franciosa, Anthony, 67
Free Shakespeare in the Park, 7, 138
French Revolution, 9, 41, 245
Freud on Broadway, 153
Freud, Sigmund, 31, 40, 149, 151–52, 164, 242
Freudianism, vii–ix, 13, 62, 68, 80–81, 129–30, 152–53, 162, 169, 253. *See also* psychology
Friedan, Betty, 128
From Here to Eternity, 65
Fry, Christopher, 40
Fuchs, Klaus, 205
Fuller, Charles, 289, 299
Funny Girl, 287
Funny Thing Happened on the Way to the Forum, A, 52
Furth, George, 294

Galbraith, John Kenneth, 232
Galileo, 274, 282
Garfein, Jack, 89
Garland, Robert, 47–48, 95, 97
Gazzara, Ben, 67, 72–73, 76, 86–88, 93, 99, 100, 112, 116, 121
Gazzo, Michael, xi, 1, 50, 66–67, 73–79, 81–82, 86, 101
Gelber, Jack, 7
Generation of Vipers, 149
Genet, Jean, 7, 55
Gentleman's Agreement, 141, 253
Getting Out, 293
GI Bill, 2, 60, 72
Gideon, 39, 213
Glaspell, Susan, 42
Glass Menagerie, The, 104, 139, 167, 173
Glengarry Glen Ross, 296
God and the H-Bomb, 249
Godspell, 291
Godzilla, 56, 211

Gone With the Wind, 92, 104
Graham, Billy, 208–9
Graham, Martha, xi, 38, 52, 215–20, 224–30, 235–38, 240, 242–43, 246–50, 254, 257–58, 279, 286
Grass Harp, The, 139
Great God Brown, The, 42
Green Pastures, The, 138
Greenberg, Clement, 241
grotesque, 104–10, 113–14, 117–19, 123–25, 225, 232, 295–96, 314
Group Theatre, 27, 47, 88–89, 262
Guys and Dolls, 172
Gypsy, 37, 145, 177, 195

Hagen, Uta, 214
Hair, 291–92, 294
Hairy Ape, The, 42
Half-Human, 245
Hallelujah Baby, 287
Hamers, Fanny Lou, 197
Hamlet, 28, 161, 169
Hampden, Walter, 266, 280
Hansberry, Lorraine, xi–xii, 53–54, 138, 178–97, 265, 281–82, 293, 322
Harris, Jed, 266
Harris, Julie, 259
Harrison, Rex, 158
Hastings, John, 192
Hatful of Rain, A, xi, 1, 18, 38, 50–51, 66–68, 72–84, 86, 88, 99, 101, 107, 116, 121–22, 164, 215
Hawkins, Erick, 216–17, 228–29
Hawkins, William, 48, 95, 97, 107–8, 113, 268
Hayes, Helen, 52
Hays, David, 172
Hayworth, Rita, 71, 230
Hedgman, Anna Arnold, 196
Heffner, Hugh, 101–2, 144
Hegel, G. W. F., 31
hegemonic masculinity, 65, 201–2, 207, 229–30, 260, 264
hegemony, 7, 27, 30, 53, 55, 63–64, 83, 119, 123, 128, 136, 138, 197
hegemony theory, 3–4, 7, 15, 304
Heidegger, Martin, 219

Index 339

Heidi Chronicles, The, 294
Heiress, The, 138
Hellman, Lillian, 42, 53, 107, 172, 214–15, 274
Hello, Dolly!, 145, 287
Henley, Beth, 293
Herberg, Will, 211
Hersey, John, 235–36, 245, 265, 275
Heston, Charleton, 201
Hewes, Henry, 148, 192, 222
Highest Tree, The, 214
Hingle, Pat, 147, 215–16, 242–43
Hiroshima, 200, 207–8, 220, 230, 235–37, 241–42, 244–45, 264, 275
Hiroshima, 245
Hiroshima Maidens, 275–76, 298
historiography, vii–xi, 8, 10, 12, 15–16, 23–29
Hitchcock, Alfred, 145, 207
Hoffman, Theodore, 88, 99
Hofstadter, Richard, 277
Holden, William, 35, 146, 201, 229
Hollywood, 5–6, 8, 12, 57, 64, 67, 71–72, 87, 92, 98, 129–30, 137, 146, 148, 159–61, 170, 175, 205–6, 213, 216, 247, 250–52, 254, 260, 262–63, 292
Holocaust, 213, 215, 245–46, 288–89
Home of the Brave, 66
homosexuality, xi, 54, 60–61, 64–65, 73–75, 107, 111, 114–17, 123, 129, 140, 145, 149, 151, 161, 166, 173, 205, 261, 288, 296, 298. *See also* othering
Honeymooners, The, 138
Hook, Sidney, 179–80
Horan, Robert, 218, 237
Hot L Baltimore, The, 294
Hotel Universe, 42
House Un-American Activities Committee (HUAC), 205, 250–52, 261–64, 269, 276, 281
How to Succeed in Business without Really Trying, 38
Hudson, Rock, 57
Hughes, Langston, 178, 184
Human Rags, 245
Hurok, Sol, 218–19

I Am a Camera, 53
I Do! I Do!, 287
I Love Lucy, 137
I Remember Mama, 138
Ibsen, Henrik, 42, 108, 271
Iceman Cometh, The, 299
ignorance effects, 10, 118, 124
Immoralist, The, 37
imperialism, 54, 136–37, 155–56, 195, 197, 299
Incident at Vichy, 288
Incredible Shrinking Man, The, 201
Inge, William, xi, 50–51, 107, 139–40, 146, 148–49, 151–53, 160–62, 167–69, 197, 261
Inherit the Wind, 213
Inner Sanctum Mysteries, 34
Invaders from Mars, 56
Invasion of the Body Snatchers, The, 56, 73–74
Ionesco, Eugene, 124–25, 281
Ives, Burl, 110, 112–13, 118, 121

J.B., vii, xii, 18, 37, 40, 50, 52, 54, 215–16, 219–24, 227, 230–35, 238–40, 242–44, 246–50, 253, 256, 258, 260–61, 263, 268, 273
Jamaica, 138
Jeffers, Robinson, 213
Joan of Lorraine, 37, 214
Joe Turner's Come and Gone, 290
Johnson, Mark, viii, x, 10–17, 19–21, 23, 25–26, 36, 38, 54, 63, 82–84, 102–3, 164, 247, 273, 303, 305. *See also* ethics; metaphor; psychology, cognitive; realism, philosophical; schema
Johnson Wax Hour, The, 33
Jones, Jennifer, 203
Joyce, James, 220
Jung, Carl, ix, 218, 220, 234
Juno and the Paycock, 181, 186

Kaye, Danny, 57, 218
Kazan, Elia, xii, 18, 48, 52–53, 88–90, 93–95, 97–98, 106–11, 113–18, 123–24, 146, 148, 151–52, 166, 173, 215, 229, 231, 233, 238–39, 242–

43, 250–64, 270, 274, 279, 313; and HUAC 250–52, 260–64
Kelly, George, 42
Kennedy, Arthur, 45–46, 266, 280
Kennedy, John F., 144
Kenyatta, 186
Kermode, Frank, 208
Kerr, Deborah, 259
Kerr, Walter, 1–2, 87, 113, 115–16, 166–67, 193, 222, 266–67
Khrushchev, Nikita, 102
Kid from Brooklyn, The, 218
Kikuchi, Yuriko, 230
King and I, The, vii, xi, 18, 37–38, 50–51, 140–44, 148, 151, 153–66, 169–72, 175, 193–94, 230, 299
King Lear, 239
Kinsey Report, 61, 68, 117, 203
Kipling, Rudyard, 33
Kirchwey, Freda, 267
Kiss Me Deadly, 276
Kissinger, Henry, 155–56
Klein, Melanie, 84–85
Kopit, Arthur, 296–97, 299
Korean War, 66, 72, 75, 77–78, 129, 137, 156, 204
Kronenberger, Louis, 95–97
Kushner, Tony, 297

Laban, Rudolph von, 236, 250
Lacan, Jacques, vii, ix
Lady and the Tramp, 139
Lakoff, George, viii–x, 10–17, 19–21, 23, 25–26, 36, 54, 63, 82–84, 102–3, 164, 247, 273, 303–5. *See also* ethics; metaphor; psychology, cognitive; realism, philosophical; schema
Land Beyond the River, A, 138
Lansberry, Angela, 145, 287
Lapine, James, 295
Lardner, John, 175
Lark, The, 53, 172, 214, 274
Last of the Red Hot Lovers, The, 286–87
Laughton, Charles, 52
Laurents, Arthur, 66
Lawrence, Gertrude, 141–42, 145, 162
Lawrence, Jerome, 213
Lee, Robert E., 213

Lewis, R. W. B., 59
liberal melodrama, 115–16, 118
liberal tragedy, 106–8, 115, 118, 271–72
Lie of the Mind, A, 293
Life magazine, 111, 127, 200–1, 221, 225, 241, 243, 249
Life with Mother, 138
Lights Out, 34
L'il Abner, 40
Lincoln Center Repertory Theater, 251, 257
Living Theatre, 7
Logan, Joshua, 137, 146, 168
London Merchant, The, 78
Lonely Crowd, The, 59
Long Day's Journey into Night, 139, 299
Long, Hot Summer, The, 139
Look Homeward, Angel, 37, 172
Look Magazine, 203
Luce, Henry, 221
Lundberg, Ferdinand, 130
Lunt, Alfred, 52

Ma Rainey's Black Bottom, 289–90
Machinal, 49
MacLeish, Archibald, xi, 50, 52, 215–16, 219–22, 224, 230–35, 238–40, 242, 246–48, 256, 261
Madwoman of Chaillot, The, 214
Magdalena, 40
Mailer, Norman, 88
Malcolm X, 197
Malina, Judith, 7
Mame, 145, 287
Mamet, David, 295–96
Man and Superman, 40
Man in the Gray Flannel Suit, The, 58, 202–3, 230, 259
Man of LaMancha, The, 288
Man on a Tightrope, 252
Man Who Knew Too Much, The, 207
Manchurian Candidate, The, 77
Marshall Plan, 59
Marshall, Thurgood, 134
Martin, John, 237
Marx Brothers, 103
Massey, Raymond, 215, 234

Mattachine Society, 61, 117
McCarthy, Sen. Joseph, 34, 53, 56, 74, 266, 276, 297
McCarthyism, 12, 54, 74, 81, 114, 116, 204–5, 214, 261, 265–69, 271–77, 279, 281
McClain, John, 86, 108, 113, 115, 190, 221, 276
McNeil, Claudia, 182, 190, 192, 194–95
McQueen, Steve, 167
Me and Juliet, 37
Mead, Margaret, 126–27, 130, 203, 249
Meany, George, 248
Medea, 38, 213, 237
Member of the Wedding, The, 37, 138–39, 195, 215
Merman, Ethel, 145–46, 195
metaphors, x, 10–20, 23, 25–27, 33–34, 37, 41, 46–47, 54, 71, 73, 78, 83, 90, 129, 143, 153, 199, 212, 230, 237–40, 276, 283–84, 297–98. See also schema
metatheatricality, 28–29, 36–37, 41–43, 46, 49–50, 70, 159–61, 173, 197, 215, 222, 224, 240, 291
Method acting, xii, 18, 21, 51, 65, 86–93, 98–100, 116, 141, 163, 198, 227, 251, 255, 295
Michener, James, 137
Mielziner, Jo, xii, 18, 47–48, 51, 108–9, 118, 146, 159, 167–75, 177
militarization, 10, 42, 50–51, 57, 59–62, 81, 128, 285
military-industrial complex, 60
Mill, John Stuart, 164–65
Miller, Arthur, xi–xii, 8, 43–44, 46–48, 50, 53–54, 66, 107, 118, 183, 204, 264–79, 281, 288–89, 298
Miller, Jason, 289
Milton, John, 39
Miracle Worker, The, 139
Mister Roberts, 66
Moby Dick, 138
modernization, 17, 134–36, 156, 183
momism, 149, 153, 229, 260

Monroe, Marilyn, 67, 71, 144, 146, 230
Moon for the Misbegotten, A, 139, 299
Moon Is Blue, The, 113
Morehouse, Ward, 46, 95, 97
Morgan, Thomas, 257
motherhood, xi, 44, 50–51, 73–74, 81, 83, 113, 128, 129, 130–32, 141–46, 148–53, 160, 162, 164–66, 175–77, 183, 193–94, 197, 205, 216, 227–28, 243–44, 255–56, 258–59, 262, 274, 287–88, 293–94
Mr. Roberts, 38
Mrs. McThing, 138
Murrow, Edward R., 33–34
Museum of Modern Art, New York, 127, 177
Music Man, The, 66, 86, 139
musical comedy, 5, 8–9, 18, 37, 40, 42, 51–52, 66, 139–46, 149, 155, 157–60, 162, 165, 170, 175–78, 287–88, 291, 294
My Fair Lady, 37, 140
My Son John, 81
Myrdal, Gunnar, 134–135, 138, 180–81, 183, 187, 193, 195

narcissism, 84–88, 92–93, 97–98, 100–3, 116–17, 122, 125, 294–95; culture of, 85–86
narcissistic gaze, 98, 100
narrative, xi, 13–14, 18, 22–23, 26, 28, 35, 38–41, 43, 46–50, 63, 105, 118, 123, 138, 153, 159, 164, 175, 189, 194, 203, 206, 208, 215–16, 219, 221–22, 225, 227, 238–40, 245, 253, 258, 264, 267–68, 275–78, 283, 287, 292, 294; of apocalypse, 52, 125, 208–10, 212, 235, 238; conspiracy, 206, 208, 276–79; Empty Boy, 22, 67–68, 72, 81–82, 94, 101, 106–8, 158; Everyman, 48–49, 78; Family Circle, 22, 137–40, 148, 153, 164–66, 177, 185, 188–89, 194; Fragmented Hero, 22, 202–03, 205–8, 212–25, 225, 227, 233–34, 242, 258, 270–71; jeremiad, 52, 54, 210–15, 231–35, 242, 258, 269,

342 Index

271–73, 277–78, 296–98; personal, 105, 119–24; restoration narrative, 207–11
Nathan, George Jean, 124
National Association for the Advancement of Colored People (NAACP), 133
national character, 58–59
National Mental Health Act, 62
national security, 9–10, 56–57, 59–63, 82, 200, 205–6, 248–49, 264, 276
National Security Act, 9–12, 57, 59
National Security Council, 9, 206
Navasky, Victor, 204, 261, 263
New York Drama Critics' Circle Award, 86, 124, 192, 286, 289
Newsboy, 42
Niebuhr, Reinhold, 243
Night Journey, xi, 18, 38, 52, 215–20, 224–29, 231, 235–38, 240, 242–44, 246–50, 258, 268, 273
'Night Mother, 293
Night of the Auk, 214
Night of the Iguana, The, 53
Nixon, Richard, 102, 276
Noguchi, Isamu, 216, 235
Norman, Marsha, 293
North Atlantic Treaty Organization (NATO), 59
Norton, Elliot, 73, 142
novels, 37, 58, 74, 107, 202, 283
nuclear family, 51, 126, 128–29, 137, 177, 290, 293
nuclearism, 52, 199, 201–2, 204, 206–8, 212, 214–15, 237–38, 240, 242–43, 245, 250, 253–54, 258, 265–66, 275, 281–82, 296–97
Nugent, Elliot, 67
nymphomaniac, 75, 95

Obie Award, 198
Obler, Arch, 214
O'Casey, Sean, 181, 183–84, 195
O'Connor, Flannery, 104–5
Odd Couple, The, 286
Odets, Clifford, 42–44, 47, 183, 190, 195, 214, 287
Oedipus, 224, 247

Oenslager, Donald, 172
Off-Broadway, 2, 7, 8, 54, 124–25, 138, 198, 266, 286–87
Off-Off-Broadway, 283
Oh! Calcutta!, 291
Oh Men, Oh Women, 66
Oklahoma, 140–41, 225
On the Waterfront, 81, 250–53, 256, 259–61, 263–64
O'Neill, Eugene, 42, 49, 108, 139, 299
Oppenheimer, J. Robert, 265
Osborn, Paul, 253, 261
othering, 18, 20–22, 34, 53, 74, 103, 131, 178, 197, 201, 212, 289; abject Other, 53–54, 309; female Other, 52, 54, 144, 229–31, 274–75; homosexual Other, 54, 74, 114, 163; racial Other, 54, 126–27, 133, 135–40, 151, 156–57, 161–62, 165–66, 189, 212
Our Mr. Sun, 211
Our Town, 36, 65, 299
Ozzie and Harriet, 137, 295

Packard, Vance, 12
Pajama Game, The, 5
Papp, Joe, 7, 138
Park, Robert, 134–35
Parks, Rosa, 184
Parsons, Talcott, 16–17, 129
Patterson, Neva, 67
Peale, Reverend Norman Vincent, 209
Peck, Gregory, 202–3, 243
Penn, Arthur, 90
performative orality, 105, 123
Performing History, 245
Petrified Forrest, The, 42
Phantom of the Opera, The, 298
phonograph, 30–32, 49, 68, 103, 122
photographic realism, 293
photography, x, 27–32, 38, 41–43, 47, 49–50, 53, 160, 170, 174, 200, 236, 240–41, 246, 253–54, 258, 279, 281, 283–84
Piano Lesson, The, 290
Picnic, 40, 66, 139, 146, 167–70, 172
Pilgrim's Progress, 48, 78
Pinter, Harold, 35, 119

Pippen, 291
Pirandello, Luigi, 21, 37, 231
Place in the Sun, A, 65, 87
Plato, 16
Platonism, 17–18, 32–36, 40–42, 49, 58, 60, 68, 82, 89, 91–92, 105, 111, 126, 128, 131, 135, 172, 186, 189, 192, 198, 220, 222, 224, 227, 252–54, 258, 281, 283, 285, 291, 297–98
Playbill, 1
Playboy, 101
Plummer, Christopher, 215
Poe, Edgar Allan, 241
Point of No Return, 37
Poitier, Sydney, 182, 190, 192–93, 195
Pollock, Arthur, 142
Popular Front, 19, 63, 178–79, 187, 190, 195
postmodernism, 200, 284, 292
Potter, David, 59, 232
presence of actors, 21–23, 122, 174
Preston, Robert, 86
Price, The, 288
Private Lives, 52
Progressive Era, 3
projection, viii, 23, 25–26, 52, 54, 84, 89, 91, 99; advisory, 20–22, 82, 100, 103, 148–49, 269; empathetic, 20–21, 24, 51, 82, 145–46, 148, 176, 195, 248, 269
proscenium stage, 118, 168–69, 173–75
Prowler, The, 5
psychic numbing, 249
psychological identity, 73, 81
psychologization, 49, 57, 64–66, 81, 99, 134–35, 167–68, 180
psychology, viii–x, 1, 10, 14, 32, 35, 40, 44, 46, 48–50, 56–57, 61–68, 70, 72–73, 75, 77–79, 81–82, 84–85, 87, 95, 100–11, 116, 122, 129, 131, 134–35, 139–42, 148–49, 151, 163, 167, 169, 173, 177, 198, 200, 203, 207–8, 218, 235, 242, 250, 254–55, 261, 264, 288–90, 292, 296; cognitive, viii–x, 10–16, 19–27, 36, 38–39, 41–43, 54, 63, 77–78, 83, 159, 173–74, 186, 202, 219, 239, 283–86, 295, 299, 304, 332; ego, 62–63; gestalt, xi, 21; psychoanalysis, 12, 32, 35, 49, 51, 61–63, 73, 84–85, 129, 149, 152, 160–61, 164, 167, 259. *See also* Freudianism
Pulitzer Prize, 124, 215, 286, 289
Purlie Victorious, 138

Quinn, Anthony, 94
Quo Vadis?, 209

Rabe, David, 295–96, 299
race, 2–3, 5, 7, 51, 54, 60, 84, 144, 126–27, 132–33, 138–40, 144, 158–59, 161, 163, 165–66, 176–81, 183, 187–89, 191–98, 202, 285
racism, 53, 133–34, 136, 138, 178, 180–82, 184–85, 188, 193, 289–91, 296
radio, xi, 1, 27–38, 41, 43, 46, 48–50, 68, 70, 79, 85, 101, 103, 122, 130, 164, 206, 209, 120–21, 218, 283–85, 297; broadcasting, 29, 32–35, 37–39
radiophony, xi, 28, 32, 34–35, 48–50, 70, 79, 85–86, 122–23, 164, 172, 189, 222, 240, 254, 258, 281, 307
Rainmaker, The, 139
Raisin in the Sun, A, 50, 53–54, 138, 178–79, 181–97, 215
Randolph, A. Philip, 133
Reagan, Ronald, 297–99
realism: philosophical, x, 15–17, 19, 29–33, 36, 50, 68, 89, 95, 155–56, 206, 241, 252, 283, 285, 290; disembodied, 19; embodied, 13–15, 19, 21, 23, 305
realist theater, xi, 19, 21, 27–28, 30, 36–37, 39, 41–42, 46–49, 53–54, 72, 79, 89, 92, 104–5, 108, 117, 119, 125, 170, 172, 174, 183, 195, 197, 153, 165, 292–94
Rear Window, 207
Rebel without a Cause, 87, 132, 144
Red River, 65
Red Scare, 204–7, 215, 282
Reeves, George, 201
Reinhardt, Max, 257

Reisman, David, 59, 101
religiousness, 211–12
Rich, Frank, 158
Richards, Lloyd, 190
Rivera, Chita, 145
Robbins, Jerome, 153, 159
Robe, The, 209
Roberts, Meade, 91
Robeson, Paul, 178–79
Rogers and Hammerstein, xi, 51, 66, 137, 140–44, 155, 157–59, 175
Romeo and Juliet, 160
Roosevelt, Eleanor, 133
Roosevelt, Franklin Delano, 33
Roosevelt, Teddy, 57
Rose Tattoo, The, 104, 139
Rosenberg, Ethel, 273, 279
Rosenberg, Julius, 205, 273
Rosenthal, Jean, 167–68
Ross, Bertram, 229
Ruth, Babe, 57
Ryder, Mark, 216

Sabin, Robert, 237
Saint, Eva-Marie, 259
Salt of the Earth, The, 5
Sambo, 291
Sandberg, Carl, 127
Sandhog, 7, 301
Sands, Diana, 182, 190
Sartre, Jean-Paul, 262
Saussure, Ferdinand de, viii
Sayonara, 137
Schary, Dore, 214
schema, viii, 13–14, 73, 173, 215, 285, 290, 292, 294; of attraction, 42; of balance, 11, 13, 42, 174; of compulsion, 24, 37–38, 41–42, 44, 49–50, 52, 58, 71, 78, 163–64, 206, 208, 215, 222, 225, 234, 262–64, 283, 285, 288, 292–93, 295; of containment, viii, ix–xii, 5–6, 9–12, 14, 16–18, 24–25, 27, 34, 36–42, 44, 46, 49–54, 57, 59–60, 71, 78, 90, 114, 117, 123, 126, 129, 132, 138, 143, 156–57, 159, 164–65, 173–75, 178, 195, 199, 206, 208, 212, 215, 222, 227, 237–39, 243, 245, 254, 275, 283, 285–86, 288–89, 291–93, 296–99, 332; of counterforce, 14, 24, 41, 51, 71–72, 75, 81, 86, 105, 121, 125; of full-empty, 14; of iteration, 14, 24, 42, 284, 290–95; of link, 284–85, 290–95; of mass-count, 42; of part-whole, 24, 41, 143, 148, 165, 185–86; of restraint removal, 41, 208, 215, 288; of source-path-goal, 13, 15, 22; of surface, 42, 284, 290–96. *See also* metaphor
Schlesinger, Arthur, Jr., 75
Schulberg, Budd, 261
Schweitzer, Dr. Albert, 134
Search, The, 65
Selznick, Irene, 251
semiotics, vii–viii, 17, 19–21, 26, 98
Serpent, The, 290
Seurat, Georges, 295
Seven Brides for Seven Brothers, 299
Seven Year Itch, The, vii, xi, 18, 39, 49–50, 66–72, 78–84, 86, 99, 101, 117, 121–22, 164, 267
sexuality, 12, 18, 57, 60, 66–67, 82, 95, 97, 101, 104, 111, 113, 118, 124, 130, 140, 153, 163, 166–69, 225, 227–28, 234, 237, 243–44, 248, 250–52, 258–60, 269–70, 276–77; androgynous, 54, 60–61, 98, 114–16, 123, 125; female, xii, 54, 70, 80, 95, 144–45, 148, 151, 203, 214–16, 227–29, 231, 238, 258, 274–75, 289, 296; male, 44, 51, 68, 71, 80, 107, 117, 229. *See also* homosexuality
Shadow, The, 34–35
Sharaff, Irene, 159
Shaw, George Bernard, 40, 214, 272–73, 281
Sheen, Monsignor Fulton, 209
Shepard, Sam, 292–93, 299
Sherwood, Robert E., 42, 103
Shrike, The, 39, 138
Sievers, W. David, 157
Silent Night, Lonely Night, 67
Silver Chalice, The, 209
Silvera, Frank, 67, 76
Simon, Neil, 286–87

Simonson, Lee, 172
Sinatra, Frank, 57
Singin' in the Rain, 299
Six Characters in Search of an Author, 37
Skin of our Teeth, The, 251
Slave Ship, 290–91
Sleep of Prisoners, A, 40
Snow White and the Seven Dwarfs, 175–76
socialism, 178–80, 184, 187, 189
Socrates, 274, 281
Soldier's Play, A, 289
Sondheim, Stephen, 294–95, 299
Sophocles, 224, 235
Sound of Music, The, 140, 145
South Pacific, 37, 66, 140, 143
Soviet Union, 11, 17, 58–60, 102, 133, 204–6, 208, 213–14, 238, 263, 287
Spellman, Cardinal Francis, 74
Spillane, Mickey, 74–75, 276
Splendor in the Grass, 146
Spock, Dr. Benjamin, 131, 148–49, 151
St. Joan, 214, 272–74
Stalin, Josef, 156
Stallings, Laurence, 42
Stanislavski, Konstantin, 86, 88–90, 257
Starkey, Marion, 278
Starlight Express, 298
Steichen, Edward, 127–28, 177
Steinbeck, John, 253
Stevenson, Adlai, 128
Stewart, Jimmy, 113, 207–8, 210, 243
Sticks and Bones, 295
Stieglitz, Alfred, 241
Stomp, 291
Strand, Paul, 241
Strangers on the Train, 145
Strasberg, Lee, 67, 86, 88–92, 99
Strategic Air Command, The, 207
Streamers, 296
Streetcar Named Desire, A, 40, 53, 86–87, 93–98, 100, 104, 106, 167, 172, 174, 229, 250–52, 255, 261
suburbs, 5, 12, 51, 85, 101, 127–28, 131–33, 136, 169–70, 175–78, 194, 210, 249, 293, 295
Sullivan, Harry Stack, 62

Summer and Smoke, 167, 172
Sunday in the Park with George, 295
Sundown Beach, 66
Sunset Boulevard, 35, 144
Sunshine Boys, The, 287
Sweet Bird of Youth, 53
Sweet Charity, 287
Swiss Family Robinson, 137

Taft-Hartley Act, 6
Take a Giant Step, 138
Talbot, William Henry Fox 241
Tales of the South Pacific, 137
Tandy, Jessica, 95–97
Tarkington, Booth, 65
Taylor, Robert, 207
Tea and Sympathy, 66, 113–14, 250, 259–61, 263–64, 274
Teahouse of the August Moon, The, 37, 140
telephone, xi, 30–31, 81, 85, 122–23
television, xi, 1, 5, 8, 24, 27, 34–36, 67, 78, 85, 87, 101–3, 122, 130–31, 137–38, 169, 177, 189, 200–1, 209, 220, 274, 283–85, 291, 294–95, 299, 332
television culture, 285, 290–91, 294, 298
Ten Commandments, The, 209–10
Tenth Man, The, 39, 213
Terkel, Studs, 57, 184, 189
Terry, Walter, 237
That Championship Season, 289
Theatre '47, 8
theater of the absurd, 118, 124–25, 184, 281
Them!, 56, 144, 209, 211, 238
Thing, The, 56
This Was Burlesque, 52
Thomas, Dylan, 111
Thurber Carnival, A, 80
Thurber, James, 80
Time Limit, 66
Time magazine, 126, 200, 221
Timebends, 264–65, 273
Tobacco Road, 103–4, 138
togetherness, 127, 130–31, 145, 153, 165, 169, 234, 292–93, 295

346 Index

Tony award, 216, 266, 286
Tooth of Crime, The, 292
Tower beyond Tragedy, The, 213
Toys in the Attic, 40, 172
Traitor, The, 39, 214
Tree Grows in Brooklyn, A, 172
Trouble in Mind, 7, 138, 139
Truckline Café, 66
True West, 292
Truman, Harry, 9, 59, 62, 133, 205, 208
Truman Doctrine, 59
Turner, Mark, 22, 190
Two by Two, 287
Two for the Seesaw, 67
Two Trains Running, 290
Tynan, Kenneth, 235, 263
typification, 38–43, 48–49, 385

Uncle Tom's Cabin, 153, 157, 164, 191
union leaders, 6, 56
United Nations, 133, 136

Valentino, Rudolph, 151
Vertigo, 113, 207
Vidal, Gore, 114
Viet Rock, 290
Vietnam, 135–36, 142–44, 216, 295–96
Vietnam War, 285
View from the Bridge, A, 39, 266, 289
Visit, The, 38, 52
Voice of America, 134
voice-over techniques, 34–36, 48–49, 221–22

Waiting for Godot, 257
Wallace, Henry, 179
Walt Disney, 137, 139
Wasserstein, Wendy, 294
Watergate, 285
Watts, Richard, Jr., 74, 86, 108, 190, 194
Watts, Steven, 177
Weales, Gerald, 192
Webber, Andrew Lloyd, 298

Welles, Orson, 34, 354
West Side Story, 140
Westward Ho the Wagons, 137
What Use Are Flowers, 281–82
Whistler, The, 34
White, W. D., 233–34
whiteness, xi, 136, 138, 140, 161–63, 165–66, 180, 197–98
Who's Afraid of Virginia Woolf, 53, 125
Wilde, Oscar, 105
Wilder, Thornton, 36–37, 42
Will Success Spoil Rock Hunter?, 66
Williams, Raymond, 15, 271, 304
Williams, Robert Moore, 249
Williams, Tennessee, xi–xii, 8, 16, 50, 53–54, 95, 97, 103–7, 110–11, 113–25, 139, 167, 173, 220, 251, 257, 260–61, 265, 293, 313–14
Williams, William Carlos, 265
Wilson, August, 289–90
Wilson, Charles, 248
Wilson, Lanford, 294, 296–97
Wilson, Sloan, 202
Winchell, Walter, 221
Wings, 296–97
Winters, Shelley, 67, 76
Winterset, 170, 172
Witchfinders, The, 274
Wittgenstein, Ludwig, 15, 20, 26
Wiz, The, 287, 299
women as irrational Others, 52
Wood, Audrey, 105
Wooster Group, 281
Wouk, Herman, 214
Wright, Theresa, 147–48, 150
Wylie, Philip, 149, 151, 201

Yeats, William Butler, 110
Yoko, Ota, 244–45, 265
You Can't Take It with You, 299
Young Progressives Association, 179

Zanuck, Darryl, 252
Zooman and the Sign, 289
Zorba, 299